THE COMMON ASPHODEL

Asphodel

THE
COMMON
ASPHODEL

COLLECTED ESSAYS ON POETRY

1922–1949

by

ROBERT GRAVES

HASKELL HOUSE PUBLISHERS LTD.
Publishers of Scarce Scholarly Books
NEW YORK, N. Y. 10012
1970

First Published 1949

HASKELL HOUSE PUBLISHERS Ltd.
Publishers of Scarce Scholarly Books
280 LAFAYETTE STREET
NEW YORK. N. Y. 10012

Library of Congress Catalog Card Number: 78-117590

Standard Book Number 8383-1023-0

Printed in the United States of America

CONTENTS

INTRODUCTION

DURING the 'reconstructive' period which followed the First World War I published four short books about poetry, alternating them with collections of poems. They are coloured by the contemporary view of humanity as convalescent after a serious nervous break-down and resolved on a complete reorganization of its habits and ideas. It was easy to identify myself closely with convalescent and reconstructive humanity. Still in a neurasthenic state from my own war experiences, I was starting life again, at the age of twenty-three, free of pre-War commitments. My hope was to help the recovery of public health of mind, as well as my own, by the writing of 'therapeutic' poems; and to increase their efficacy by a study of the nature of poetry 'from subjective evidence.'

As a neurasthenic, I was interested in the newly expounded Freudian theory: when presented with English reserve and common sense by W. H. R. Rivers, who did not regard sex as the sole impulse in dream-making or assume that dream-symbols are constant, it appealed to me as reasonable. I applied his case-history method of accounting for emotional dreams to the understanding of romantic poems, my own and others', and found it apt enough; though poems were obviously complicated, I wrote, by 'the secondary elaboration that the poet gives them when no longer in a self-hypnotized condition.' My findings are recorded in *On English Poetry* (1922), in the final chapter of *The Meaning of Dreams* (1924),[1] and again in *Poetic Unreason* (1925). In my foreword to *On English Poetry* I describe my work as no more than an 'irregular approach to the problem of the nature of the poetic art: workshop notes.'

The awkward position into which I had put myself by too close an interest in morbid psychology, and then in philosophy, did not appear clearly until I tried, in *Poetic Unreason*, to elaborate these notes for academic purposes: the book was to serve as a thesis for a literary degree at Oxford, the subject offered being 'The Illogical Element in

---

[1] The substance of this chapter is incorporated in Chapter 24 of my *White Goddess* (Faber & Faber, 1948).

English Poetry, with a study of its modification by Classical and its Exploitation by Romantic writers.' I record in the *Foreword* that I recast it nine times; but it remained a tangle of contradictions or difficult evasions of contradiction.

The 'universal' applicability of a poem was, I wrote, an illusion, because of the perpetual flux of human opinion since the historical process began. Though acknowledging poetry itself as the dominating ideal I described it as being as remote and unrealizable an ideal as perfection. A poem could not escape the taint of contemporaneity, and the innumerable and scarcely satisfiable demands made on the poet, by the contemporary interests which he claimed to reconcile, changed as soon as he satisfied them. There were therefore neither 'good' nor 'bad' poems in any final sense: poems could not be legitimately criticized except as they stated or did not state, untangled or did not untangle, on some specific occasion, this or that public emotional knot. As soon as a poem was written it lost its interest for the poet: he realized that it was only an approximation to poetry. Poetry was impossible. This impossibility should not, however, discourage the true poet: rather it should brace him and keep him continually on the move, always again trying to make to-day catch up with to-morrow by a rapid casting back of to-days into yesterday. But in his continuous studies of poems, both his own and other people's, he should destructively analyse the effects of poetic magic by the same rationalistic tests that he would himself apply to illusionism. For though he might achieve, for his time, a satisfying sensation of enlightenment by the skilful control of words, this would be only temporary and further sensations depended on the supersession of previous ones.

Poetic Unreason contains a chapter on poetic genius with the thesis that the so-called 'supreme genius' is one whose life symbolizes and includes the principal conflicts of his own historical period, and in whose work occurs the solution of these conflicts or the most favourable attitude towards them that hitherto has been found; but that genius is not a constant quality, since the court of poetic judgment lies with the changing historical needs for poetry. This conclusion was out of keeping with my natural poetic preferences: I maintained it chiefly as an argument against contemporary poetic manifestos of an intellectual *poésie pure*, or 'absolute poetry,' which was to be written within history but insulated against the changing temperatures of time by a vacuum-bottle trick of abstractness. I was saying no more than that until the Day of Judgment no values but human values are ascertainable; a Day which cannot be anticipated. 'One goes plodding on and hoping for a miracle,' I wrote.

The difficulty lay in my attempt to satisfy myself by satisfying everyone as if myself. I was trying to reconcile the psychological view with my own poetic conscience; the relativist view of good and bad with a strong personal bias towards the good; and a sentimental love of humanity with an unappeasable mistrust of the individuals that composed humanity. If the poet must be regarded as a chairman of these sub-personalities representing every legitimate human interest the further question came up: what about the representatives of definitely anti-poetic interests, such as philosophical absolutism? The answers I gave were: that the psychological view could be challenged by postulating true poetry as a post-Classical Romanticism—a writing of poetry in the Romantic mode of apparent unreason, but with full awareness of its symbolic connotations as 'sensorial hieroglyphs'; that the relativist view of good and bad could be argued against philosophical absolutism; and that the personal bias towards good could be excused as a human limitation which the assiduous practice of poetry might in time remove. But these conclusions were not confidently drawn.

The remaining two books, *Contemporary Techniques of Poetry* and *The Future of the Art of Poetry*, were concerned with questions of poetic craftsmanship. They were published at a time when the popular interest in poetry, revived by the stresses of an unusually horrible war, had not yet subsided and the triangular feud between Victorian conservatists, 'Georgian' liberals and post-Georgian anarchists was being fought in the columns of scores of literary magazines. My attitude had become increasingly historical. *Contemporary Techniques of Poetry* was a review of modern poets as writing behaviouristically according to the political camps into which they were divided. I welcomed the modernistic tendency as an effort towards the conversion of to-day into to-morrow; though recognizing the irony, which was the keynote to modernism, as a passing historical phenomenon. *The Future of the Art of Poetry* was an attempt to historicize even the future towards which modernism was tending.

Re-reading these four books in the reconstructive period which follows the Second World War, I find that my practical observations were, on the whole, sound: mixed up with the unsound theories and written in a less uncertain prose style, are a good many scattered notes and two entire essays which seem worth republishing. They appear here as 'Observations on Poetry (1922–25),' 'The Future of Poetry' and 'The Sources of *The Tempest*.' My wholehearted devotion to poetry has not altered in the interval, but I no longer use psychological or philosophical terms when writing about it, and for the last twenty-two years have abandoned the view that the poet is a public servant ministering to the caprices of a world in perpetual flux. I now regard him as independent of fashion and public service, a servant only of the true Muse, committed on her behalf to continuous personal variations on a single pre-historic, or post-historic, poetic theme; and have thus ceased to feel the frantic strain of swimming against the stream of time.

In 1926 I entered into a literary partnership with Laura Riding (now Laura Jackson) which was not dissolved until 1939. In 1926–27 we collaborated in *A Pamphlet Against Anthologies* and *A Survey of Modernist Poetry*, both word-by-word collaborations. She has since given me permission to reprint any of our various collaborations and include them with work of my own, at my discretion, on the ground that they no longer interest her. What I reprint here of the two books is not the full text—I have left out the literary polemics and much else that is no longer topical though retaining the excusably savage *Perfect Modern Lyric* chapter. My comment on *A Survey of Modernist Poetry* will be found on page 166. Most of the remaining essays, especially those published in *Epilogue*, an annual which we edited between 1934 and 1936 and which commanded increasing inattention in literary circles, owe a great deal to her criticism. Two of them, *Poetic Drama* and *Poetry and Politics*, are collaborations with her. They are all re-printed here more or less as they were written and call for no autopsy.

I have included *The Ghost of Milton* as a minority report justifying my dismay at the recent revival of Milton-worship. To me Milton has always been a monster and a renegade who, as soon as he had perfected himself in the *trivium* of verse-writing, abandoned his half-hearted allegiance to the Muse and set himself up as a grand quadrivial anti-poet.

The Common Asphodel links this volume with my recently published *The White Goddess*, which is a historical grammar of poetic myth; it emphasizes my contention that poets must know exactly what they are writing about in the most practical sense, if they are not to be mistaken either for fools or for rhetoricians.

The title of this book, suggested by the last essay, is shorthand for saying that the popular view of what poetry is, or ought to be, has for centuries been based on sentimental misapprehensions: most people think of asphodel, and of poetry, as a rare, fragrant, soporific flower from a fanciful midsummer meadow. They know nothing of its genus, of its flowering season, of its sovereign virtues, of the harsh rocky soil in which it grows, or of its roots and seeds, and have only the vaguest notion of its magical associations with life, doom and immortality. The botanical drawing which appears as the practical frontispiece of the book does not, of course, explain the nature of the common asphodel—a hardy, tall, tough, unscented and commercially value-less plant—any more than these essays explain the nature of poetry; it does not even give a clue to its geographical distribution. But it may at least help the curious to distinguish asphodel, when they see it, from orchid, lavender and poppy.

Deyá   R.G.
  Mallorca
  1949

OBSERVATIONS ON POETRY
(1922–1925)

I

THE POETIC TRANCE

THE nucleus of every poem worthy of the name is rhythmically formed in the poet's mind, during a trance-like suspension of his normal habits of thought, by the supra-logical reconciliation of conflicting emotional ideas. The poet learns to induce the trance in self-protection whenever he feels unable to resolve an emotional conflict by simple logic. If interrupted during this preliminary process of composition he will experience the disagreeable sensations of a sleep-walker disturbed; and if able to continue until the draft is completed will presently come to himself and wonder: was the writer really he?

As soon as he has thus dissociated himself from the poem, the secondary phase of composition begins: that of testing and correcting on commonsense principles, so as to satisfy public scrutiny, what began as a private message to himself from himself—yet taking care that nothing of poetic value is lost or impaired. For the reader of the poem must fall into a complementary trance if he is to appreciate its full meaning. The amount of revision needed depends largely on the strength and scope of the emotional disturbance and the degree of trance. In a light trance, the critical sense is not completely suspended; but there is a trance that comes so close to sleep that what is written in it can hardly be distinguished from ordinary dream-poetry: the rhymes are inaccurate, the phrasing eccentric, the texture clumsy, the syntax rudimentary, the thought-connexions ruled by free-association, the atmosphere charged with unexplained emotion.

The classical instance of a poem composed in deep trance is Coleridge's *Kubla Khan*. Though the thought-connexions in the published version remain characteristically obscure, it is clear that Coleridge revised the first draft considerably after his unfortunate interruption by the 'gentleman from Porlock.' I believe that if it could be recovered we should find, for instance, that *Abora* rhymed with *dulcimer*:

> I saw an Abyssinian maid
> And on a dulcimer she played—
> A damsel with a dulcimer,
> Singing of Mount Abora.

The published version runs:

> A damsel with a dulcimer
> In a vision once I saw:
> It was an Abyssinian maid,
> And on her dulcimer she played,
> Singing of Mount Abora.

Here *saw* is too self-conscious an assonance, and too far distant from *Abora*, to have been part of the original laudanum-dream.

Poetry as the reconciliation of conflicting emotional ideas may be illustrated by crucial lines from Elizabethan and Jacobean drama. When Lady Macbeth complains:

> All the perfumes of Arabia will not sweeten this little hand.

the conflict is between her ambition to command the luxuries of queenship and her fear of divine retribution as a murderess: between 'All the perfumes of Arabia will sweeten my little hands' and 'Nothing will ever cleanse this hand of blood.'

When Ferdinand views the dead body of the Duchess of Malfi, in Webster's play, and says:

> Cover her face: mine eyes dazzle: she died young.

the word 'dazzle' conveys two simultaneous emotions: sun-dazzled awe at loveliness, tear-dazzled grief for early death.

When Marlowe's Doctor Faustus is waiting for the clock to strike and the Devil to exact his debt, he cries:

> That Time may cease and midnight never come!
> *O lente, lente currite noctis equi.*

Prosaic commentators have remarked on the inappropriate oversweetness of the quotation, 'Go slowly, slowly, coursers of the night,' originally spoken by an Ovidian lover with his arms around the mistress from whom he must part at dawn. But Marlowe has chosen it both to mark the distance which the scholar Faustus has travelled since his first dry Latin quotation:

Bene disserere est finis logices.
('Is to dispute well, Logick's chiefest end.')

and to combine in a single expression mawkish sensuality with agonized fear of the eternal bonfire.

Such poetry has a therapeutic effect on the minds of readers similarly disturbed by conflicting emotions. The Greeks presented this notion mythically in the fable of Perseus, the hero who rode Pegasus. The polished shield given him by the Goddess Athene mirrored the Gorgon with no hurtful effect and enabled him to behead her at his ease. Poetic drama to the Greeks was thus a rite of spiritual cleansing.

II

PROSE AND POETRY

Prose is the art of manifest statement: the periods and diction may vary with the emotional mood, but the latent meanings of the words that compose it are largely disregarded. In poetry a supplementary statement is framed by a precise marshalling of these latent meanings; yet the reader would not be aware of more than the manifest statement were it not for the heightened sensibility induced in him by the rhythmic intoxication of verse.

III

FAKE POETRY AND BAD POETRY

Fake poetry results from pretending to have undergone the profound mental disturbance that calls poetry into being: the faker draws on the experiences of real poets, thieving peculiar turns of speech and metrical irregularities in the hope of conveying a conviction of genuineness. It must be distinguished from ordinary bad poetry, which results from a failure to transform a private poetic occasion into a public one by critical commonsense. It is characteristic of the bad poet that he cannot understand why nobody appreciates his work, which he knows to be genuinely poetic in inception, and is bitterly resentful of the fake poet's popular success.

Q. When is a fake not a fake?
A. When hard-working and ingenious conjurers are by common courtesy billed as magicians.
Q. But when is a fake not a fake?
A. When it's a Classic, and organ-music, and all that.
Q. But when is a fake not a fake?
A. When lapse of time has obscured the original sources of borrowing and when the faker is so competent in his trick of synthesizing the occasional 'beauties' of usually indifferent poets that even the incorruptible porter of Parnassus winks and says 'Pass, friend!' This sort of hermit-crab, secure in his stolen armour, becomes a very terror among the simple whelks.

IV

SCHOOLS

Most histories of English poetry are a record of 'schools,' 'political tendencies,' and metrical fashions. But poets appear spasmodically, write their best poetry at uncertain intervals, owe nothing to schools and, in so far as they are behaving poetically, steer well clear of politics. Schools are formed by the fakers who try to formalize the magic of the real poets; and the history of such set forms as the sonnet, the Spenserian stanza and the heroic couplet is of no greater importance to the student of poetry than is the history of numismatics to the student of finance.

Poetry is not a science but an act of faith. Mountains are moved by it against all the rules laid down by the professors of dynamics—only for short distances, admittedly; still, beyond dispute, moved. The one possible test of the legitimacy of this or that technical method is the practical question: 'Did the mountain stir?' Yet the same mountain will never move twice at the same word of command.

V

RHYME

Rhymes properly used are the good servants whose presence at the dinner-table gives the guests a sense of opulent security; never awkward or over-clever, they hand the dishes silently and professionally. You can trust them not to interrupt the conversation or allow their personal disagreements to come to the notice of the guests; but some of them are getting very old for their work.

Milton, Spenser and Campion all used rhyme though agreeing to condemn it as a barbarism, there being no rhymes in the Greek and Latin classics which were regarded as the foundation of civilized literature. Now that English poetry is accepted as an independent tradition, rhyme is generally approved even by Classicists, but with the proviso that it must on no account appear to guide the sense: it must come unexpectedly and yet inevitably, like presents at Christmas, and convey the comforting sense of free will within predestination. The chimes must answer one another harmoniously and clearly, whatever the poetic context; and though there are licensed exceptions to this rule, known as near-rhymes and sight-rhymes—e.g. *have* and *grave; earth* and *hearth; love* and *remove*—where the pronunciation of one or other of the words has changed in the course of the last four centuries, the Classicist professes to be outraged by such 'Cockney' rhymes as *dawn* and *morn, thought* and *sort.* He far prefers 'French rhymes,' i.e. *groan* and *grown, poor* and *pour,* which at least have the authority of Chaucer.

Modern anti-Classicists either reject rhyme as an impediment to free poetic expression—a 'silly ornament' Mr. Flint has lately called it— or modify the harmony of its chimes to suit the context. It has been found, for example, that to rhyme a stressed syllable with an unstressed, e.g. *spent* with *moment, dish* with *famish,* or one unstressed syllable with another, e.g. *melon* with *Mammon* and *Babylon,* gives the effect of uncertainty, incompleteness, suspense. Wilfred Owen's use of assonantal French rhymes in 'Strange Meeting': *escaped, scooped; groined, groaned; bestirred, stared*—to convey the heavy, fateful, nightmarish atmosphere of the Hindenburg Tunnel in which the meeting took place—has been much admired and imitated. Miss Edith Sitwell and others use rhyme as a means of arraigning the ethical and philosophical structure on which Classicism rests: not only using half-rhymes, French rhymes, assonances, Cockney rhymes, e.g. *board* and *fraud*, and false rhymes, e.g. *bath* and *laugh*, but letting the rhymes seem to guide the sense:

> The wind's bastinado
> Whipt on the calico
> Skin of the Macaroon
> And the black Picaroon
> Beneath the galloon
> Of the midnight sky . . .

—thus advancing a view of life as founded in error, boredom and ugliness and ruled by caprice. Granted, Miss Sitwell does not regard herself as a revolutionary and will even on occasion proclaim herself a traditionalist; but that is no more than bearing lightly home the handle of the family pitcher which has gone to the well once too often.

VI

ARIPHRADES

When Aristotle, who was not a poet himself, laid down that poets describe what might be, whereas historians describe what has been, and that poetry is 'of more philosophic, graver import than history because its statements are of a universal nature,' that was well said. But he went on to explain 'what might be' as meaning what is 'probable and necessary' according to every-day experience of life; and here we must dissent. Aristotle was trying to free poetry from the language of myth in which it originated and to confine it within logical and educative limits; it was to him only an intuitive imitation of how typical men think and react upon one another when emotionally stimulated. Yet he defended poetical properties that would correspond nowadays with 'floweret gay,' 'vernal choir,' 'leafy bowers' and so forth, on the ground that 'it is indeed a great thing to make proper use of these poetic forms as also of compounds and strange words. The very fact of their not being in ordinary speech gives the diction a non-prosaic character.' One Ariphrades had been ridiculing the tragedians for the use of these forms. Aristotle saw that archaic diction and the display of theatrical masks and buskins surprised and hypnotized simple-minded theatre-goers and served as a reminder to the intelligent ones that 'imitation' was not realism. But he did not see that as soon as a single Ariphrades had ridiculed what was no longer a surprise the time had come to discard the convention; ridicule is catching.

A strange superstition survives among Classicists that some flowers are poetical and others are not. Thus Mr. Reginald Cripps recently in a description of a villa garden:

> Indian cress, unknown to verse
> And yet a glory; nought of grace
> Is wanting to this humble place.

Apollo is implored to include the plant in a post-Edwardian edition of his poetical register.

VII

VERS LIBRE

Writers of *vers libre* claim that their work, composed in natural rhythms, is untainted by such irrelevant or decaying images as constantly infiltrate into poems written in set metres.

But this apparent advantage is offset by a loss of control over the poem; for the rhythmic part of poetry consists in emotional variations on a given metrical norm. So my neighbour Dr. Robert Bridges told me downrightly the other day that in his opinion *vers libre* was a contradiction in terms. At any rate, the standard which the leading exponents of *vers libre* set themselves is not a high one. With rhythmic freedom so dearly bought one would expect a more intricate poetic meaning than that found in poems of strict metre; but all that one gets is American-French rhetoric.

'Natural rhythms' need no laborious search. A queer, wayward, broken-kneed rhythm often runs through whole sentences of standard prose. The following news item has not had a word changed since I found it in the *Daily Mirror*:

John Frain
Of Ballaghadereen
Was indicted at Roscommon
For the murder of his father.

He battered his father, an old man, to
    death with a pounder.

The jury found him
Unable to plead
And he was committed
To an asylum.

One doesn't 'listen' when reading standard prose; it is only in poetry that one looks out for metre and rhythmic variations on it. The writers of *vers libre* rely on their printers to call your attention to what is called 'cadence' or 'rhythmic relation' (not easy to follow) which might have escaped you if printed as prose; *this* sentence, you'll find, has its thumb to its nose.

In Latin verse a word can scan only in a single way: quantity dominates accent. In English verse, accent dominates quantity. The Latin quantitative scansion, for example, of the line:

I am outcast of Paradise

would be—to disregard elision:

Ī am ōutcast ōf Părădīsē.

This does not correspond with the English accentual scansion—which is not even fixed, but varies with the mood of the speaker. Here is the same line introduced into nonsense rhymes of three different metres:

Satan to the garden came,
Found his Lordship walking lame.
'Give me manna, mead and spice;
I am outcast of Paradise.'

He asked his Lordship then
    For manna and mead and spice.
'I am Chief of the fallen Ten,
    I am outcast of Paradise.'

> Wonderful dainties
>   Around me I see.
> I am outcast of Paradise.
>   Give·them to¯me!

And if the line were introduced into *vers libre* it would be impossible to decide how the author intended it to be scanned.

VIII

THE HOUNDS OF SPRING

As a boy I had been often told that Swinburne was 'absolutely wonderful,' that I would be carried away by him, that the opening chorus of *Atlanta in Calydon* was the most melodious verse in English. Eventually I felt bound to read it:

> When the hounds of Spring are on Winter's traces
> The Mother of months in meadow and plain . . .

I was not carried away. For a time I concluded that the fault was mine, that I had no ear; but one day I began asking myself whether in the lines just quoted, the two *in*'s of *Spring* and *Winter* and the two *mo*'s of *Mother* and *months* did not come too close together for euphony; and who exactly was the Mother; and whether the heavy alliteration in *m* was not too obvious a device; and whether *months* was not a stumbling-block in galloping verse of this sort . . .

I am glad to be confirmed in my judgment of Swinburne's technical competence by Dr. Bridges, who has given me an amusing account of how he misread *Hertha*, the opening lines of which run:

> I am that which began;
>   Out of me the years roll;
> Out of me, God and man;
>   I am equal and whole;
> God changes, and man, and the form of them bodily; I am the soul.

He began reading them as though they had four beats apiece:

> Í am that ‖ whích begán;
> Oút of mé ‖ the yeárs róll;
> Oút of mé ‖ Gód and mán;
> Í am équal ‖ ánd whóle;

and thought this noble and imposing, though 'équal ánd whóle' seemed a trifle brass-bandish. Only when he reached the conclusion of the stanza did he realize that he had made a mistake, and that they were two-beat lines after all. 'It was Swinburne's impudence in putting the Almighty's name in an unaccented place and accenting the name of man that put me on the wrong track.' Swinburne's fault, I agree, was in his wrong sense of material: trying to make muslin do the work of camel's hair cloth. He was, as usual, imposing a metre on the theme rather than letting the theme determine it.

IX

THE OUTWARD AND INWARD EARS

Though the poet ought to write as if his work were intended to be read aloud, in practice the reading aloud of a poem distracts attention from its subtler properties by emphasizing the more obvious ones. The outward ear is easily deceived. A beautiful voice can make magic even with bad or fraudulent poetry which the eye, as the most sophisticated organ of sense, would reject at once; for the eye is in close communication with the undeceivable inward ear.

X

SECONDARY ELABORATION

The technical process of revision can be conveniently illustrated by the later drafts of a poem I recently wrote, called *Cynics and Romantics*; I do not claim that it has lasting value and three or four lines are sufficient for the purpose.

1st *Draft:* In club or mess-room let them sit,
            Let them indulge salacious wit
            On love's romance, but not with hearts
            Accustomed to those healthier parts
            Of grim self-mockery . . .

Consideration: There is an angry jerkiness in 'Let them indulge' and a roughness in 'indulge salacious' which do not suit the opening of the poem; for a whiie it must proceed as suavely as possible.

2nd Draft: In club or mess-room let them sit
        Indulging controversial wit
        On love's romance, but not with hearts
        Accustomed . . .

Consideration: Now the first two lines both start with 'In,' which catches the eye unnecessarily. And in 'sit indulging' two short *i*'s come close together; the vowel sounds must be more varied. 'Controversial' is not quite the word that is needed: these wits are too blasé to indulge in genuine controversy. And 'love's romance' is too telegraphic a phrase; 'the romance of love' is what was meant, but the metre forbade it. Better to put merely 'love' and let the context supply the sense of 'romance.' 'But' is not strong enough for the task assigned to it.

3rd Draft: In club or mess-room let them sit
        At skirmish of salacious wit,
        Laughing at love, yet not with hearts
        Accustomed . . .

Consideration: 'Skirmish' is good because it conveys the unserious atmosphere of a military mess, but we now have too earnest an alliteration in *s*, so 'salacious' can come into the poem later. And now there are two *at*'s close together; one of them must go.

4th Draft: In club or mess-room let them sit
        With skirmish of destructive wit,
        Laughing at love, yet not with hearts
        Accustomed . . .

Consideration: But now one of the two *with*'s must go; obviously the first, which makes an ugly assonance with 'wit.' Restore the first 'at' and remove the second; then if 'deriding' is substituted for 'laughing at' there is a better variation of vowels in the line—'laughing' and 'hearts' are too much alike in sound—and the over-earnest alliteration in *l* is avoided.

5th Draft: In club or mess-room let them sit
        At skirmish of destructive wit,
        Deriding love, yet not with hearts
        Accustomed . . .

Consideration: But now '*de*structive' and '*de*riding' come too close together. 'Ingenious' is far better than 'destructive.' It improves the sound of the lines with its long *e*, and suggests that the derision was really witty not merely dirty. The two *in*'s are now far enough separated not to catch the eye or irritate the ear. 'Accustomed' is too blank a word; one can be accustomed to a thing which one dislikes. A more accurate word is 'accorded,' since the syllable *cor* means 'heart'; and its use further varies the vowels.

6th Draft: In club or mess-room let them sit
            At skirmish of ingenious wit,
            Deriding love, yet not with hearts
            Accorded . . .

Consideration: That is better; now for the next lines. But it is possible that they will dictate a further revision of the first three.

The considerations of euphony illustrated above are modified or forgone in certain contexts, especially where the prevailing mood is one of obscurity, difficulty, emotional stress or monotony. Leigh Hunt records:

I remember Keats reading to me with great relish and particularity, conscious of what he had set forth, the lines describing the supper [in *The Eve of St. Agnes*] and ending with the words:

         And lucent syrops, tinct with cinnamon;

Mr. Wordsworth would have said that the vowels were not varied enough; but Keats knew where his vowels were *not* to be varied.

Keats was imitating with his succession of short *i* sounds a gourmet's fastidious pursing of lips. Leigh Hunt continues:

On the occasion above alluded to, Wordsworth found fault with the repetition of the concluding sound of the participles in Shakespeare's line about bees:

         The *singing* masons *building* roofs of gold.

This, he said, was a line which Milton would never have written. Keats thought, on the other hand, that the repetition was in harmony with the continued note of the singers, and that Shakespeare's negligence, if negligence it was, had instinctively felt the thing in the best manner.

Wordsworth was right. The manipulation of vowels and consonants is, for poets in the Virgil-Dante-Milton tradition, a matter of achieving abstract musical grandeur without consideration of the emotional context. Virgil would never have permitted himself to write a line so playfully imitative of galloping horses as:

Quadrupedante putrem sonitu quatit ungula campum

if he had not remembered, and felt obliged to emulate, Homer's similar line about the bounding stone which cheated Sisyphus.

I forget the name of the old Italian portrait-painter who, when dying, gathered his friends and pupils to his bedside and bequeathed them this legacy of wisdom, the fruit of a lifetime's experience:

The art of portrait-painting consists in putting the high-lights of the eyes at exactly the right spot.

When I come to die I shall have an equally important message to deliver:

The art of poetry consists in knowing exactly how to manipulate the letter *S*.

XI

THE ARROGANCE OF POETS

The arrogance of the poet is based on his courageous dedication to a thankless profession, the difficulties and humiliations of which he alone fully realizes. Even where others think that he has succeeded memorably, he knows that he has failed; for the practice of poetry is conditional on an awareness that only an approximation to poetic truth is ever possible. Yet he forgets this condition in the moment of writing, when it always seems that at last something of perpetual value is being achieved.

XII

SCIENTIFIC ENGLISH

Of all classes of writers, poets are the most accurate in the use of ordinary words; scientists the least, even those research professors who are at pains to improvise a supplementary vocabulary of extraordinary ones. *Instinct and the Unconscious* by Dr. W. H. R. Rivers, a most important contribution to modern psychological research, contains a passage about the unaccountable foreknowledge shown by certain grubs of the needs that they will have to meet after their metamorphosis into moths. He writes:

This grub, after a life completely spent within the channels in a tree-trunk which it itself manufactures . . .

'Yes,' he said, when I questioned the sentence, 'somehow the two *it*'s coming together look a bit awkward, but I have had a lot of trouble with that sentence, and come to the conclusion that I'd rather have it clumsy than obscure.'

I suggested that 'tree-trunk which it itself manufactures' was surely not what he meant, but that the fault of the writing lay deeper than the mere omission of commas: it was a failure to visualize the event described. Although in prose the latent associations of words may be disregarded, their manifest meaning at least must be respected. A grub cannot *manufacture* a channel. Even an artisan who can manufacture a boot or a boot-box cannot *manufacture* a channel; he can only scoop, or dig, one or lay it with manufactured tiles. And a channel can be found only on the surface of a tree-trunk; channels, once they penetrate it, become *tunnels*, which are *driven* or *bored*. And a grub can be *within* a tree-trunk, but not within a channel; 'within' implies overhead cover. The sentence should have run:

The grub, after a life completely spent within a tree-trunk, in tunnels bored by itself . . .

Dr. Rivers explained good-humouredly: 'Scientists are, or should be, functionally incapable of such visualization; normal visualization is dangerous, abnormal visualization fatal, to scientific study, as offering imaginative vistas of hypothetic events unconfirmed by investigation.'

XIII

TEXTURE

Classicists pay great attention to the texture of poetry; their aim is euphony and, within the strict metrical patterns approved by tradition,

variety. 'Texture' covers the interrelations of all vowels and con-
sonants in a poem considered as mere sound. The skilled craftsman
varies the vowel sounds as if they were musical notes so as to give an
effect of melodic richness; uses liquid consonants, labials and open
vowels for smoothness; aspirates and dentals for force; gutturals for
strength; sibilants for flavour, as a cook uses salt. His alliteration is not
barbarously insistent, as in Anglo-Saxon poems or *Piers Plowman*,
but concealed by the gradual interlacement of two or three alliterative
sequences. He gauges the memory-length of the reader's inward ear
and plants the second word of an alliterative pair at a point where the
memory of the first has begun to blur but has not yet faded. He varies
his word-endings, keeping a careful eye on *-ing* and *-y*, and takes care
not to interrupt the smooth flow of the line, if this can possibly be
avoided, by close correspondence between terminal consonants and
the initial consonants that follow them—e.g. *break ground, maid's
sorrow, great toe*. Non-Classicists either disregard texture as another of
the heavy chains clamped on the naked limbs of poetry, or use their
understanding of it for deliberate exercises in cacophony or dislocation:
by judicious manipulation of vowels and consonants a line can be made
to limp, crawl, scream, bellow and make other ugly or sickening noises.
In a passage from *The Waste Land* Mr. T. S. Eliot, though a master
craftsman of musical verse, amuses himself by letting a line snuffle
and clear its throat realistically:

> Madame Sosostris, famous clairvoyante,
> *Had a bad cold, nevertheless*
> Is known to be the wisest woman in Europe.

In *Ancient History* (I quote the earlier version) Mr. Siegfried Sassoon
writes:
> . . . he thought of Abel, soft and fair,
> A lover with disaster in his face
> And scarlet berries twisted in his hair.

Here the sense of Abel's weakness is conveyed by the similar termina-
tions of *lover* and *disaster* and by the succession of short *i*'s in 'berries
twisted in his.' The contrast is with the boisterous and alliterative:

> He was the grandest of them all, was Cain,
> A lion laired in the hills whom none might tire,
> Swift as a stag, a stallion of the plain,
> Hungry and fierce with deeds of huge desire.

And Mr. D. H. Lawrence, in his description of the bat circling round his room and refusing expulsion, writes:

> Go, but he will not . . .
> Round and round and round
> In an impure haste
> Fumbling, a beast in air,
> And stumbling, lunging, and touching the walls, the bell-wires
> About my room.

Here the ugly sequence of *fumbling, stumbling, lunging, touching* suggests the awkwardness and giddiness of the baffled pursuer.

XIV

FASHIONS IN POETRY

One age values emotional intensity in poems, another values sophistication and restraint; one, a high standard of craftsmanship, another, an anarchic abandon of grammatical or logical control. We are passing from a phase in which no poet was respected unless he had published poems many thousands of lines long; and soon we may limit ourselves like the Japanese to five or three lines a poem. Artificial extravagance of conceits is sometimes valued, at other times a simpleness verging on infantility; and so on. We can now read the history of the recent War, with its immediate sequel of peace and depression, without prejudice and see that the literary canons of good and bad in England corresponded closely with, and were no more stationary than, national political sentiment. From 1914 to the end of 1915 the idealism of the Government poster 'Your King and Country Need You,' the love of battle as voiced by a professional soldier like Julian Grenfell, the spirit of sacrifice as voiced by the patriotic Rupert Brooke, were necessary for the public inspiration of a militarily unorganized power engaged in a death-struggle with a highly organized one. But as soon as 'There is some corner of a foreign field that is for ever England' had achieved its end and this England had adopted universal military service, when every man was a compulsory hero, when love of battle in prospect had become loathing in retrospect, when 'Your King and Country Need You' could be a trench joke for pulling corpses out of sump-pits by their boots, then sentiment changed: Siegfried Sassoon became the popular laureate of disillusion and suffering realistically conveyed. Brooke's contribution began to be questioned as early as April 1915, when Charles Sorley wrote:

He is far too obsessed with his own sacrifice, regarding the going to war of himself (and others) as a highly intense, remarkable and sacrificial exploi., whereas it is merely the conduct demanded of him (and others) by the turn of circumstances where non-compliance would have made life intolerable. He has clothed his attitude in fine words: but he has taken the sentimental attitude.

Sorley was killed at Loos in October 1915 before trench warfare had embittered him, as it almost certainly would have embittered Brooke. But Sassoon, Herbert Read and Wilfred Owen were still serving in France in 1918 (Owen was killed just before the end) and, until the pressure of war was removed by the Armistice, poetry of idealism stank in the nostrils of all who had done any serious fighting.

With the Armistice and Peace, realistic war-poetry immediately lost its market, and now until the confident poetry of reconstruction can appear in Western Europe, the public laurels will be transferred either to civilian poets of scepticism and cynicism, Messrs. Hardy and Housman of the elder, Messrs. Aldous Huxley and T. S. Eliot of the younger generation, or to the poets of temporary escape, Mr. De la Mare, Mr. Blunden, the later Masefield and the middle Yeats.

XV

'BREAD I DIP IN THE RIVER'

Stevenson's famous ballad in praise of the Open Road is not what it seems to be. All he asks is Heaven above and the road before him; bread dipped in the running river will be sufficient subsistence for him as long as he lives. It is in fact, an invalid's poem: expressing an over-powering desire for freedom and a disgust with sickroom diet. A professional tramp told the other day, with horror, of the condition known as bread-sickness; after two or three months of unrelieved bread diet the stomach revolts and even the smell of a baker's shop causes vomiting. As for cold water . . .

XVI

HÉLAS, C'EST VICTOR HUGO

When English poetry goes Classical it goes French, and when it goes French it goes wrong. The French themselves are uncomfortably aware that the English by a failure to regularize their themes, diction and metre have contrived to leave the door open for a sudden unforeseen advent of poetry. M. André Gide, when asked recently 'who is the greatest of your poets?' hesitated, and then answered ruefully: '*Hélas, c'est Victor Hugo.*'

There is a story about Hugo in his dreadfully vigorous old age. A young subaltern was ordered to join his regiment in Madagascar. He had said all his good-byes and found himself with two or three hours to spend in Paris between trains. A courageous thought struck him: why not visit the great poet, whom he had never had the privilege of meeting, and pay his farewell respects? He took a fiacre to Hugo's house and was graciously admitted to his presence; there with tears in his eyes he explained that he was to be removed from his fatherland for a number of years, and craved as a souvenir of all that France represented—*la culture, la gloire, la liberté* and so on, to take into exile some poetic sentiment written in the hand of his *cher maître*.

Hugo was touched. Expatiating in his best style on *la gloire, la culture, la liberté, la civilisation* and so on, he seized his pen and wrote with a flourish on a strip of parchment:

> *La vie, c'est l'amour.*
> Victor Hugo

It happened two years later that the same officer's younger brother was also ordered abroad, this time to 'Les Indes.' His good-byes said, he found himself in Paris with the same two or three hours on his hands. It occurred to him: 'My brother was well received by the great Victor Hugo. Why should I be any the less welcome?' He took a fiacre to Hugo's house and explained his business with tears in his eyes.

Hugo was touched. He expatiated in his best style on *la gloire, la culture, la liberté, la civilisation, l'esprit, la jeunesse* and so on and presently seized his pen and wrote with a flourish on another strip of parchment:

> *L'amour, c'est la vie.*
> Victor Hugo

XVII

SHAKESPEARE'S FAIR COPIES

The act of composition is not one of communication between the poet and his public, but an intercommunication of different selves within him. This is proved by the rough and often almost illegible scrawl of the first draft of a poem—for instance, Trelawny records that Shelley's first drafts were 'frightful.' As soon as the poet comes out of his trance and can see the poem objectively he copies it out in neat and regular lines, crosses every *t* and dots every *i*, and signs his name boldly underneath. By this time the poem has fulfilled its primary function, that of informing the poet himself of the nature of a poetic experience; he sends it on its travels as a public record of the event and as a marketable commodity. It is recorded that Shakespeare never blotted a line. The inference drawn from this, that his first drafts were the last, is contradicted by the variant texts of the plays and sonnets; perhaps the meaning was merely that he wrote out his fair copies with extreme care and allowed no cancellations to appear in them.

XVIII

THE GROSSER SENSES

In my experience, poetic imagery concerned only with the visual sense is far less cogent than that concerned with the so-called 'grosser' senses of hearing, touch, taste and smell.

Shelley's imagery is remote and almost wholly visual and, whatever effect it may have on others, leaves me unmoved; Keats' imagery is sensuous, intimate, and, to me, unforgettable. Shelley was a volatile creature of air and fire: he seems never to have noticed what he ate or drank, except sometimes as a matter of vegetarian principle. Keats was earthy, with a sweet tooth and a relish for spices, cream and snuff, and in a letter mentions peppering his own tongue to bring out the delicious coolness of claret. His well-known lines in *The Eve of St Agnes*:

> The arras, rich with horseman, hawk, and hound,
> Flutter'd in the besieging wind's uproar;
> And the long carpets rose along the gusty floor.

appeal less to my visual sense than to my senses of hearing and touch. I identify myself with Porphyro and Madeline in their guilty flight and grope with them down the 'darkling corridor,' recognizing my whereabouts by touching with my fingertips the heavily embroidered outlines of horseman, hawk and hound on the flapping arras. The historically improbable 'long carpets' give me the horrible sensation of movement underfoot as my soft shoes grope hesitantly forward. The wind rumbles in the chimneys and howls around the corners of the castle.

In the earlier scene, where Porphyro courts Madeline with jellies and candied fruit, Keats records what Shelley would have described in wholly visual and probably rather sketchy terms, the strong moonlight streaming through stained glass on Madeline's breast as she sleeps:

> A casement high and triple-arch'd there was,
> All garlanded with carven imag'ries
> Of fruits, and flowers, and bunches of knot-grass,
> And diamonded with panes of quaint device,
> Innumerable of stains and splendid dyes,
> As are the tiger-moth's deep-damask'd wings;
> And in the midst, 'mong thousand heraldries,
> And twilight saints, and dim emblazonings,
> A shielded scutcheon blush'd with blood of queens and kings.

> Full on this casement shone the wintry moon,
> And threw warm gules on Madeline's fair breast . . .

As I read this I mentally finger the antique stone carving—its roughness of texture is suggested by 'bunches of knot-grass'—and the raised leadwork which frames the diamond-shaped panes, and the hinges of the handle and catch of the historically improbable 'casement'—Shelley would have been content to call it a window. The heraldic scutcheon is not merely 'of a field *gules*': it blushes with the blood of queens and kings. I feel a shivering alternation of heat and cold when I reach the last lines quoted above. For the only source of light is the wintry moon, yet Madeline's breast, exposed to the bitter cold of the castle room, is seemingly kept warm by the crimson light streaming upon it through the cold glass. The word 'stains' becomes illogically connected in my mind with the 'fruits, and flowers, and bunches of knot-grass' and is there translated into the smells and tastes of a hot summer—bruised flowers and grasses, crushed blueberries and raspberries. The imaginative appeal of 'the tiger-moth's deep-damask'd wings' I find irresistible. The savagery and stealth of *tiger*, the gentleness and vagueness of *moth*, contribute jointly to the atmosphere of suppressed fear that animates the poem. 'Damask'd' conveys similarly contradictory associations: the hardness, coldness and sharpness of a damascened blade, the soft warm texture of damask silk, the richness of a scented damask rose.

When Shelley in *Prometheus Unbound* mentions:

> The yellow bees in the ivy-bloom,

he does not conjure up, as Keats would have done, the taste of the last hot days of the dying English year, with over-ripe blackberries, ditches full of water, and the hedges grey with old man's beard. He is not aware of the veteran bees whirring their frayed wings or sucking rank honey from the dusty yellow blossoms of the ivy. Instead:

> He will watch from dawn to gloom
> The lake-reflected sun illume
> The yellow bees in the ivy-bloom . . .

They are to him merely yellow specks in silent motion across the darker ivy, greatly etherealized by being reflected in the limpid and somewhat unreal waters of Lake Como.

XIX

CENTENARIES

The Keats, Shelley and Byron centenaries have been most amusing: their spectacle of antique dons and savants ceremoniously prostrating themselves before the youthful rebels of the past, with side glances of reproach for the Keatses, Shelleys and Byrons (conceited young puppies!) of their own day.

The critics of the *Quarterly* deserve no blame for sending Keats back to his gallipots after reading his first volume or for patronizing his second: literature had not yet taken the turn that made him a figure of crucial importance. Such criticism was unavoidable, and the best which they could give; even Keats' supporters praised him for what we now call the wrong motives. It was the same with Shakespeare: the shrewdest critic of that age, Ben Jonson, in his private conversations with Drummond of Hawthornden, was content to remark that 'Shakespeare wanted art.' (His commendatory verses prefixed to the *First Folio* should be read as a generous public tribute to an old friend and rival, not as literary criticism.) Francis Meres in his eulogy of contemporaries at the expense of the Classics gave him no precedence above his brother playwrights; and the solitary Barnefield who declared 'our fellow Shakespeare puts them all down' was plunging wildly.

An anonymous reviewer in the *Westminster Gazette* of 1874 declared, after reading a new volume of poems, that readers who, like himself, were tired of the trivialities of Mr. Tennyson, the harshness and infelicity of Mr. Browning, and the naughtiness of Mr. Swinburne, would find the true sacred flame of poetry still burning brightly in a volume entitled *Puck on Parnassus*, by H. Cholmondeley Pennell. Who knows whether posterity may not make a solitary and glorious Barnefield of this *Westminster Gazette* reviewer? And as for the pure and limpid English of the Authorized Version, 'the standard of all good writing,' only suppose that the Euphuists had been entrusted with the original Hebrew and Greek texts for free translation and poetical expansion; and the result ordered to be read in the churches! What sort of language would we be talking now, and what would be the 1925 standard of good writing?

XX

HAMLET

Shakespeare's *Hamlet* is an example of the complexity of poetry written under great emotional stress. It is supra-logical and written in defiance of the Aristotelian unities of time and space and probability.

Miss Lilian Winstanley in her *Hamlet and the Scottish Succession* proves that there are close historical analogues between the story of *Hamlet* and the political events of 1600, the year in which it was written, particularly the abortive Essex revolt that had been intended to further the succession of James VI of Scotland to the English throne then occupied by the aged Elizabeth. She accounts for Hamlet's contradictory nature by suggesting that he represents at once King James and the Earl of Essex, ill-matched associates in the same cause. Shakespeare, she says, has taken from James the central traits of Hamlet's character: the hatred of bloodshed, the irresolution, the philosophic mind, the fear of action, the hesitation to punish which is half weakness and half generosity. She writes:

> In so far as Hamlet is Essex, we see that he is one of the most brilliant and wittiest of courtiers. We see his unsuspiciousness and the generous but misplaced confidence which led him to his doom, his instability of character, his rashness, his passionateness, but through it all his nobility and the pathos of his fate.

Miss Winstanley well asks: if Hamlet was only the philosophic prince disliking bloodshed, why did young Fortinbras say of him at the end of the play that the one fitting funeral for him was 'the soldiers' music and the rites of war'? And if he was only the courtier 'unmatched in form and stature,' 'the glass of fashion and the mould of form,' how could he be also, but for this doubling of the parts, a despiser of dress and habiliments, a lover of privacy, a hater of the tricks of courtiers, and according to his own mother, 'fat and scant of breath'?

Miss Winstanley suggests three possible explanations for these historical analogues:

1. They belong to the atmosphere of the time and get in 'unconsciously.' Shakespeare sees these things around him and without knowing it incorporates them in his drama.

2. He is writing a literary drama in which he deliberately incorporates a certain amount of contemporary history.

3. He is dramatizing in a mythological way.

She holds that (1) can be rejected absolutely. The analogues are so important, numerous, detailed and close, that it does not seem to her that they can have got in by any form of accident, and that 'when we reflect moreover that they were all events of immediate interest the supposition is practically impossible.'

But that they are not accidental seems to me consistent with their having been introduced into the play without a full realization of their poetic significance. To Shakespeare in 1600, everything seemed to have crashed in ruins. Although he still had property at Stratford and elsewhere, his prosperity had received a rude, and it might prove a fatal, check. His patron, the Earl of Southampton, was awaiting execution in the Tower, where Essex, also his patron and recently instru-

mental in getting him the coveted distinction of a coat-of-arms, had
already lost his head. He and his disgraced company were obliged to
go on tour in the provinces and, as we learn from contemporary sneers
by the rival playwrights, to part with their stage clothes in order to
eat. Their place was taken in London by the 'little eyases' of which we
hear in the play-scene. Shakespeare's friend of the *Sonnets* and the
Dark Lady of the *Sonnets* had both deceived him, but he was still
clinging desperately to the hope that his friend was true to him in spite
of appearances; it was the sheet-anchor of his existence. That mood
appears in Sonnet 29, 'When in disgrace with Fortune and mens
eyes,' which I take to be contemporary with *Hamlet*.[1]

It is unfortunate that the original *Hamlet* play, based on the old
Danish saga of Almeth, which had been written some years before,
possibly by Kidd, possibly by Shakespeare himself, is no longer in
existence; a comparison between this and Shakespeare's rewriting of it
in 1600 would be illuminating. The only comparison that can now be
made is between the barbaric saga-story and the rewritten play. The
saga is certainly more consistent than the play and Shakespeare could
easily have turned it into a straightforward *History* had he felt inclined
to do so. In Shakespeare's Histories the poetry is only occasional; the
rest is drama and rhetoric. In his Tragedies it is dominant. Granted that
the historical analogues are not accidental, it is clear at least that he
did not sit down with the deliberate aim of welding the natures of
James and Essex into so inconsistent a character as Hamlet. No
Elizabethan dramatist was ever deliberately inconsistent.

I think it most unlikely that he knew beforehand how the rewritten
Hamlet would develop, but he knew at least that he had to write a good
'get-penny' touring play for his company during their exile from
London, and he probably also knew that the play would be somehow
expressive of the emotional distress in which he was labouring. As
each scene developed he must have become aware of the political
allusions occurring in it, but I cannot believe that he realized what
now seems obvious enough: that Hamlet was a political allegory of
his own disharmony. His professional misfortunes, that is to say,
were directly due to the failure of the Revolt, which was, in turn, due
to the failure of James and Essex to concert together for a common
political end. There was an irreconcilability of temperament: Essex
was magnanimous, passionate, reckless, courtier-like; James was mean,
slatternly, retired, timorous and scholarly. Prince Hamlet was smo-

---

[1] This subject is treated more fully in the next essay.

thered and battered by the wash and undertow of these same irrecon-
cilables; and Hamlet, as I read the story of the *Sonnets*, was a surrogate
of Shakespeare himself.

It is not only in Prince Hamlet that a fusion of characters occurs.
In the grave-digger's scene, the skull of the dead jester Yorick seems
to be in part representative of Shakespeare's dead self, the jaunty author
of the recent brilliant Comedies; but in treating of the grave-digger's
song:

> In youth when I did love, did love,
>   me thought it was very sweete . . .

the traditional approach of literary critics has merely been to note
'Comic relief, a fantastic curtailment of Lord Vaux's well-known
ballad published in Tottel's *Miscellany*,' or even to suspect it as an
interpolation of some theatrical hack-writer. The scene certainly is
often acted as a comic incident and accepted as such by an undiscerning
audience, but to Shakespeare it was as little comical as the mad scene
in *King Lear*; and is not relief in the sense that its content is less painful
or less related to the central emotional conflict than the 'To be or
not to be' soliloquy. Lord Vaux's poem is a most moving one:

> I loathe that I did love
> In youth that I thought sweet.

The question must be asked: 'Why did Shakespeare garble the song
in that particular way? And over an open grave?' To suggest that the
garbling is accidental or that he could not have had access to the
original version, or that he failed to appreciate its poetry, seems absurd.
At this period of Shakespeare's life the thought of suicide is constantly
occurring in the plays as a possible escape from the tangle of things,
but nowhere so painfully as in *Hamlet*. His fortunes being so low he
was not strong enough to face reality, as he faced it after they were
restored at the accession of King James, to admit that his friend was
actually 'as black as hell, as darke as night.'

The lyric irresolution of:

> In youth when I did love, did love,
>   me thought it was very sweete . . .

is made the stronger by recollection of the downright original 'I
loathe that I did love,' a sentiment to which he cannot afford to confess.

The scene has been thought to refer to the death of Tarleton, a
famous comedian of Shakespeare's company; but Miss Winstanley

thinks that the incident of the insult to the dead body refers to the Essex execution, Essex having been a brilliant jester and the executioner having painfully bungled his task. Essex, moreover, had been haunted by the dread of ignominy done to his body if he died on the scaffold, and had repeatedly spoken of this. In a letter to the Queen on May 28th, 1600 he wrote that he felt 'as if I were thrown into a corner like a dead carcase; I am gnawed upon and torn by the basest and vilest of creatures upon the earth. The tavern haunter speaks of me what he lists. Already they print me and make me speak to the world and shortly they will print me in what forms they list upon the stage.' Thus the dead Yorick is at least a treble character, comprising Essex, Tarleton and Shakespeare himself; but it seems incredible that this treble significance was logically premeditated.

THE SOURCES OF *THE TEMPEST*
(1925)

THE SOURCES OF THE TEMPEST

In a recent volume Professor Schücking, of Breslau, has done rather more than make a collection of well-known psychological inconsistencies in Shakespeare's plays which have puzzled commentators both in England and Germany: brushing aside all attempts to explain them away he assumes that Shakespeare was often a little inconsistent in order to achieve certain dramatic effects. He argues:

> We need hardly insist on the fact that on the whole he is most successful in making his plays coherent, and that the rather independent effect of some of the scenes does not actually lead to disorder and chaotic composition. But still we cannot help observing that even his work manifests what we may call a tendency to episodic intensification. Even when he is bent upon securing the highest effect which the subject will admit, to bring it home in the most convincing manner and make it irresistibly capture and hold the spectator's imagination, he sometimes introduces or amplifies details which cause us to lose the sense of a connected whole . . . 'It is evident,' says Rumelin, 'that he worked in scenes.'

This view Professor Schücking supports by an examination of the manuscript of *Sir Thomas More*, where it is evident that a number of playwrights parcelled out the work among themselves, several scenes being entrusted, probably by Shakespeare himself, to collaborators who were so vague about the general plan of the play that they did not even know the most important characters appearing in it and were sometimes obliged to write in the margin 'Another.' But even while proposing that this 'episodic writing' principle is characteristic of Elizabethan drama, both in one-man plays and in collaborations, the professor is surprised that in *The Tempest*, of which he has, as a result, no very high opinion, the character of Miranda is so changeable. First we are expected to see her as a child of nature who has never met a young man of any sort except the demi-devil Caliban, and then we find her generalizing merrily on the ways of the world. Again, the island is first obviously one of the Bermudas, but then is transplanted to the Adriatic. 'It really won't do,' he complains, in effect. 'Shakespeare has forgotten his *Poetics*.'

The Tempest cannot be fairly judged by Aristotelian standards. Shakespeare never listened kindly to the advice of his brother playwrights who upheld the dramatic conventions of Sophocles or Seneca: He was the 'master poet' who insisted on his 'own absurd courses,' and carried on something of the city-mystery tradition in which each guild contributed an episode of a topical or humorous kind strung on a loose thread of Scriptural history.

It is now generally acknowledged that there are three main sources of *The Tempest*: the first, an earlier play by Jacob Ayrer, a Nuremberger who died in 1605, or a lost variant of this play; the second, a Spanish romance by Ortunez de Calahorra; the third, a fairly large body of literature dealing with adventure in the New World. Ayrer's play, *Von der schönen Sidea*, accounts pretty completely for the Ariel-Ferdinand-Miranda-Prospero relations, and where there is interplay between these characters it only differs from *The Tempest* in being staged in a remote forest as opposed to a remote island. Shakespeare is likely to have heard about Ayrer's play from a member of one of the two companies of English actors who visited Nuremberg in 1604 and 1606.

An account of *Von der schönen Sidea* is given by Mr. Thomas in his *Three Notelets on Shakespeare*:

It is true that the scene in which Ayrer's play is laid and the names of the personages differ from those of *The Tempest*; but the main incidents of the two plays are all but identically the same. For instance, in the German drama Prince Ludolph and Leudegast supply the places of Prospero and Alonzo. Ludolph, like Prospero, is a magician, and like him has an only daughter, Sidea—the Miranda of *The Tempest*—and an attendant spirit Runcifal who, though not strictly resembling either Ariel or Caliban, may well be considered as the primary type which suggested to the nimble fancy of our great dramatist those strongly yet admirably contrasted beings. Shortly after the commencement of the play, Ludolph having been vanquished by his rival, and with his daughter Sidea driven into a forest, rebukes her for complaining of their change of fortune, and then summons his spirit Runcifal to learn from him their future destiny and prospects of revenge. Runcifal who, like Ariel, is somewhat 'moody' announces to Ludolph that the son of his enemy will shortly become his prisoner. After a comic episode we see Prince Leudegast, with his son Engelbrecht—the Ferdinand of *The Tempest*—and the councillors, hunting in the same forest; when Engelbrecht and his companion Famulus, having separated from their associates, are suddenly encountered by Ludolph and his daughter. He commands them to yield themselves prisoners. They refuse, and try to draw their swords; when, as Prospero tells Ferdinand:

> For I can here disarme thee with this sticke,
> And make thy weapon drop.

so Ludolph, with his wand, keeps their swords in their scabbards, paralyses Engelbrecht, and makes him confess his

> ... Nerues are in their infancy againe,
> And haue no vigour in them.

and when he has done so gives him over as a slave to Sidea to carry logs for her.

The resemblance between this scene and the parallel scene in *The Tempest* is rendered still more striking in a late part of the play, when Sidea, moved by pity for the labours of Engelbrecht, in carrying logs, declares to him:

> I am your wife, if you will marry me,

an event which in the end is happily brought about and leads to the reconciliation of their parents, the rival princes.

Mr. de Perott in *The Probable Source of the Plot of Shakespeare's 'Tempest,'* and Mr. Henry Thomas in his recent *Spanish and Portuguese Romances of Chivalry*, both point the resemblance between *The Tempest* and the *Mirror of Princely Deeds and Knighthood*, translated from the Spanish of Ortunez de Calahorra, and printed in 1580. That Shakespeare knew the book is proved by Falstaff's reference to it in *King Henry the Fourth*. Various princely magicians occur there, especially Polistes, Prince of Phrygia, who lives on an island with his two children, and practises magic. There is also a reference to another island called 'Artimaga' after its mistress, the most wicked and abominable among women, who worshipped only the Devil and had by him a son called Fauno, at whose birth she died. The island passed to this son and was frequented by devils. The name Claribel, the princess who in *The Tempest* marries the King of Tunis, also occurs here, as well as accounts of ships moved and tempests called up by magic.

The New World adventure part of the play is largely taken from books, but also, I believe, from talks with returned adventurers. Eden's *History of Travaille*, published in 1577, gives an account of a voyage to Patagonia, in the course of which certain natives kidnapped by the voyagers began to cry out to Setebos, 'chief devil of the many they worship,' to deliver them. In this work occur also the names Alonso, Ferdinand, Sebastian, Gonzales (which appears in *The Tempest* as Gonzalo), and Antonio. Direct allusions have also been found in the play to Sir Walter Raleigh's *Discoverie of the Large, Riche and Beautiful Kingdom of Guiana*, 1596. From another pamphlet Shakespeare drew the form 'Bermoothes' for Bermudas. But he borrowed most from contemporary accounts of a sensational voyage to the Bermudas, of which the fullest is Silvester Jourdain's *A Discoverie of the Barmudas, otherwise called the Ile of Divils, by Sir Thomas Gates, Sir George Sommers and Captayne Newport with divers others*, published in 1610. Jourdain was a survivor of this voyage, in the course of which the Admiral's ship parted from the rest of the fleet in a tempest and was driven on the Bermuda reefs. The sailors gave themselves up for lost, but the vessel, wedged between the rocks, did not founder, and since the storm passed as quickly as it came they were able to get ashore. Not a single person had perished and the sailors, having fallen asleep from exhaustion and awakened to find all well and their clothes dried by the tropical sun, began to talk of enchantment. The other ships were dispersed by the storm but the greater part met again and returned in consort to Virginia, where they gave out that the Admiral's ship was lost with all aboard. A few months later Sir George Sommers and his men returned to Virginia in two cedar vessels which they had built on the island.

A supplementary account of the same wreck is given by Purchas from the narrative of William Strachey, a Virginian official, who was also a poet and a friend of poets, particularly of Chapman and Jonson. In Strachey's account the antics of Ariel are anticipated:

Only upon the Thursday night [just before the storm] Sir George Sommers being upon the watch had an apparition of a little round light like a faint starre trembling and streaming along with a sparkeling blaze halfe the height upon the Maine Mast, and shooting sometimes from shroud to shroud.

He also relates that during Sommers' enforced stay on the island, described as uninhabited, several conspiracies took place and a 'sea monster in shape like a man' was seen, 'having at his elbows large fins like fish.'

These main sources then, the Spanish romance, Ayrer's drama, and Sommers' voyage, have been fused into a single theme, the nearest points of association being the desert island scene, the common atmosphere of conspiracy and the enchantment in which all three stories are wrapped—for Jourdain in a subsequent edition of his book took pains to deny that the Bermudas were enchanted, probably at the request of the Council of Virginia, who did not want maritime adventure discouraged.

When these themes are extracted from *The Tempest*, what is left?

There is, of course, the Masque, but that is no more than a spectacle
—the 'creaking throne come down the boys to please,' as Jonson has
it—and though not irrelevant, principally intended to bolster up the
thinness of the play which even with its aid is the shortest that Shake-
speare wrote. What else? The drunken sailors Trinculo and Stephano,
and the plot against Prospero, which has no connexion with the main
plot of brother pitted against brother; and Caliban. His name is a
variant form of 'Carib' or 'Cannibal' or 'Galiba,' the name of a
fierce West Indian tribe. So far he is only a vague sea monster seen in
the Bermudas—almost certainly a dugong or sea-cow, an animal for
which the term 'moon-calf' is extremely appropriate—spiced with a
hint of the Devil in a Spanish romance. And there also remains Ariel,
who so far is a rather colourless German fairy in one tale and a pyro-
technic display in another. And there is Sycorax, the Devil's mother;
although she never appears in person in the play, her malignant spirit
colours the whole plot; and, like Caliban and Ariel, she is given a
particular history which cannot be discovered in any of the three
sources noted.

Let what remains of *The Tempest* by removal of the easily trace-
able materials be told as a story by itself, and let it be remembered
that tradition has always identified Prospero with Shakespeare himself:
when the magician breaks his wand, drowns his book, dismisses his
familiar and returns to his native land where 'every third thought shall
be my grave,' he is Shakespeare on the point of departure for Stratford
saying good-bye to the enchanted lands of drama. According to this
view, *The Tempest* with its 'heavenly music' and 'airy charm' is the
last work of his genius, in which he 'abjures the rough magic' of his
previous tragedies. The Ferdinand and Miranda part of the story
corresponds with this identification, if Miranda can be regarded as a
type of Shakespeare's daughter Susannah; Susannah had recently
married and Shakespeare was fond enough of her and her husband,
John Hall of Stratford, to make them, rather than his wife, his executors.

To begin with Sycorax. Her name, which occurs nowhere else in
Elizabethan literature, evidently means Pig Raven. She is dead when
the play begins; her only relics are a legacy of fear and hate and her
monstrous son, Caliban, begotten on her by the Devil. Her skin was
swarthy (for she was born in Algeria) and her eyes blue-rimmed with
debauch. Through her devil-god Setebos, she exercised great power in
her native country—such power, indeed, as to control the Moon
herself, 'make ebbs and flows and deal in her command.' Her witch-

crafts were so many and terrible that she was eventually banished from Algiers. But 'for one thing she did' (we are never told what) 'they would not take her life.' On an island where she was marooned for twelve years, when with child of Caliban, she pent in a tree an airy spirit called Ariel who was too delicate 'to act her earthy and abhorred commands.' Ariel afterwards became the familiar spirit of Prospero who had set him free; Caliban exercised no dominion over him.

Caliban had at first been by no means so unattractive as one might expect of a 'freckled whelp hag-born,' a true son of the Devil. Prospero used to stroke and make much of him, lodging him in his own cell and educating him; but Caliban repaid him with enormous ingratitude and became the vilest monster that could be conceived, finally making an attempt to seduce Miranda. Caliban claimed, however, that Prospero was as much beholden to him as he to Prospero, because he had shown him all the qualities of the island, which was his own through Sycorax, such as fresh springs, brine pits and fertile places, without knowledge of which Prospero might have perished. Now Prospero had lodged him in a sty and made him a servant as a punishment for doing such wickedness as, indeed, he rejoiced in having done. Ariel, moreover, used to torment him if he shirked the work he hated; so he was overjoyed when two shipwrecked sailors, Stephano and Trinculo, taught him to drink and undertook with his aid to dispossess Prospero of the island. Ariel and Prospero discovered the plot, and the conspirators, made ridiculous by their theft from a clothes-line of glistening apparel, Prospero's magic robes, were chased by Ariel's fairy hounds until they howled for mercy. Caliban then made a recantation:

> . . . what a thrice double Asse
> Was I to take this drunkard for a god?
> And worship this dull foole?

which carries as little conviction as his fear that the arts of Prospero were such that they would even have made a vassal of Setebos.

In the year 1600, Shakespeare's *Sonnets* were published, in jumbled order, with the following dedication over the initials of T.T. (Thomas Thorpe, a publisher) and an assurance that they had never before been printed:

To the onlie begetter of these insuing sonnets Mr. W. H. all happinesse and that eternitie promised by our ever-living poet, wisheth the well-wishing adventurer in setting forth.—T.T.

I accept the general outlines of the story behind the *Sonnets* as reconstructed by Samuel Butler in his edition of 1899, though I question his dates, which are ten years earlier than those of other commentators, as well as his theory that some of the sonnets addressed to the Dark Lady were written by Shakespeare for W.H. to pass on as his own.

Here is their history as I read it. About 1593 Shakespeare made the acquaintance of a boy who was certainly named Will, and very probably Hughes or Hews, as we read from the punning sonnets (20 and 135), in which both the words *Will* and *Hews* are italicized. Already Shakespeare had a mistress of whom we know only that she was swarthy and black-eyed, and no longer young in 1599 when Shakespeare's two sonnets, each with variant readings from Thorpe's copy, were published by Jaggard in *The Passionate Pilgrim*. The boy was handsome and unresponsive to Shakespeare's affection which was of an extravagant kind in the manner of the day. Shakespeare in Sonnet 94 charges him with being temperamentally incapable of loving, 'Vnmooued, cold, and to temptation slow'; and it looks as if he tolerated Shakespeare only because he gave him presents and flattery.

To judge from Sonnet 104, Shakespeare has been sending W.H. amatory sonnets for some three years when he decides (Sonnets 2, 3 and 6) that the 'Master Mistris' of his passion (20) has now turned twenty and ought to marry and father children as beautiful as himself. He treats him in the same elder-brotherly style as Falstaff (of whom he was writing at the time) treated Prince Hal. The plea is not disinterested; Shakespeare is jealous of rivals and an arranged early marriage, as we learn from the *Autobiography of Lord Herbert of Cherbury*, is the Elizabethan recipe for curbing youthful follies. But his advice comes too late. The Dark Lady grows as amorous of W.H. as Shakespeare himself, who makes his grand mistake of standing aside and letting her seduce him with: 'Take all my loues, my loue, yea take them all' (40). This part of the story corresponds with the 'Venus and Adonis' sonnets printed in *The Passionate Pilgrim* in 1599, and more completely in the 'Venus and Adonis' poem of 1593. Shakespeare seems to have envisaged a *ménage a trois*, and may even for a while have attained it, for he bargains with the Dark Lady that she may have her 'Will' if she gives Shakespeare his. But with Adonis safely in her arms Venus has no need for any other man; she goes off with him. Shakespeare never seems to have thought it possible that he would be deserted by both, though in Sonnet 35 where he reproves W.H. for the abduction of his mistress he plainly admits himself accessory to the sensual fault. They seem to have written him a conciliatory letter, dictated by the Dark Lady, in which they assure him that theirs is the love which really counts, and that while continuing to esteem him highly, they intend to remain together; for Shakespeare in Sonnet 119 swallows his pride and says with a gesture of nobility that he can admit no impediment to the marriage of true minds.

He continues to write to W.H. and send him sonnets; but he hears rumours which (70) he does not at first believe, that the boy is living a scandalous life. When he finds they are true he grieves greatly. While pretending to pardon these youthful excesses, and in Sonnet 58 disclaiming any right to control them, he knows in his heart that W.H. does not sin with any sportiveness: he is a calculating sinner who sins only to advantage. An important phase of their relations is marked by the other sonnet published in 1599, apparently without Shakespeare's consent (144 in Thorpe's edition): 'Two loues I haue of comfort and dispaire,' namely the angel and the devil. W.H. was the angel whom the 'woman collour'd il' was corrupting to be a devil like herself—'Wooing his purity with her fowle pride.' Shakespeare hoped against hope that W.H. might be better than he seemed; but the tragedy of love grew darker. Presently W.H. with the assistance, probably, of a rival playwright and the Dark Lady, laid a trap for Shakespeare, inviting him to a rendezvous. Shakespeare came, anxious to fall in with any suggestion his friend might make, and W.H. arranged for Shakespeare to be surprised and assaulted when about to compromise himself grotesquely. I agree with Butler that Shakespeare was roughly handled by W.H.'s accomplices, who seem to have been responsible for the lameness of which he afterwards complains. The catastrophe is marked by the sonnets: 'Fvll many a glorious morning haue I seene' (33), 'Why didst thou promise such a beautious day' (34), and 'Tis better to be vile then vile esteemed' (121). In the last of these he asks bitterly why the false adulterate eyes of others should have been allowed to give salutation to his sportive blood, or why on his frailties have there been frailer spies? The 'salve' which he is offered is worthless.

Shakespeare having rashly given his soul to W.H. makes desperate efforts to repair the breach in the friendship between them. They seem to have met intermittently, but W.H. delights in tormenting Shakespeare, saying that he prefers the poetry of a rival—almost certainly Chapman, as Professor Nimmo has deduced from the lines about the 'affable familiar ghost' and the 'compiers by night' (86), which can refer only to a poem written by Chapman in 1594. But next (if this is the correct order of events) we find him rebuking Shakespeare for neglecting him and not writing often enough; perhaps at the time he needed Shakespeare's money or protection. The affair drags on and what has happened to the Dark Lady we do not learn.

In Sonnet 29 Shakespeare refers to his disgrace and absence from his friend, almost certainly a result of the Essex rising; in Sonnet 107 to the death of Queen Elizabeth in 1603 and the happy accession of James I, which obliterated the memory of Essex's failure and secured the despaired survival of Protestantism as the State religion. Shakespeare makes this an occasion for renewing the old bonds of friendship, but affection is waning and the end comes when W.H. gives evidence against him in some high quarter and so prevents him from carrying a canopy in a ceremonial procession. In Sonnet 125 Shakespeare pretends not to care about the canopy; but that ambition for social advancement was his Achilles' heel is shown by the frequency with which his enemies satirized it. This incident made what I think was the final breach, even after Sonnet 147 which calls him 'black as hell, as darke as night': 'Hence, thou subbornd *Informer*,' he writes, 'a trew soule When most impeacht, stands least in thy controule.' Suborned by whom?

The best authority for dates are the dramas. From the wanton light-hearted world of the early histories and comedies, we pass through the middle comedies to the tragedies and so to *The Winter's Tale* and to *The Tempest*, which is the goal of our enquiry. Every commentator has remarked on the cloud that darkened Shakespeare's life about 1601 when he began writing the tragedies; but I should be inclined to date it two or three years earlier, with the middle comedies. There are two alternative reactions to the torments of love—flight and fight, comedy and tragedy. *As You Like It* and *Twelfth-Night* are romantic escapes from love, an acknowledgment of defeat, and in both cases the girl disguised as a boy gives a clue to what was in Shakespeare's thoughts at the time. With the tragedies, he makes a determined effort to gain control of himself, but the flame of passion was not finally quenched, I believe, until 1609, when W.H. allowed Thorpe to publish a collection of sonnets, both those addressed to himself and those addressed to the Dark Lady. Revenge for this piratical publication, which must have rubbed salt in Shakespeare's wounds, seems to me one of the chief motives for the writing of *The Tempest*. The extravagance of Sonnet 57:

> Being your slaue what should I doe but tend,
> Vpon the houres, and times of your desire?

and of Sonnet 18:

> Shall I compare thee to a Summers day?
> Thou art more louely and more temperate:

and of Sonnet 116 about love looking on tempests and never being shaken, and bearing it out even to the edge of doom, demanded a recantation as violent as the statement.

It was apparently a passage in *Isaiah* that engendered *The Tempest*. In the twenty-ninth chapter of *Isaiah* and in the eighth of *Ezra* occurs the name Ariel. In the first case it appears as the name of a town, the city of Jerusalem; in the second as the name of a man among several others of no special significance. The only other known mention of the word in Elizabethan literature, though Ariel occurs frequently as a spirit in the Gaelic runes, is in Heywood's *Hierarchie of the Blessed Angells* where he is a spirit not of air but earth. This has confused commentators in view of Ariel's title in the *dramatis personæ* of the *First Folio*, 'Ariell, an ayrie spirit,' and in view of Shakespeare's statement that Ariel was too delicate a spirit to perform Sycorax's earthy behests. But perhaps Heywood's Ariel does not come into the story: Professor Lefranc has suggested that Shakespeare was acquainted with the contents of a magical book written in Latin by a monk of Spanheim In this book, *Steganographia*, published in 1606, the year in which Shakespeare's preoccupation with witches and familiars is manifested in *Macbeth*, occurs a magician Zachariel with three familiars—Ariel, Raphael and Amael; their relationship with Zachariel is that of Ariel with Prospero.

The chapter from *Isaiah*, however, supplies a number of associative links between Shakespeare's personal story, as we read it in the *Sonnets* and elsewhere, and the main literary sources of *The Tempest*. Nobody familiar with the processes of romantic creation can well deny that this passage with its references to Ariel, to the familiar spirit, to the conspiracy, to the tempest and flame of devouring fire, to the vision of the book, to the drunken enemies, to the deep sleep, which all appear in the first few verses of this chapter, must have crystallized into dramatic form all the fluid material in Shakespeare's mind.

> 1. Woe to Ariel, to Ariel, the city *where* David dwelt! add ye year to year; let them kill sacrifices.

2. Yet I will distress Ariel, and there shall be heaviness and sorrow: and it shall be unto me as Ariel.

3. And I will camp against thee round about, and will lay siege against thee with a mount, and I will raise forts against thee.

4. And thou shalt be brought down, *and* shalt speak out of the ground, and the speech shall be low out of the dust, and thy voice shall be, as of one that hath a familiar spirit, out of the ground, and thy speech shall whisper out of the dust.

5. Moreover the multitude of thy strangers shall be like small dust, and the multitude of the terrible ones *shall be* as chaff that passeth away: yet, it shall be at an instant suddenly.

6. Thou shalt be visited of the Lord of hosts with thunder, and with earthquake, and great noise, with storm and tempest, and the flame of devouring fire.

7. And the multitude of all the nations that fight against Ariel, even all that fight against her and her munition, and that distress her, shall be as a dream of a night vision.

8. It shall even be as when an hungry *man* dreameth, and, behold, he eateth; but he awaketh, and his soul is empty: or as when a thirsty man dreameth, and, behold, he drinketh; but he awaketh, and, behold, *he* is faint, and his soul hath appetite: so shall the multitude of all the nations be, that fight against mount Zion.

9. Stay yourselves, and wonder; cry ye out, and cry: they are drunken, but not with wine; they stagger, but not with strong drink.

10. For the Lord hath poured out upon you the spirit of deep sleep, and hath closed your eyes: the prophets and your rulers, the seers hath he covered.

Shakespeare, when he read this beautifully-worded but utterly obscure prophecy, can have had no knowledge of the historical setting or of the experience behind it. Yet he felt its direct application to his own case. There had been a conspiracy against himself, he had been brought down low—'in disgrace of Fortune and mens eyes'—and his voice was as of one that has a familiar spirit. Especially he could respond to verse 8, reminding him of his own dreams:

> Be not affeard, the Isle is full of noyses,
> Sounds, and sweet aires, that giue delight and hurt not:
> Sometimes a thousand twangling Instruments
> Will hum about mine eares; and sometime voices,
> That if I then had wak'd after long sleepe,

CA: D

> Will make me sleepe againe, and then in dreaming,
> The clouds methought would open, and shew riches
> Ready to drop vpon me, that when I wak'd
> I cri'de to dreame againe.

His own airy spirit had been oppressed by the Terrible One, of a later verse in the same chapter, and there was a heaviness and sorrow on Ariel—'and it shall be unto me as (unto) Ariel.' This verse is important as confirming the intimate connexion between Prospero and Ariel. Ariel being identified in Shakespeare's mind with the Ariel of the *Steganographia*, the sentence: 'It shall be unto me as Ariel' thereupon detaches itself from the context and becomes an interpolation of the suffering man, Prospero, whose spirit is being oppressed by the Terrible One. The only Terrible One in *The Tempest* being Sycorax, I feel that the connexion between Sycorax and Shakespeare is more intimate than appears in the play: really it was Prospero whom Sycorax oppressed for twelve winters, and continued to oppress even after her death. (Thus, as with morbid dreams, the emotional stress is shifted from the primary object of importance to the secondary.) It is notable that twelve years is the space of Prospero's oppression by his brother and that Shakespeare wrote *The Tempest* twelve years after his desertion by the Dark Lady and W.H.

Isaiah continues:

> 11. And the vision of all is become unto you as the words of a book that is sealed, which *men* deliver to one that is learned, saying, Read this, I pray thee: and he saith, I cannot; for it *is* sealed;
> 12. And the book is delivered to him that is not learned, saying, Read this, I pray thee: and he saith, I am not learned.
> 13. Wherefore the Lord saith, Forasmuch as this people draw near *me* with their mouth, and with their lips do honour me, but have removed their heart far from me, and their fear toward me is taught by the precept of men:

These verses confirm the impression that *The Tempest* is a book similarly sealed and that Shakespeare, applauded alike by the courtiers and the playhouse mob, who have never realized how much of a poet he is, determines to make it his most magnificent play, in which he will 'abjure the rough magic' of the past (the magic of the great tragedies which were forced out of him by the malignancy of Sycorax) and end his cycle of plays, instead, with an airy music. He is appealing to posterity. The eighteenth to twenty-first verses run:

18. And in that day shall the deaf hear the words of the book, and the eyes of the blind shall see out of obscurity, and out of darkness.

19. The meek also shall increase *their* joy in the Lord, and the poor among them shall rejoice in the Holy One of Israel.

20. For the terrible one is brought to nought, and the scorner is consumed, and all that watch for iniquity are cut off:

21. That make a man an offender for a word, and lay a snare for him that reproveth in the gate, and turn aside the just for a thing of nought.

The last two verses pertinently bridge the story of the *Sonnets* with that of *The Tempest*.

With Caliban for W.H., Sycorax for the Dark Lady, and Ariel as an emanation of Shakespeare himself, the drunken sailors Trinculo and Stephano discover themselves in this personal setting as Chapman and Jonson, with a suggestion of Marston. Caliban takes 'this drunkard for a god,' and worships 'this dull foole'; then Stephano must be Chapman the rival poet, and Trinculo with his love of sack and dropsical tendencies, Jonson. My reasons for this identification are as follows: Shakespeare introduced Ben Jonson to the public by producing his first play. A year or two later Jonson joined a rival company and a coolness ensued between them. Jonson made two slighting remarks to Caliban, one in *Bartholomew Fair* in 1616, and one in the prologue attached to *Every Man out of his Humour* when he published it in its altered form. Mr. Percy Simpson believes that this prologue was written shortly after the appearance of *The Tempest*, and it looks as if Jonson knew that he was being satirized in Trinculo. The passage in *Bartholomew Fair*:

> But these Master Poets they will have their own absurd courses; they will be informed of nothing! He has (sir-reverence) kicked me three or four times about the Tyring-House, I thank him, for but offering to put in with my experience . . .

would be explained in this context where Trinculo is hunted about the stage when discovered in Prospero's tiring-house putting on his robes.

My reason for suggesting Marston as contributing to the caricature figures of these sailors is that Jonson, Chapman and Marston in 1605 produced a successful comedy called *Eastward Ho!*, which has a good deal to do with the creation of *The Tempest*; and that while Chapman and Jonson were originals, Marston was perpetually 'stealing by line

and level' Shakespeare's glistening apparel. *Eastward Ho!* contains a
footman named Hamlet, who must have been a skit on Shakespeare's
already famous hero, and an apprentice named Quicksilver who leaves
his master Touchstone—apparently a caricature of Shakespeare—and
goes off to join a company of drunken sailors bound on a voyage of
adventure for Virginia; the sequel is a comic shipwreck on the Isle of
Dogs and discomfiture all round. Jonson, Marston and Chapman
incurred the severe displeasure of King James for a jeering reference to
the Scots in the play and nearly lost their ears and noses.

W.H. was associated with this rival Blackfriars company in Shake-
speare's mind; possibly he was, as Mr. Frank Harris believes, an actor.
Sonnet 126 suggests that W.H. had acted, probably in some Court
Masque; as I read the story the Dark Lady had died in disgrace—
'banished from Argier'—and W.H., left in the lurch, joined the rival
company of actors to spite Shakespeare. What the occasion of W.H.'s
informing against Shakespeare was we do not know, but it is likely
that they suborned him.

As Mr. Acheson points out in *Shakespeare's Sonnet Story*, Thorpe
the bookseller had long been publishing books for Chapman and his
clique, and never before or afterwards published anything of Shake-
speare's; and it seems probable that the publication of the sonnets was
arranged by Chapman through W.H. as an act of hostility to Shake-
speare, following their enmity of ten years. Mr. Acheson writes:

> It is evident, however, as in the case of Marston, that Jonson's attacks
> upon Shakespeare were instigated largely by Chapman's persistent malevo-
> lence. Shakespeare's provincial breeding, the fact that his father was a
> butcher and his grammar school education were the principal basis of
> aspersions of the scholars against him all through his London career . . .

Shakespeare's application through his father, in 1596, for the confirma-
tion of an alleged grant of arms made to his forebears was finally granted
late in 1598 or early in 1599. As the scholars for years past had cast
slurs upon his social standing and had twitted him in *Histriomastix*
and elsewhere in his quality as an actor with being 'within the Statute'
against vagabonds and sturdy beggars, the legal status of 'gentleman'
which he now attained through the influence of the Earl of Essex
added new fuel to their envy. This continued to be shown in poems
and plays written by Marston, Jonson and Chapman both singly and
in collaboration between 1600 and 1609.

Jonson's *Every Man out of his Humour* contains a parody of

Shakespeare's armorial bearings and a reference to his father's trade as a butcher:

> SOG [reads]: *On a chief argent, a boar's head proper, between two ann'lets sable.*
>
> CAR: Slud, it's a hog's cheek and puddings in a pewter field, this.
>
> SOG: How like you them, signior?
>
> PUNT: Let the word be '*Not without mustard*: your crest is very rare, sir.'
>
> CAR: A frying-pan to the crest had had no felloe.

Mr. Acheson writes:

> It is apparent that such a palpable parody of Shakespeare's *Non sans Droict* as Jonson's 'Not without Mustard' and, in fact, the whole passage quoted, must have been added or restored after the play had been presented by Shakespeare's company . . .

However acrimonious the early dispute between Jonson and Marston may have been before the end of 1599, from that time forward until about 1606 and 1607 they were friends, and indeed a part of Jonson's satire against Marston written in this earlier period was later revised as a satire upon Shakespeare and his supporters.

To sum up. Shakespeare after an unhappy marriage and a precarious life in theatrical London became a popular dramatist, and took up with a lady of wit and fashion. He developed his poetic gift late, as a result, he believed, of a passionate attachment to a boy named Will Hughes, which first 'taught . . . heauie ignorance aloft to flie' (78), and showed him all the qualities of the Isle of Poetry, the quick freshes and the brine pits (that is, comedy and tragedy). The lady fell in love with the boy; Shakespeare condoned and even encouraged the affair and as a result was deserted by both, and not only deserted but plagued and insulted for a number of years. The woman, who was powerful at Court in the last years of Elizabeth's reign through some personal quality or power, deified as Setebos, so that she could control the moon herself—that is the Queen—'make ebbs and flows and deal in her command,' eventually fell into disgrace but did not lose her life 'for one thing she did,' and died in 1607 or so, 'with Age and Enuy . . . growne into a hoope.[1]

The boy, who seems to have chafed under the domination of the Dark Lady (133), was appealed to by Shakespeare on the death of the

---

[1] I like to think that she was the lady-in-waiting who sent Sir Edward Cary secret news of the Queen's death and thus enabled him to prepare King James for the succession before any other claimants appeared.

Queen and James's accession and asked to rejoin him. But he went over to Shakespeare's rivals at Blackfriars and, to judge from the suicide element in *Hamlet* and *King Lear*, and Sonnet 66, 'Tyr'd with all these for restfull death I cry,' Shakespeare had frequent thoughts of drowning himself; later he seems to have played with the notion of leaving England altogether and living in some remote island. In 1609, as a last act of spite in concert with Shakespeare's rivals, W.H. published the sonnets, both those addressed to himself, and those addressed to the Dark Lady which came into his possession at her death. Shakespeare, searching for some worthier object of his affections, rediscovered his daughter Susannah, whom he celebrated in *Pericles* as Mariana, in *The Winter's Tale* as Perdita, and in *The Tempest* as Miranda. He patched up a reconciliation with his wife, as we guess from the two former plays, and decided to return to Stratford and live with his family again; Susannah had just raised him to the dignity of grandfather.

At this point he read the chapter in *Isaiah* and pored over it as over some Sibylline leaf that could give the clue to his whole life. He would do this marvellous work, write this sealed book. Ayrer's play suited his mood up to a point, but he preferred the setting of the Spanish romance because of the Devil Island and because his enemies, the drunken sailors of *Eastward Ho!* would be more at home there. The dugong sea-monster of Jourdain's *Discoverie* became Caliban; the Dark Lady became Caliban's mother, because she could not appear as his mistress, because they were mother and son in the Spanish romance, and because she was certainly much older than he was. The familiar spirit of *Isaiah* became the Ariel of *Steganographia*, and took the form of Sommers' vision of St. Elmo's fire playing on the shrouds before the storm. (It is possible that Ariel was also, in the personal context, an acquaintance of Shakespeare's, perhaps a boy actor who at the time of the writing of *The Tempest* wanted to leave the theatre, but whom he persuaded to stay on for one more part.) The Spanish romance and Ayrer's play largely determined the dream-framework of *The Tempest*, but the wicked brother, who had no personal significance in Shakespeare's mind although occupying a prominent place in the play, remains a lay-figure, while Sycorax, though dead and a *muta persona*, stands out strongly in the romantic imagination as the real villainess of the piece. Caliban's attempted seduction of Miranda is an incident in the war between the evil angel and the good angel.

[Addition 1946—I have since found a fourth main source of *The Tempest*: the *Mabinogion* legend of Taliesin, a version which Shakespeare (my guess is) had been told by his Welsh schoolmaster at Stratford Grammar School. It begins on 'an island in the midst of the Lake Tegid' where there lived a magician named Tegid Voel, his witch-wife Caridwen and their children Creirwy, the most beautiful girl in the world and Avagddu, the ugliest youth in the world. Caridwen, 'the black screaming hag,' set a child called Little Gwion to stir a magic cauldron, the contents of which were intended to compensate her son for his ugliness with the gift of great wisdom; but by accident Gwion, not Avagddu, benefited from the potion and in revenge Caridwen pursued him, caught him despite his many rapid magical transformations, swallowed him, bore him again as the miraculous child Taliesin and finally imprisoned him in a leather bag which she threw into the sea.

The rest of the story is concerned with Taliesin, not with Tegid Voel, Creirwy and Avagddu. It is likely that in the version told to Shakespeare Avagddu attempted to rape his sister and Tegid Voel banished him with his mother to Anglesey; in the *Mabinogion* version Caridwen was also due for punishment at the plea of one Morda whom she had wantonly blinded, but the sequel is not given. The origin of the story is a myth about the Goddess Caridwen, the Welsh Demeter who is associated with pigs and ravens, Tegid Voel the Welsh Poseidon and Gwion, the Welsh Zagreus who was yearly torn in pieces and eaten by Caridwen after going through his customary transformations; its end, to judge from parallel Greek legends, must have been Tegid's triumph over her. Lusi in Arcadia, where Demeter fled from Poseidon, was the last seat of the old cannibalistic rites in Greece; in Wales it was Anglesey. If Avagddu attempted to rape Creirwy, this would be paralleled by Greek myths in which Satyrs (devotees of the Pelasgian Demeter) carry off the daughters of Poseidon-worshipping Achaean chiefs.]

Ariel's song, 'Full Fathom Five' and Prospero's Epilogue to the play remain to be examined. The Epilogue contains a curious plea to the public, or perhaps to posterity. It amounts to this: 'I have ended my cycle of plays with a gesture of forgiveness and reconciliation. Now I want you, by sympathetic understanding of the sufferings which made the play, not to let this remain a mere imaginary island of melodrama but show that you have caught my meaning; then I shall not feel that I have suffered in vain. I am soon returning to Stratford. I trespassed, but forgive those who trespassed against me; pray for my soul.' Pray we do, though we note that Prospero's forgiveness of his brother is the easy forgiveness of an imaginary person, while his forgiveness of the more important Stephano, Trinculo and Caliban is as perfunctory and unconvincing as their apologies; and the gigantic broomstick shadow of Sycorax still lies across the page.

My knowledge of *The Tempest* has broadened since I recently met Miss Lilian Winstanley of Aberystwyth University, who has been working on the political references in it. The chief importance of her claim is this. The sudden murder of Henry IV of France, in whom all Protestant Europe trusted as its protector against Spanish aggression, came as a great blow to Shakespeare. The joyful atmosphere of the Masque, which may have served the purpose of celebrating the marriage of King James' daughter Anne to the Protestant King of Bohemia, is clouded by Henry's death. Sycorax in the political sense is Catherine of Medici, a reputed witch, accused of digging up corpses with her nails and of controlling the moon; with a contributory suggestion of Mariana, the Jesuit. Caliban is Jesuitism, which Henry had tolerantly admitted to his Court to be his own ruin, and at the same time, Ravaillac, who was brought up by the Jesuits, inflamed by Mariana's book and entrusted with Henry's murder. Ravaillac is written of by political pamphleteers as a spotted monster, a degenerate, a dunce; and he was first racked and then pinched to death with red-hot pincers in punishment for the murder—as Caliban was pinched by Ariel.

In 'Full Fathom Five,' Shakespeare is evidently recording a story he has heard, how looking down through clear lagoon waters one sees what appear to be the bones of drowned sailors encrusted with coral —really the skeleton-like coral formation itself. To me 'Those are pearles that were his eies,' recalls the romantic shock of seeing under a glass case in a Catholic cathedral the jewel-studded skulls of saints; perhaps Shakespeare had the same experience in mind. If so, 'Thy Father' is not merely Prospero's wicked brother, nor is the song addressed merely to Ferdinand. 'Thy Father,' I regard as Shakespeare's old self, father of the Shakespeare who wrote *The Tempest*. This regenerate Shakespeare sees the skeleton of his old self sanctified by suffering and transformed into something rich and strange. The poem suggests that a contemplated suicide by drowning, and a profound dissatisfaction with the nymphs of earth, have been succeeded by a period of comparative calm; Shakespeare concludes that poetic beauty is born of great suffering. A *De Profundis Clamavi* peace has succeeded the painful bitterness of mind, especially bitterness against sex in all its aspects, which dates in Shakespeare's plays from the opening of the new century and appears to mark the disillusionment stage in the story of the *Sonnets*. The cathedral and the lagoon are both types of quiet, one a religious and the other a secular escape from the unhappiness of this world; the jewelled bones of martyrs and the sea-jewelled bones of storm-tossed sailors correspond emotionally. The skull of the dead jester Yorick, or the skull of the happy-go-lucky early Shakespeare, has now, after ten years, lost its charnel smell and grown pearls in its eye-sockets.

Miss Winstanley admits the connexion of *Eastward Ho!* with *The Tempest*, the former being a satire against the expansionist policy of Southampton, Shakespeare's patron, with sly digs at Shakespeare himself. Quicksilver is Raleigh; his personal badge having been a figure of Mercury. James' anger against the dramatists was probably roused by this discrediting of a policy which he himself supported, rather than by the sneer at the Scots.

Prospero in this sense is an ideal king with characteristics of both James and Henry: James as being Anne's father, Henry in a variety of ways. Besides the Ravaillac connexion, Henry is Prospero because he was believed to have magic powers and even admitted possessing them. He is credited in Pierre Mathieu's panegyric, which Shakespeare seems to have read, with wind-like swiftness, flight through the air like Pegasus, unexpected appearances, all-observant watchfulness, meteorlike brilliancy and the qualities of St. Elmo's fire. Prospero's familiar, Ariel, is represented in these very terms. Miss Winstanley has found political counterparts for the other subsidiary characters, and Miranda's arrival on the island in a small boat and her peaceful upbringing there were borrowed by political writers to symbolize the Reformed Faith as it found shelter in England. The Gonzalo-Antonio conversation about Claribel (Clara Isabella the Infanta) teems with veiled political references. Miss Winstanley accepts the *Isaiah* connexion and finds in 'the city where David dwelt' a reference to Henry IV who was referred to by Pierre Mathieu as 'David the Shepherd King.' She believes that Shakespeare was acting as political agent for the Earl of Southampton, first in his attempts to secure the succession of King James to the throne of England, and later in his *Westward Ho!* propaganda: this had as its object the founding of a

Protestant Empire in the New World as a means of combating the Catholic combination which drew its strength from American revenues.

Miss Winstanley has produced irresistible evidence that there is a close correspondence between the imagery of Shakespeare's dramas in the new century and the imagery of contemporary Huguenot and anti-Spanish pamphleteers. I do not go so far as she does and suggest that the plays were written as propaganda; but it is clear that this imagery could not have been introduced into his plays unless the political interest in his life had been a powerful one. Shakespeare, it has lately been discovered, lodged with a Huguenot family in London, and three legends about him appear credible in the light of the suggestion that he worked for the counter-espionage system against Spain: first, the legend of the private letter which King James wrote to him complimenting him on his plays; second, that of the £1,000 which Southampton gave him for the purchase of a plot of ground (though he never paid more than £320 for any such purchase); third, the suspicion that he died of poison. The size of his estate at his death, in view of the sneers of rival playwrights against his lavishness in providing dinners for his lickspittle friends, may also be explained by this theory. The Venetians said that the King of Spain swore revenge on the English dramatists; and yet, apart from Middleton's *Game of Chess*, very little direct anti-Spanish propaganda occurs in Elizabethan drama. Why this desire for revenge?[1]

The Continental pamphleteers wrote under initials or pseudonyms for fear of the horrible fate that would overtake them if Spanish agents discovered their authorship. One of the most prominent, Boccalini, an Italian (who on one occasion visited London), called himself Orpheus. An Englishman, Sir William Vaughan, who called himself 'Orpheus Junior' to underline his connexion with Boccalini, published in 1626, three years after the appearance of Shakespeare's *First Folio*, a book of secret political history called *The Golden Fleece*. From this book Miss Winstanley has given me the following remarkable extracts:

From PART I

Above all the magnificent courts which the sun beholdeth from East to West and from the one Pole to the other, it is noticed that Apollo as it were by sympathy of some heavenly influence, beares particular affection to the

---

[1] It has since been proved that the occasion of Marlowe's death was not a vulgar tavern brawl, but political intrigue.

Royall Court of Great Brittaine and tenders the welfare thereof as of his own Parnassus. Insomuch that his Imperiall Majesty foreseeing that Guy Faux and his damned confederates would have blown up the Parliament House, with the King and Estates there assembled upon the fifth day of November, 1605, and that they afterwards intended to set up their Romish religion hee first caused one of the Aeriall Spirits to insinuate into Tressam's braine and by often nibbling on his imagination to procure from him that Aenigmaticall letter wrote his brother-in-law, the Lord Mounteagle.

Then out of his divine love towards this monarchy he assisted the Genius of the learned and most noble King James to discover the whole plot, by unlocking with the Key of Prophecie the Mysterie of that intricate Letter more intricate and dark than Sphinx his riddle, so odious appeared this Butcherly and Diabolicall Treason unto his Sacred Spirit. But for all his examinations and vigilant cares Apollo could by no means ferrit out the Fox; for the Devill had transformed the beast into an Angel of Light, until Ravaillac that monster of Mankind had massacred the great Hercules of France, King Henry the Fourth. Upon which accident One, Peter Ramus . . . informed Apollo that the said Ravaillac the very morning of the same day when he committed this lamentable murther, was heard to maintaine that Paradox: how justifiable and glorious an act it were for a Sibyll to kill a Tyrannical or Hereticall Prince.

Apolloe's griefe conceived by this assassinate and Tragicall event became somewhat assuaged when he knew the cause of this inhumane butchery proceeded through the King's owne credulite and tenderness of heart in admitting the Jesuits into France, against the will of the Sorbonnists and afterwards fostering them, like Æsope's snake, in the Louvre his Royall Palace, whose common maxime he knew to be: One God in Heaven, One God on Earth and one Catholick King.

. . . Apollo commanded Robert Earl of Essex Lord High Marshall of his Empire and Sir Philip Sidney, the Provost Marshal of his Court, to make diligent search and enquire within the Precincts of his Territories for the body of Mariana.

. . . [of Charles I]. His Highness devoted himself and his Kingdom to bee perpetually governed by the Lawes, Charters and Prescriptions of Apollo's Court.

[Mariana the Jesuit is tried before Apollo's Court] . . . Ye have most traitorously infringed God's peace in plotting to blow up the King and Estates of Great Brittaine. This sacred bond have ye cancelled when Ravaillac that devill of men by the instigation of your seditious booke, did massacre the Prince of his native soyle, Victorious Henry the under-miner of that Catholick Monarchie which the Spaniards dreamed of. This chaine of charitie have ye violated and torn asunder when at sundry times you whetted on simple creatures more silly than sheep to take arms against their native prince.

PART II

[Apollo exhorts King James to put the laws in joint:]
Yet now is come Astraia's Golden Age
A King of Denmark's Bloud, Lawes out of joint
As there in written Booke's hee shall appoint.
None then shall wrest, as would King James ordaine
A secret law hatcht in one Lawyer's braine.

PART III

[Apollo urges the English to colonize the Bermudas and Newfoundland: Newfoundland especially, because there they will get plenty of wood and fish.]

1. First, this Trade of Fishing multiplyeth shipping and mariners, the principall props of this Kingdom.
2. It is near unto Great Britaine, the next Land beyond Irland, in a temperate Aire, the south part thereof being of equall Climate with Little Britaine in France.
. . . To this I add the great benefit which may be made by woods, being pine, birch, spruce.
. . . No place in the world brings naturally more store of gooseberries filberts etc.
[Apollo also advises the colonists to get rid of all lawyers. He encourages the colonization of the Summer Isles in the Bermudas.]
All these hopeful projects did his Majestie lay before our Britaines, exhorting them to become more industrious, to cast by the hideous coat of Poverty, and with an undaunted courage to sail into the uttermost Ocean.

It is hard to say what is meant by Apollo's Court; very likely the playwrights of the anti-Cecilian clique were allied in the counter-espionage business for which the theatres were the best possible centres of information. That Shakespeare assisted in the discovery of the Gunpowder Plot is a startling notion, but I cannot see where else this argument leads; the reference to Hamlet is clear enough.

The poetic nucleus of *The Tempest* seems to have originated in a dream or deep trance. It is impossible to say how far Shakespeare understood after writing each scene what it was about—how far, for instance, he recognized in Caliban these various components: the ugly boy of Welsh legend, an Adriatic devil from a Spanish romance; a sea-cow seen in the Bermudas; Jesuitism incarnate in Ravaillac;

Mr. W. H.; the *Malus Angelus* of a morality play; with Trinculo under his gaberdine, a *tableau vivant* caricaturing the Two-Headed League; and when talking of his dreams, the natural genius of poetry, true heir to the magical island through his witch mother, whom Prospero by his scholarly arts has deprived of his birthright and turned into a dull drudge.

My object has been to account for those fanciful and irregular forms occurring in romantic poetry, which classical tradition ascribes merely to 'poetic madness'; not to anatomize *The Tempest* with the fallacious notion that by presenting a certain phenomenon in terms of others one can arrive at a knowledge of its unique character. *The Tempest* may be in one aspect a play of revenge on Shakespeare's personal enemies, in another his farewell to the stage; in another a political satire; in another (as Mr. John Still has suggested) a religious mystery; in another a theatrical spectacle to please the common people and make money; in another a loyal tribute paid to the King on the marriage of his daughter. Yet even if every such aspect, and every historical source, has been discovered and isolated, there still remains the poetic event, *The Tempest*, which transcends its components.

THE FUTURE OF POETRY
(1926)

THE FUTURE OF POETRY

Mr. Robert Trevelyan in his *Thamyrïs, or Is there a Future for Poetry?* is chiefly concerned with the change that has come over poetry since it ceased to be chanted to music and began to be first recited, then read aloud, then read silently. These are important changes, though not at all so recent as Mr. Trevelyan makes out. English poets have not chanted their poems since the time of Caedmon, and the silent reading of poetry dates back far behind the invention of printing in the fifteenth century to the time of the great copying-schools of Hellenistic Greece, which made it possible for private people to build up large libraries. However, it is true that since the beginning of this century public recitations have become rarer, the habit of reading aloud in the home has declined and poetic drama is on its last legs. Unless some new mechanical contrivance enables us to listen to recorded poems as quickly and casually as we turn the pages of a book of verse —but neither the gramophone nor the radio can yet do that for us— poetry will be written more and more for the eye and the inner ear, rather than for the ear and the inner eye.

In primitive times the rhythmic swaying of the poet, the tap of his foot on the ground and the twanging of his harp were needed to induce in an audience the necessary trance which enabled them to think in poetic terms. The trance is now induced by typographical conventions: the division into lines each beginning with a capital letter, the leaving of a space between stanzas, the use of wide margins and large print; wherever these conventions are dispensed with, or modified, it is difficult to read poetry with perfect attention. No similar convention is used in public recitals of poetry except the stage voice and the stage manner, which are apt to antagonize sensitive listeners; and most poets when they read their own work aloud affect a lugubrious and toneless drone like a man confessing to a crime under hypnotic influence.

We are not accustomed to listening attentively to long recitations of verse-romances or epics and have a far shorter aural memory than our ancestors, but the inward ear can be trained not only to remember rhymes and structural sign-posts of various sorts but to become aware of the texture of verse that is being silently read. Besides, when a poem is printed, one can always glance back to confirm the meaning of a passage and still keep the continuity of the rhythm in one's head. With a recitation this is impossible; also the reciter rarely adjusts the tempo of the lines to the sense or distributes the emphases correctly. Personally, I dislike the sound of my reading voice only less than I dislike professional elocution, and cannot bear to hear a stage-performance of any poetic play of Shakespeare's or Marlowe's.

Altogether, I think, Mr. Trevelyan is wrong to regard the abandonment of the 'singing tradition' in English poetry as a bad thing. One can appreciate a printed poem fully without the mediation of the interpretative artist; just as trained musicians get a purer delight from reading an orchestral score than from hearing it played by even a good orchestra. And, granted equal inspiration and intelligence, poetry composed and transmitted orally always sets itself a lower standard of technical accomplishment than poetry composed with the help of pen and paper and transmitted in print. (It would be unfair to quote the poems of Homer in evidence to the contrary, because they were given a careful literary editing at the court of King Pisistratus of Athens and were further refined by Alexandrian scholars.)

Mr. Trevelyan discusses the future of verse forms and comes to the conclusion that anything may happen, but hopes sincerely that it won't. Some of his statements are wildly unhistorical, e.g. 'Blank verse is the oldest of our verse forms'—it was not introduced until Tudor times—and 'The conscious principle according to which English verse has been written from the time of Chaucer until recent years has been syllable-counting.' Syllable-counting is a principle of Continental prosody imposed on English by the Norman-French invaders; in the earlier native prosody the metre was determined by the stress-centres of the line and the time-intervals between them. This earlier prosody has never been abandoned by popular poets and is frequently used by poets of culture. Its most familiar use is in nursery rhyme and country ballads:

> Misty, moisty was the morn,
>   Chilly was the weather;
> There I met an old man,
>   Dressed all in leather,
> Dressed all in leather
>   Against the wind and rain.

It was, how do you do? and how do you do?
And how do you do? again.

At Wednesbury there was a cocking,
    A match between Newton and Scroggins;
The colliers and nailers left work,
    And all to old Spittle's went jogging.
To see this noble sport,
    Many noblemen resorted;
And though they'd but little money,
    Yet that little they freely sported.

Though the syllables number most irregularly, nobody can deny that
the pieces scan. I write of stress-centres rather than of stresses, because
often the stress is not on one syllable but, as in *how do you do? and how
do you do?* spread over two or three. Anglo-Saxon verse was all
alliterative and stressed, its syllables uncounted. William Langland, a
contemporary of Chaucer's, though the most famous of the middle
English poets to revive the Anglo-Saxon alliterative metre was by
no means the only one. In the sixteenth century John Skelton wrote
in the native style as often as in the Continental, though reducing
the alliteration and adding rhyme. In the seventeenth century, Shake-
speare, who had been dominated at first by the Continental prosody in
vogue at the London theatres, gradually rediscovered his native
inheritance, and transformed the foppish blank verse which Surrey and
Wyatt had brought from Italy into a metre in which both principles,
native and Continental, interacted; it was a metre capable at times of
stresses as turbulent as those in *Beowulf*, while at others it could still
strut syllabically like an Italianate courtier.

The two principles of prosody correspond in a marked way with
contrary habits of life and political principles: the calm, feudal prin-
ciple of preordained structure, law and order, culture spreading down-
wards from the king and peers; the communal principle, threatening
the feudal scheme from below—impulsive, emotional, headless, un-
foreseeable. The rare poets who have contrived to reconcile the two
principles have always, like Shakespeare and Skelton, had one foot
firmly planted in the Court and the other equally firmly in the market.
The feudalism of the eighteenth century made for conscientious
syllable-counting; the Romantic Revival, intimately connected with
the French Revolution, re-introduced stress-prosody. The future of

English prosody depends on the political outcome of the class warfare now declared.

Classical prosody is tinged with what Dr. Scripture calls the typographical fallacy, namely, that the space between printed letters and the space between printed words represent an actual time-interval, or at least that it is possible to divide a verse into feet by driving wedges between syllables; whereas, except for pauses indicated by punctuation marks, spoken verse is really one continuous flow of the voice-stream, and when a sensitive instrument is set to record it, there is nothing of a regular rise and fall in the resultant wavy line to indicate either syllables or feet. Most of English classical verse, while conforming typographically to the syllable-counting principle and to the rigid dualism of 'short or long?' which goes with it, derives its quality from a far subtler musical scheme than that of an ordered sequence of approximately identical iambs, dactyls and what not; in fact, the musical delight we derive from, say, Gray's *Elegy* is not and never was one of elementary arithmetic, but is based on the variations of distance, pitch and sonority between what custom arithmetically marks off as identical feet. This is not to rule out the useful convention of the syllable. Its adoption in classical verse has meant the calming and slowing down of rhythm, suitable for grave and reflective thought; its neglect, in the prosody of stress-centres, has made for fury and turbulence.

Mr. J. B. S. Haldane in his *Daedalus, or The Future of Science,* has a few lines to spare for the future of poetry. While lavish of his quotations from poets living and dead, he takes a gloomy view of the poetic scene. He affirms that the decay of poetry to-day is due to the defective education of the poets; that at present not a single competent poet understands industrial life, and that no poet since Shelley has been up to date in chemical knowledge, and that if we want poets to interpret physical science, which is, he says, vastly more stimulating to the imagination than are the Classics, we must see that our potential poets are instructed in science and economics.

Not until our poets are once more drawn from the educated classes (I speak as a scientist) will they appeal to the average man by showing him that beauty in his own life, as Homer and Virgil appealed to the street urchins who scrawled their verses on the walls of Pompeii.

But is poetry in decay? Decay presupposes a prime; and poetry has never had a prime in which it has been in touch with the 'average man,' except in primitive societies where it serves magical purposes, or in advanced societies where, during a common calamity, distinctions of class, education and occupation temporarily disappear.

And is Science the interest of the average Englishman any more than Poetry? There are a few intellectuals really interested in its developments, many commercials less interested in it than grateful for the comforts it provides, and very many manual workers wholly indifferent to it, except as its development affects wages and prices. And, in any case, what does 'average' mean? Until a cerebral index can be established to decide intelligence even as accurately as a cephalic index decides race, and until poems can be subjected to a critical analysis as readily as physical substances are to spectral analysis, we cannot scientifically assume that an average can in either case be struck.

I don't know what 'competent poet' means to Mr. Haldane. Professional scientists, he says, have no perception of literary form; and since he is now writing as a scientist, the only meaning which he can rightly attach to 'competent' is 'approved in literary circles'—but literary circles are notoriously fallible. Mr. Haldane is misinformed about the education of living English poets who are 'competent' in this sense. Among them are to be found an architect, a mining engineer, an economic expert, a navvy, a scavenger, a senator, a natural historian, a museum official, a professional soldier, a clerk in the Standard Oil Company, a tramp, a dog-breeder, a peer, a seaman, and a metaphysician. As an instance of a poet who has been up to date in Science since Shelley, what about Francis Thompson? At one time it was his chief interest. Mr. Haldane suggests that really competent poets interpret life: therefore well-educated poets of the future will achieve great poetry mainly by interpreting Science and Industry, which are the only forms of activity not at present suffering from decay. When a scientist talks about interpretation absurdities sprout. The nearest he can get to interpretation is a simplifying of technical language into something rudely resembling unlearned speech: *Einstein Made Easy*, *Mendelism at a Glance*. The scientific method is consistently one of accurate equations and reasonable cross-references, e.g. 'the sum of the squares on the smaller sides of a right-angled triangle is equal to the square on the hypotenuse side'; or 'water is formed of two parts of hydrogen gas to one part of oxygen'; or 'the negroid races are characterized by black skin, broad lips, and curly black hair.' When therefore a scientist speaks of a poet 'interpreting' industrial life he expects the interpretation to be as simple as Pythagoras' interpretation of the two sides of the right-angled triangle in terms of the hypotenuse, or any other interpretative formula of the physicist or anthropologist. Now, while it may be discovered that legitimate cross-references can be made between the images or rhythms of a poem, and the physical and imaginative context in which the poet was situated at the time of composition, the scientist cannot expect, even in traditional poems, to find any constant formula equating the poem with its context. He must not expect, for instance, that because the original *Royal George* did go down, as Thomas Campbell relates, with Admiral Kempenfeldt and his twice four hundred men on board, the original 'schooner Hesperus' was also wrecked. As it happens, she reached Boston harbour with a damaged bowsprit only; the *female lashed to a mast*, which Longfellow noted in his diary account of the same storm, belonged to a vessel whose fate was never 'interpreted.' And Longfellow's phrase about the old moon having the young moon on her arm is salvage from another wreck altogether, that of Sir Patrick Spens' White Ship on its return from 'Norraway o'er the faem.' And Sir Patrick Spens himself, if it comes to that, had nothing whatever to do, historically speaking, with either of the two voyages which, fused together, form the subject of the ballad which bears his name.

That Mr. Haldane is unaware how well educated, in his sense, many 'competent poets' are is probably due to their refusal to interpret scientific or industrial experience in the way he intends; and, the fact is, purely literary poets are those who appeal most to scientists, as Mr. Haldane's own quotations prove. I cannot imagine that he would have much use for a modern *Purple Island* in physiology, a *Loves of the Plants* in botany, or a *Polyolbion* in geography; and I have not noticed him rushing into print with a retraction of his statements on account of Mr. Alfred Noyes' recent accomplished epic, *The Torchbearers*, which purports to record the triumphs of Science throughout the ages.

But those urchins of Pompeii: were they really so entranced with the *Iliad* and *Aeneid* that they could not contain themselves when they saw a blank wall? A simpler explanation would be that they were showing off their handwriting, and the first things that occurred to them were the lines of verse which had been beaten into them that day at school. On the nursery wall next door, as I write, this inspiring legend is chalked:

Dame Trot was an old woman with kind blue
eyes and a white . .

for I have two urchins learning to read and write, and their School Primer opens with Dame Trot. And does Mr. Haldane remember the Greek epigram of the doctor who objected to his son learning Homer? He complained that the boy came home with a rigmarole about one Achilles, who sent many valiant souls down to Hades. 'What good does that stuff do him? Why, I myself, in the course of my profession, have done as much as Achilles.' The doctor anticipated (by two thousand years) Mr. Haldane's view that the Classics were played out; and that was even before Virgil's time.

However, I agree with Mr. Haldane that poetry is in a bad way these days. The working classes do not read poems: they read little except the Sunday newspapers. This is because elementary education is aimed at increasing the industrial efficiency and the civic obedience of the masses, not at humanizing their culture. The necessarily uninspired teaching of poetry in elementary schools has disinclined the children to continue their acquaintance with it after the leaving age. But at least they have learned to spell, and in their Sunday's leisure they read lurid accounts of the world to which they do not belong, the world of moneyed folly, of unnatural vice, of sordid crime, of political intrigue. The commercial classes have had a somewhat better schooling. They do not read poetry either, except in regions where the old-fashioned parlour tradition survives: there John Oxenham's books of verse are laid out on the table next to devotional tracts and the novels of Dickens and Charles Garvice, and perhaps read. Those of them who have had secondary school education are supposed to know something of English literature; and have 'done' Shakespeare, along with French and geometry. They do not read poetry either: they are deeply suspicious of it as something concerned with boring messages about truth and beauty. They read light modern novels, short stories and the more ebullient daily papers.

Open any monthly magazine of commercial fiction. Each story is thoroughly workmanlike. The local colour is carefully applied, the plot well handled, the characters plausible, and considerable demands are made on the reader's observation and memory as the *dénouement* approaches. But the general run of verse chosen to fill up the blank spaces between these stories is as banal, nerveless and amateur as could be. The reason is that there is a genuine and sincere demand for the short story but no such demand for verse; its appearance in the magazine is a quaint survival from the days of the early Victorian *Keepsake* annual.

The public which is acquiring a short-story sense and a film-sense and a traffic-sense and a radio-sense is neither dull nor lazy. The enthusiasm for the difficult crossword puzzle and the home-made radio-set proves that. I see no justification for the theory that because the demands of industrial or commercial life are so fatiguing poems must necessarily be narcotic and simple in the extreme if they are to find a large public. On the contrary, any stimulant to adventurous thought is welcomed by the victims of business routine; but it happens that poetry is no longer in fashion, and the poetry-sense has not been cultivated correspondingly with these other senses. Yet it is only a hundred years ago since crowds queued up for a new canto of Byron's *Don Juan* and a publisher could offer Thomas Moore 3,000 guineas in advanced royalties for *Lalla Rookh*. As a marketable commodity verse has entered a vicious circle: the less it is wanted the duller it gets, and the duller it gets the less it is wanted. Its temporary boom during the War was artificial and did not affect the larger reading public.

This brings us to the professional class, with money and a background of university education and foreign travel, which feels bound in duty to follow the work of a few poets who show some originality —but not to the extent of paying them a living wage; so that they fall too easily into the temptation of wooing, futilely, a larger and less discriminating public. And to fashionable Society, whose function is to indulge literary and artistic caprice, and therefore supports, or half-supports by indirect patronage, one or two modernist poets who are experimentally amusing, like designers of hats or ballet *décor*. Their experiments are based on analogous experiments in painting and music. Though expressive only of the present come-what-may transitional stage—alternately stoical and defeatist but always ironical—from the solid nineteenth-century tradition to the not yet formulated tradition of the twentieth, this is the most interesting work now being published. In structure it is Protean, in subject it admits no limits; in syntax it acknowledges no duty to the grammarians; in diction it will not be disciplined—Mr. Eliot's *The Waste Land* varies from the archaic literary to the commercial and the squalidly obscene, and Miss Sitwell confuses the senses with 'shrill grass' and 'clucking flowers'; in allusion it is often wilfully obscure and indirect. Its chief value is its courageous demonstration of how far one can, or cannot, modify poetic tradition without falling into arhythmic nonsense.

But experimental work, as such, has no future. Last year's experimental poem is as out of date as last year's hat and there must come a time, perhaps not very many years hence, when there will be a nostalgic reaction from futurism to some sort of traditionalism, and in the end, back will come the Miltonic sonnet, the Spenserian stanza and the mock-heroic epic in the style of Pope.

MODERNIST POETRY

with Laura Riding

(1926)

I

MODERNIST POETRY
AND THE PLAIN READER'S RIGHTS

LET us assume for the moment that poetry not characteristically 'modernist' presents no difficulty to the plain reader: for the complaint against modernist poetry turns on its differences from traditional poetry. These differences would seem to justify themselves if their effect were to bring poetry any nearer the plain reader; even traditional poetry, it is sometimes charged, has a tendency to withdraw itself from him. But the sophistications of advanced modern poetry seem only to widen the breach. In the poetry of Mr. E. E. Cummings, for example, who may be considered to illustrate the divorce of advanced contemporary poetry from the standards of ordinary common sense, is to be found apparently not only a disregard of common sense, but an insult to it. Such poetry seems to say: 'Keep out! This is a private performance.'

But does the poet really mean to keep the public out? If, after a careful examination of poems that seem only to be part of the high-brow's game of baiting the low-brow, they still resist all reasonable efforts to understand him, then we must conclude that such work is, after all, merely a joke at the plain reader's expense and return him to his newspapers and his Shakespeare—let us assume for the moment that he has no difficulty in understanding Shakespeare. But if, on the other hand, we are able to extract from these poems the experiences which are expected of poetry, or at least see that the poet originally wrote them in all sincerity, then the plain reader must modify his critical attitude. In the first place, he must admit that what is called common intelligence is the mind in its least active state: that poetry demands a more vigorous imaginative effort than he has hitherto been willing to apply to it; and that, if anthologies compiled to refresh tired minds have indulged his lazy reading habits, poets can be pardoned for using exceptional means to make him do justice to their poems. Next, he must ask himself whether such innovations have not a place in the normal course of poetry-writing, and if he decides that they have, he must question the depth of his understanding of poetry which, like Shakespeare's, is taken for granted and aᴗk whether a poet like Mr. Cummings must not be taken seriously, at least for his effect on the future reading of poetry of any age or style.

To begin with, we shall choose one of Mr. Cummings' earlier and simpler poems, which will nevertheless excite much the same hostility as his later work. It is unusually suitable for analysis, because the subject is of just the kind that the plain reader looks for in poetry. It appears, moreover, in Mr. Louis Untermeyer's popular *Anthology of Modern American Poetry* side by side with the work of poets more willing than Mr. Cummings to defer to the intelligence-level of the plain reader. It is all the more important to study because Mr. Untermeyer seems personally hostile to Mr. Cummings' work and yet to have been forced by the pressure of more advanced critical opinion to include it in a book where modernism in poetry means, in his own definition, simplicity ('the use of the language of everyday speech' and the discarding of that poetical padding which the plain reader and the plain critic enjoy more than Mr. Untermeyer would admit). But Mr. Untermeyer is speaking of a modernism no longer modern, that of such dead movements as Georgianism and Imagism which were supposedly undertaken in the interests of the plain reader. We are dealing here with a modernist who seems to feel no obligation to the plain reader, and to work solely in the interests of poetry.

SUNSET

stinging
gold swarms
upon the spires
silver

   chants the litanies the
great bells are ringing with rose
the lewd fat bells
                 and a tall

wind
is dragging
the
sea

with

dream

-S

With so promising a title—though supplied, it appears, by Mr. Untermeyer, since none of the poems in Mr. Cummings' own volumes have titles—what barriers does the poem raise between itself and the plain reader? In what respect does it seem to sin against common intelligence?

The lines do not begin with capital letters. The spacing does not suggest any regular verse-form, though it seems to be systematic. There are no punctuation marks. But even if one can overlook these technical oddities, it still seems impossible to read the poem as a logical sequence. Many words essential to the coherence of the ideas suggested have been deliberately omitted; and the entire effect is so sketchy that the poem might be made to mean almost anything. If the author once had a precise meaning he seems to have lost it while writing the poem. Let us, however, assume for the sake of this argument that it is possible to discover the original poem at the back of the poet's mind; or at least to gather enough material from the poem as it stands from which to construct a poem that will satisfy all formal requirements, the poem that he perhaps meant to hint at with these fragments. As the naturalist Cuvier could reconstruct an extinct animal in full anatomical detail from a single tooth, let us restore this extinct poem from what Mr. Cummings has permitted to survive.

First, we must decide whether there are any positive features in *Sunset* which will allow it to be judged as a formal poem and which must occur with much the same emphasis in the proposed rewriting. The title might be amplified because of a veiled literary reference in lines five and six to Rémy de Gourmont's *Litanies de la Rose*. It might reasonably include some acknowledgment of the poet's debt to French influences, and read: 'Sunset Piece: After Reading Rémy de Gourmont.' The heavy *s* alliteration in the first seven lines, confirmed in the last by the solitary capitalized *S*, cannot be discarded: the context demands it. The first word, *stinging*, taken alone, suggests merely a sharp feeling; its purpose is to supply an emotional source from which the other *s* ideas may derive. In the second line *swarms* develops the alliteration; at the same time it colours *stinging* with the association of golden bees and softens it with the suppressed idea of buzzing. We are now ready for the more tender *s* word, *spires*, in the third line. *Silver*, the single word of the fourth line, brings us back to the contrast between cold and warm in the first and second lines (*stinging* suggests cold in contrast with the various suggestions of warmth in the *gold swarms*) because *silver* reminds one of cold water as gold does of warm light. Two suppressed *s* words play behind the scenes in this first part of the poem, both disguised in *silver* and *gold*, namely *sea* and *sun*. *Sea* does not actually occur until the twelfth line, when the *s* alliteration has flagged: separated from alliterative associations, it becomes the definite image *sea* around which the poem is to be built up. But once it has appeared there is little more to be said: the poem trails off, closing with the large *S* echo of the last line. The hyphen before this *S* detaches it from *dream* and sets it apart as the alliterative summary of the poem; in a realistic sense -*S* might stand for the alternation of quiet and hiss in wave movement. As a formal closing it leaves us with much the same feeling as at the start, but less acute, because the ʒ sound has prevailed over the *s* sound with which the poem began. The sunset is over, the final impression is darkness and sleep, though the -*S* vaguely returns us to the two sharp *s*'s of the opening.

Another feature which would recur in the rewriting of the poem is the deceleration of the rhythm in the last half indicated by the shortening of the lines and by the double spacing. In regular verse this would naturally mean line-lengthening, the closing of a ten-syllable stanza series with a twelve-syllable couplet, for example. No end-rhymes occur in the poem as it stands but the rhyme element is strong. Though the only obvious rhyme-sympathy is between *stinging* and *ringing*, many suppressed rhymes are present: not only *swinging* accompanying the idea of bells but *bees* and *seas*, *bells* and *swells*, *spires* and *fires*. In the rewritten poem a formal metrical scheme would have to be employed, but the choice would be governed by the character of the original poem. The rhythm would be gentle and simple, with few marked emphases. Monosyllables would prevail, with a noticeable recurrence of *ing* words; and *bells* would be repeated. Here, then, is a poem embodying the important elements of Mr. Cummings' poem, but with normal spacing and punctuation and a regular verse-form. It contains no images not directly suggested by the original, but links up grammatically what appears to be an arrangement based on caprice.

SUNSET PIECE

After reading Rémy de Gourmont

White foam and vesper wind embrace.
The salt air stings my dazzled face
And sunset flecks the silvery seas
With glints of gold like swarms of bees

And lifts tall dreaming spires of light
To the imaginary sight,
So that I hear loud mellow bells
Swinging as each great wave swells,
Wafting God's perfumes on the breeze,
And chanting of sweet litanies
Where jovial monks are on their knees,
Bell-paunched and lifting glutton eyes
To windows rosy as the skies.

And this slow wind—how can my dreams forget?—
Dragging the waters like a fishing-net.

Mr. Cummings, it may be assumed, felt bound to write the poem as he did in order to prevent it from becoming what we have made of it. To treat an old subject like sunset and avoid all the obvious poetical formulas, the poet must write in a new way if he is to evoke any fresh response in his readers at all. Not only does the rewritten version demand much less attention than the original, but it is difficult to feel respect for a poem that is full of reminiscences not only of Rémy de Gourmont, but of Wordsworth ('To the imaginary sight'), Milton (in the metrical variations taken from *L'Allegro*), Messrs. Belloc and Chesterton ('Where jovial monks . . .' etc.) and Tagore in English translation ('Dragging the waters like a fishing-net'). Stale phrases such as 'vesper wind' and 'silver seas' have come to mean so little that they scarcely do their work in the poem. And yet we shall see that such phrases cannot be avoided if we are to revise the poem for the plain man. 'White foam' is understood from the sea setting, the movement of the poem, and the cold hissing implied in the sequence of *s*'s. 'Vesper wind' is suggested by *sunset, spires, monks, bells, tall wind*. 'Salt air,' besides resulting from the embrace of 'white foam' and 'vesper wind,' is built up from *stinging, sea* and *wind*. The transformations in the next three lines are fairly obvious. 'Imaginary sight' is necessary to remind the plain reader that the poem is not to be taken literally, a hint which Mr. Cummings disdained to give. It should be noticed that 'imaginary' is the longest and slowest word in the poem yet adds nothing to the picture; in fact, makes it less real. The seventh and eighth lines express the connexion between bells and waves which Mr. Cummings leaves the reader to deduce, if he pleases. The ninth line is the expansion of the rose idea demanded by the context: *monks, spires, litanies* are all bound up with the Catholic symbolism of the rose; and in rewriting the poem it is impossible not to develop the literary associations of the rose as well (*wafting, perfumes*). The rose-windows of cathedrals are also obviously suggested. Unfortunately *lewd*, too strong a word for a formal sunset piece, has to be broken up into *jovial* and *glutton*, recalling the Christmas-annual type of monk. The analogy between *great bells* and *fat monks* has to be emphasized, thus introducing gratuitous words like *mellow, bell-paunched, on their knees*, etc. Instead of taking advantage of the natural associations latent in certain highly pictorial words, we have had to go over much un-necessary ground and have ended by merely being banal. In lengthen-ing the metre of the last two lines to match the slowing down in the original piece, many superfluous words and images have had to be introduced here too. First of all, *slow* itself, as weakening to the con-centration of the poem as the line 'To the imaginary sight.' Then, '—how can my dreams forget?—', to account grammatically for the vivid present tense in which the whole poem is written, and to put *dream* in its more logical position, since in the original poem it is doing double duty for a specific image (*fishing-net*, following from *dragging*) and the vagueness with which the image is felt.

The conclusion to be drawn from this exercise might be that poems must in future be written in skeleton style if poetry is not to die out. But the poetry of Mr. Cummings is clearly more important as a sign of local irritation in the poetic body than as a model for a new tradition. The important thing to recognize, in a time of popular though super-ficial education, is the need of bringing home to the reading public the differences between good and bad poems, the very differences that we have been pointing out here. Poets in such a time, indeed, may forget that they have any function other than to teach the proper approach to poetry: there is an exaggerated though excusable tendency to suspend the writing of all poetry that is not critical in intention. (Rare exceptions, of course, occur: poets whose writing is so self-contained that they are not affected by staleness in traditional poems or obliged to attack them or escape from them.) Mr. Cummings in this poem was really rewriting the other poem, the one we gave, into a good poem. But for the rarer poet there is no 'other poem'; there is only the poem which he writes. Mr. Cummings' experimental tech-nique, indeed, if further and more systematically developed, would become so complicated and so elaborate that the principal interest in his poems would be mathematical. Real poets, however, do not pursue innovation for its own sake: they are conservative in their methods so long as these ensure the proper security and delivery of the poem.

A poem's virtue does not lie in the way in which it is set down on paper, as a picture's does in the way it is set down on canvas. Method in poetry is not anything that can be discussed in terms of physical form. The poem is neither the paper, nor the type, nor the spoken syllables. It is as invisible and as inaudible as thought; and the only method that the real poet cares to use is one that will present the poem without making it either visible or audible: without turning it into a substitute for a painting or for music. Yet when conservatism of method, through its abuse by slack-minded poets, comes to mean the supplanting of poems by exercises in poet-craft, then there is a reasonable place for any innovation which brings up the important question: 'How should poetry be written?' and acts as a deterrent against writing in a worn-out style. Our suggestion is not that poets should imitate Mr. Cummings, but that the appearance of poems like his and the attention they demand should make it harder for poetical exercises to be passed off as poetry. We may not accept his experimental version of the sunset piece, but once we have understood it we cannot return with satisfaction to the formal one.

Turning back for a closer comparison of the two versions, we see how much of the force of the original has been lost in the rewriting. We have begun each line with a capital letter, but the large final *S* which was one of the most important properties of the original has thus been eliminated, and a look of unnecessary importance has been given to words like *And*, *To* and *So*. In our use of normal spacing and verse-form we have had to disregard the significance of the double spacing and indentation, and of the variation in the length of the lines. Formal indentation can either be a guide to rhyming pairs or a sign that the first part of a line is missing, but it cannot denote musical rests of varying value as in the original of the poem. We have also expanded the suggested ideas by grammatic means and supplemented them with the words which seem to have been omitted. But in so doing we have sacrificed the compactness of the original and dispelled its carefully devised dreaminess. In fact, by formalizing the poem we have not added anything to it but on the contrary detracted from its value.

The expansion of the original by the addition of the suppressed words has necessarily multiplied the number of *s*'s, because the suppressed words show a high proportion of these. This alliteration, sustained over several couplets, does not match the alliteration of the original, especially since we have been obliged to use many *s*'s that have no sort of alliterative significance ('To windows rosy as the skies'). Neither has the gradual slowing down of the rhythm in the last half of the poem been effectively reproduced. In the original the slowing down extends over the sestet of this fragmentary sonnet (the fragmentary line, -*S*, being an alliterative hang-over). But because in the formal version the original simple octave develops a prolixity which destroys the proper balance between it and its sestet, we have had to abandon the sonnet-form and pack into two lines words which should have had the time-value of six. The best we have been able to do is to keep fourteen lines (or rather seven rhyming couplets, one of which has an extra line). The rhymes, too, in the formal version have mutilated the sense: they express the remoteness of the scene by a series of echoes rather than by silences—for the original lines can be regarded as sonnet-lines filled out with musical rests. By transposing the poem into a form in which a definite metrical scheme can be recognized we have entirely altered the character of the poem. We have not even been able to save the scraps of regular iambic rhythm with which we started.

Certain admissions must therefore be made. We must not only reject the formal version in favour of the original: we must admit that the original itself is an intensely formal poem. Indeed, its very virtuosity has caused it to be mistaken for a mere assemblage of words, a literary trick. But since it is proved capable of yielding the kind of experiences customarily expected from poetry, in fact the most ordinary of such experiences, our conclusion must be that the plain reader's approach to poetry is adequate only for poems as weak as the critical effort which he is ready to apply to them; and that Mr. Cummings (to disregard the satiric hilarity in which many of his poems are written) really means to write serious poetry and to have it read with the critical sympathy it deserves. The importance of any new technical methods which he employs to bring this about lies not in their ultimate permanence or impermanence, but in their establishment of what the poet's rights are in his poem: how free he is to disregard the inferior critical efforts to which the poem will be submitted by the greater part of the poetry-reading public. What, then, of the plain reader's rights? They are, like the poet's, whatever his intelligence is able to make them.

It must be admitted that excessive interest in the technique of the poem can become morbid both in the poet and the reader, like the composing and solving of crossword puzzles. Once the sense of a poem with a technical soul, so to speak, is unriddled and its patterns plainly displayed, it is not fit for re-reading: as with the Sphinx in the fable, to allow the riddle to be guessed is equivalent to suicide. A poem of this kind is nevertheless able to stave off death by revealing, under closer examination, an unexpected reserve of new riddles; and so long as it is able to supply these it may continue to live as a poem. But clearly its surprises cannot last for ever; nor can we, as when reading the indestructible poem whose soul is not technical, go back to the beginning when we have done and start all over again as with a new poem.

How much more life is left in *Sunset* at this point? Have we come to an end? Or are there further reasons why it should continue to be called a poem, since it is a poem only so long as there is a possibility of its yielding still more meaning? Did we not, without assuming any formal verse-pattern, give a satisfactory explanation of the poem? Did we not also find it possible to give an entirely new view of it on the basis of its being a skeletonized sonnet? Did we not accept it as a non-grammatic construction, yet still make sense of it? But could we not show it to be potentially or even actually grammatic and make sense of it because it was so? Why not read *swarms* and *chants*, which we have been regarding as nominative plural nouns, as third person singular verbs, and read *silver* and *gold* as nouns, not as adjectives? The poem will then stand grammatically as follows:

Stinging gold swarms upon the spires.
Silver [i.e. a voice or tone of silver] chants the litanies
The great bells are ringing with rose—
The lewd fat bells—
And a tall wind is dragging the sea with dreams.

And even if we had explored the technical possibilities in this poem of thirty-one words—the grammar, the metre and other technical aspects, the context and the association of images—we should still be left with the fact that it has thirty-one words, and perhaps find in it another formalism. Can it be a coincidence that this is also the standard length of the *tanka*, the dominant verse-form in Japanese poetry—thirty-one syllables, each of word value? The Japanese influence is further intimated by Mr. Cummings' tendency to suggest and symbolize rather than to express in full. In Japanese, according to the conventional arrangement of the thirty-one word-units in lines of five, seven, five, seven, seven, this poem would be set down like this:

CA: F

stinging gold swarms upon the
spires silver chants the litanies the great
bells are ringing with rose
the lewd fat bells and a tall
wind is dragging the sea with dreams.

But stronger than the Japanese influence in modern English and American poetry is the French, which in turn has borrowed much from the Japanese. Mallarmé, the father of symbolism, turned the act of suggestion in poetry into a science. He found the tradition of French poetry so exhausted by sterile laws of prosody that he had to practise poetry as a science to avoid malpractising it as an art. Rimbaud, with all Mallarmé's science behind him and endowed with a natural poetic mind, was able to practise poetry as an art again. Similarly Mr. Cummings and other experimentalists—he is to be regarded rather as an inspired amateur than a scientist—may be preparing the way for an English or American Rimbaud. As M. Paul Valéry, the French critic and poet, says of Mallarmé and Rimbaud, discussing their employment of the vehicles of sense in poetry: 'What is only a system in Mallarmé becomes a domain in Rimbaud.' So modernist poets are developing resources to which a future poet will have easy access when he turns the newly opened-up territory into a personal poetic domain.

Although an elaborate system of poetic technique may come to flower in the work of a natural poet like Rimbaud, it may on the other hand fossilize in a convention as tyrannic as the one it was invented to supplant. There is more danger of this, however, in French poetry than in English. M. Paul Valéry has even been made a member of the French Academy, in recognition of his formal influence on contemporary poetry. Although as traditional in form as Mr. Cummings is modernist, he relies, like him, almost entirely on the effectiveness of images—on their power to evoke sensations, and on their strangeness. To describe how night hid from Narcissus his own beloved image in the fountain, he says that night slid between him and his image like 'a knife shearing a fruit in two.' What he means is that Narcissus and the image formed a whole as symmetrical as the halves of an apple before they are divided. Mr. Cummings' images are as strange and as vivid as this ('gold swarms' or 'ringing with rose,' for example); but there is no question of making an academician of him or calling his most recent and more methodical phase 'Pope-ian,' as M. Valéry's last phase is known by his admirers as 'Racinian' after the master-craftsman of the most formal period in French poetry.

English modernist poets also imitate the French in the use of combinations of sounds to create a musical picture. This is, of course, nothing new in English poetry. Gray, one of the most traditional of English poets, wishing to give the picture of slow and painful descent down a steep mountain, writes:

> As down the steep of Snowdon's shaggy side
> He wound with toilsome march his long array.

But this usage has never been applied except as an occasional trope, and even as such has been discouraged rather than encouraged by criticism. It is considered tolerable only where the combinations of sounds add musicalness without taking away from the meaning; never where they over-represent or distort the meaning.

Musicalness in modern French verse means something else: the treating of word-sounds as musical notes in which the meaning itself is to be found. This takes poetry even farther from its natural course than the Victorians took it with their coloratura effects. The bond between the Victorian poet and his reader was at least that of a common, though not an original, sentiment. The meaning of a poem was understood beforehand from the very title, and the persuasiveness of the word-music was intended to keep the poem vibrating in the memory long after it had been read. The bond, however, between the French modernist poet and his reader is one of technical ingenuity: the poet setting the meaning down in combinations of sounds, the reader interpreting words as combinations of sounds rather than as words. Actually, there is little poetic thought in Victorian poetry because of the compromise it makes between ideas and their pleasurable expression. But the compromise in modern French poetry, though less apparent, is still more destructive of poetic thought. It is between ideas and typography and as such implies the domination of ideas by mechanics. By giving the letters of words a separate personality we have a new psychology of letters entirely distinct from the psychology of images. A striking illustration of the attempt to reconcile these two psychologies is a poem of Rimbaud's on the colours of the vowels. It is plain that the colours associated with vowels will vary widely with the individual and may be determined by so irrelevant a cause as the colour of the alphabet-blocks which one used as a child. A better case might perhaps be made for the meaning-associations of consonants, particularly of combinations of consonants such as *st*, as in *stinging*, *strike*, *stench*, to denote sharp assault, and the final *nch*, as in *clinch*, *munch*, *wrench*, to denote strain. But it is only occasionally that the letters of a word imitate its meaning in this way; no general rule can be drawn from these examples. There are many more instances of letters out of harmony with word-meanings than of letters in harmony with them. Take the word *kiss*, for instance. Is this *iss* any gentler than the *iss* of *hiss*? Or is the *k* in *kiss* gentler than the *k* of kick? Logically, such a theory should mean that a French poem written in this way would produce the same effect on a person who did not understand French as on one who did.

When it is remembered how such theories crowd the literary air, it will be realized what great restraint Mr. Cummings has imposed on himself in the matter of alliteration and other tricks with letters. He would not, we feel, let such theories run away with him to the extent of forcing his choice of words to depend more on the sense of their sounds than on the sense of their images. His choice of *swarms*, for instance, is primarily determined by the three meanings combined in the word (the crowding sense, the bee-buzzing sense, and another hitherto not noted—the climbing sense associated with *spires* and the eye looking up to the light); not by the occurrence of *s* and *ʒ* or by the presence of *warm* in *swarms*, though these are accidents of which he takes every advantage. And this is the way such things should happen in poetry: by coincidence. The poet appreciates and confirms rather than stage-manages. A certain amount of superstitious faith in language is necessary if the poet is to perform the sort of miracle expected of, and natural to, poetry.

II

THE PROBLEM OF FORM AND SUBJECT-MATTER

Modern French poetic theory lays a deal of emphasis on the phonetic sense of words; and has done so increasingly since the time of the Symbolists. The French, indeed, have long been dissatisfied with the progress of poetry as compared with that of music and the arts, and attempted to remedy its supposed deficiencies by bringing it closer to music. To do this they have had to insist that a musical meaning accompanies the word-meaning and to introduce a system of letter-notation similar to musical notation. Three lines from a poem by

M. Paul Valéry will illustrate this picture-making in poetry by the help of sounds:

> Il se fit Celui qui dissipe
> En conséquences son Principe,
> En étoiles, son Unité.

Since we can recognize *dissipe*, *conséquences*, *Principe* and *Unité* by their English parallels, we must rewrite these lines, if we want to test their direct phonetic value, in some practical phonetic notation which will completely divorce them from any associated meaning:

> Eel s' fee s' lwee kee deesseep p'
> Ahng kohnsaykahng s' sohng Prangseep p',
> Ahng aytwal l', sonn Ewneetay.

This is the closest approximation to the sounds that can be made in English spelling without the use of a formal phonetic system. We are immediately impressed by the recurrence of the strong *s* and *ee* sounds, as we were supposed to be. This might denote a number of things: a man whetting a scythe, a child writing on a slate, or a serpent trying to talk. On the other hand, such sounds might have nothing to do with the subject; as in the couplet:

> See: fleecy sheep we leap
> Across this grassy sweep

the *s* and *ee* sounds are contrary to the sense. Suppose, however, that we did choose the idea of a serpent's talking, as we are meant to do, have we any clue to what the serpent is talking about? Or are the lines supposed merely to represent a serpent talking, without any collateral meaning? As a matter of fact, they represent a serpent talking about God. But how are we to deduce God from the sound of the poem or know whether the alliteration is supposed to indicate the subject or the elocutionist? Granted that for the special purpose of imitating a serpent's sneers at God such odd sound combinations may be wittily employed. But as a general poetic practice this sort of thing becomes no less tiresome and puerile than the incessant puns and jokes of Goldsmith, Hood or Calverley. Wit in poetry should be devoted to the irony of ideas rather than of phonetics. If phonetics get the upper hand in a poem, they turn it into an exercise in elocution.

Let us try another Valérian specimen, one in which there is no speaking in character:

Vous me le murmurez, ramures! . . . O rumeur déchirante!

Because *murmurez* and *rumeur* are suggestive of their meanings in English, we might be able to get something of the intended sense (the murmur of wind among leaves) and even make a good guess at the meaning of the other words; if only because we have Tennyson's:

> . . . immemorial elms
> And murmur of innumerable bees,

as a class-room quotation to help us. Could we not, however, easily improvise a line of the same musical character but with a totally different meaning:

> More ordure never may restore our midden's pure manure

to show how misleading to the sense letters can be? We suspect that the aim of such poetry as this, is to cast a musical enchantment un-allied with poetic meaning. The meaning becomes merely a historical setting for the music, of which readers need not be aware. We are made to feel that M. Valéry would not object to readers' adopting the same attitude to his poems as his own *Mme Teste* to lofty and abstract questions: instead of being bored, she was musically entertained by them. M. Valéry, perhaps realizing the strain put upon readers by the preciousness of his images, holds their attention by the masterly skill of these musical distractions.

The chief claim of poetic impressionism is that any realistic truth may be better conveyed by the impressions it gives the observer, however disjointed or irrelevant they may seem, than by systematic reasoning or study. Impressionist poetry describes an object by creating in the reader the indefinite feelings he would have on first seeing it, not by giving definite facts about it. This is a method formally recom-mended by Poe, borrowed from him to justify and explain the changes that began to affect French poetry with Baudelaire, and reimported into America when the French had carried Poe's theory far beyond his intentions, which had to do more with the sentiment than with the technical theory of poetry. Poe defined poetry as a combination of music with an idea, resulting in indefinite feelings. But this was, after all, only a restatement of the Classical definition of the aim of poetry, namely to create a sublime effect for the reader; whereas the Impres-sionists aim at a technical correctness—they wish the reader to have the same frame of mind as the poet had when he wrote, they wish to help him rewrite the poem for himself with the poet's mind. These so-called 'indefinite' feelings of impressionism, therefore, must be expressed in painstakingly precise images, since the effect of the poem depends on an accurate identity of the reader's feelings with the poet's.

If, then, the poet practises impressionism according to its literal meaning, it is unfair to call him an Impressionist in the loose, colloquial sense of the word. He rejects reason and logic as poetic aids, not because they encourage definite feelings, but because the feelings they encourage are not definite, not subtle enough for his purpose. 'Indefinite' should be understood in its opposite sense, namely, not defined in prose because not definable; so *definite*, in fact, that ordinary methods of measurement are not accurate enough for them. Images in poetry which seem strained and obscure are often like distances so small or so large that though they are real one has to discard the foot-rule and work in abstract mathematics. Suppose a poet wishes to describe a sunset. He could say in substance: 'It was beautiful. The sea was flecked with gold as the sun sank behind it. Overhead floated rosy clouds. In the foreground hissed the silvery foam. Somewhere bells were ringing. There was a salt taste in the air and the evening breeze blew slowly in from the sea as night drew on.' Or he could say: 'It was beautiful. At first I felt invigorated. My eyes ached with the dazzle of the sun and the saltiness of the air. As I looked up to the rosy glory above me, a great religious feeling overcame me; I seemed in the presence of God. There was a ringing in my ears. I felt warm and cold at once. But after a time the wind made me feel sleepy, so I turned in.' It would be possible to call either of these descriptions impressionist in the colloquial sense, for they would record the poet's impressions objectively or subjectively with a view to reproducing them in the reader. In reality, however, they would convey only a vague and somewhat insincere atmosphere, as does the formalized version of Mr. Cummings' sunset poem; for an actual experience of this sunset one would have to go to some such poem as his original. In it would be found a complicated recipe for a sunset experience, as if for a pudding, not merely a description of what the pudding looked like or how it tasted. And such a method turns the reader into a poet.

Strictly speaking, then, *Sunset* is not Mr. Cummings' poem, but the poem of anybody who will be at pains to write it. What at first glance strike the plain reader as external peculiarities which hinder him from approaching its meaning—the oddness of the form—now appear as the poet's means of avoiding that conventional form which generally stands between the reader and the poetic experience. Indeed, if we look upon form as distinct from the subject-matter of a poem, in this sense true impressionist poems usually lack form, or are capable of adopting a new form with every reader. The poet unites the subject of the poem with the feelings it arouses in him. This unity makes the poem a living whole; it is impressionistic, but not because the subject and the feelings it arouses become indefinite in the combination. They blend without blurring.

Looking on impressionism as one of the earliest manifestations of the general modernist tendency to overcome the distinction between subject-matter and form, we realize that M. Valéry draws the same old-fashioned line between *music* and *idea* that Poe did: he subscribes, in fact, to the Classical conception of poetry. He is a classicist in the musical associations which he weaves into his poems, all intricately designed to arouse 'indefinite feelings' in the reader. Although he is a modernist in his choice of the images through which he conveys poetic ideas, images apparently intended to arouse *definite* feelings, these feelings come closer to one's physical sensation of a thing than to one's mental concept of it. To the definite feelings provoked by the images, or the thought, of a poem of M. Valéry's, the indefinite feelings provoked by the *sounds* of the words form a musical background. Paradoxically, it is in this musical background that the ideas are suggested rather than in the logical sequence of the images, for M. Valéry deliberately suppresses Reason in poetry. It is this which makes him a classicist in form and a modernist in the thought-content of his poems. He handles the modernist problem of achieving a unity between form and subject-matter by letting form suggest the subject of the poem and thought-content do all that form is ordinarily supposed to do. The sole reason for calling this method impressionistic is that it does not, and could not, succeed in arriving at an ingenious balance between the two sets of feelings, definite and indefinite, which theoretically combine to give the poetry meaning; all that it results in is the vague blur that impressionism has come to stand for in its colloquial sense.

M. Valéry provides only one example of those modern French theories of poetry which have had such an abnormal and unwholesome influence on the younger poets of America and England. In Mr. Cummings' defence it should be said that, though his poetry by its immediate effect of oddness does invite labelling, it can be understood without reference to labels: one does not have to explain the sunset poem as impressionistic, although it makes a very strong case for impressionism. Any fairly good poet can be quoted to justify a theory of poetry, however inadequate a theory it may be by which to write poetry. Shakespeare, indeed, can be quoted to justify impressionism or any other poetic theory, simply because he is such a good poet. It would be as reasonable to explain Shakespeare, who was independent of poetic theory, in terms of impressionism as in terms of any poetic theory prevailing at his time. Though one should not overlook the influence on Shakespeare of contemporary theorists, it would be false to say that he wrote as he did from a conscious use of their theories. If he had been critical in the way a poet is generally supposed to be, then we should expect to find him continually demonstrating well-chosen poetic theories. As a matter of fact, his work was such a clearing-house of good and bad elements in contemporary poetry and drama that they cannot have been introduced by conscious critical choice.

It would be as absurd to say that Mr. Cummings sat down to write a poem with all the rules of impressionism before him as to say that Shakespeare sat down to write a play with all the theories of the so-called 'university wits' before him. These men—Lodge, Peele, Greene, Nashe, Lyly and Marlowe—had to set themselves the deliberate task of compromising between the old popular type of play, which was violent, disorderly and exciting, and the new blank-verse play on the classical model, which was orderly and dull. They had for the time being to treat the drama as a literary problem. But when we get past Marlowe's early work and past Kidd's *Spanish Tragedy* we find the drama no longer treated as a problem: it is already a successful convention. The London theatres are paying concerns, and Shakespeare, fortified by his long theatrical apprenticeship, has nothing to worry about. These dramatic experimenters left him a legacy; but he was their natural heir by the right of his genius. What were conscious theories in the dramatists of the previous generation became in him instinctive habits. There are no technical innovations in his plays or poems. The nearest approach to invention in Shakespeare is his original use of other people's innovations. The wits had introduced the Court Fool on their stage, as a link between the old farce and the new classical tragedy; Shakespeare used the part not as mere comic relief but as a living element of the tragedy. Similarly with the sonnet: though pre-Elizabethan experiments with the sonnet, which little by little removed it from the Italian model, were made by Wyatt and Surrey, the

Elizabethan sonnet is nevertheless called after Shakespeare, though he made no experiments with it, and though by the time it reached him it had been successfully used by all the Elizabethan small fry. Yet the sonnet theory can be proved in Shakespeare's sonnets as all pre-Shakespearian dramatic theories can be proved in his plays.

No genuine poet ever called himself after a theory or invented a name for a theory. And it was surely a critic who first pointed out the distinction between subject-matter and form, and from this began to philosophize on form; as it is surely criticism which has always stood between poetry and the plain reader, made possible the writing of so much false poetry and, by giving undue prominence to theory, robbed the reader of his power to distinguish between what is false and what is true.

The struggle on the part of poets to make subject-matter and form coincide in spite of criticism is an old one; as old, perhaps, as the first critic. It should not be confused with attempts to make form suit subject-matter (as the Pindaric ode was designed to contain any stately flattery); or to suit subject-matter to a popular form (as the sonnet has become a general utility form designed to suit a variety of subjects). The trend of modern poetry is towards treating poetry like a sensitive substance which should be allowed to crystallize by itself rather than poured into prepared moulds; and this is why modern critics, no longer able to discuss questions of form, try to replace them by obscure metaphysical reflections. Modern poets are groping for some principle of self-determination to be applied to the making of the poem—not lack of government, but local government. Free verse has been one of the most powerful movements towards this end. But too often it means not local government but complete *laissez-faire*, a licence to metrical anarchy instead of a harmonious enjoyment of liberty. Strangely enough, when we come upon an example of free verse which shows clarity, restraint and proportion, we do not think of it as free verse, though on the other hand we do not think of it as poetry of a traditional form. And this is as it should be.

The opening of a poem by Mr. Hart Crane, *Passage*, is a case in point:

> Where the cedar leaf divides the sky
> I heard the sea.
> In sapphire arenas of the hills
> I was promised an improved infancy

The rhyme between *sea* and *infancy* is not strong enough to mislead one into construing this as a regular stanza. The impression of regularity comes from a careful alternation of images, from a regularity of design more fundamental than verse regularity. Passages in the Authorized Version of the Bible which were originally written as poetry provide the most familiar example of this:

> The beauty of Israel is slain upon thy high places;
> How are the mighty fallen!
> Tell it not in Gath,
> Publish it not in the streets of Ascalon;
> Lest the daughters of the Philistines rejoice,
> Lest the daughters of the uncircumcised triumph.

The effect of regularity is here again achieved by the recurrence of ideas in varying alternations to show the movement of the poem. As in Mr. Crane's poem the imaginative experience of the first two lines is carried, by a parallelism between first and third, second and fourth, to a more specialized meaning, from which the direction of the remainder of the poem is taken; so in David's lament over Saul and Jonathan there is a parallelism between *The beauty of Israel* and *the mighty*, and between *slain upon thy high places* and *fallen* of the first and second lines. The scorn with which the last four lines here quoted must be pronounced is dictated by the ironic contrast between the *high places* of Israel and the *streets* of Gath and Ascalon (the streets of these Philistine cities were trenches below ground-level) and between the God-fearing *beauty of Israel* and the sexually promiscuous *daughters of the Philistines*. In Mr. Crane's poem the sympathetic connexion between the first four lines and the rest of the poem depends not so much on the technical symmetry of the poem as on the use of the images stated directly in these lines, and more indirectly and complicatedly in those that follow. Poetry so treated is no more than a single theme subjected to as many variations as its first or simplest statement will allow, even to the point where it ironically contradicts itself. There is in it no room, and no reason, for a separate element of form. Form arbitrarily imposed on a poem, unless the poem is deficient in the balance of its ideas, is like architectural dressing that spoils the natural proportions of a building and has no structural usefulness to excuse it.

How does the question of form affect the long poem? Let us compare Tennyson's *In Memoriam*, which embroiders the theme of his friend's death in a sequence of episodes, with Mr. T. S. Eliot's *The Waste Land*, which enlarges the introductory theme of the death and decay implicit in Spring to embrace the death and decay implicit in all forms of hopeful human energy. In the first, the same rhymed stanza is maintained through all the varying moods of the poem; in the second the progress of the poem is marked by the most sensitive changes in metre, rhythm and diction—not only from episode to episode but from incident to incident. The poetic quality is to be tested at the delicate transitions from one mood to another. No such transitions are to be found in Tennyson's poem, written wholly in the same stanza, or for that matter in a poem like the *Aeneid*: length in such poems means bulk. The poem is as long as the poet's endurance and the reader's patience permit. Just how long this will be depends on the period in which it was written: long poems generally occur when poetic themes are limited to a few approved subjects, such as war, religion, or mythological history. The length of the poem is then only a sign of the subject's dignity.

A long poem of this sort is not thought to need the same unity as a short poem: the unchanging metre serves to keep the loosely connected parts together. But *The Waste Land* has to be read as a short poem: that is, as a unified whole.

> When lovely woman stoops to folly and
> Paces about her room again, alone,
> She smooths her hair with automatic hand,
> And puts a record on the gramophone.

This formal rhymed stanza, reminiscent of Goldsmith, Mr. Eliot ironically applies to a sordid modern love-scene. He will return us from here to a romantic picture of Queen Elizabeth and Leicester in amorous progress down the Thames, the same Thames across whose waters the noise of this gramophone is now carried. How is the transition between these two passages made? The ten-syllabled iambic line of the stanza quoted turns into blank verse beginning with a romantic quotation from *The Tempest*, getting more and more ragged as the music is interrupted by Thames-side noises, and finally trailing off with syncopated phrases suggested by a mandoline.

> 'This music crept by me upon the waters'
> And along the Strand, up Queen Victoria Street.
> O City city, I can sometimes hear
> Beside a public bar in Lower Thames Street,

> The pleasant whining of a mandoline
> And a clatter and a chatter from within
> Where fishmen lounge at noon: where the walls
> Of Magnus Martyr hold
> Inexplicable splendour of Ionian white and gold.

The change from the riverside to the river is now made by allowing the rhythm to break up into short verse units proper to a river song:

> The river sweats
> Oil and tar
> The barges drift
> With the turning tide
> Red sails
> Wide
> To leeward, swing on the heavy spar.
> The barges wash
> Drifting logs
> Down Greenwich reach
> Past the Isle of Dogs.
>   Weialala leia
>   Wallala leialala

The lyrical quality of this passage is, according to Mr. Eliot's explanatory note, to be associated with the song of the Rhine-daughters in *Die Götterdämmerung*. And this operatic atmosphere imposed on a modern river-scene makes a fitting transition to the picture of Elizabeth and Leicester seated not in a barge foul with oil and tar but in a gilded barge of state:

> Elizabeth and Leicester
> Beating oars
> The stern was formed
> A gilded shell
> Red and gold
> The brisk swell
> Rippled both shores
> Southwest wind
> Carried down stream
> The peal of bells
> White towers
>   Weialala leia
>   Wallala leialala

In contrast with this apparently irregular transition, let us consider three successive sections of *In Memoriam*: 119, 120, 121. The first is a return in reverie to the early days at Cambridge when Tennyson and his dead friend were undergraduates. Arthur Hallam seems to stand before him as in life:

> And bless thee, for thy lips are bland,
>   And bright the friendship of thine eye;
>   And in my thoughts with scarce a sigh
> I take the pressure of thine hand.

This stanza closes the first section. The sections are separated by a double space and a new number. Section 120, though it seems to belong to an entirely different poem, continues in the same mercilessly uniform metre:

> I trust I have not wasted breath:
>   I think we are not wholly brain,
>   Magnetic mockeries; not in vain,
> Like Paul with beasts, I fought with Death;
>
> Not only cunning casts in clay:
>   Let Science prove we are, and then
>   What matters Science unto men,
> At least to me? I would not stay.
>
> Let him, the wiser man who springs
>   Hereafter, up from childhood shape
>   His action like the greater ape,
> But I was *born* to other things.

We find him in the midst of an elementary discussion on rationalism and the materialistic conception of the universe. We may be supposed to read in this the triumph of mind over matter as illustrated by Tennyson's obstinacy in regarding his friend as still alive; there may also be a reminiscence here of undergraduate discussions on the same subjects. But we make these suppositions only in default of a logical connexion between the separate sections. This is not a case of the energetic poet who makes a lazy reader think and work along with him, but of the lazy poet who takes advantage of his reader's faith and industry. Section 121 begins:

> Sad Hesper o'er the buried sun
> And ready, thou, to die with him,
> Thou watchest all things ever dim
> And dimmer, and a glory done:

Here again no strict connexion can be construed. The strain in which the section opens is probably a reaction against the scientific language used in the previous one. Casting about for a more elegiac tone, Tennyson naturally remembers Milton's *Lycidas*, from which he borrows the image of the setting sun, emblem of his dead friend. The rest of the section he devotes to a truistic identification of the evening star with the morning star, as an analogy (which does not quite work out) between his own past and present.

The division into sections has certainly done away with the padding that would have been necessary had the poem been treated as a continuous piece, but deprive it of these, deprive it of its metrical regularity and grandiose diction, and it will appear the sentimental, ill-assorted bundle of lost ideas that it really is. Such feeble material would not be tolerated in a poem which, like *The Waste Land*, has to improvise its metrical changes as it goes along.

Nowadays a poem must give good reason for being of unusual length: it must account strictly for every line that at first sight would appear to be more properly contained in a footnote. The apology for a long poem should be: 'This is really a long *short* poem.' Poe was the first modern critic to explode the dignity of the long poem of major poetry. In *The Poetic Principle* he writes:

> That degree of excitement which would entitle a poem to be so called at all, cannot be sustained throughout a composition of any great length. After the lapse of half an hour, at the very utmost, it flags—fails—a revulsion ensues—and then the poem is, in effect, and in fact, no longer such.

Although he held that the long poem was necessarily weak in structure, that length in itself was destructive of poetic form, by poetic form he meant that metrical uniformity imposed on subject-matter which we have here been questioning in both the short and long poem. Modernist poetry seems to be composed chiefly of short poems—*The Waste Land*, one of the longest modernist poems, runs to only 433 lines. Yet this is not because of a belief in the short poem *per se* as against the long poem, but because of a sense that form and subject-matter are structurally identical whatever the length of the poem. Well-controlled irregularity substituted for uncontrollable regularity makes 'short' and 'long' obsolete critical standards. The very purpose of this 'irregularity' is to let the poem find its own natural length in spite of the demands put upon poetry by critics, booksellers and the general reading public.

III

A STUDY IN
ORIGINAL PUNCTUATION AND SPELLING

The objections raised against the 'freakishness' of modernist poetry are usually supported by quotations from poems by Mr. E. E. Cummings and others which are not only difficult in construction and reference but are printed oddly on the page. The reader naturally looks for certain landmarks in a poem before he can begin to enjoy it: as the visitor to Paris naturally sets his mental map of the city by the Eiffel Tower, and if the Eiffel Tower were to collapse, would have difficulty in finding his way about for a few days. Modernist poets have removed the well-known landmarks and the reader is equally at a loss. The reasons for this removal are, apparently, that landmarks encourage the making of paths, that paths grow to roads, that roads soon mean walls and hedges, and that the common traveller who keeps to the roads never sees any new scenery.

> because
> you go away i give roses who
> will advise even yourself, lady
> in the most certainly(of what we
> everywhere do not touch)deep
> things;
>   remembering ever so . . .

This is the beginning of one of Mr. Cummings' poems. The first obvious oddity is the degrading of the personal pronoun 'I' to 'i.' This has a simple enough history. The 'upper case' was once used for all nouns and proper names and the adjectives formed from them; but since the eighteenth century has been reserved for the Deity; for Royalty (in 'We' and 'Our'); for certain quasi-divine abstractions such as Mystery, Power, Poetry; sometimes for 'She' and 'Thou' and so on, where love gives the pronoun a quasi-divine character. Mr. Cummings protests against the upper case being also allotted to 'I': he affects a humility, a denial of the idea of personal immortality responsible for 'I.' Moreover, 'i' is more casual and detached: it dissociates the author from the speaker of the poem. The use of 'i' is in keeping with his use of 'who,' instead of 'which,' to qualify the roses; the roses become so personal as to deserve the personal rather than the neutral relative. His next idiosyncrasy is his denial of a capital letter to each new line of the poem. Now, if this convention were not so well established, it would seem as odd and as unnecessary as, for instance, quotation marks seem in eighteenth-century books when they enclose each line of a long speech. The modernist rejection of the initial capital letter can be justified on the grounds that it gives the first word of each line, which may be a mere 'and' or 'or,' an unnatural emphasis. If for special reasons the poet wishes to capitalize the first word, the fact that it is capitalized in any case, like all the other initial 'And's' and 'Or's,' makes any such niceness impossible.

Later in the poem a capital letter occurs at the beginning of a new sentence to call attention to the full stop which might otherwise be missed: but the 'because' at the beginning of the poem need not be capitalized since it obviously *is* the beginning. Similarly, the conventional comma after 'lady' is suppressed because the end of the line makes a natural pause without the need of punctuation. Commas are used to mark pauses, not merely as the geographical boundaries of a clause. Mr. Cummings has even inserted one in another poem between the *n* and *g* of the word 'falling' to suggest the slowness of the falling. Colons, semicolons and full stops he uses to mark pauses of varying length. To indicate a still longer pause he leaves a blank line. In the quotation just given, the new line at 'remembering' is to mark a change of tone, though the pause is no longer than a semicolon's worth. He uses parentheses for *sotto voce* pronunciation; or if they occur in the middle of a word, as in:

the taxi-man p(ee)ps his whistle

they denote a certain quality of the letters enclosed—here the sharp whistling sound between the opening and closing (the two *p*'s) of the taxi-man's lips. When this system of notation is carried to a point of great accuracy we find lines like the following:

CA: G

with-ered unspea-king:tWeNtY,f i n g e r s,large

which, if quoted detached from their context, seem to support any charge of irrational freakishness, but in their context are completely intelligible. Moreover, Mr. Cummings is protecting himself against future liberties that printers and editors may take with his work, by using a personal typographical system which it will be impossible to revise without destroying the poem.

He has perhaps learned a lesson from the fate of Shakespeare's sonnets: not only have his editors changed the spelling and pronunciation, but certain very occasional and obvious printer's errors in the only edition printed in Shakespeare's lifetime have been made the excuse for hundreds of unjustifiable emendations and 'modernizations.' Mr. Cummings and Shakespeare have in common a deadly accuracy. It frightens Mr. Cummings' public and provoked Shakespeare's eighteenth-century editors to meddle with his texts as being too difficult to print as they were written. We shall find that though Shakespeare's poems have a more familiar look than Mr. Cummings' on the page, they are more difficult in thought: Mr. Cummings accurately expresses, in a form peculiar to himself, what is common to everyone; Shakespeare expressed, as accurately but in the common form of his time, what was peculiar to himself.

Here are two versions of a sonnet by Shakespeare: first, the version found in *The Oxford Book of English Verse* and other popular anthologies whose editors may be assumed to have chosen this sonnet from all the rest as being particularly easy to understand; next, the version printed in the 1609 edition of the *Sonnets* and apparently copied from Shakespeare's original manuscript, though Shakespeare is most unlikely to have seen the proofs. The alterations, it will be noticed in a comparison of the two versions, are with a few exceptions chiefly in the punctuation and spelling. By showing what a great difference to the sense the juggling of punctuation marks has made in the original sonnet, we shall perhaps be able to persuade the plain reader to sympathize with what seems typographical perversity in Mr. Cummings. The modernizing of the spelling is not quite so serious a matter, though we shall see that to change a word like *blouddy* to *bloody* makes a difference not only in the atmosphere of the word but in its sound as well.

I

Th' expense of Spirit in a waste of shame
Is lust in action; and till action, lust
Is perjured, murderous, bloody, full of blame,
Savage, extreme, rude, cruel, not to trust;
Enjoy'd no sooner but despisèd straight;
Past reason hunted; and, no sooner had,
Past reason hated, as a swallow'd bait
On purpose laid to make the taker mad:
Mad in pursuit, and in possession so;
Had, having, and in quest to have, extreme;
A bliss in proof, and proved, a very woe;
Before, a joy proposed; behind, a dream.
    All this the world well knows; yet none knows well
    To shun the heaven that leads men to this hell.

II

Th' expence of Spirit in a waste of shame
Is lust in action, and till action, lust
Is periurd, murdrous, blouddy full of blame,
Sauage, extreame, rude, cruell, not to trust,
Inioyd no sooner but dispised straight,
Past reason hunted, and no sooner had
Past reason hated as a swollowed bayt,
On purpose layd to make the taker mad.
Made In pursut and in possession so,
Had, hauing, and in quest, to haue extreame,
A blisse in proofe and proud and very wo,
Before a ioy proposd behind a dreame,
    All this the world well knowes yet none knowes well,
    To shun the heauen that leads men to this hell.

First, to compare the spelling. As a matter of course the *u* in *proud* and *heauen* changes to *v*; the Elizabethans had no typographical *v*. There are other words in which the change of spelling does not seem to matter. *Expence, cruell, bayt, layd, pursut, blisse, proofe, wo*—these words taken by themselves are not necessarily affected by modernization, though much of the original atmosphere of the poem is lost by changing them in the gross. Sheer facility in reading a poem is no gain when one tries to discover what the poem looked like to the poet who wrote it. But other changes designed to increase reading facility involve more than changes in spelling. *Periurd* to *perjured*, and *murdrous* to *murderous*, would have meant, to Shakespeare, the addition of another syllable. *Inioyd*, with the same number of syllables as *periurd*, is however printed *Enjoy'd*; while *swollowed*, which must have been meant as a three-syllabled word (Shakespeare used *ed* as a separate syllable very strictly and frequently allowed himself an extra syllable in his iambic foot) is printed *swallow'd*. When we come to *dispised*, we find in the modern version an accent over the last syllable. These liberties do not make the poem any easier; they only make it less accurate. The sound of the poem suffers through re-spelling as well as through alterations in the rhythm made by this use of apostrophes and accents. *Blouddy* was pronounced more like *blue-dy* than *bluddy*; the *ea* of *extreame* and *dreame* sounded like the *ea* in *great*; and *periurd* was probably pronounced more like *peryurd* than *pergeurd*.

But it is the changes in punctuation which do the most damage: not only to the atmosphere of the poem but to its meaning. In the second line a semicolon substituted for a comma after the first *action* gives a longer rest than Shakespeare gave; it also cuts the idea short at *action* instead of keeping *in action* and *till action* together as well as the two *lust*'s. A comma after *blouddy* makes this a separate characterization and thus reduces the weight of the whole phrase as rhythmic relief to the string of adjectives; it probably had the adverbial form of *blouddily*. Next, several semicolons are substituted for commas; these introduce pauses which break up the continuous interpenetration of images. If Shakespeare had intended such pauses he would have used semicolons, as he does elsewhere. Particularly serious is the interpolation of a comma after *no sooner had*, which confines the phrase to the special meaning 'lust no sooner had *past reason* is hated past reason.' Shakespeare did not write in the syntax of prose but in a sensitive poetic flow. The comma might as well have been put between *reason* and *hated*; it would have limited the meaning, but no more than has been done here. On the other hand a comma is omitted where Shakespeare was careful to put one, after *bayt*. With the comma, *On purpose layd* —though it refers to *bayt*—also looks back to the original idea of *lust*; without the comma it merely continues the figure of *bayt*. In the original there is a full stop at *mad*, closing the octave; in the emended version a colon is used, making the next line run on and causing the unpardonable change from *Made* to *Mad*. The capital 'I' of *In* shows how carefully the printer copied the manuscript. Evidently, Shakespeare first wrote the line without *Made*, and then, deciding that such an irregular line was too dramatic, added *Made* without troubling to change the capital 'I' to a small one. In any case *Made* necessarily follows from *make* of the preceding line: 'to make the taker mad, made (mad)'; but it also enlarges the mad-making bayt to the generally extreame-making lust. The change from *Made* to *Mad* limits the final *so* of this line to *Mad* and provokes a change from comma to semicolon—'Mad in pursuit and in possession so (mad)'—whereas *mad* is only vaguely echoed in this line from the preceding one. The meaning of the original line is: 'Made In pursut and in possession as follows,' and also: 'Made In pursut and in possession as has been said.'

The comma between *in quest* and *to have extreame* has been moved forward to separate *have* from *extreame*. This line originally stood for a number of interwoven meanings:

1. The taker of the bait, the man in pursuit and in possession of lust, is made mad: is so made that he experiences both extremes at once. (What these extremes are the lines following show.)

2. The *Had, having and in quest*, might well have been written in parentheses. They explain, by way of interjection, that lust comprises all the stages of lust: the after-lust period (*Had*), the actual experience of lust (*having*), and the anticipation of lust (*in quest*); and that the extremes of lust are felt in all these stages (*to have extreame*—i.e. to have in extreme degree).

3. Further, one stage in lust is like the others, is as extreme as the others. All the distinctions made in the poem between *lust in action* and *till action lust*, between lust *In pursut* and lust *in possession* are made to show that in the end there are no real distinctions. *Had, having and in quest* is the summing up of this fact.

4. *Had* and *having* double the sense of *possession* to match the double sense of *action* implied by *Th' expence of Spirit in a waste of shame*; and *in quest* naturally refers to *In pursut*, which in turn recalls *till action*.

5. Throughout the poem it must be kept in mind that words qualifying the lust-interest refer interchangeably to the man who lusts, the object of lust and lust in the abstract. This interchangeability accounts for the apparently ungrammatical effect of the line.

With the emended punctuation the line has only one narrow sense, and this not precisely Shakespeare's; the semicolon placed after *so* of the preceding line, cuts the close co-operation between them. The shifting of the comma not only removes a pause where Shakespeare put one, and thus changes the rhythm, but the line itself loses point and does not pull its weight. In this punctuation the *whole* line ought to be put into parentheses, as being a mere repetition. The *to have* linked with *in quest* is superfluous; *extreme* set off by itself is merely a descriptive adjective already used. Moreover, when the line is thus isolated between two semicolons, *Had, having*, etc., instead of effecting a harmony between the interchangeable senses, disjoints them and becomes ungrammatical. *Mad in pursuit, and in possession so* refers only to *the taker mad*. The next line, *A blisse in proofe and proud and very wo*, should explain *to have extreame*; it is not merely another parenthetical line as in the emended version. To fulfil the paradox implied in *extreame* it should mean that lust is a bliss during the proof and after the proof, and also *very wo* (truly woe) during and after the proof. The emended line, *A bliss in proof, and proved, a very woe*, which refers only to lust in the abstract, not equally to the man who lusts, means that lust is a bliss during the proof but a woe after the proof—and thus denies what Shakespeare has been at pains to show all along, that lust is all things at all times.

Once the editors began repunctuating the line they had to tamper with the words themselves. A comma after *proof* demanded a comma after *provd*. A comma after *provd* made it necessary to change *and very wo* so that it should apply to *provd* only. Another semicolon which they have put at the end of this line again breaks the continuity of the sense: the succeeding line becomes only another antithesis or rhetorical balance ('a joy in prospect, but a dream in retrospect,' to repeat the sense of 'a bliss during proof but woe after proof'), instead of carrying on the intricate and careful argument that runs without a stop through the whole sestet The importance of the line is that it takes all the meanings in the poem one stage further. Lust in the extreme goes beyond both bliss and woe: it goes beyond reality. It is no longer lust *Had, having and in quest*; it is lust face to face with *love*. Even when consummated, lust still stands before an unconsummated joy, a proposed joy, and proposed not as a joy possible of consummation but as one only to be known through the dream by which lust leads itself on, the dream behind which this proposed joy, this love, seems to lie. This is the over-riding meaning of the line. It has other meanings, but they all defer to this. For example, it may also be read: 'Before a joy can be proposed, it must first be renounced as a real joy, it must be put behind as a dream'; or: 'Before the man in lust is a prospect of joy, yet he knows by experience that this is only a dream'; or: 'Beforehand he says that he proposed lust to be a joy, afterwards he says that it came as involuntarily as a dream'; or: 'Before (in face of) a joy proposed only as a consequence of a dream, with a dream impelling him from behind.' All these and even more readings of the line are possible and legitimate, and each reading could in turn be made to explain precisely why the taker is made mad, or how lust is *to have extreame*, or why it is both *a blisse* and *very wo*. The punctuated line in the emended version, cut off from what has gone before and from what follows, can mean only: 'In prospect, lust is a joy; in retrospect, a dream.' Though a possible contributory meaning, when made the *only* meaning it presents as the theme of the poem that lust is impossible of satisfaction, whereas the theme, as carried on by the next line, is that lust as lust *is* satisfiable but that satisfied lust is in conflict with itself.

The next line, if unpunctuated except for the comma Shakespeare put at the end, is a general statement of this conflict: the man in lust is torn between lust as he well knows it in common with the world and lust in his personal experience which crazes him to hope for more than lust from lust. The force of the second *well* is to deny the first *well*: no one really knows anything of lust except in personal experience, and only through personal experience can lust be known *well* rather than 'well-known.' But separate the second *well* from the first, as in the emended version, and the direct opposition between *world* and *none*, *well knowes* and *knowes well* is destroyed, as well as the word-play between *well knowes* and *knowes well*; for by the removal of the comma after the second *well*, this becomes an adverb modifying *To shun* in the following line—*well* now means merely 'successfully' in association with *To shun*, instead of 'well enough' in association with *knowes*. This repunctuation also robs *All this* of its significance, since it refers not only to all that has gone before but to the last line too: 'All this the world well knowes yet none knowes well' the moral to be drawn from the character of lust (i.e. to shun the heaven that leads men to this hell). The character and the moral of lust the whole world well knows, but no one knows the character and the moral really well unless he disregards the moral warning and engages in lust: no one knows lust well enough to shun it because, though he knows it is both heavenly and hellish, lust can never be recognized until it has proved itself lust by turning heaven into hell.

The effect of this emended punctuation has been to restrict meanings to special interpretations of special words. Shakespeare's punctuation allows the variety of meanings he actually intends; if we must choose any one meaning, then we owe it to Shakespeare to choose at least one he intended and one embracing as many meanings as possible, that is, the most difficult meaning. It is always the most difficult meaning which is the most nearly final. No prose interpretation of poetry can have complete finality, can be difficult enough. Shakespeare's editors, in trying to clarify him for the plain man, weakened and diluted his poetry and in effect deprived him of clarity. There is only one way to clarify Shakespeare: to print him as he wrote or as near as one can get to this. Making poetry easy for the reader should mean showing clearly how difficult it really is.

Mr. Cummings safeguards himself against emendation by setting down his poems, which are not complex in thought, so that their most difficult sense strikes the reader first. By giving typography an active part to play he makes his poems fixed and accurate in a way which Shakespeare's are not; but in so doing he forfeits the fluidity that Shakespeare kept by not cramping his poems with heavy punctuation and by placing more trust in the reader—a trust that may have been merited in his own day, though betrayed later. It is important to realize that the *Sonnets* were first circulated in manuscript 'among his private friends' and not intended for popular publication; the 1609 edition is now generally regarded as a piracy. The trouble with Mr. Cummings' poems is that they are too clear, once the reader sets himself to work on them. Braced as they are, they do not present the eternal difficulties that make poems immortal; they merely show how difficult it is for Mr. Cummings or for any poet to stabilize a poem once and for all. Punctuation marks in any poem of his are the bolts and pins that make it a foolproof piece of machinery requiring common sense rather than poetic intuition for its working. The outcry against his typography shows that it is as difficult to engage the common sense of the reader as his imagination. A reviewer of Mr. Cummings' recent book *is 5*, writes:

I know artists are always saying that a good painting looks as well upside down as any other way. And it may be true. The question now arises: does the same principle apply to a poem? But it is not necessary to answer the question; if a poem is good, people will gladly stand on their heads to read it. It is conceivable, if not probable, that the favourite poetic form of the future will be a sonnet arranged as a cross-word puzzle. If there were no other way of getting at Shakespeare's sonnets than by solving a cross-word puzzle sequence, I am sure the puzzles would be solved and the sonnets enjoyed. But what about Mr. Cummings? Can his poems surmount such obstacles? Well, perhaps if they cannot survive as poems they can survive as puzzles.

This may be the immediate verdict on Mr. Cummings' typography, but he can be sure of one thing which Shakespeare could not: that three centuries hence his poems if they survive (and worse poets' have) will be the only ones of the early twentieth century reprinted in facsimile, not merely because he will be a literary curiosity but because he has edited his poems with punctuation beyond any possibility of re-editing. The Shakespeare to whose sonnets this reviewer makes a rhetorical appeal is the popular Shakespeare of the anthologies and not the facsimile Shakespeare. How many of our readers have ever before seen the original version quoted here? So few, surely, that it is safe to conclude that no one is willing to stand on his head to understand Shakespeare, that everyone wants a simplified Shakespeare as well as a simplified Cummings. Indeed, very few people can have looked at Shakespeare's sonnets in the original since the eighteenth century, when the popular interest in his high-spirited comedies sent a few dull commentators and book-makers to his poems. In 1766 George Steevens printed the *Sonnets* in the original and without annotations, apparently because he thought they deserved none. Twenty-seven years later he omitted the *Sonnets* from an edition of Shakespeare's works 'because the strongest Act of Parliament that could be framed would fail to compel readers into their service.' Edmund Malone, who undertook in 1780 to justify the *Sonnets* to an apathetic public by simplifying the difficult originals, was considered by Steevens to be 'disgracing his implements of criticism by the objects of their culture.' Steevens' view was the general one. Chalmers reaffirmed it as late as 1810, and if Malone had not defied the general critical opinion of the *Sonnets* by emending the texts and presenting them, well-filleted, to the plain man of the eighteenth century, the plain man of the twentieth would be unaware of their existence. Unlike Mr. Cummings' poems, Shakespeare's *Sonnets* would not even have 'survived as puzzles.'

Thus far does a study of Shakespeare's typography take one: to the difficulties of a poet with readers to whom his meanings are mysteries and for the most part must remain mysteries. A modernist poet like Mr. Cummings handles the problem by trying to get the most out of his readers; Shakespeare handled it by trying to get the most out of his poem. Logically the modernist poet should have many readers, but these with an elementary understanding of his poems; Shakespeare only a few readers, but these with an enlarged understanding of his poems. The reverse, however, is true because the reading public has been so undertrained on a simplified Shakespeare and on anthology verse, that modernist poetry seems as difficult as Shakespeare really ought to seem.

Only a few points of the original sonnet have been left uncovered by our typographical survey, and these occur principally in the first few lines, which suffer from fewer emendations than the rest of the poem. The delicate inter-relation of the words of the two opening lines should not be overlooked: the strong parallelism between *expence* and *waste* and *Spirit* and *shame* expressing at once the terrible quick-change from lust as lust-enjoyed to lust as lust-despised; the double meaning of *waste* as 'expense' and as 'wilderness,' the *waste* place in which the Spirit is *wasted*; the double meaning of *expence* as 'pouring out' and as the 'price paid'; the double meaning of *of shame* as 'shameful,' i.e. 'deplorable' and as *ashamed*, i.e. 'self-deploring'; the double meaning of *shame* itself as 'modesty' and 'disgrace'; and the double meaning of *lust in action* as 'lust unsuspected by man in his actions because disguised as shame' (in either sense of the word), and as 'lust in progress' as opposed to 'lust contemplated.' All these alternate meanings interacting on one another, and other possible interpretations of words and phrases besides, make as it were an oracle which can be read in many senses at once, none of the senses, however, being incompatible with any others. The intensified inbreeding of words continues through the rest of the poem. *Periurd* is another example, meaning both 'falsely spoken of' and 'false.' Again, *heaven* and *hell* have the ordinary prose meaning of 'pleasure' and 'pain'; but 'heaven,' for Shakespeare, was the longing for a temperamental stability which at the same time he mistrusted; his 'hell' was akin to Marlowe's hell, which

> . . . hath no limits nor is circumscribed
> In one selfe place, for where we are is hell.

The reader who complains of the obscurity of modernist poets must be reminded of the intimate Shakespearian background with which he needs to be familiar before he can understand Shakespeare. The failure of imagination and knowledge in Shakespeare's editors has reduced his sonnets to the indignity of being easy for everybody. Beddoes, an early nineteenth-century imitator of Shakespeare, said:

About Shakespeare. You might just as well attempt to remodel the seasons and the laws of life and death as to alter one 'jot or tittle' of his eternal thoughts. 'A Star,' you call him. If he was a star all the other stage-scribblers can hardly be considered a constellation of brass buttons.

Few of the modernist poets are Stars, but most of them are very highly polished brass buttons and entitled to protect themselves from the sort of tarnishing which Shakespeare, though a Star, has suffered.

Shakespeare's attitude towards the perversely stupid reorganizing of lines and regrouping of ideas is jocularly shown in the satire in repunctuation given in the prologue of *Piramus and Thisby* in *A Midsummer Night's Dream*:

QUINCE: If we offend, it is with our good will.
            That you should thinke, we come not to offend,
            But with good will. To shew our simple skill,
            That is the true beginning of our end.
            Consider then, we come but in despight.
            We do not come, as minding to content you,
            Our true intent is. All for your delight,
            We are not heere. That you should here repent you,
            The Actors are at hand; and by their show,
            You shall know all, that you are like to know.
THESEUS: This fellow doth not stand vpon points.

      ·   ·   ·   ·   ·

LYSANDER: His speech was like a tangled chaine: nothing
            impaired, but all disordered . . .

IV

THE UNPOPULARITY OF MODERNIST POETRY

Poetry was clarified to the mid-eighteenth-century reading public by the way in which new poems were written and early English and Classical poems rewritten or translated. But this was a period with a very limited recipe for poetry: for metre the heroic couplet, which broke thought up into short lengths; for language a stock poetical vocabulary of not more than three or four thousand words. Anyone could write that correct sort of poetry, if he obeyed the rules, without necessarily being a poet. In the nineteenth century, because of a reading public enlarged by democracy, clearness meant not so much obeying rules as writing for the largest possible audience. The reaction in

twentieth-century poetry against nineteenth-century standards is not
against clearness and simplicity, but against rules for poetry made by
the reading public rather than by the poets themselves; this is why so
many modern poets are forced into a nostalgic sympathy with the
eighteenth century. Now the quarrel is between the larger reading
public and the modernist poet over the definition of clearness. Both
agree that perfect clearness is the end of poetry; but the larger reading
public insist that no poetry is clear unless it can be understood at a
glance, whereas the modernist poet insists that the clearness of which
the poetic mind is capable demands thought and language of a far
greater sensitivity and complexity than the reading public permits it
to use. To remain true to his conception of what poetry is, he has to
run the risk of seeming obscure or freakish, if he is to have any readers
at all; even of writing what the reading public refuses to call poetry,
in order to remain a poet. The main fault to be found with Mr. Cum-
mings is that he has tried to do two things at once: to remain loyal to
poetic requirements of clearness, and to persuade the reading public
to call the result 'poetry.' He has tried to do this by means of an
elaborate system of typography, but his ungrateful public considers
him freakish and obscure because of this typography.

Here is another poem of his, describing sunset seen through a
railway carriage window in Italy.

> Among
>
>> these
>>> red pieces of
> day(against which and
> quite silently hills
> made of blueandgreen paper
>
> scorchbend ingthem
> -selves-U
> pcurv E,into:
>>> anguish(clim
> b)ing
> s-p-i-r-a-
> l
> and,disappear)
>>> Satanic and blasé
>
> a black goat lookingly wanders

There is nothing left of the world but
into this noth
ing il treno per
Roma si-gnori?
jerk.
ilyr,ushes

The cleverness of this as mere description can be shown by turning the poem into ordinary prose with conventional typography; and afterwards showing how the unconventional typography improves the accuracy of the description:

Among these red pieces of day (against which—and quite silently—hills made of blue and green paper, scorch-bending themselves, upcurve into anguish, climbing spiral, and disappear), satanic and blasé, a black goat lookingly wanders. There is nothing left of the world; but into this nothing 'il treno per Roma signori?' jerkily rushes.

'Red pieces of day' suggests sunset fragments—the disintegration of the universe as the train moves towards night. The hills become as unreal as blue and green paper. The rocking of the train seems to give their rounded outlines, as they stream past, the sort of movement which a long strip of paper has when it curls up in the heat of fire, or the pen when it writes coppɛrplate *u*'s and *e*'s. As the train comes close up to the hills their rounded outlines seem to spiral upward against the red pieces ('into anguish') because the eye strains itself in looking up at them: they can only just be seen by pressing the face against the window, and as the train gets nearer still they are no longer visible. The eye is forced to drop to the foreground and there exchanges glances with a devilish-looking goat. The traveller is bewildered by these perceptual experiences: when the line of hills which he has been watching is snatched from his eyes it seems like the end of the world, like death, and the goat like the Devil greeting the dead. He pulls himself together. 'Where am I?' The rocking and jerking continues. He remembers the last words he has heard spoken, the question 'The Rome train, gentlemen?' which is all that he can think of to account for the motion.

A prose summary cannot *explain* a poem; otherwise the poet, if he were honest, would give the reader only a prose summary, and no poem. The above is rather the expansion, the dilution, even the destruction, of the poem which one reader may perform for another who is unable to face its intensity and compactness. The indignity of popular literary criticism lies largely in its having had to perform this levelling service for generations of plain readers. It has never yet performed any services for poetry itself, which it tries to justify either to the philosopher or to the plain reader. Poetry cannot be judged by its adaptability to a philosophical system, and critics have spoiled the plain reader by encouraging him in his democratic vanity and in his demand for poems to be written down to his level. However, from our prose-expansion of the poem, the spoiled reader may perhaps be able to infer the greater accuracy and truthfulness of the poetic version. The irregularity of Mr. Cummings' lines is intended to convey two movements in one: the jerking and the rocking of the train. 'Blueandgreen' is printed as a single word to show that it is not parti-coloured paper but paper which is blue and green at once, the colours run together by the rocking motion. The phrase 'scorchbend-ingthem' represents the up-and-down rhythm of the diagonal spiral movement; '-selves-' stresses the realistic character of this movement. The capitalized *U* and *E* enlarge the mounting copperplate curves. The parentheses enclosing the syllable 'climb' may mean a catch of the breath at that point. The comma after the *E* and the colon after 'into' are used as pauses of a certain length marking the rhythm of the spirals. The word 'spiral' is distended by hyphens to mark the final large spiral which sweeps the sky out of view at the letter *l*. 'Satanic' is capitalized to make the goat personally devilish. The full stop after 'jerk' marks a sudden jolt back to a consciousness of the inside of the train and of the journey's purpose.

There is no experience here with which the plain reader cannot sympathize, and only a little imaginative recollection has been needed to make this analysis; no key from the author except the poem itself. The poem combines two qualities of clearness: clearness of composition in the interests of the poem as a thing in itself, clearness of transmittance in the interests of the reader. It is obvious that the poet could have given the poem this double accuracy in no other way. Has he perhaps been wrong in paying too much attention to the rendering of the poem for the reader? If he had allowed it to be more difficult, if he had concentrated exclusively on the poem as a thing in itself, would it not have seemed less freakish?

That the modernist poet is often charged with 'freakishness' and abnormality of feeling is not because this is no age for poetry and therefore to write poetry at all is a literary affectation. The trouble is rather that modern life is full of the stock feelings and situations with which traditional poetry has continually fed popular sentiment; that most commonplaces of everyday speech are the detritus of past poems; so that the enlarged reading public must regard the poet who has an original experience to express as either unliterary or anti-literary. It is always the poets who break down antiquated literary definitions of people's feelings and try to make them self-conscious about formerly ignored or obscure mental processes for which an entirely new vocabulary has to be invented. The appearance of freakishness in poetry generally means that the poets are not trying to write 'things often felt but ne'er so well expressed,' as Pope wanted them to do, but discovering what it is that they are really feeling.

One of the first modernist poets to feel the need of expressing his feelings with such meticulous, more than scientific, clearness as to make of poetry a higher sort of psychology, was Gerard Manley Hopkins, a Catholic poet writing in the 'eighties. We call him a modernist because of the extraordinary strictness of his language and the unconventional notation he used for his poems: they had to be understood as he meant them to be, or understood not at all—which is the crux of the question of 'difficult' poetry. Hopkins cannot be accused of trying to antagonize the reading public. In 1883 he wrote about his use of typography to explain an unfamiliar metre and an unfamiliar grammar:

There must be some marks. Either I must invent a notation throughout, as in music, or else I must only mark where the reader is likely to mistake, and for the present this is what I shall do.

In 1885 he wrote again:

This is my difficulty, what marks to use and when to use them: they are so much needed and yet so objectionable. About punctuation my mind is clear: I can give a rule for everything I write myself, and even for other people, though they might not agree with me perhaps.

These lines from a sonnet written in his peculiar metre will show the extent of his modernism:

Soul, self; come, poor Jackself, I do advise
You, jaded, let be; call off thoughts awhile
Elsewhere; leave comfort root-room; let joy size
At God knows when to God knows what; whose smile
's not wrung, see you; unforeseen times rather—as skies
Betweenpie mountains—lights a lovely mile.

First of all *Jackself.* Here the plain reader will get no help from the dictionary, he must use his wits and go over the other uses of *Jack* in combination: jack-screw, jackass, jack-knife, Jack Tar, Jack Frost, Jack of all trades, boot-jack, steeple-jack, lumber-jack, jack-towel, jack-plane, roasting-jack. From these the central meaning of *jack* becomes clear. It represents a person or thing that is honest, patient, cheerful, hard-working, undistinguished—but the one that makes things happen, and does things nobody else would or could do. (Tom in English usage is the mischievous, rather destructive, impudent and often unpleasant fellow—tomboy, tomcat, tomfoolery, tomtit, peeping Tom, Tom the piper's son, etc.) 'Jackself,' then, is this workaday self which he advises to knock off work for a while: to leave comfort or leisure, crowded out by work, some space to grow in, as for flowers in a vegetable garden; to have his pleasure and comfort whenever and however God wills it, not, as an ordinary Jackself would, merely on Sundays. (Hopkins uses 'God knows when' and 'God knows what' as just the language a Jackself uses.) God's smile cannot be forced from him; that is to say, happiness cannot be postponed until one is ready for it. Joy comes as suddenly and unexpectedly as when, walking among mountains, one comes to a point where the sky shines through a cleft between two peaks and throws a shaft of light over a mile of ground thus unexpectedly illuminated. We must appreciate the accuracy of the term *Betweenpie.* Besides being again, the sort of homely kitchen language which the Jackself uses to describe how the sky seems pressed between two mountains, it is also the neatest possible way of combining the patching effect of light —as in the word 'pied,' or in 'magpie'—with the way that this light is introduced between the mountains.

Dr. Robert Bridges, Hopkins' editor, who postponed publication of the poems for thirty years, thus making him even more of a modernist poet, writes:

Apart from faults of taste . . . affectations such as where the hills are 'as a stallion stalwart very-violet-sweet' or some perversion of human feelings, as, for instance, the 'nostril's relish of incense along the sanctuary side,' or 'the Holy Ghost with warm breast and with ah! bright wings,' which repel my sympathy more than do all the rude shocks of his purely artistic wantonness—apart from these there are faults of style which the reader must have courage to face. For these blemishes are of such quality and magnitude as to deny him even a hearing from those who a love a continuous literary decorum.

What Dr. Bridges calls a fault of taste, an affectation, in the description of hills as 'a stallion stalwart very-violet-sweet,' can, with the proper sympathy for Hopkins' enthusiasm, be appreciated as a phrase reconciling the two seemingly opposite qualities of mountains: their male, animal-like roughness and strength and their ethereal qualities under soft light—of which the violet in the gentle eye of the horse is exactly the right symbol. What Dr. Bridges and other upholders of 'literary decorum' most dislike in a poet is not, as a matter of fact, either 'faults of taste' or 'faults of style' (in Hopkins, supposedly, his clipping of grammar to suit the heavily stressed metre) but a daring which makes the poet socially rather than artistically objectionable. As a reviewer in *The Times Literary Supplement* states the grievance against modernist poetry:

> It is as if its object were to express that element only in the poet's nature by virtue of which he feels himself an alien in the universe, or at least an alien from what he takes to be the universe acknowledged by the rest of mankind.

Yet the truth is that 'the rest of mankind' is for the most part unaware of the universe and constantly depends on the poet for a second-hand sense of the universe through language. This language passes gradually into current use, where it becomes stereotyped and loses its meaning; and the poet is again called upon to remind 'the rest of mankind' what the universe really looks and feels like—what language means. If he does this conscientiously he must always use language in a fresh way or even invent new language. But in either case he will antagonize for a while those who ask poetry to do their more difficult thinking for them; they claim a proprietary interest in the old language, however stale it may have become, and do not realize that it must be brought up to date or even entirely recast if poetry is to remain a living thing. How irate they become can be seen from a further statement by the same reviewer:

> Language itself is an accepted code: and if the poet is really to be the man who cannot accept what others do, he ought to begin squarely at the beginning and have nothing to do with their conventional jargon.

But if the poet begins squarely at the beginning in order to discover whether there is anything to accept, the cry will immediately be raised: 'Language is an accepted code.'

It is easy in any period to look back with satisfaction on the growth of poetic language and, for instance, to blame the early nineteenth century for being so slow to recognize the services done to poetry by Wordsworth, Coleridge, Shelley and Keats in their refreshment of language and metre. But every period regards itself as the final flowering of everything that has come before it, so that *The Times Literary Supplement* reviewer can imagine new poets, of an originality equal to Wordsworth and others in their own day, only as writing now exactly as they wrote then. The same is true in music: the charge of freakishness has been brought by critics in their time against Debussy, Wagner and even Brahms. It is a paradox that literary critics who find modernist poets freakish often tolerate modernism in contemporary music, as conservative musical critics will not be so hard on modernism in literature; their proprietary interests are not threatened in either case.

The plain reader stands in the vortex of this conflict between orthodox criticism and unorthodox poetry. His attitude towards poetry has to be one of self-defence. He must be cautious in his choice of books: he must not read anything that will waste his time, anything not likely to last for long years, not destined to be a classic. Forced to be on his guard, he is inclined to emphasize the value of the 'practical' things which are not poetry, such as time in the quantitative, financial sense; and so develops a shrewd sense of the 'practical' value of poetry. He avoids new work about which no final judgment has yet been made, whatever its emotional appeal may be—poetry which seems too different from the reputable poetry of the past to be a good investment. He will prefer an unoriginal but undisturbing poem to an original but disturbing one.

The reader who may be said to occupy an enlightened middle position towards the various historical changes he must face in life is generally many generations behind himself in poetry and in religion. This is not because of spiritual incapacity, but because he realizes that the demands put upon him by poetry and religion are too pressing and too personal for him to meet decently. It is a case of all or nothing. So it is nothing; because no common Christian would seriously turn the other cheek when smitten or sell all that he had and give it to the poor, as no common reader of poetry could bring himself, without a cruel effort, to meet the demands of thought put upon him by an authentic poem. An advocacy of the turning of the other cheek and of the communalizing of private property would be regarded as an obnoxious modernism in the most devout Christian; as an increase in the demands put upon the plain reader would antagonize him against modernist poetry no matter how devoutly he might love poetry in general. Poetry, then, like religion, has to be dissociated from practical life, except as a sentimentality: a saint or a poet is given lip-service, but only lip-service, particularly if he is still living, for it is only time that reveals which of the saints or poets are genuine and which are charlatans. The plain Christian will prefer a popular preacher of the orthodox type to a 'fanatic' like General Booth of the Salvation Army; this preserves his self-respect.

We make the analogy between poetry and religion because, though false, it is a traditional one and largely accountable for readers' mistrust of modern poetry. Religion may be in active conflict with social principles; to turn the smitten cheek, for instance, is to abandon the virtue of self-pride and to compromise 'honour.' Poetry, on the other hand, makes no demands of a social nature, no demands which exceed the private intimacy of the reader and the poem; particularly when, as now, the poet asks for neither personal bays nor public banquets. But the plain reader, though afraid of the infringements that modernism in religion may imply, is even more afraid of modernism in poetry. For the greatest possible interference with anyone's privacy is a demand for his complete attention, intimacy and confidence.

When Wordsworth and Coleridge were writing their best poetry the plain reader would have nothing to do with them but was reading safe writers such as Shenstone and Mickle, now mere names in literary history; when Keats and Shelley were writing their best he was reading Thomas Moore and Samuel Rogers; when he should have been reading the early Tennyson he was reading Mrs. Hemans and Martin Tupper; when he should have been reading Whitman he was reading Robert Montgomery and the later Tennyson. And so on to the present day: when even the plain reader who wants to keep up with contemporary poetry will be more likely to choose a poet such as Mr. Carl Sandburg or Mr. John Drinkwater, belonging to dead movements which have reached their limits and will expire with the death of their authors, than one belonging to a live movement (such as Mr. Cummings or Mr. John Crowe Ransom) which asks him to risk his critical judgment.

Let us compare a poem of Mr. Sandburg's, who has tried to create a democratic poetry in the spirit of the American Middle West by using free verse, slang and sentimental lower-class subjects, with a poem of Mr. Ransom's who, without making a sensational appeal to the locality in which he lives or to a particular social class, yet has a colloquial dignity and grace which may be called Southern aristocratic.

Strangely enough, it is Mr. Sandburg whose work is in the natural course of events shelved among the dull relics of dead movements and Mr. Ransom, though his poems are a formal and careful evasion of violence, whom the plain reader regards as the sensational modernist. Here is the Sandburg poem, especially designed to match the intelligence-level of the plain reader. It presents him with no allusions which might mystify him.

MAMIE

Mamie beat her head against the bars of a little Indian
    town and dreamed of romance and big things off
    somewhere the way the railroad trains all ran.
She could see the smoke of the engines get lost down
    where the streaks of steel flashed in the sun and
    when the newspapers came in on the morning mail
    she knew there was a big Chicago far off, where all
    the trains ran.
She got tired of the barber shop boys and the post office
    chatter and the church gossip and the old pieces the
    band played on the Fourth of July and Decoration Day.
And sobbed at her fate and beat her head against the bars
    and was going to kill herself,
When the thought came to her that if she was going to
    die she might as well die struggling for a clutch of
    romance among the streets of Chicago.
She has a job now at six dollars a week in the basement
    of the Boston Store
And even now she beats her head against the bars in the
    same old way and wonders if there is a bigger place
    the railroads run to from Chicago where maybe
    there is
            romance
            and big things
            and real dreams
            that never go smash.

This poem shows why the plain reader prefers bad contemporary poetry which can give him as much innocent enjoyment as a good short story or his newspaper or an up-to-date jazz-band, to good contemporary poetry which demands a kill-joy effort of criticism. Poetry, like fashions in clothes, has to be 'accepted' before the man in the street will patronize it. Next to the traditionally 'accepted' literature, the plain reader places literature of dead movements of his own time—for which 'modern' poetry he has a good-humoured tolerance because he does not have to take it seriously. 'Modernist' is his way of describing the contemporary poetry which perplexes him and which he is obliged to take seriously without knowing whether it is to be accepted or not. The plain reader's cautiousness gives employment to the literary critic who, thinking the plain reader more stupid than he really is, becomes in his turn cautious about what he recommends to him, being anxious not to earn his disapproval. Much modernist poetry has therefore been confined to limited editions for connoisseurs whose taste is not dependent on the literary critic; and this further antagonizes the plain reader, since whatever is patronized by a *few* seems self-condemned as a snobbish cult. He gets the impression that this poetry is not meant for him and is only too glad to leave it alone; it seldom reaches him except in pieces torn from their context for ridicule by the literary critic. The modernist poet, left without any public but the connoisseur, does not hesitate to embody in his poems remote literary references which are unintelligible to a wider public and which directly antagonize it. Here is Mr. Ransom's *Captain Carpenter*, an example of the sort of poetry which, because it is too good, has to be brushed aside as a literary novelty.

CAPTAIN CARPENTER

Captain Carpenter rose up in his prime
Put on his pistols and went riding out
But had got wellnigh nowhere at that time
Till he fell in with ladies in a rout.

It was a pretty lady and all her train
That played with him so sweetly but before
An hour she'd taken a sword with all her main
And twined him of his nose for evermore.

Captain Carpenter mounted up one day
And rode straightway into a stranger rogue
That looked unchristian but be that as may
The Captain did not wait upon prologue.

But drew upon him out of his great heart
The other swung against him with a club
And cracked his two legs at the shinny part
And let him roll and stick like any tub.

Captain Carpenter rode many a time
From male and female took he sundry harms
He met the wife of Satan crying 'I'm
The she-wolf bids you shall bear no more arms.'

Their strokes and counters whistled in the wind
I wish he had delivered half his blows
But where she should have made off like a hind
The bitch bit off his arms at the elbows.

And Captain Carpenter parted with his ears
To a black devil that used him in this wise
O Jesus ere his threescore and ten years
Another had plucked out his sweet blue eyes.

Captain Carpenter got up on his roan
And sallied from the gate in hell's despite
I heard him asking in the grimmest tone
If any enemy yet there was to fight?

'To any adversary it is fame
If he risk to be wounded by my tongue
Or burnt in two beneath my red heart's flame
Such are the perils he is cast among.

'But if he can he has a pretty choice
From an anatomy with little to lose
Whether he cut my tongue and take my voice
Or whether it be my round red heart he choose.'

It was the neatest knave that ever was seen
Stepping in perfume from his lady's bower
Who at this word put in his merry mien
And fell on Captain Carpenter like a tower.

I would not knock old fellows in the dust
But there lay Captain Carpenter on his back
His weapons were the old heart in his bust
And a blade shook between rotten teeth alack.

The rogue in scarlet and grey soon knew his mind
He wished to get his trophy and depart
With gentle apology and touch refined
He pierced him and produced the Captain's heart.

God's mercy rest on Captain Carpenter now
I thought him Sirs an honest gentleman
Citizen husband soldier and scholar enow
Let jangling kites eat of him if they can.

But God's deep curses follow after those
That shore him of his goodly nose and ears
His legs and strong arms at the two elbows
And eyes that had not watered seventy years.

The curse of hell upon the sleek upstart
Who got the Captain finally on his back
And took the red red vitals of his heart
And made the kites to whet their beaks clack clack.

This is a ballad, and the plain reader will insist that ballads in the old style, such as *Chevy Chace* or *Sir Patrick Spens* or the Robin Hood cycle, may be imitated by a modern hand, but imitated only with an affected simplicity like that of Longfellow's *The Schooner Hesperus*. In *Captain Carpenter* Mr. Ransom makes use of an old ballad metre and of an archaic vocabulary. But this is not enough for the plain reader: the poet has committed the unpardonable modernism of giving him the choice of several different reactions to the poem. It is the balance of these various reactions which should form his critical attitude towards the poem. But the plain reader does not want a critical attitude; he wants to have poetical feelings of simple pleasure or sorrow rather than to understand poetry. He wants to know whether he is to laugh or cry over Captain Carpenter's story, and if he is not given a satisfactory clue he suspects the sincerity of the poet and leaves him alone. He makes two general categories for poetry: the realistic (the true), a literary register of the nobler sentiments of practical life; and the non-realistic or romantic (the untrue), which covers his life of fantasia and desires in a world that he is morally obliged to treat as unreal. Now, in this particular poem fact and fancy have equal value as truth. Captain Carpenter is both the realistic hero or knight-errant, who is bit by bit shorn of his strength until there is nothing left but his hollow boasts, and the fairy-tale hero who is reduced bit by bit to a tongue; and the double meaning has to be kept in mind throughout. The reader trained to expect a single reaction in himself is upset, and modernist poetry becomes the nightmare from which he tries to protect his sanity.

Captain Carpenter contains a few literary echoes of the old ballads, such as the use of *twined* for 'robbed' and *jangling* for 'making a discordant noise,' typically eighteenth-century words like *rout* for 'dance,' Victorian expressions like *with gentle apology and touch refined*, and unmistakably modern usages like *the shinny part, like any tub*. This mixture of styles is only an amiable satire of styles (as more violently employed in prose by James Joyce, in the second part of *Ulysses*, against successive period styles) which adds to the charm of Captain Carpenter's character, thus seen as a legendary figure of successive ages. But the plain reader's chief resentment will be that Captain Carpenter is not an easily defined or felt subject, neither a particular historical figure nor yet a complete allegory; that Mr. Ransom has confounded the emotions instead of simplifying them and provided no answer to the first question which will be asked: 'Who or what, particularly, is Captain Carpenter?' The chief condition the reader makes is that a poem must not force him to think in an unaccustomed and therefore unsettling way; he is afraid of his own mind. The poet is expected to respect this fear if only because he himself is supposed to have a mind more than normally obsessed with imaginative terrors and stalking ghosts: he must refrain from troubling the reader with the more disturbing thought-processes which are vaguely known to be involved in the writing of poetry but not supposed to be evident in its reading. Caliban is a mental ghost of Shakespeare's, but once he becomes incarnate in a dramatic performance of *The Tempest*—'airy nothing' given 'a local habitation and a name'—and prances grotesquely on the stage, he becomes more realistic, less real. The stricter modernist poet neither conceals his private mind nor lets his Calibans and Hamlets become realistic stage figures while he remains behind the scenes himself. His mind, as it were, puts in a personal appearance; and it is the shock of this contact which the plain reader cannot bear.

V

DEAD MOVEMENTS

The refusal of the reading public to spend time on contemporary poetry is to some extent excusable when we recall the decrepitude to which poetry was reduced in Edwardian and early Georgian times.

By allowing its fangs to be drawn and domesticating itself in order to be received into the comfortable homes of the larger reading public, poetry had grown so tame, so dull, that it could no longer compete with other forms of social entertainment, especially with the active new religion of sport. Callow or learned echoes of accepted poetry have now [1926] become as unattractive to the plain reader as the poetry which he would classify as dangerous. And he does not realize that the alarming 'new' poetry with which he has been confronted is at least a deterrent against the writing of old-fashioned trash: that modernist poetry, if nothing else, is an ironic criticism of false literary survivals.

The dullness of the poetry which survived the great Victorians who had enfeebled it caused a general depression in the market of all verse not intended for academic or devotional purposes. To choose between such lines as John Drinkwater's:

> O fool, o only great
> In pride unhallowed, O most blind of heart.
> Confusion but more dark confusion bred,
> Grief nurtured grief, I cried aloud and said,
> 'Through trackless ways the soul of man is hurled,
> No sign upon the forehead of the skies,
> No beacon, and no chart
> Are given to him, and the inscrutable world
> But mocks his scars and fills his mouth with dust.'

and Marianne Moore's *To a Steam Roller*:

> The illustration
> is nothing to you without the application.
>   You lack half wit. You crush all particles down
>   into close conformity, and then walk back and forth on them.
>
> Sparkling chips of rock
> are crushed down to the level of the parent block.
>   Were not 'impersonal judgment in aesthetic
>   matters a physical impossibility,' you
>
> might fairly achieve
> it. As for butterflies, I can hardly conceive
>   of one's attending you, but no question
>   the congruence of the complement is vain, if it exists.

involves an effort of criticism which the plain reader does not think it worth his while to make, when so many other possibilities of entertainment are offered besides poetry. The first passage obviously takes him nowhere. The second, an insulting address to a man with a steam-roller mind, who lacks that half of wit which is to leave the whole unsaid, assumes that the reader is willing to part with the deteriorated sentimental part, the decayed flesh of poetry, and to confine himself to the hard, matter-of-fact skeleton of poetic logic. He may be brought to admire Miss Moore for having resisted the temptation to write emotional abuse in the style of Mr. Drinkwater, by conveying her meaning as drily and unfeelingly as a schoolmistress would explain a problem in arithmetic. But he can feel no interest in the technical discipline to which poetry may need to be submitted; and Miss Moore's poetry is wholly concerned with such discipline. Thus he will not sympathize with the prose quotation which she thought necessary as the documentary justification of her tirade, nor appreciate the logical application of *butterflies*—butterfly being the mathematical complement to steam-roller, and emphasizing the extreme, unrelieved dullness of this particular steam-roller mind which has no possible complement, even in metaphor. Anything, indeed, that reveals the poet at work, that reveals the mechanism of his wit, is obnoxious to the plain reader, who likes to keep the poetic process a mystery. Miss Moore, who turns her poetry into matter-of-fact prose demonstrations in order to avoid mystery, expresses in the following lines the plain reader's antagonism to poetry which perplexes rather than entertains. He may not understand her sympathy, but he will at least agree with her sentiments.

POETRY

I too, dislike it:
there are things that are important beyond all this fiddle.
The bat, upside down; the elephant pushing,
a tireless wolf under a tree,
the base-ball fan, the statistician—
'business documents and schoolbooks'—
these phenomena are pleasing,
but when they have been fashioned
into that which is unknowable,
we are not entertained.
It may be said of all of us
that we do not admire what we cannot understand;
enigmas are not poetry.

It would be foolish to ask the plain reader to accept poetry which he does not understand; but unless he is willing to make the effort of criticism he might perhaps be persuaded to refrain from critical comments such as 'this is incomprehensible.' And if he does make it, much that at first glance antagonized him will appear not incomprehensible but only difficult or, if not difficult, only different from what he has been accustomed to consider poetical. He may even train himself to read a few contemporary poets with interest; or, if he persists in keeping the critical process separate from the reading process, have at least a historical sense of what is happening in poetry.

An important distinction must be drawn between peculiarities in the work of modern poets resulting from a deliberate attempt to improve the status of poetry by jazzing up its programme and those resulting from a concentration on the poetic process itself. The first sort constitutes a commercial advertising of poetry; the second, while equally caused by the cloud under which poetry has fallen, is concentrated on curing its sickness, even if that means making it temporarily more unpopular than ever. The plain reader has an exaggerated antagonism towards peculiarities of this second sort: he seems to be presented with clinical observations rather than with the benefits resulting from the cure. He is more likely to be seduced by the first sort, which are expressive of a dead movement in literature.

A dead movement is one which never had, nor can have, a real place in the history of poets and poems: some passing or hitherto unrealized psychological mood in the public has offered a new field for exploitation, as sudden fashion crazes come and go, leaving no trace but waste material. Since mid-Victorian times there has been a succession of such dead movements: pre-Raphaelitism, the literary counterpart of a novel theory of painting; the use of playful French forms for drawing-room occasions, of which the triolet became the most popular, by Austin Dobson, Arthur Symons and Sir Edmund Gosse; the wickedness movement of the 'nineties, also of French origin, with its vocabulary built around such words as *lutany, arabesque, vermilion, jade, languid, satyr*; then the long end-of-the-century lull; then a new train of dead movements, more interesting only because they belong to a more alarming phase of world history. None of these movements, which we call 'dead' because they never had any real poetic excuse for being, has made any lasting contribution to English poetry: they were all glossy advertisements of the same old product of which the reader had long wearied.

Imagism is one of the earliest and the most typical of these twentieth-century dead movements. It had the look of a movement of pure experimentalism and reformation in poetry. But the issuing of a public manifesto of Imagism, the organization of the Imagists as a literary party with a defined political programme, the war they carried on with reviewers, the annual appearance of their Imagist anthology—all this showed that poetic results to them meant a popular demand for their work, not the discovery of new values in poetry with an indifference to its recognition by the public. The Imagists had decided what kind of poetry was needed by the time: a poetry to match certain up-to-date movements in music and art. They wanted to be *new* rather than to be poets; which meant that they could go only so far as to say, in a slightly different style, what had already been often said. 'Imagism refers to the manner of presentation, not to the subject.' Authentic 'advanced' poetry of the present day differs from such programmes for poetry in its concern with a reorganization of the matter (not in the sense of subject-matter, but of poetic thought as distinguished from other kinds of thought) rather than the manner of poetry. This is why the plain reader feels so balked by it: he must enter into that matter without expecting to be given a cipher-code to the meaning. The ideal modernist poem is identical with its own clearest, fullest and most accurate meaning. Therefore since his poem does not give a rendering of a poetical picture or of an idea existing outside itself, the modernist poet does not need to talk about the use of images 'to render particulars exactly,' but presents the very substance of poetry. His poem has the character of an independent creature. In Imagism, on the other hand, and all other similar dead movements, it is taken for granted that poetry is a translation of certain poetic subjects into the language which will bring the reader emotionally closest to them. It is assumed that a natural separation between the reader and the subject can be bridged by the manner in which it is presented.

Georgianism was an English dead movement contemporary with Imagism and politically affiliated with the then dominant Liberal party. Although not so highly organized, it had a great vogue between the years 1912 and 1918 and was articulate chiefly upon questions of style. The Georgians' general recommendations were the discarding of archaistic diction such as 'thee' and 'thou' and 'floweret' and 'whene'er' and of poetical constructions such as 'winter drear' and 'host on armed host' and of pomposities generally. It was also understood that, in reaction to Victorianism, their verse should avoid all formally religious, philosophic or improving themes; and all sad, wicked, café-table themes in reaction to the 'nineties. Georgian poetry was to be English but not aggressively imperialistic; pantheistic rather than atheistic; and as simple as a child's reading book. These recommendations resulted in a poetry which could be praised rather for what it was not than for what it was. Eventually Georgianism became principally concerned with Nature and love and leisure and old age and childhood and animals and sleep and similar uncontroversial subjects.

There was no outstanding figure either among the Imagists, the Vers Librists generally, or the Georgians—if we except W. H. Davies, a half-educated Welsh 'natural'—capable of writing new poetry within these revised forms. All that happened was that the old stock-feelings and situations were served up again, though with a different sauce; and poetry soon became more insipid than ever. The extent of this insipidity was concealed by the boom which the War brought about in poetry, as part of the general mobilization of public industries. Many poets who would otherwise never have been heard of were carried to popular recognition on the wave of war-sentiment. Rupert Brooke and his American counterpart Alan Seegar are examples of this temporary immortalization. War-poetry was Georgianism's second wind, for the contrast between the grinding hardships of trench-service —which, as a matter of fact, none of the original Georgians experienced —and the Georgian stock-subjects already enumerated was a ready poetic theme. Imagism also profited by the War, though, as it was an American rather than an English product, and the United States missed the first half of the war, it was mobilized for war-service only when Georgianism had already made a good start. Two other dead movements arose in the United States, not organized or heralded by a manifesto, but distinguishable as those of daintiness and daring. The 'dainty' poets, mostly women, evoked an Elizabethan or Cavalier atmosphere as a relief from the War; they were also 'cute,' arch, sly and naughty and the impression which their poems left was of an argument that they always won by having the last word. The 'daring' poets used for the most part free, very free, verse, and under the influence of war-excitement indulged in bursts of self-revealing confidence. Imagism may be said to have engaged only the top layer of the plain reading public. But Georgianism in England and the daintiness and daring movements in the United States made poetry pay a decent dividend until about three years after the Armistice, when somehow both poets and plain readers grew simultaneously tired. It may be said unreservedly that of all that creative and reading enthusiasm *nothing* survives except a few shadowy names. Of the War poets whose works were temporarily advertised by their death in action only three can be regretted as poets: Sorley, Rosenberg and Owen.

All dead movements are focused on the problem of style. Style may be defined as that old-fashioned element of sympathy with the reader which allows a poem to be used as an illustration to the text of the reader's experience; and much modernist poetry may be said to be literally without style. The modernist poet does not need to issue a programme declaring his intentions towards the reader, or an announcement of tactics. He does not need to call himself an individualist (as the Imagist poet did) or a mystic (as the poet of the Anglo-Irish dead movement did) or a nature-lover (as the poet of the Georgian dead movement did). He does not have to describe or docket himself for the reader, because now the importance of poetry does not lie in its style, namely the personality of the poet as expressed by a poem, but in the personality of the poem itself, namely its independence of both reader and poet once the poet has separated it from his personality by making it complete—a new and self-explanatory creature.

The most striking characteristic of modernist poetry is that it declares the independence of the poem. This implies a new sense of the poem's rights comparable with the new sense in modern times of the independence of the child, and a new respect for the originality of the poem as for the originality of the child. It is no longer considered proper to keep a child in its place by repressing its personality or laughing down its strange questions until it turns into a rather dull and ineffectual edition of the parent; the modernist poet is similarly freeing the poem of repressive nursery rules and, instead of telling it exactly what to do, encouraging it to do things, even queer things, by itself. He pledges himself to take them seriously on the principle that the poem, being a new and mysterious form of life, has more to teach him than he it. It is a popular superstition that the poet is the child; really the child is the poem and the most that the poet can be is a wise, experimenting parent.

Experiment, however, may be interpreted in two ways. In the first and better sense it is a delicate alertness directed towards the discovery of something to which some slight clue has been given; and system in such experiment means only the constant shifting and adjustment of the experimenter to the unknown creature as it becomes more and more known—the constant readiness to change system. The important element is the initial clue or, in old-fashioned language, the inspiration. The true scientist should have power equal to the poet's, with the difference that the scientist is inspired to discover things which exist already (his results are facts), while the poet is inspired to discover things which are created by his discovery of them (his results are not statements about things already known to exist, or knowledge, but truths which existed before only as potential truths). Experiment in the second and worse sense is the use of a system for system's sake and brings about, whether in science or poetry, only limited results. As the scientific genius is alone capable of using experiment in the first of these senses, and since the personnel of science is necessarily far more numerous than that of poetry, experiment in the second sense is the general method of the systematic, as opposed to the inventive, side of science; perhaps properly so.

Poets, then, who need the support of a system—routine labourers pretending to be inventors, since poetry, unlike science, has no place or use for routine—are obliged to adopt not only the workshop method of science, but its whole philosophical attitude, which directly contradicts that of poetry. For in science no personality is granted to the things discovered, which are looked upon as soulless integers of a soulless aggregate, with no independent rights of their own. Such poets, therefore, produce poems which are at best only well-ordered statements about chosen subjects, not new, independent living organisms; facts, not truths; examples of literature, not distinct poetic personalities. Poetry of this sort (and there has been little poetry of any other sort, because there have been few real poets) is thus the science of poem-coercion rather than the art of poem-appreciation. The real poet is proved by his creative vision of the poem, as the real parent is proved by his creative vision of the child: authorship is not a matter of the right use of the will but of an enlightened withdrawal of the will to make room for a new one.

It is this watchful withdrawal of the author's will at the right moments which gives the poem, or the child, an independent spirit—though several poets, anxious to be modernists, have misunderstood the principle and forced their poems by violent training to behave independently when they have no natural independence.

If the poem is left to shift entirely for itself and its independence is only a sign of the irresponsibility of the poet, poetry becomes a form of automatic writing, which inevitably leads to the over-emphasis of the dream element in its writing. Granted, dreams seem to exercise the same kind of control over the mind as the poem over the poet. But in dreams uncreative thought runs itself out to a solution in sheer inertia unrefreshed by any volitional criticism; a solution which is like the negative image of the one that creative volitional thought would reach. The automatic poem is a very poor substitute for the poem resulting from the deliberate adjustment of the creative will to a solution which seems to come nearer and nearer as this will grows more and more discreet.

Thus the question, how to prevent poetry from sinking into a still more dangerous decline than at present, cannot be answered by recommending a greater sense of responsibility in the poet towards the reader, as evidenced in the use of a carefully designed 'style.' The right answer is that the poet should feel a watchful responsibility for the development of the poem according to its own natural bent; yet its dependence on him until it is complete should not be seen as a weakness after it has been completed. So also childhood should survive in a grown man as the element of continuous newness in him, not as the permanent bad effect of discipline which made him less, rather than more, independent as he grew up.

VI

THE MAKING OF THE POEM

A declaration of the poem's independence naturally changes the attitude of the poet towards himself. It is not that he regards himself as no longer important; but that he acquires a sense of privacy which his former relations to the poem made impossible. He laughs at the public laurels of the traditional poet-cult and at the abnormal sense of self-importance displayed in the official programmes of such dead movements as Imagism. Mr. Cummings' foreword to his volume *is 5* is clearly inspired by a distaste for the sentimental display by which the poet has hitherto been expected to advertise himself; and perhaps explains his tendency, the modernist tendency in general, to let the poem take precedence over the poet:

On the assumption that my technique is either complicated or original or both, the publishers have politely requested me to write an introduction to this book.

At least my theory of technique, if I have one, is very far from original; nor is it complicated. I can express it in fifteen words, by quoting 'The Eternal Question And Immortal Answer of burlesk,' viz. 'Would you hit a woman with a child?—No, I'd hit her with a brick.' Like the burlesk comedian I am abnormally fond of that precision which creates movement.

If a poet is anybody, he is somebody to whom things made matter very little—somebody who is obsessed by Making. Like all obsessions, the Making obsession has disadvantages; for instance, my only interest in making money would be to make it. Fortunately, however, I should prefer to make almost anything else, including locomotives and roses. It is with roses and locomotives (not to mention acrobats Spring electricity Coney Island the 4th of July the eyes of mice and Niagara Falls) that my 'poems' are competing. They are also competing with each other, with elephants and with El Greco.

Ineluctable preoccupation with The Verb gives a poet one priceless advantage: whereas non-makers must content themselves with the merely undeniable fact that two times two is four, he rejoices in a purely irresistible truth (to be found, in abbreviated costume, upon the title page of the present volume).

Mr. Cummings, then, writing according to what would seem to the reader to be a most carefully constructed poetic system, refrains from delivering a critical key to his poems except as a semi-prefatorial confidence. Indeed, the more independent poems become, the less sense there is in providing them with an interpretative escort. This may read as though the more difficult poems become, the less chance there is of understanding them, but it means only that the reader has a chance of becoming less and less separated from poetry by the technique hitherto concentrated on connecting him with it. Technique itself has taken on a different character; it is no longer the way a poem is presented to the reader, but the way its elements correspond in every respect with the governing sense. In making a poem the poet may be said to be ruled by this sense, and in this foreshadowing, inevitable sense the poem exists even before it is recorded on paper, before the poet is aware of anything more definite than that there is a poem to be written. It is this that Mr. Cummings means, or should mean, by 'the obsession of making' and it is with this that a reader must reckon while the present poetic tendency continues of inviting him inside the framework of the poem and there making him study the stages by which it came to be. Thus technique in the modernist definition is no code of rules by which a poem is written but an awareness of its evolutionary history. 'The Eternal Question And Immortal Answer of burlesk' are in literary terms: 'Do you write poems with a prearranged technique?—No, I

CA: I

write them with a pen.' Meaning: the question of technique in a poem is irrelevant to the writing of it, but if one must talk about poems as being mechanically contrived by the poet, then the pen is the instrument used. Like the brick, it is the only practical answer to a theoretical question irrelevantly burdened with a practical qualification.

This brings us to the adjustments which have to be made between poetry itself and the reader of poetry who would welcome intimacy with a poem but is embarrassed by the thought of the poet's presence in it. He is not at his ease with the poem: it is never entirely his own—he reads it with the uncomfortable feeling that the poet's eyes are on him and that he will be expected to say something afterwards. He cannot rid himself of the notion that the poet had designs on him in writing the poem, to which he must respond. With traditional poetry he is less embarrassed because, although he is formally aware of the poet as author, he is not made self-conscious by him. We may compare traditional poetry in this sense with the conservative, well-appointed restaurant where the customer is placed in a soft light, the waiters address him in a respectful monotone and he is left to himself to eat. Modern poetry of the dead-movement sort resembles the 'artistic' tea-room where the plain eater finds himself affronted by orange curtains, Japanese prints, hand-painted furniture, art-china and conversational waitresses in smocks who lend the personal touch with a cultured accent: the sort of tea-room which soon runs down and becomes a dead movement. Modernist poetry at its most uncompromising seems inaccessible to the plain reader: the reader who approaches it feels as though he were walking into the front garden of a private house and expected to lunch tête-à-tête with the eccentric owner. He hesitates, and returns to the conservative restaurant where he can at least reduce the personality of the waiters to a minimum. One might think that if he could conquer his initial embarrassment he would find in modernist poetry an interior where he could be on completely impersonal terms with poetry: he would find himself alone with it. However, he does not really want to be placed in this position. He is scared by the mental ghosts with which only poets are supposed to have natural commerce. The real discomfort which he finds in modernist poetry is the absence of the poet as his protector from the imaginative terrors that lurk in it.

What the reader calls the clearness of a poem often means merely its freedom from those terrors which in blind self-defence he attacks as obscurities. Clearness to him is the suppression of everything in the poem over and above the normal height of comprehension—of everything likely to disturb his mental ease. A poem which is potentially above the normal height of comprehension and which, because the poet disregards such heights, fulfils all its potentialities, makes its real meaning clearer and clearer as it becomes more and more obscure to the average reader. The trouble is not with the reader or with the poem but with the government of criticism by the sales-principle, which in assuming standardized public taste allows for the most backward readers of each of the three reading classes corresponding with the three different levels of popular education. If a variable standard of comprehension were admitted, the poet could let his poem develop to the degree of clearness corresponding with the comprehension of the most advanced readers, and the word *obscure* would disappear from the vocabulary of criticism except as denoting the obscurity of particular references. *Bad* would be the only possible critical term by which a poem could be categorically dismissed; at the present time, it is enough for the critic to call a poem *obscure* to relieve himself of the obligation of criticizing it as good or bad according to the standards it suggests.

Here is an example, in the first eighteen lines of what might be called a modernist poem,[1] of the obscurity which would probably make the critic lay it aside after the customary two-minute reading:

> The rugged black of anger
> Has an uncertain smile-border.
> The transition from one kind to another
> May be love between neighbour and neighbour;
> Or natural death; or discontinuance
> Because so small is space,
> The extent of kind must be expressed otherwise;
> Or loss of kind when proof of no uniqueness
> Strikes the broadening edge and discourages.
> Therefore and therefore all things have experience
> Of ending and of meeting,
> And of ending, that much being
> As grows faint of self and withers
> When more is the intenser self
> That is another or nothing.
> And therefore smiles, when least smiling—
> The gift of nature to necessity
> When relenting grows involuntary.

[1] By Laura Riding.

His reaction will be one of 'blank incomprehension,' perhaps coloured with antagonism because of the didactic impression which the poem makes. 'What, in so many words,' the critic will ask, 'is this all about?'

To tell what a poem is all about in 'so many words' is to reduce the poem to so many words, to leave out all that the reader cannot at the moment understand in order to give him the satisfaction of feeling that he has understood it. If it were possible to convey the complete force of a poem in a prose summary, then there would be no excuse for writing it: in a complete poem the 'so many words' are, to the last punctuation mark, the poem itself. Before further discussing *The Rugged Black of Anger*, let us quote the beginning of a ballad by Mr. Ezra Pound which, like much of what passes for poetry nowadays, is no more than the rewriting in poetical language of a prose fancy.

BALLAD OF THE GOODLY FERE[1]

Simon Zelotes speaketh it somewhile after the Crucifixion

Ha' we lost the goodliest fere o' all
    For the priests and the gallows tree?
Aye, lover he was of brawny men
    O' ships and the open sea.

When they came wi' a host to take Our Man
    His smile was good to see,
'First let these go!' quo' our Goodly Fere,
    'Or I'll see ye damned,' says he.

Aye, he sent us out through the crossed high spears,
    And the scorn of his laugh rang free,
'Why took ye not me when I walked about
    Alone in the town?' says he.

Oh, we drank his 'Hale' in the good red wine
    When we last made company,
No capon priest was the Goodly Fere
    But a man o' men was he.

I ha' seen him drive a hundred men
    Wi' a bundle o' cords swung free
When they took the high and holy house
    For their pawn and treasury . . .

[1] Mate or companion.

Stripped of their imitated antiqueness, these five stanzas could be simply summarized as follows:

It would be false to identify the Christ of the sentimentalists with the Christ of the Gospels. So far from being a meek or effeminate character he strikes us as a very *manly* man, and his disciples, fishermen and others, must have reverenced him for his manly qualities as much as for his spiritual teaching. His action in driving the money-changers from the Temple with a scourge of cords is a proof of this. So is his courageous action when confronted by the soldiers of the High Priest sent to take him—he mockingly enquired why they had not dared arrest him previously when he walked about freely in the city of Jerusalem, and consented to offer no resistance on condition that his disciples were allowed to escape. The Last Supper was surely a very different scene from the Church Sacrament derived from it, where a full-fed priest condescendingly officiates; it was a banquet of friends of which the Dearest Friend was Our Saviour.

Here we see that the poeticalization has in fact weakened the historical argument. By using the ballad setting Mr. Pound has made the fishermen of Galilee into North-country sailors of the Patrick Spens tradition and given them sentiments more proper to the left wing of the Y.M.C.A.

The extravagant use of metaphor and simile is thus seen to be governed by the necessity of making a poem of this sort equal the prose summary which is dictating it. This practice is founded on two fallacies: the first, that the poet is not saying what he means but something *like* what he means in prettier language than he uses to himself about it; the second, from which the first is deduced, that the ideas of truth in which the poet deals are not agreeable in themselves, so that he has to make a distinction between what is pretty and not pretty, poetical and not poetical. When, therefore, naked ideas are found in poetry instead of ideas dressed up in rhetorical devices, such poetry is naturally accused of being didactic. But all that has happened is that the poet has made the poem out of the poem itself: its final form corresponds with its first intuitive conception in the poet's mind, uncorrupted by hints to the reader, familiar asides to make it less terrifying, or conceits to flatter, entertain, and display the poet's virtuosity. But it is almost impossible for a poet who really means what he says to make the literary critic believe that he does: the more he means what he says and the more earnest he is to make that clear, the more he will be thought to be concealing his meaning in clever evasions of 'obscurity.'

If, then, the author of *The Rugged Black of Anger* were pressed to
employ some familiar metaphor or simile to explain them, this would
be to demand some such insult as: 'At your request I shall make my
poem into a bad imitation of itself. I shall, in fact, call this version *your*
poem, and the more yours the sillier it will be. But you must promise
not to deceive yourself that this is what the poem really means.'

If one assumes that the first two lines of the poem do not mean what
they say, but refer satirically to the popular sentiment:

> Look around and you will find
> Every cloud is silver-lined.

one is brought into a sentimental personal atmosphere in which *anger*
is anger as felt by someone, or bad luck seen as the anger of providence
or fate, and in which *smile-border* is either personal happiness or good
luck. But if one consults the poem one finds, after the first two lines,
that such an interpretation does not fit: *anger* means nothing but
anger, *smile-border* nothing but smile-border. So much do they mean
just what they say that the rest of the poem is developed from their
saying what they do: *anger* equals anger, *smile-border* equals the smiling
border of anger which separates it from some other concept, whose
border separating it from anger might equally be called an 'anger-
border.' What is one to do, then, since the poem really seems to mean
what it says? All that can be done is to let it interpret itself, without
introducing any new associations or, if possible, any new words.

> The rugged black of anger
> Has an uncertain smile-border.
> The transition from one kind to another,
> As from anger, rugged black,
> To what lies beyond its smile-border,
> May be love between neighbour and neighbour
> (Love between neighbouring kind and kind);
> Or natural death (death of one,
> Though not of the other); or discontinuance
> (Discontinuance of kind,
> As anger ceases to be anger)
> Because so small is space
> (So small the space for kind and kind and kind), that
> The extent of kind must be expressed otherwise
> (The extent of kind beyond its border
> Is end of kind, because space is so small

There is not room enough for all
Kinds: anger when *angrier* has to be
Expressed otherwise than by anger,
Therefore by an uncertain smile-border) . . .

This will serve to illustrate the method of letting the poem interpret itself. It has been done without introducing any words not belonging to the poem, without throwing any of the poem away as superfluous padding and without having recourse to a prose version: the poem as interpreted is practically itself repeated at three times its own length. Readers may object that it is still not entirely clear, but not that it is not *any* clearer, or that it could not be made clearer still by an increase in length proportionate to their needs. For instance, if they are puzzled by the sixth of the original lines and cannot at the first reading persuade themselves that *Because so small is space* really means *Because so small is space*, yet see that it can mean nothing else, they can repeat to themselves:

Because so small is space,
Because so small is space,

until they are convinced; or, perhaps:

Because space is so small,
Because space is so small,

an inversion less gratuitous than, for instance, the philosophical summary: 'Because so small is Space or the Universe or the Human Mind, that Ideas cannot reach their full development but are crowded into cramped quarters where they have difficulty in keeping their independence and are often completely extinguished.'

A wider application of this method to the reading of poems which really mean what they say—obviously it could not be applied to poems that do not—would reveal that much of the so-called obscurity of modernist and other poems is created by the laziness of the plain reader, who wishes to hurry through poetry as quickly as through prose; he does not realize that he is dealing with a kind of thought which, though it may have the speed of prose to the poet, he must himself follow with a slowness proportionate to how much he is not a poet. Increasing the time-length of reading is one way of getting out of the prosal and into the poetic state of mind, of developing a capacity for minuteness, for seeing all there is to see at a given point and for carrying it along with one.

But the plain reader, while he does not object to the poetic state of mind in the poet, has a fear of cultivating it in himself. This is why he prefers the prose summary to the poem itself, and thinks of the poem, in its first occurrence to the poet's mind, as a genial prose idea free of those terrors which the poet is supposed to keep to himself or carefully disguise.

The 'making' poet does not write because of the demand of the reader to be fed with poetry but because certain poems demand to be written and the poet is 'somebody who is obsessed by Making.' Once the poems are 'made,' his personal activity in them ceases. They begin a life of their own towards which he has no responsibility: it is an affair entirely between them and the reader.

The purpose of printing a poem which is construed in this private sense is not to convert it into a selling product, but to give it a separate identity. The poet finds it practically impossible to read his own work intelligently until he has separated it from himself, and the easiest and most obvious way to bring this about is to have it set down in print, since his own handwriting is almost a physical part of himself: the printed page acts as a mirror. This may explain the mystery of Shakespeare's failure to have his poetic plays uniformly printed in his lifetime: they had become sufficiently externalized by being presented on the stage. But the more important aspect of externalization is the poet's duty towards the poem. His curiosity to see his own poems in print is legitimate; though too often externalization means only that he wishes narcissistically to see in print something that bears his name.

In traditional poetry the problem of externalization is a simpler one because there is a whole apparatus of metrical conventions at the poet's service ready to give it a formal literary independence of him. Independent poems can of course be written in traditional forms; but metrical conventions tempt poets to be lazy and tempt non-poets to write verses which look like poems. The finality of traditional verse-forms can make an incomplete poem—'incomplete' in the sense of 'not thoroughly separated from the poet'—seem complete. Poetry closely bound by literary conventions is destined sooner or later to grow shabby; and attempts to smarten it up only substitute new conventions for the old without challenging the fundamental fallacy that what turns out good poems is completeness of method, rather than an indefatigable obsession for making until the poem is made.

If the poet has poems in him they will get themselves made regardless of his literary training. No technical method, whatever its merits, can extract poems from a non-poet: a method can seem to make, it cannot make. The Imagists, for example, did not make new poems; they only evolved a new kind of stanza which seemed to them more real than traditional stanza-forms because it was new. When Mr. Cummings says that his 'poems are competing with locomotives and roses' he means that they have been made as real entities, whether mechanical or natural. He does not claim to have an infallible method for manufacturing poems, but is irresistibly besieged by poems, even of contradictory natures and of contradictory principles of growth, each with its own separate method of getting made. The poet who relies on method for repetitively producing verses which resemble locomotives or roses whenever he pleases is only saying over and over again that twice two is four. The making poet has no method, only a faculty for allowing things to invent themselves, and cannot write a poem unless there is one to write. He is incapable of repeating himself and declares with each new poem a new truth, a complete truth, even a contradictory truth. He is allowing twice two (or truth) to become whatever it is possible for it to be, since truth cannot be reduced to a fixed mathematical formula any more than poetry to a fixed literary method: twice two, like poetry, may be everything or anything.

VII

MODERNIST POETRY AND CIVILIZATION

Modernism is used as a term of condemnation by the stolid critics for whom poetry is centred in the past; but as a boast by the energetic young intellectuals who hold that it should keep pace with new developments in painting, music and philosophy, and with civilization in general. Between the two parties poetry becomes a matter of temperamental politics, and in the ensuing battle of words both lose sight of the main issue: may a poet write as a poet or must he write as a period? Genuine modernism is not part of a 'modernist' programme of contemporary mannerisms but a natural personal manner and attitude in the poet to his work; he accepts the term 'modernist' because he believes that there is now a new spirit struggling at great odds to free poems of the cramping traditional habits which have prevented them from realizing their full capacities. If this spirit is kept in mind, more excuse can be found for applying the term 'modernist' to poems than to the poet. Yet no matter how restrained and impersonal a literary attitude modernist poets may adopt it is difficult for them to resist the temptation of making converts, especially when they are defamed. Literary loose-ends are always anxious to acquire character and reputation by attaching themselves to a cause, and liberal-minded readers who regard civilization as a steady human progress which does not exclude the idea of a modernist, historically advanced, poetry offer themselves as ripe for conversion. It is difficult when clarifying some aspects of genuine poetic modernism to avoid appealing to this progressive population—that is to say, presenting poetry as an instrument of historical progress—or to avoid the appearance of condoning that false modernism which disguises feebleness with eccentricity. It is at first difficult, in fact, to distinguish false modernism, or faith in history, from genuine modernism, or faith in the immediate performances of poems as not necessarily derived from history. Modernist poetry need mean no more than poetry sprung from honest invention rather than from conscientious attendance on the time-spirit.

Francis Thompson, in his essay on Coleridge, complained that:

... the charge of affectation has been hurled in turn at the outset of their careers against Coleridge, Wordsworth, Shelley, Keats, Tennyson and Browning. Wordsworth wrote simple diction and his simplicity was termed affected; Shelley gorgeous diction and his gorgeousness was affected; Tennyson cunning diction and his cunning was affected; Browning rugged diction and his ruggedness was affected. Why Coleridge was called affected passes the wit of man, except it be that he did not write like Pope or the elegant Mr. Rogers—or, indeed, that all critical tradition would be outraged if a mere recent pet were not labelled with the epithets made and provided for him by wise critical precedent.

Now, it suits Thompson, who is here incidentally defending his own ornate poems against the charge, to hint that for a poet to be called affected—as both the genuine and the false modernists are to-day— is a proof of genuineness; he does not, therefore, stop to enquire how many of these charges of affectation were justified at the outset of the careers of the six poets he names. As a matter of fact, Shelley is the only one who can be fairly exculpated of the charge, as being the only one free of authorial ambition: his political and philosophical enthusiasms soon absorbed what professional literary enthusiasm he may originally have had. Wordsworth's early simplicity *was* affected:

A simple Child, dear brother Jim,
  That lightly draws its breath,
And feels its life in every limb,
    What should it know of death?

I met a little cottage Girl;
  She was eight years old, she said;
Her hair was thick with many a curl
  That clustered round her head.

Keats' early richness *was* affected:

              . . . here is cream
Deepening to richness from a snowy gleam;
Sweeter than that nurse Amalthea skimm'd
For the boy Jupiter: and here, undimm'd
By any touch, a bunch of blooming plums
Ready to melt between an infant's gums:
And here is manna pick'd from Syrian trees,
In starlight, by the three Hesperides.

Tennyson's early cunning *was* affected:

The streams through many a lilied row
  Down-carolling to the crisped sea,
Low-tinkled with a bell-like flow
  Atween the blossoms, 'We are free.'

Browning's early ruggedness *was* affected:

And on that young round cheek of thine
I make them recognise the tinge,
As when of the costly scarlet wine
They drip so much as will impinge
And spread in a thinnest scale afloat
One thick gold drop from the olive's coat
Over a silver plate whose sheen
Still through the mixture shall be seen.

Similarly, Coleridge's early work was disfigured with Gothick affectations and affectations of primitive piety:

'This Hermit good lives in that wood
Which slopes down to the sea.
How loudly his sweet voice he rears!
He loves to talk with marineres
That come from a far countree . . .'

The history of these affectations is that of the social demands made of poetry by the intelligent plain reader devoted to the idea of human uplift; and of the conforming by poets themselves to popular notions about the place of poetry in this uplift. Poetry is viewed as supplying an elegance and refinement which must necessarily be neglected in the practical business of life. Since common affairs are not genteel, poetry is expected to feed a hunger in common man for the high polish of civilization. Another of these demands has been that poetry shall be romantically progressive, that it shall advertise civilization: a task to which Tennyson devoted his mature powers in *The Princess* and other sumptuously phrased verse tracts. In this sense the poet is still regarded as a tribal prophet; and that Tennyson could foresee air warfare in 'navies grappling in the central blue,' or the League of Nations in 'The Parliament of Man, the Federation of the World,' contributed greatly to his success with the liberal reader. Another demand is for poetry as a gauge of intellectual, rather than social or political, advancement: poetry as deeper and deeper thinking. Browning exemplifies the poet who appreciated and indulged the popular weakness for profundity, appearing to be profound without really being so, keeping the required illusion by various technical devices such as unnecessarily protracted sentences and an over-clipped grammar.

Poetry is thus converted into a rapidly expanding institution which embodies from period to period all novel forms of specialized knowledge, and broadens its definition to include psychology, applied theories of music and painting, philosophy, physical science and so on. The poet feels obliged to present himself as a sage; as Tennyson, when he became Poet Laureate, conscientiously sent himself to school again and kept to a weekly curriculum of self-imposed studies, which included science, foreign languages, mathematics and philosophy. In this view, which is based on an untenable view of civilization as continuously developing in the direction of an absolute and perfect end, not only is the nature of the poet expected to change in a scheme of minute daily adjustment to history, but poetry itself is supposed to undergo historical evolution: if it keeps up with the times this is read as a sign of its good behaviour and its worthiness to be listed among the material evidences of progress. Thus a poet of to-day who considers himself a modernist because he is successfully keeping up with his date is, however low his opinion of Tennyson may be, merely an earnest Tennysonian.

A strong distinction must be drawn between poetry as something developing through civilization and as something developing organically by itself. Civilization develops only in the sense that one thing follows another, not in the sense that things become progressively better or more harmonious because they follow on one another's heels. Poetry does develop in the sense that it is contemporaneous with civilization; but it has to protect itself from contemporaneous influences rather than woo them, since there is no merit in believing in modernism for modernism's sake. One must always therefore keep this distinction in mind: between what is historically new in poetry because the poet is acting as a barker for civilization, and what is intrinsically new in poetry because the poet is an original interpreter of the fortunes of mankind.

Very many of the poems of to-day are written in defiance of the demands made on the poet by civilized society; though the defiance, it must be admitted, is often trivial and undignified. One of the refinements of contemporary poetry is the reaction against those very refinements of civilization which it is generally expected to cultivate. Even such a sentimentalist as Rupert Brooke mentioned love and seasickness in the same breath:

> The damned ship lurched and slithered. Quiet and quick
>   My cold gorge rose; the long sea rolled; I knew
> I must think hard of something, or be sick;
>   And could think hard of only one thing—*you*!
> . . . Do I forget you? Retchings twist and tie me,
>   Old meat, good meals, brown gobbets, up I throw.
> Do I remember? Acrid return and slimy,
>   The sobs and slobber of a last year's woe . . .

At the declaration of the War there was a national demand for heroics to which Brooke and his contemporaries succumbed. Then experience of the horrors of war provoked in poetry both genuine and insincere examples of a defiant reaction against heroics. These lines of Wilfred Owen's describe with painful literalness a man dying from poison-gas:

> . . . If in some smothering dreams, you too could pace
> Behind the wagon that we flung him in
> And watch the white eyes writhing in his face,
> His hanging face, like a devil's sick of sin,
> If you could hear, at every jolt, the blood
> Come gargling from the froth-corrupted lungs
> Bitten as the cud
> Of vile, incurable sores on innocent tongues . . .

And Edward Thomas reacted less sincerely in:

> This is no case of petty right or wrong
> That politicians or philosophers
> Can judge. I hate no Germans, nor grow hot
> With love of Englishmen, to please newspapers.
> Beside my hate for one fat patriot
> My hatred of the Kaiser is love true . . .

To the demand for elegance we find close juxtapositions of elegance and vulgarity in the same poem—as in Mr. Eliot's *The Waste Land.* The lines:

> The hot water at ten.
> And if it rains, a closed car at four.
> And we shall play a game of chess,
> Pressing lidless eyes and waiting for a knock upon the door

are immediately followed by:

> When Lil's husband got demobbed, I said—
> I didn't mince my words, I said to her myself,
> HURRY UP PLEASE IT'S TIME
> Now Albert's coming back, make yourself a bit smart.
> He'll want to know what you done with that money he gave you
> To get yourself some teeth . . .

To the demand for romantic progressiveness there is a reaction of hopeless and unpurposed pessimism, as in Miss Nancy Cunard's *Parallax*, an imitation of T. S. Eliot:

> In the rooms
> A sombre carpet broods, stagnates beneath deliberate steps.
> Here drag a foot, there a foot, drop sighs, look round for nothing, shiver.
> Sunday creeps in silence
> Under suspended smoke
> And curdles defiant in unreal sleep.
> The gas-fire puffs, consumes, ticks out its minor chords—
> And at the door
> I guess the arrested knuckles of the one-time friend
> One foot on the stair delaying, that turns again.

To the demand for deep thinking the reaction is a frivolousness like Mr. Wallace Stevens':

La—la! The cat is in the violets
And the awnings are let down.
The cat should not be where she is
And the awnings are too brown,
Emphatically so.

To the demand that poetry shall combine all arts and sciences into a master-art the reaction is praise of either silliness or simpleness, as in Mr. Witter Bynner's:

I'm a-building my house
    On a mountain so high,
A good place to wait
    For my love to come by.

Go 'way now, all of you,
    Leave me alone
On the peacefullest mountain
    Ever was known.

or Æ's:

Cloistered amid these austere rocks
A brooding seer, I watched an hour
Close to the earth, lost to all else,
The marvel of a tiny flower.

To all these demands, and particularly to this last, there is a more complex reaction. Many contemporary poets not only snap their fingers at civilization; they elaborate their superior attitude by casually proving that they can not only keep up with civilization but outstrip it. This is by way of counter-attack against cock-a-hoop scientists who agree with Mr. J. B. S. Haldane that 'not until our poets are once more drawn from the educated classes (I speak as a scientist), will they appeal to the average man by showing him the beauty in his own life.'

Exploitation of modern musical theory appears in the poetry of W. J. Turner, of modern painting theory in that of Edith and Sacheverell Sitwell, of psychological theory in that of Herbert Read and Archibald Macleish, of modern sex-engrossment in that of D. H. Lawrence, of philosophical theory in that of Conrad Aiken, of encyclopediac learning in that of Marianne Moore and T. S. Eliot—and so on and so on. This reaction inspires not only an emulative display of modernist learning, but also a cultivation of fine writing to prove that this generation can beat the most cunning Elizabethan, Romantic

Revivalist or Victorian at his own game. Here is Sacheverell Sitwell doing what John Fletcher might be doing were he alive now: taking liberties with blank verse and poetic imagery under the influence of modern painting and music, while still remaining recognizably a late-Elizabethan dramatist:

> Who can have trod, before, this field of fire
> The huge floor of ocean, unfoamed, shining,
> Lit with loud stars and mellow harvest moon?
> The sea-nymphs swimming by the galleon's side
> Have never shone, golden, in its wake before:
> Like winds they play among the corn's gold tide
> Loosing those windy locks, or down they dive
> Through amber furrows lifted by the keel,
> Past starlight, crackling to the sad shell note
> Of scalèd Tritons in deep water depths.

His modernism appears in such lines as the second and fifth, which the Elizabethans or Jacobeans, large as were the liberties they took with blank verse (far larger than those taken by Milton or the Victorians), could not have included in a gentle lyrical passage. They would have put instead:

> The hugy floor of ocean foamless shining

and:

> Have ne'er shone golden in its wake before.

The first of these lines of Mr. Sitwell's must be read:

> The húge flóor of ócean (pause) unfoámed (pause) shíning

and the next:

> Have néver shóne (pause) gólden (pause) in its wáke befóre.

The influence of modern music appears in the readiness with which Mr. Sitwell varies the monotony of the metrical pattern. The pictorial element is also modern. 'The loud stars,' 'the corn's gold tide,' the nymphs who dive 'crackling' down, are not Elizabethan conceits but verbal equivalents of a modern picture in which the size and shape of the stars, the cornfield aspect of the sea, the sharpness of the water-flurry when the nymphs dive would be anti-realistically represented to suggest just these figures. Fletcher would have written 'bright stars' and:

> Like winds that wanton in the yellow corn,
> So do they wanton in this golden tide.

and:

> . . . shivering the sad shell note

and so on.

The following lines from *The Waste Land* further illustrate the modernist tendency to outdo the past in elaborate and elegant writing:

> In vials of ivory and coloured glass
> Unstoppered, lurked her strange synthetic perfumes,
> Unguent, powdered, or liquid—troubled, confused
> And drowned the sense in odours; stirred by the air
> That freshened from the window, these ascended
> In fattening the prolonged candle-flames,
> Flung their smoke into the laquearia,
> Stirring the pattern on the coffered ceiling.
> Huge sea-wood fed with copper
> Burned green and orange, framed by the coloured stone,
> In which sad light a carvèd dolphin swam.

Keats is pale beside him:

> Of wealthy lustre was the banquet-room,
> Fill'd with pervading brilliance and perfume:
> Before each lucid pannel fuming stood
> A censer fed with myrrh and spiced wood,
> Each by a sacred tripod held aloft,
> Whose slender feet wide-swerv'd upon the soft
> Wool-woofed carpets: fifty wreaths of smoke
> From fifty censers their light voyage took
> To the high roof, still mimick'd as they rose
> Along the mirror'd walls by twin-clouds odorous.
>
> (From *Lamia*)

Literary internationalism—the incorporation of foreign tongues and atmospheres—is another method of civilizing and enlarging poetry. French is the most common language introduced to this end, with Italian and Spanish closely following. Mr. Eliot not only makes free use of French side by side with English: he has written poems entirely in French. An even greater enlargement is made by a cultivation of the more remote classics. Some poets are able to maintain a sense of balance and dignity in this, if only because they are good scholars; but not so Mr. Ezra Pound. In a single volume of his, *Lustra*, occur literary references to Greek, Latin, Spanish, Italian, Provençal and Chinese

CA: K

literature—several of these incorrectly quoted. Mr. Eliot, a more serious scholar, refers in *The Waste Land* to Greek, Latin, Spanish, Italian, French, German and Sanskrit literature. The English poets quoted or referred to are no longer those to whom the Victorians and post-Victorians paid tribute: not Chaucer, Spenser, the stock Shakespeare, Milton, Burns, but others known only to the cognoscenti— Peele, Kidd, Lyly, the less familiar Shakespeare, Webster, Marvell, Dryden, Swift, Darley, Beddoes. The same enlargement is made with the Greek, Latin, Italian and French poets.

Among the few unexploited elegances left to poetry, as opposed to drama, is an affectation of the vocabulary of low life. Wordsworth's use of the language of simple men was, in a conservative way, a similar counter-elegance; but modernist poets outdo Wordsworth in literary slumming. Whereas he wrote:

> And now the same strong voice more near
> Said cordially, 'My Friend, what cheer?
> Rough doings these! as God's my judge,
> The sky owes somebody a grudge!
> We've had in half an hour or less
> A twelve month's terror and distress!'

Mr. Eliot writes unexpurgated and unsentimentalized cockney, and Mr. Cummings:

> ... some
> guys talk big
> about Lundun Burlin an gay Paree an
> some guys claims der never was
> nutn like Nooer Leans Shikahgo Sain
> Looey Noo York an San Fran dictaphones
> wireless subways vacuum
> cleaners pianolas funnygraphs skyscrapers an safety razors
>
> sall right in its way kiddo
> but as fer I gimme de good ole daze ...

In this way much modernist poetry, attempting to justify itself to civilization, the civilization of the progressive reading public, succeeds so well that it is rejected as over-advanced; whereupon it turns to a smaller audience or to no audience at all, consoling itself with its own advancement.

Of some contemporary poets 'modernist' is used merely to describe

a certain independence of mind, without definitely associating them
with modernism as a literary cause: though content to stay in the main
stream of poetry, they make judicious splashes to show that they are
aware of the date. This has been the tactical position adopted both by
those whose modernism consists in a studied aloofness from literary
politics and by those who have had neither the courage nor the
capacity to go the whole way with modernism and yet do not wish to
be left behind. To the first class belong such poets as Mr. Siegfried
Sassoon, and Mr. Robert Frost whose nature-poems are, with the
exception of two or three of Mr. Frank Prewett's, perhaps the only
unaffected ones of our period. (Mr. Edmund Blunden's show accurate
observation but grow more and more literary.) The following is from
Mr. Frost's *Runaway*, describing a foal afraid of his first sight of snow.
The faint modernism of the poem consists in its complete casualness
and matter-of-factness:

> Once when the snow of the year was beginning to fall,
> We stopped by a mountain pasture to say, 'Whose colt?'
> A little Morgan had one forefoot on the wall,
> The other curled at his breast. He dipped his head
> And snorted at us. And then he had to bolt . . .
> And now he comes again with clatter of stone,
> And mounts the wall again with whited eyes
> And all his tail that isn't hair up straight.
> He shudders his coat as if to throw off flies . . .

Mr. Sassoon who, like Mr. Frost, has not struggled to keep up with
literary fashions and who, when he yields to the temptation of poetical-
ness, adopts the manner of a generation ago, writes as follows about
a Founder's Feast held in St. John's College, Cambridge, shortly after
the war ended. The poem carries on the indignation of his war-poems
against the General Staff. Modernism in Mr. Sassoon is an intelligent,
satiric reaction to contemporary political and social Bluffs; it is not a
literary policy:

> . . . Gowns, rose and scarlet in flamingo ranks,
> Adorned the dais that shone with ancient silver;
> And guests of honour gazed far down the Hall
> With precognition of returning thanks. .
> There beamed the urbanest Law-lord on the Bench,
> Debating with the Provost (ceremonious
> In flushed degrees of vintage scholarship)
> The politics of Plato—and the French.

> But on the Provost's left, in gold and blue
> Sat . . . O my God! . . . great Major-General Bluff
> Enough enough enough enough enough!

To the second class belong poets like Mr. Yeats who, observing that his old poetical robes had worn rather shabby, recently acquired a new outfit. But confirmed literary habits are not so easily discarded: even when he writes of 'Lois Fuller's Chinese Dancers'—a high-brow Vaudeville turn—instead of Eire and the ancient ways, And the Red Rose upon the Rood of Time.

Such are the shifts to which poets are driven in trying to cope with civilization and in rejecting or keeping up with the social requirements which seem to be laid upon poetry. In the confusion which results it is clear at least that modernist verse, however much it has been weakened or perverted by its race with civilization, embodies the best and most enduring contemporary poetry. 'Modernist' should describe a quality in poetry which has nothing to do with the date or with reacting to the demands of civilization, though the poets in whose works this quality is most evident are not so stupid or unhumorous as to ignore their contemporaneous universe. Evidences of time naturally occur in their writing; but its modernism always lies in its independence, in its not relying on any of the traditional devices of poetry-making nor on any of the effects artificially achieved by using the atmosphere of contemporary life and knowledge to startle or to convey reality; the most intelligent attitude towards history is not to take one's own date too seriously. If a topical institution, person or object happens to be mentioned by these poets, this is only because it supplies an image more accurately suited to the particular requirements of a poem than another less recent one. Their work is especially characterized by a lack of strain, by an intelligent ease. Not only are its references simple and natural, no matter how untraditional, but it does not have to rely on realistic short-story material as in the poem we quoted of Mr. Sandburg's, or in this of Mr. Pound's:

> Like a skein of loose silk blown against a wall
> She walks by the railing of a path in Kensington Gardens,
> And she is dying piece-meal
>   of a sort of emotional anaemia . . .

Even poetry which is modernist only in the historical sense—even Mr. Pound's or Mr. Sandburg's—has accomplished at least this: it has widened the limits of reference, diction and construction in poetry. By extending the poet's curriculum it has also extended his acceptable scope, so that poetry which is modernist only in the personal sense has some chance of attention, its frowardness being taken for historical modernism.

Many common symbols of civilization are, in any case, naturally absorbed by poetry, although to begin with they cannot be used without self-consciousness. The naturalness with which some new invention or scientific discovery may be mentioned in poetry depends on its newness. There is even an assessable time-limit before any such novelty becomes a common object and until the completion of which one cannot write of it in poetry without a certain affectation. This time-limit varies with the nature of the novelty. During the period of acclimatization its name gradually loses the initial capital or the italics with which it was originally printed, and comes to be pronounced without any sense of strangeness or second-thought.

The train, for example, has passed from a stage of strangeness to one of complete familiarity. Wordsworth was the first established poet to take notice of it, but as a curiosity rather than as a common object and on the theory that poetry should take cognizance of modern scientific development. Although his view was that poetry was conferring a favour on the scientists in recognizing their products, it will be seen from the following lines that he admitted minutely and specifically the various demands which civilization puts upon poetry; material progressiveness, literal prophecy, intellectual advancements, 'future change' and, finally, elegance, which he achieved by calling Steamboats, Viaducts, Railways by other than their own names ('Motions and Means,' 'Nature's lawful offspring').

STEAMBOATS, VIADUCTS, AND RAILWAYS

Motions and Means, on land and sea at war
With old poetic feeling, not for this,
Shall ye, by Poets even, be judged amiss!
Nor shall your presence, howsoe'er it mar
The loveliness of Nature, prove a bar
To the Mind's gaining that prophetic sense
Of future change, that point of vision, whence
May be discovered what in soul ye are.
In spite of all that beauty may disown
In your harsh features, Nature doth embrace

> Her lawful offspring in Man's art; and Time,
> Pleased with your triumphs o'er his brother Space,
> Accepts from your bold hands the proffered crown
> Of hope, and smiles on you with cheer sublime.

Tennyson was forced to accept the train, though he handled it gingerly. *Lady Godiva* has a short prelude to show his broadmindedness; but it is only a foil to the romantic story:

> I waited for the train at Coventry;
> I hung with grooms and porters on the bridge,
> To watch the three tall spires; and there I shaped
> The city's ancient legend into this:—

In '*Mechanophilus*—in the time of the first railways' he frankly romanticizes:

> Now first we stand and understand,
>   And sunder false from true,
> And handle boldly with the hand,
>   And see and shape and do.

> Dash back that ocean with a pier,
>   Strow yonder mountain flat,
> A railway there, a tunnel here,
>   Mix me this Zone with that! . . .

> As we surpass our fathers' skill,
>   Our sons will shame our own;
> A thousand things are hidden still
>   And not a hundred known . . .

Browning was rather more courageous; and the first to introduce the train as a commonplace into poetry, but through the back door, in what was known as serio-comic verse. The following lines are from *Christmas-Eve and Easter-Day*:

> A tune was born in my head last week,
> Out of the thump-thump and shriek-shriek
>   Of the train, as I came by it, up from Manchester;
> And when, next week, I take it back again,
> My head will sing to the engine's clack again,
>   While it only makes my neighbour's haunches stir . . .

By the use of rhymes like 'back again' and 'engine's clack again,' 'Manchester' and 'haunches stir,' he is saying in effect that a train is no proper subject for true poetical feelings; that as it is a part of modern life we must include it in our poems but in the low style proper to it. Emily Dickinson was perhaps the first to confess to a feeling of personal affection for the train as such:

> I love to see it lap the miles,
> And lick the valleys up,
> And pause to feed itself at tanks;
> And then prodigious, step
> Around a pile of mountains
> And, supercilious, peer
> In shanties by the sides of roads . . .
>
> And neigh like Boanerges;
> Then, punctual as a star,
> Stop—docile and omnipotent—
> At its own stable door.

To John Davidson it was an appealing creature, too, although more terrible; in no way comic. His *Song of the Trains* begins:

> A monster taught
> To come to hand
> Amain,
> As swift as thought
> Across the land
> The train.
> . . . O'er bosky dens
> By marsh and mead,
> Forest and fens
> Embodied speed
> Is clanked and hurled . . .

In a poem of Mr. Robert Nichols' we find the train treated with more modern nonchalance. *The Express: Hereford to London* begins:

> On sways the tilting train:
> We feel the carriage bluffly sideways blown,
> We see the chill shower brighten on the pane,
> We hear the high wind through the lantern moan,
> We three borne ever through the wind and rain,
> We three who meet here not to meet again,
> We three poor faring fools who sit alone.

But towards the end a romantic lapse excuses the liberties taken:

But the giant train begins a confident song
'Why be so meek, so proud, when both are wrong.'

Mr. Sacheverell Sitwell can write even more casually of the train.
Apparent romantic lapses like the following in his *At Breakfast*:

A railway engine ran across the field
Galloping like a swift horse down the rails.
As it came quicker the window-panes rattled,
The roof shook side to side: all its beams trembled,
Thundering hoofs were upon us—glass chariots.

are not real lapses like Mr. Nichols' but a half-satiric 'Look: modernist
though I am, I can still be romantic about old-fashioned subjects like
the railway train.' It is now not a 'monster' but a charming early-
Victorian *objet de vertu* under a glass dome.

Miss Marianne Moore describes expanding book-cases and books
printed on india-paper in a serious poem, without self-consciousness:

the vast indestructible necropolis
of composite Yawman-Erbe separable units;
the steel, the oak, the glass, the Poor Richard publications
containing the public secrets of efficiency
on 'paper so thin that one thousand four hundred and twenty
pages make one inch.'

Without self-consciousness? Perhaps that is too much to say when so
short a space of years separates poetry of this sort from the once-
advanced poetry of, say, Richard Le Gallienne, a 'decadent' of the
'nineties still alive and writing literary criticism in the same city as Miss
Moore—a city where there must be large backward sections of the
reading public to whom Mr. Le Gallienne is still an advanced writer
because he has, perhaps, written familiarly of the Devil and the sweets
of sin.

But is it necessary for the poet to come to the point, after slowly
acclimatizing his verse to what were once considered unpoetical
subjects, where he can, with Miss Moore, bring himself to insert in
his poem fourteen unrevised and consecutive words straight from a
newspaper advertisement, and put them into quotation marks as well?
Though a feat of poetic self-martyrdom and perhaps the logical
conclusion of giving civilization what it wants—verse actually inter-
pretative of what is called 'the poetry of modern business'—it is bad
for both poetry and business: the quotation would have been much

more effective if left in the original setting to compose the daily synthetic advertisement-poem of the morning paper.

True modernist poetry can appear equally at all stages of historical development from Wordsworth to Miss Moore. And it does appear when the poet forgets what is the correct literary conduct demanded of him in relation to contemporary institutions (by civilization speaking through the literary critic) and can write a poem which has the power of survival in spite of its disregarding these demands; a poem of a certain old-fashionedness, if only because the policy of the popular newspapers has long been to shrink the current vocabulary to a few thousand words and because popular novelists have followed suit. If the poet is to allow his poem to achieve its full meaning he must often use words which are practically obsolete. English has never been so rich and flexible, so capable of conveying nice shades of meaning, as it was in Ben Jonson's day. Yet it would be absurd for a poet to disregard all that has since happened to the language. Poems which deserve to endure are at once old-fashioned and modernist. It is hard to decide offhand how much of modernist poetry is merely evidence of the poet's conversion to the last-minute salvationism of Progress, and how much is in need of no such conversion but working out its own salvation. The proportions vary with individuals. With Mr. Pound the former sort of writing predominates; with Mr. Cummings, though he is more 'daring' than Mr. Pound, there is much less of this than appears at first sight; with Mr. Archibald Macleish, an industrious imitator of Mr. Cummings, much more.

A danger in any discussion of modernist poetry which may reach the plain reader is that as a result of pointing out how many of its characteristics are inspired by necessity, sincerity or truthfulness, these characteristics may endear themselves to him not because of their necessity, sincerity or truthfulness but only because he can understand them as up-to-date; the danger, in fact, that the plain reader may fall in love with this poetry's up-to-dateness. If modernist poetry were seen and applauded as part of the movement of civilization, the demands made upon it would become intensified. There is such a great gap between Victorian poetry and the poetry of just before the War, and again between this poetry and advanced modern poetry, that the converted plain reader might fail to see that the theories governing the leading poets of 1860 or 1910 or 1926 have nothing to do with the essential goodness of poetry, however much they may have to do with its up-to-dateness.

VIII

VARIETY IN MODERNIST POETRY

The reader whose introduction to poetry comes not through personal compulsion or curiosity but through the systematic requirements of his education, naturally associates it with the utilitarian point of view, which must dominate any formal educational process. If his school-masters have happened to be old-fashioned and so used poetry merely as a means of teaching grammar, or as 'lines' to be learned by heart for disciplinary purposes, he is likely either to renounce it for ever as a dreary pedagogical invention or to rediscover it as something so different from the 'lines' of the classroom as to forget all its unpleasant associations. Schoolmasters of a 'liberal school-system,' however, do not leave poetry, as poetry, alone. They attempt to interest their pupils in its 'values'; and the pupils will be likely either to subscribe to these values and accept poetry because of them, or reject it because of them. 'Beauty' is the term of approval which they are asked to apply to the 'values' of poetry; and character-formation, or if not character-formation at least a wholesome relief from its ardours, is indicated as its practical end.

The elder, and on the whole preferable, system, has been generally superseded in English-speaking countries: the official report *The Teaching of English in England* (1919) stresses the folly of the teacher in 'throwing away an important weapon,' if he refuses to win his pupils' hearts by making the literature lesson interesting, particularly through a study of Shakespeare. The authors of the report, in reply to an objection that 'Shakespeare is over the heads of the children,' approve a professor-witness who replied: 'He is over all our heads'— as though that made matters any better. In this system all poetry is seen as tending towards the same general tone and purpose—Spiritual Elevation.

It is unimportant to decide whether education since the time of Aristotle has caused the spread of this view of poetry; or whether it has been caused by the numerical predominance of poets who have written most of their poetry in its support over poets who have either dissented or refused to commit themselves. The fact remains that this has always been the academic view and the view of orthodox literary critics; even a self-proclaimed dissenter like Poe defined the end of poetry as spiritual elevation. The mass-impressiveness of Classical poetry is largely due to the uniformity with which this principle was once accepted. And though we know from history that between romantics like Byron, Wordsworth, Keats, Coleridge and Shelley there was as much personal dissimilarity as could possibly be found between contemporary poets, yet the lip-service which they all paid to the principle often induced in them a corresponding pen-service. Here are descriptive passages by six more or less contemporary early nineteenth-century writers:

> . . . the hoar
> And aery Alps towards the North appeared
> Through mist, an heaven-sustaining bulwark reared
> Between the East and West, and half the sky
> Was roofed with clouds of rich emblazonry
> Dark purple at the Zenith, which still grew
> Down the steep West into a wondrous hue
> Brighter than burning gold, even to the rent
> Where the swift sun yet paused in his descent
> Among the many folded hills . . .

> It was no marvel—from my very birth
> My soul was drunk with love—which did pervade
> And mingle with whate'er I saw on earth.
> Of objects all inanimate I made
> Idols, and out of wild and lonely flowers
> And rocks, whereby they grew, a paradise.

> Woodlark may sink from sandy fern—the Sun may hear his lay;
> Runnels may kiss the grass on shelves and shallows clear,
> But their low voices are not heard, though come on travels drear;
> Blood-red the Sun may set behind black mountain peaks;
> Blue tides may sluice and drench their time in caves and weedy
>   creeks.

> Mournfully breaks the north wave on thy shore,
>   Silent Iona, and the mocking blast
>   Sweeps sternly o'er thy relics of the past,
>   The stricken cross, the desecrated tomb
> Of abbots, and barbarian kings of yore . . .

Since risen from ocean, ocean to defy,
Appeared the Crag of Ailsa, ne'er did morn
With gleaming lights more gracefully adorn
His sides, or wreathe with mist his forehead high:
Now, faintly darkening with the sun's eclipse,
Still is he seen, in lone sublimity . . .

I stood on Brocken's sovran height, and saw
Woods crowding upon woods, hills over hills,
A surging scene, and only limited
By the blue distance. Heavily my way
Downward I dragged through fir groves evermore . . .

These pieces are by Shelley, Byron, Keats, Tupper, Wordsworth and Coleridge, in that order: but what reader could off-hand ascribe them correctly? Who would not credit the first to Keats, the second to Wordsworth and stumble over the last four?

The extraordinary sameness in the less inspired work of poets with such entirely different temperaments comes from the limitations imposed on them by 'spiritual elevation' in the academic sense: they wrote authentic poetry only when off their guard. The sameness was accentuated by the nationalistic element: each poet wrote, first, as an Englishman bound by the use of his language to a policy of increasing the national heritage of song, not of developing a strictly personal idiom. He also wrote as a member of the governing class. One of the last surviving rewards of the poet as a privileged member of the community was that, whatever his birth, by writing acceptable poetry he became a gentleman; and this tradition obtained even in the narrowly aristocratic eighteenth century. Stephen Duck, the 'Thresher Poet,' whose works pleased George II's Queen, was officially confirmed in his gentility by being presented with a country benefice. Burns was, for a while at least, given the freedom of smart Edinburgh society and encouraged to write familiar epistles to members of the aristocracy.

Poetical ideas and poetical technique have always been class-institutions, and poets born from the labouring or shop-keeping classes have with very few exceptions tried to elevate themselves by borrowing ideas and techniques to the enjoyment of which they were not born. Even revolutionary ideas are, by a paradox, upper-class ideas, a rebound from excesses of decorum. Burns' romantic sympathy with the French Revolution in its earlier stages could be read as a sign of natural good breeding, the gentlemanly radicalism of the literary *jeunesse*; the social gap between the crofters and the gentry was, moreover, not so wide in Scotland as in England, and he soon learned the trick of drawing-room writing. Keats, not being, like Burns or Clare, an obvious example of peasant genius, or an aristocrat like Shelley, always had difficulty in discovering his temperamental biases. The son of a tradesman, he could not afford to be politically so radical as those inferior or superior to him in class, though he went with Leigh Hunt as far as he dared. Blake, another tradesman's son, was also a radical: one of the few Englishmen who dared walk about London wearing a cap of Liberty. But Blake is the rare instance of a poet who could afford not to learn a class-technique: he was on intimate terms with the angels and wrote like an angel rather than like a gentleman. His radicalism was part of his personal religion, not, like Wordsworth's early radicalism, a philosophical affectation. If a man has complete identity with his convictions, then he is tough about them; if not, his convictions are a sentimental weakness, however strongly he may press them. The Romantic Revivalists were all spoiled as revolutionaries by their gentility. Blake was not one of them; he was a seer and despised the gentry in religion, literature and painting equally, which is why there is little or nothing of his mature work that could be confused with that of any contemporary or previous writer. He neither forfeited his personality by submitting to any conventional medium, nor complained of the neglect of his poems by the larger reading public.

The sameness of poetry is increased rather than diminished by the spirit of competition. Once a tacit or written critical agreement is reached as to the historical form proper to the poetry of a period, all the poets of fashion or taste vie with one another in approximating to the perfect period manner. In the eighteenth century such major poets as Pope and Shenstone were only to be distinguished from such minor ones as Ambrose Philips and Richard Graves by being more willing to polish away every vestige of personal eccentricity from their work. The case is made worse by the imitators of the major poets, who try to synthesize their styles in a single period style.

Such monotony springs from the necessity of having socially secure convictions. Poetry is for the poets of the school-room tradition the instrument and illustration of their convictions, whether (to take examples only from the nineteenth century) patriotic as with Campbell, moral as with Tupper, religious as with Aubrey de Vere, philosophical as with Wordsworth and Whitman, genial as with Thomas Moore, artistic as with Poe and the pre-Raphaelites. Even the decadents at the end of the last century were decadent from conviction rather than from wilfulness or inertia. Decadence introduced no variety. It merely substituted self-satisfied pessimism for self-satisfied optimism; and one nationalism for another by moving the seat of English poetry from London to Paris.

When Decadence decayed and was succeeded by the spurious Chestertonian healthiness of the country-rambler, beer-drinker and patriot, and this in turn fell out of fashion about the year 1917, the spirit of scepticism began seriously to invade poetry. It had already found expression in the poems of Mr. Thomas Hardy, pilloried by Mr. Chesterton as 'the village atheist gibbering on the village green,' and of Mr. A. E. Housman; but with certain important conservative reservations in the former, while in the latter it was confused with the shy, or aggressive, anti-religiousness of the eighteen-nineties. The new scepticism is of a different order. The conscious bravado of anti-social or anti-idealistic writing has disappeared. The poet does not feel cut off from his fellow-men by the loss of his more bigoted convictions, since he can assume that an increasingly large part of the educated classes is in private agreement with him. At the time of the Romantic Revival, though the debaucheries of Byron could be sympathetically discounted because of his rank, a confessed atheist like Shelley was not admitted into polite society: it was assumed that every reader at least professed allegiance to Christianity, however lax his private life. But the modernist poet assumes that his readers owe no emotional allegiance to any religious or social or national institution, even that they have emerged from the combative stages of mere 'doubt' or 'naughtiness' and are organizing their lives intellectually; that to them the consistent and humane atheism of Shelley, or the consistent and humane saintliness of Traherne or Vaughan, is preferable to the vulgarly incongruous lives of Byron and Wilde as reflected in their poetry. The school-room may remain the citadel of convictions, and Byron and Wilde may be morally whitewashed because their poetry abounds in old-fashioned convictions; but the modernist poet does not write for the school-room.

Genuine modernists do not make individual style their object: they try to write each poem in the way which fits it best. But the sum of their work has individuality because of their natural variousness; like the individuality of the handwriting of all independent-minded men or women, however clearly and conventionally they form their letters.

True style is the personal handwriting in which poetry is written; if it can be easily imitated or reduced to a formula it should be at once suspect to the poets themselves. Pseudo-modernists pursue individual style because they know they cannot make a name without it; but if they had lived in the eighteenth century their sole object would have been to write correctly, to conform to the manner of the period. In practice, their conforming individualism means an imitation, studiously concealed, of the eccentricities of poems which really are individual.

'Groups' may spring up in the old style around a poet, though the genuine modernist who has by accident become popular or notorious and still retains a sense of personal dignity would shrink from being made a *cher maître*. It is not, as Mr. Philip Guedalla suggests, that there is no English equivalent for *cher maître*, but merely that the modern English poet good enough to be one can treat the literary scene only casually. Much sifting and grading of personalities and groups within a complicated hierarchy does, however, occur where modernism is a professional purpose rather than a personal trait, and the complication is increased by the efforts of professional modernists to make genuine modernists accept a place in the hierarchy. In every modernist group the members are aware who is the dog and who are the fleas; and fleas which are ambitious to become dogs hop energetically from one group to another. Hence the facile synthetic styles which are offered to the general public as large-scale exercises of originality, a contemporary grand manner.

To-day the poetic scene appears to the interested but perplexed reader a chaos of free-lance originality and group originality: a restless multitude of types, imitation of types, antitheses and syntheses of types. The cult of variety, the most characteristic general feature of contemporary poetry, not only encourages poets themselves to free experiment but encourages the non-poets to literary competition. In periods where a single poetical type prevailed non-poets found it easier to write verse than they do now, yet more non-poets are writing to-day than ever before. A competitive hunt for originality drives them to seek inspiration in foreign literatures: in eighteenth-century French, in seventeenth-century Spanish, in Demotic Greek, in mediaeval Latin, in Chinese or Javanese or Aztec; in various low dialects— Bowery, Whitechapel, journalese; in the works of ancient religious writers, particularly the Early Fathers and the Buddhist saints. Even when one has withdrawn from critical consideration all backward verse directly imitative of Keats or Tennyson or Wilde or Swinburne or Francis Thompson or Whitman, and all ordinary adolescent verse of distinguishable male and female varieties, there still remains an enormous mass of miscellaneous verse to be reviewed. Literary criticism, reared for centuries in the faith of the technical and philosophical consistency of poetry, cannot cope with such a task; as it could a hundred years ago, when the possible varieties of poetical composition could be counted on the fingers and toes and the most daring were either imitators of Chaucer, Ossian or Spenser, or affectations of country simplicity. It is impossible now for the most industrious critic to be sure who is the inventor of any particular poetical mannerism, and who is the copyist, or to what extent striking resemblances between poems by different authors are attributable to unconscious contemporary sympathy.

When modernist poetry, or what not so long ago passed for modernist poetry, can reach the stage where the following piece by Mr. Ezra Pound:

PAPYRUS
Spring . . . .
Too long . . .
Gongula . . . . .

is seriously offered as a poem, there is some justification for the plain reader and orthodox critic who shrinks from anything that may be labelled 'modernist' either in terms of condemnation or approbation. Who or what is Gongula? Is it the name of a person? Of a town? Of a musical instrument? Or is it the obsolete botanical word meaning 'spores'? Or is it a mistake for Gongora, the Spanish poet from whose name the word 'gongorism' is formed, meaning 'an affected elegance of style'? And why 'Papyrus'? Is the poem a fragment from a real papyrus? Or from an imaginary one? Or are these Mr. Pound's thoughts about either a real or imaginary fragment? Or about Spring seeming too long because of the gongula of the papyrus-reeds? Rather than answer any of these questions and be driven to the shamefaced bluff of making much out of little, the reader retires to safer ground. Better, he thinks, that ten authentic poets should be left for posterity to discover than that one charlatan should be allowed to steal into the Temple of Fame.

If a poet is to achieve even the smallest reputation to-day his work must suggest a style capable of being exploited by a group; or he must either be a brilliant group-member or quick-change parasite. Otherwise he is likely to be lost to the literary news-sheets of every critical colour and not even to occur as a subject of the plain reader's suspicion and the critic's caution: to exist, in fact, only unto himself. But this, should the poet appreciate the joys of privacy, is not so bad a fate as it may sound. Never, indeed, has it been possible for a poet to remain unknown with so little discredit and dishonour as at present. The prima donna reputation acquired by Mr. Humbert Wolfe with work of the most crudely histrionic and imitative brilliance (his original comma-effects in *Kensington Gardens* began it) should not only comfort the true poet but drive him further into decent obscurity.

IX

THE HUMOROUS ELEMENT

The motto to Mr. Hemingway's modernist novel *The Sun Also Rises* is: ' "You are all a lost generation"—Gertrude Stein, in conversation.' The title is taken from the passage in *Ecclesiastes* which contains the better-known text: 'Vanity of vanities, saith the Preacher, vanity of vanities; all is vanity.' This is also the conclusion of most modernist poets, though not a counsel of altogether unrelieved gloom. Miss Sitwell's chief message, if she may be said to have one, is the endless, minute triviality of adult life. Mr. Eliot's *The Waste Land* is prefixed by a quotation from Petronius: how the Cumaean Sibyl, when asked by the acolytes what her wishes were, replied (exhausted by her prophetic visions): 'I wish to die.' But in general, although the total effect of modernist poetry on the reader may be gloomy because it does not shine with the convictions and grandeurs that once made poetry a beacon of seldom-failing optimism, the vanity of the world seen without other-worldly compensation forces a wry cheerfulness on the poet.

The temper of this generation, however, is not to be confused with the temper of two previous lost generations, that of Byron and that of Wilde. The first was gloomy because gloom gave a tone of romantic defeat to fanciful ideals which could not be seriously maintained; the next was gloomy because gloom gave a tone of romantic defeat to a fanciful want of ideals. The poet of the 'nineties could get over his gloominess either by becoming successful or turning devoutly Catholic; or else he could blow out his brains. The present lost generation does not feel its lack of ideals as sinfulness, but rather as sophistication. It does not love itself, but neither does it hate itself. It does not think much of life, but neither does it think much of death. It is a cynically common-sense generation which would not, for example, think of dying for the freedom of a small enslaved nation or for literary fame. The gloom which it seems to cast does not come from self-pity or emotional prostration; but from the intellectuality of its humour.

Because it is a common-sense generation, it must claim to be fully experienced. Because it emphasizes the wit in common sense, and because wit is cynical, it is a cynical generation; yet not a sentimental generation, because of its common sense; nor a pessimistic generation, because pessimism is sentimental. It has tried everything and, like Ecclesiastes, found it vanity. Yet it has reached a degree of sophistication a stage beyond that of Thomas Hardy or Anatole France. It is not interested in denouncing. It is no longer grieved by the failure of Heaven to answer prayer, or by the hypocrisy of the 'unco guid,' or by the inconstancy of lovers and fortune. It announces a drastic revision of traditional values; but without the violence characteristic of writers who have reached this stage by more emotional paths. It is a generation opposed to stress; and to go on living is always easier than to die. Being above all things interested in self-preservation, it is an intensely serious generation, whose wilful cheerfulness is often mistaken for drunken frivolity: a generation which the War surprised at its most impressionable stage and taught the necessity for scepticism about the stability of all human relationships, of all national and religious institutions, of all existing moral codes, of all sentimental formulas for future harmony. From the War it also learned a scale of emotional excitement and depression with which no subsequent variations can compete; yet the experience was too nervously destructive to be wished for again. The disillusion of the War has been completed by the Peace, by the continuation of the old régime patched up with political Fascism, by the same atmosphere of suspense which prevailed from 1911 to the outbreak of nationalistic war and is now again gathering around further nationalistic and civil wars.

The other set of experiences, besides the War, which have most impressed this generation are experiences of knowledge. It has witnessed not only a variegation but a fresh synthesis of intellectual interests. As forced to write in the limelight of modernism it has a professional selfconsciousness and an over-developed historical sense.

It must not only revise traditional values; it must appreciate new ones. It is mentally uncomfortable—shrewd, nervous, suspicious of itself; it rejects philosophy and religion in the old droning sense, but would welcome an intellectual system—a permanently accessible mental cocktail—which would be a stiff, sane, steadying combination of both. What aggravates this nervousness, this superior sort of stage fright, to the modernist poet, is that in the new synthesis of values—even in the system which he is attempting to realize for himself—the historically minded modernist poet is uncertain whether there is any excuse at all for the existence of poets. He brazens out the dilemma by making cruel jokes at his own expense—jokes which he expects no one to see or to laugh at if seen.

The modernist poet, then, as a type (though a type can contradict itself in its individuals) may be said to possess a peculiar and recognizable intellectual slant. He does not commit himself wholeheartedly to any obvious conviction. He does not, on the other hand, waste himself in attacking the convictions of others. Since any choice of faith, action or habit is held to belong to the historically less developed processes of reasoning, the making of a choice seems a vulgarism. It is a point of intellectual pride with him to refrain from utilitarian choices: his choices are in the more serious realm of speculation. His aversion to indulging in feelings merely because they are temporarily pleasant, or because they are those expected of him as a poet, or because they best show off his talents, or because they are the obvious feelings to have—amounts to a severe asceticism. But, as he is aware, asceticism is an easily parodied position; and because he is a hard-headed, common-sense creature, he is also aware that asceticism is in practice impossible. Thus he is able to do what no generation of poets before him has been able to do: to make fun of himself when he is at his most serious.

Self-mockery is the feature of modernist poetry most likely to puzzle the reader or the critic who has not properly appraised its intellectual slant. A poem which is a joke at the poet's expense cannot meet with any sympathy in the reader unless he sees it as also in some respects a joke against himself; and he cannot do this unless he is at least capable of discovering in the poem clues to the poet's wit and its direction. The expected failure of wit in the reader removes from the poet that measure of *address* which an audience imposes. Relieved of the obligations of address, the modernist poet often leaps from formal drollery to unrestrained burlesque. The closing lines of a poem, *Winter Remembered*, by Mr. Ransom illustrate that drollery which is the

poet's rôle when he troubles to keep within reach of his audience's
sentiment:

> Dear Love, these fingers that had known your touch,
> And tied our separate forces first together,
> Were ten poor idiot fingers not worth much,
> Ten frozen parsnips hanging in the weather.

Mr. Ransom, though a modernist in his self-disrespect, leans rather
towards the sentimental tradition of irony. He insists upon the wit
of his reader; he makes an appeal which the reader cannot possibly
overlook. If the reader is slow in discovering the clues to this drollery,
the poet forces it on him in a way that cannot be mistaken, even to the
point of over-stepping the disrespect he wishes to do himself. It is as
if the pantomime clown had made a deep but delicate joke against
himself which the audience missed. Intent on getting them to appreciate
his mood, he slaps himself hard and makes a long face. The audience
now sees the joke and laughs. But he was obliged to brutalize his joke
in order to soften the audience towards him.

In the main, however, the modernist clown, aware of a lack of
sympathy in his audience, turns his back on it and performs his antics
without benefit of applause. We therefore find in modernist poetry many
examples of *pure* burlesque, not in the pantomime tradition, but in
the tearless, heartless tradition of the early Italian comedy. Miss Sitwell
belongs to this tradition, as much as any modernist poet.

> The wind's bastinado
> Whipt on the calico
> Skin of the Macaroon
> And the black Picaroon
> Beneath the galloon
> Of the midnight sky.
> Came the great Soldan
> In his sedan
> Floating his fan,—
> Saw what the sly
> Shadow's cocoon
> In the barracoon
> Held. Out they fly.
> 'This melon,
> Sir Mammon,
> Comes out of Babylon:
> Buy for a patacoon—
> Sir, you must buy!'

So far, so good. The poem is a fantasia, a sort of mime-show, and the antic figures are expressed by obsolete romance words like Macaroon (a clown), Picaroon (a rogue), galloon (rich embroidery), barracoon (convict-prison), patacoon (Spanish dollar). The clown and rogue come out from the shadow of the prison dressed in their white calico pierrot costumes—see the cover of Mr. Sacheverell Sitwell's *Thirteenth Caesar*—and offer a fruit to the great Soldan: as two old-style poets might offer their works to the great Public.

> Said il Magnifico
> Pulling a fico,—
> With a stoccado
> And a gambado
> Making a wry
> Face: 'This corraceous
> Round orchidaceous
> Laceous porraceous
> Fruit is a lie!
> It is my friend King Pharaoh's head
> That nodding blew out of the Pyramid . . .'

In effect, the Soldan, pulling a fico (snapping his fingers) with a stoccado (a lunge as in fencing) and a gambado (gambol) said—but this time Miss Sitwell, who has been going very fast, has left her audience far behind: they have either deserted her, or are a dozen lines behind, fumbling with the dictionary. So at this point she whips up her piebald pony and goes faster than she knows herself. Even the dictionary sense, at this speed, falls to pieces and the words themselves turn into clowns. It no longer matters that 'orchidaceous' means 'belonging to the orchid family,' or that 'porraceous' means 'belonging to the leek family,' or that (unless Miss Sitwell has a bigger dictionary than ours) 'laceous' and 'corraceous' are mere nonsense-words. By this time nothing matters and nothing makes sense, not even what the great Soldan says. Indeed the boisterous collapse is so sudden and so complete that 'laceous' and 'corraceous' may be deliberate misspellings that indicate the state of merry disintegration which the poem has reached.

Limitations in the reader's sense of humour have thus the effect of making the modernist poem more and more difficult. The poet tells himself that if the reading public is in any case bound to be a limited one, he may as well take advantage of its isolation by using references and associations which are as far out of the ordinary critic's reach as

the modernist sense of humour is. When, for example, Edith and
Sacheverell Sitwell both introduce a Captain Fracasse into their poems
as a symbol of the comic-opera sword-and-cape hero, they are going
too far for the average English reader and critic who has never heard
of Gautier's romance or of Catulle Mendes' comic-opera drawn from
it, yet would at once recognize a character corresponding to Fracasse
in English literature. Fracasse is used because French comic-opera
heroes have an eccentric quality not quite to be matched in the English
Classics; but he would certainly not have been used if a freer commerce
in humour existed between the reader and the poet. Again, when Miss
Sitwell writes of:

> ... winding
> Roads whose dust seems gilded binding

> Made for 'Paul et Virginie'—
> (so flimsy-tough those roads are), see

> The panniered donkey pass ...

the reference is to a pastoral by Bernardin de Saint-Pierre, an old-
fashioned French nursery-classic. It is a sentimental record of true
love in the picturesquely savage Isle of Mauritius, a mixed flimsiness
and toughness of story with which we may imagine the format of
Miss Sitwell's school-room copy to have been analogous—heavy gilt
binding and flimsy French paper. This is little more than a family joke,
certainly not a popular one.

A poem by Mr. Eliot may be quoted in full to show how limited the
humorous appeal of modernist verse may become. The extreme particu-
larity of some of the references may be called the teasing element of
modernist wit. We do not pretend to see all the jokes in Mr. Eliot's
poem; literary specialists will be able to follow the scent farther than
we have done, and of course Mr. Eliot himself could, if pressed, make
everything clear:

BURBANK WITH A BAEDEKER:
BLEISTEIN WITH A CIGAR

Tra-la-la-la-la-la-laire—nil nisi divinum stabile est; caetera fumus—the
gondola stopped, the old palace was there, how charming its grey and pink
—goats and monkeys, with such hair too!—so the countess passed on until
she came through the little park, where Niobe presented her with a cabinet,
and so departed.

Burbank crossed a little bridge
Descending at a small hotel;
Princess Volupine arrived,
They were together, and he fell.

Defunctive music under sea
Passed seaward with the passing bell
Slowly: the God Hercules
Had left him, that had loved him well.

The horses, under the axle-tree
Beat up the dawn from Istria
With even feet. Her shuttered barge
Burned on the water all the day.

This is modern Venice visited by two American tourists, one, who
may or may not be called Burbank after Luther Burbank the horticul-
turist famous for his 'crossings' of fruits and plants, the other a
caricature Jew. The Latin quotation means: 'Nothing is lasting unless
it is divine: the rest is smoke.' The remainder of the introduction, with
the exception of 'with such hair too!' mischievously borrowed from
Browning and a little snippet from Henry James, may be by anyone,
even by Mr. Eliot himself: we do not know.

The old palace is one of the many show-places on the Grand Canal:
possibly the one where Lord Byron's intrigue with the Countess
Guiccoli took place. The goats and monkeys may be relics of the zoo
which Lord Byron kept there; but they may also symbolize lechery.
Not only are monkeys permanent features of Venetian palaces, but they
play a symbolic part in *The Merchant of Venice*; and *The Merchant of
Venice* is a suppressed *motif* in the poem. Jessica, it will be remembered,
turned her back on Jewry, took up with Christians and at once bought
a pet monkey. The little parks are features of some of these Venetian
palaces. Niobe is the Greek symbol of sorrow: her children were slain
as a punishment for her pride in them. The cabinet is a memorial of
Niobe's sympathy with Venice, whose pride has also been brought low.
Princess Volupine evidently represents the degenerate aristocratic
romanticism of Venice: she has an intrigue with Burbank, who stands
for the sentimental element in modern civilization—a sort of sym-
bolical 'decent chap.' 'Defunctive music' comes from Shakespeare's
The Phoenix and the Turtle. The last line of the first stanza is possibly
also a quotation, like the last two of the second and the first two of the

third, but here again we leave pedigrees to more reference-proud critics than ourselves. Burbank's power leaves him. (Hercules is the Latin god of strength, and also the guardian of money.)

The third stanza marks an increase from the second in the mock-grandeur of the writing: it almost threatens to become serious. This in turn demands the sudden bathetic drop of the fourth stanza. The manner of the third stanza accounts for the artificiality of the symbols used: their grandiosity and the obscurity of their source throw a cloud over their precise significance. The horses under the axle-tree may be the horses of the sun under the axle-tree of heaven; but they may also suggest the little heraldic horses fixed at the side of every Venetian gondola, which may be said to be under the axle-tree of the gondola, i.e. the oar. So this may be a conceit which amounts to calling the sun a sky-gondola rather than a chariot. Or it may not. Istria lies east from Venice on the road to Vienna. Princess Volupine's shuttered barge burns on the water all day, a sign that she is now closeted with someone else. There is an echo here from *Antony and Cleopatra*:

> The barge she sat in, like a burnished throne,
> Burned on the water . . .

At this point the other member of the cast enters the poem: Bleistein the Jew. Burbank walks through Venice with a Baedeker, that is to say with a melancholy respect for the past; Bleistein, on the contrary, walks through Venice with a cigar, a symbol of vulgar and ignorant self-enjoyment. The name Bleistein is a caricature of the common Goldstein or 'Goldstone': it means 'Leadstone.'

> But this or such was Bleistein's way:
>   A saggy bending of the knees
> And elbows, with the palms turned out,
>   Chicago Semite Viennese.

> A lustreless protrusive eye
>   Stares from the protozoic slime
> At a perspective of Canaletto.
>   The smoky candle end of time

> Declines. On the Rialto once.
>   The rats are underneath the piles.
> The jew is underneath the lot.
>   Money in furs. The boatman smiles,

Burbank sees the strength and wealth of Venice departed, the remnants of her glory enjoyed by an upstart Chicago Jew who probably started life as a furrier's apprentice in Leopoldstadt, the Jewish quarter of Vienna. Canaletto was an eighteenth-century painter whose aristocratic pictures of Venice lie at a long remove from Bleistein's world —though Bleistein may one day carry Venice to the United States by presenting the Chicago Art Institute with an authenticated Canaletto in evidence of his good citizenship. The smoky candle end recalls the Latin motto: 'The rest is smoke.' Burbank sorrowfully pictures the Rialto of other days. The rats are underneath the piles now, and the Jew (the eternal Shylock) is the rat of rats. The jew (Jew is written with a small initial letter like rat) is a rat because he has made money and because for some reason Jewish wealth, as opposed to Gentile wealth, has a mystical connexion with the decline of Venice. This may not be Burbank's private opinion, or even Mr. Eliot's. It at any rate expresses for Burbank and Mr. Eliot the way Venice at present feels, or should feel, about the modern Jew strutting through her streets. 'Money in furs' refers not only to the fact that the fur trade is largely in Jewish hands and that this is how Bleistein made his money, but also to some proverbial witticism, perhaps about the ability of a Jew to make money even out of rats' skins, out of the very instruments of decay.

The smiling boatman, who has for centuries seen everything, stands as an ironic fate between Bleistein and Princess Volupine.

> Princess Volupine extends
>   A meagre, blue-nailed, phthisic hand
> To climb the waterstair. Lights, lights,
>   She entertains Sir Ferdinand

> Klein. Who clipped the lion's wings
>   And flea'd his rump and pared his claws?
> Thought Burbank, meditating on
>   Time's ruins, and the seven laws.

Venice, in the person of Princess Volupine (is this another French comic-opera character? Or a coined word compounded of the Latin for 'pleasure,' *voluptas*, and the name of a play of Ben Jonson's, *Volpone, the Fox*? Or a character from one of the obscurer dramatists of the *Mermaid Series*? We do not pretend to know), has now sunk so low that, no longer content with Byronic intrigues, she actually admits the Jew (in the person of Sir Ferdinand Klein, a British financier) to her embraces. Sir Ferdinand's name is an epitome of contempt and pathetic comedy: the Jew, having made money, has similarly conquered and corrupted English society; his noble Christian name is purloined from the very country which most persecuted him (now also in decay); his family name means 'little' and is, appropriately enough, from the German—there is no sentimental condolence with the Germans because, presumably, they do not suffer from this peculiarly Mediterranean type of decay. Thus, in the person of Sir Ferdinand Klein, Bleistein succeeds where Burbank fails; the implication being that the Jew is not an individual but an eternal symbol, each Jew being the entire race. 'Lights, lights!' is a Shakespearianism further evoking *The Merchant of Venice* atmosphere, though it is the cry which usually goes up just before the *dénouement* of a tragedy, not a comedy. The lion is the winged lion of St. Mark, the patron saint of Venice; but also, in a secondary sense, the British lion whose wings have been clipped by the Jew. What the seven laws are in the Venetian context will probably be found in Baedeker, or in the Classical Dictionary, or in *The Merchant of Venice* along with rats, the Rialto, cabinets and pet monkeys.

This is not, of course, popular writing. It is aristocratic writing, and its jokes are exclusive; but only exclusive if the reader has neither capacity nor interest for sharing in them: the Baedeker is common to all men, so are the Classical Dictionary and La Rousse and the plays of Shakespeare. The jokes are against modern civilization, against money, against classicism, against romanticism, against Mr. Eliot himself as a tourist in Venice with a Baedeker. One of the few privileges of the comedian is to have prejudices for which he cannot be held morally accountable; and the modernist poet, taking full advantage of this privilege, indulges his caprices without feeling obliged to render a rationalistic report on them. The anti-Jewish prejudice, for instance, occurs frequently in modernist poetry; and the anti-American prejudice also. It is part of the comedy that a Jew or an American may equally express these prejudices.

Although written in a mood of intellectual severity, modernist poetry retains the clown's privilege of having irrational prejudices in favour of a few things as well as against a few things. It assumes, indeed, the humorous championship of things which poets of the past have either hated, neglected or mishandled. Towards poetical items which have been worn out by spiritual elevation, such as motherhood, childhood, nature, national pride, the soul, fame, freedom and perfection, it maintains a policy of disinterested neutrality; not because of a prejudice against motherhood, nature, etc., but because of a feeling that they have had their day and that it is now the turn of other things, such as obscenity, lodging-house life, pedantry, vulgarity, frivolousness, failure, drunkenness, and so on, to be put into the scales. This is due to a desire for emotional equilibrium, not for sensationalism.

The only way in which traditional poets could treat drink, for example, was either with sentimental gaiety, as in Shakespeare's:

> Let the canakin clink,
> And let the canakin clink!
> A soldier's a man
> And life's but a span,
> So let the canakin clink!

or with irony, as in Gay's song from *The Mohocks*:

> Come fill up the glass!
> Round, round, let it pass,
> Till our reason be lost in our wine:
> Leave conscience's rules
> To women and fools,
> *This* only can make us divine.

or with loathing for its fatal fascination as in Lefanu's *Drunkard's Address to a Bottle of Whiskey*:

> Oh terrible darling,
> How have you sought me,
> Enchanted, and caught me,
> See, now, where you've brought me
> To sleep by the road-side, and dress out in rags.

Drunkenness, as a poetical subject, was either comic or disgusting. Comic, as in George Colman's *Toby Tosspot*: when the drunken man on his way home at midnight sees a notice on a street-door, 'Please Ring the Bell,' and does so vigorously out of sheer friendliness; disgusting, as in Mr. Masefield's *Everlasting Mercy*:

> 'Look on him there,' she says, 'look on him
> And smell the stinking gin upon him,
> The lowest sot, the drunk'nest liar,
> The dirtiest dog in all the shire.'

The modernist poet does not recognize 'poetical' subjects, since all subjects are to him commonplaces. So that when the fact of drunkenness gets into his poetry, he does not explain how he feels about drunkards, but callously and precisely explains what drunkenness is. If the poem is a 'comic' poem, it is not so because he thinks drunkenness a comic subject but because, as a shrewd mental condition, it sharpens his wit. So Mr. Cummings:

> death is more than
> certain a hundred these
> sounds crowds odours it
> is in a hurry
> beyond that any this
> taxi smile or angle we do
>
> not sell and buy
> things so necessary as
> is death and unlike shirts
> neckties trousers
> we cannot wear it out
>
> no sir which is why
> granted who discovered
> America ether the movies
> may claim general importance
>
> to me to you nothing is
> what particularly
> matters hence in a
>
> little sunlight and less
> moonlight ourselves against the worms
>
> hate laugh shimmy

The wit of drunkenness can easily be deciphered from this taxi-and-gin shorthand. Drunkenness is a mental dare-devilry; one of the few conditions, indeed, in which it is not disgraceful to be sentimental, because one feels deadly serious. All Mr. Cummings' most serious poems are drunken poems; even his love poems. He does not say here: 'Death is more than certain, fellow drunkards. Out of every hundred people born, a hundred die,' and proceed, as in *Down Among the Dead Men*:

> Then come, let us drink it while we have breath,
> For there's no drinking after death!

He clips his grammar, increases his speed, gets on with the argument, and does not stop until he has reached the conclusion that all there is left to do under the circumstances is to 'hate, laugh, shimmy'—and speculate. In drunkenness, he declares, one's mind is not less clear, but clearer than usual. It holds more, it thinks faster, it sees and understands everything; it is even like the taxi which, we gather, is assisting the poetic argument. Death triumphs, it is not left behind by the taxi (no, sir!) together with the shops, the crowds and our rake's fast thoughts. Nothing matters, therefore (and here our rake turns, perhaps, to the other occupant of the taxi) except a little bragging sunshine to show the worms we don't care and to hate, laugh and shimmy. And so Death does not triumph. This is how an old comic subject reads in nineteen twenty-six.

The intellectual slant of the modernist poet involves him in a bright game of spite against the middle-classes responsible for the front of solemn good-breeding and dullness which poetry acquired in the last century. He combines upper-class impeccability and lower-class roughneckedness into a disdainful recklessness on the road. The stalest joke of comic song (but not of poetry) is the mother-in-law. Miss Sitwell's *Fantasia for Mouth Organ* has dashingly taken the mother-in-law joke and sent it round the world to India, the North Pole and South Pole, the land of the redskins, the land of the humming-birds and the equatorial isles where the savages sank upon one knee—

> For when they saw
> My mother-in-law
> They decided not to tackle
> Me!
> She is tough as the armorian
> Leather that the saurian
> Sun spreads over the
> Sea—
> So she saved my life
> Did the mother of my wife
> Who is more than a mother to
> Me!

The humorous element in poetry, it is seen, has undergone a complete reversal and become part of the mechanism of fine writing;

Miss Sitwell's mother-in-law poem, for instance, is not offered as a comic poem. Even what appears to be an obvious comic satire of Victorianism in many of her poems is, in reality, a spiteful championship of it against the bourgeois satirist. The humorous element here lies in the spice which a much abused institution acquires when restored by impudent artifice to connoisseur sentiment. A partiality for Victorianism is one of the disingenuously irrational prejudices in which the three Sitwells indulge. The Queen becomes a robustious and slangy old lady telling Queen Venus just where to get off:

> 'For the minx,'
>   Said she,
>   'And she drinks,
>   You can see,
> Are hot as any hottentot and not the goods for me!'

Demodé Victorian fashions evoke literary enthusiasm:

> Rose castles
> Those bustles
> Beneath parasols seen!
> Flat blondine pearls
> Rondine curls
> Seem.

Even Victorian rococo architecture and interior decoration become semi-humorously aetherialized: Balmoral's towers, its pitch-pine floors and special tartan, the Crystal Palace, the Albert Memorial and the horse-hair settees of Buckingham Palace.

On the other hand this serious poem of Miss Marianne Moore's:

> Openly, yes
> with the naturalness
>   of the hippopotamus or the alligator
>   when it climbs out on the bank to experience the
>
> Sun, I do these
> things which I do, which please
>   no one but myself. Now I breathe and now I am sub-
>   merged; the blemishes stand up and shout when the object
>
> in view was a
> renaissance; shall I say
>   the contrary? the sediment of the river which
>   encrusts my joints, makes me very gray but I am used . . .

or the many various pieces of Mr. Cummings written in comic vernacular, bring the wheel round full circle to the professionally comic vein of traditional poetry. A poem by J. W. Morris, a writer of the American 'sixties, should be brought face to face with Miss Moore's poem to mark the reversal which serious and comic elements have undergone in poetry. It is called *Collusion between a Alegaiter and a Water-Snaik.* The scene is 'Guatimaly.' It should be read as a parody of 'unpoetical' poetry, even perhaps as a prophetic parody.

> Evidently a good chance for a water snaik
> Of the large specie, which soon appeared
> Into the horison, near the bank where repos'd
> Calmly in slepe the Alegaiter before spoken of
> About 60 feet was his length (not the 'gaiter)
> And he was aperiently a well-proportioned snaik.
>
> When he was all ashore he glared upon
> The island with approval but was soon
> 'Astonished with the view and lost to wonder'
> (from Watts)
> (For jest then he began to see the Alegaiter)
> Being a natural enemy of his'n he worked hisself
> Into a fury, also a ni position.
> Before the Alegaiter well could ope
> His eye (in other words perceive his danger)
> The Snaik had enveloped his body just 19
> Times with 'foalds voluminous and vast'
> (from Milton)
> ... But soon by grate force the tail was bit complete-
> Ly off ...

The mental feats required of the poet who wishes to reconcile poetry with modernism and modernism with poetry gives him an exaggerated nimbleness. Much of his superfluous energy is consumed in an ostentatious display—sometimes childish but in general harmless—of the Protean powers of poetry. The badge of the modernist poet might well be the one which the Stanley family gave to the Isle of Man— three legs conjoined and the motto 'Wherever you throw it, it will stand.' Though by his technical flexibility he may seem to be continually standing on his head, by his common sense he inclines to be all legs; and however extreme the comedy—however wilful his caprices, however grotesque the contrasts between innocence and

obscenity or brutality and preciousness—it is a point of intellectual
vanity with him to laugh last, to be found on his feet when the per-
formance is over. He completes, and in a sense contradicts, his clown-
ishness by revealing that even clownishness is a joke: that it is a joke
to be writing poetry, a greater joke to be writing modernist poetry.
By this token he belongs to the most serious generation of poets which
has ever written; with the final self-protective corollary, of course,
that it is also a joke to be serious.

Sometimes, however, the modernist poet in his grotesque panto-
mime is very nearly tempted, out of virtuosity, to leave himself stand-
ing on his head. The following is a passage from *Causerie*, a poem by
Mr. Allen Tate. It is a rambling pillow-cogitation on the vulgarization
and mechanization of the language of Homer, Catullus, Shakespeare
and Rousseau. The poem is historically interesting as a psychological
synthesis of the manners of his contemporaries, among them Messrs.
Eliot, Cummings, Ransom, Miss Moore:

> . . . Hermes decorates
> A cornice on the Third National Bank. Vocabulary
> Becomes confusion, decoration a blight; the Parthenon
> In Tennessee stucco, art for the sake of death. Now
> (the bedpost receding in stillness) you brush your teeth
> 'Hitting on all thirty-two'; scholarship pares
> The nails of Catullus, sniffs his sheets, restores
> His 'passionate underwear'; morality disciplines the other
> Person; snakes speak the idiom of Rousseau; Prospero
> Serves Humanity in steam-heated universities, three
> Thousand dollars a year;—for simplicity is obscene.
> Sunlight topples indignant from the hill.
> In every railway station everywhere, every lover
> Waits for his train. He cannot hear. The smoke
> Thickens. Ticket in hand he pumps his body
> Toward lower six, for one more terse ineffable trip,
> His very eyeballs fixed in disarticulation. The berth
> Is clean; no elephants, vultures, mice, or spiders
> Distract him from nonentity; for his metaphors are dead.
> *Notescatque magis mortuus atque magis,*
> *Nec tenuem texens sublimis aranea telam . . .*

The motto to the poem is from an American newspaper:

> . . . party on the stage of the Earl Carrol Theatre on February 23. At this
> party Joyce Hawley, a chorus-girl, bathed in the nude in a bathtub filled
> with alleged wine.

The comic technique is devoted to a controversial contrast between Imperial America and Imperial Rome, intended to prove that the mind, in being democratized, has grown swollen, complicated, vulgar and moribund. The poet's clownishness consists in swift and showy acrobatic turns, from present-day vulgar sophistication back to the comparative simplicity of classical manners, and from classical decorum forward again to twentieth-century vocabularistic vulgarity. A prejudice in favour of classical phrasing is the special privilege in which Mr. Tate indulges himself. The Latin verse from Catullus means: 'And may he when dead grow more and more famous, nor may the spider spinning its fine thread from above . . . [make a web upon the forgotten name of Allius].' The quotation, admittedly somewhat forced in its application, is from an elegy on the death of Allius, a friend who had helped Catullus in his intrigues by providing him and his Lesbia with a rendezvous at the house of his own mistress: for which Catullus thanks him with frankness and simplicity. The vultures also occur in this poem of Catullus': and 'hitting on all thirty-two'—an advertisement for a toothpaste—is probably an ironic comment in the style of Catullus' ironic comment on the fine teeth of his friend Egnatius. Prospero is the symbol of learning, not yet become humanitarian and democratic, commercialized and vulgar. The element of humour in this poem is not entirely sincere because the prejudice is somewhat too dogmatic: the poet fails to identify himself equally with both subjects of the contrast. Unwilling to be the complete clown he has very nearly left himself standing on his head.

The bourgeois character of the popular belief in human progress does indeed inspire in most modernist writers a temperamental antagonism to old-style democratic civilization; not so much out of militant opposition to bourgeois liberalism as out of peripatetic avoidance of a crowded thoroughfare. So the only flaw in the modernist poet's humour, the only turn missing in his clownish repertoire, is the failure to include the bourgeois in his intellectual scale. Indeed, James Joyce has suggested that Shakespeare's greatness lay in his power to play the bourgeois impersonally, yet as a bourgeois, neither keeping a bourgeois dummy to kick nor yet slapping his own face:

And the sense of property, Stephen said. He drew Shylock out of his own long pocket. The son of a maltjobber and moneylender he was himself a cornjobber and moneylender with ten tods of corn hoarded in the famine riots . . . He sued a fellow-player for the price of a few bags of malt and exacted his pound of flesh in interest for every money lent. How else could Aubrey's ostler and callboy get rich quick?

Death, a common bourgeois conviction, is the only progressive liberal subject which the modernist poet sometimes treats without prejudice. One contemporary poet[1] actually writes of it:

> This I admit, death is terrible to me,
> To no man more so naturally,
> And I have disenthralled my natural terror
> Of every comfortable philosopher
> Or tall doctor of Divinity:
> Death stands again in his true rank and order.

But even with Death the modernist poet is seldom at his clownish best, because he is too well aware of its bourgeois connotations: it is very difficult, considering its literary and religious history, not to treat it as a dead-earnest joke. A similar difficulty exists with Love, Death's twin in settled bourgeois conviction. In love even the most modernist of poets is bourgeois: he is narrowly idealistic and therefore incapable, except in rare cases, of making it another dead-earnest joke. The clown in this turn is afraid of not landing on his legs. A few ribald high jumps are the most he trusts himself to make.

[COMMENT 1949]

Since Laura Riding and I wrote our *Survey of Modernist Poetry* a new generation of poetry critics has grown up, the newspaper outcry against modernism has died down, and at least two or three of the maligned poets we dared to praise are now established classics. Re-reading these chapters after twenty-three years, I am surprised to find how little of importance could be added to them to-day: how few genuine modernists, as opposed to such virtuosi of the 'thirties as Messrs. W. H. Auden and Dylan Thomas, have appeared since either in Britain or the United States, and how steadfastly, on the whole, the original ones have kept on their poetic courses. Writers of the second War generation seem to have disciplined their poetic consciences but dulled their imaginations in the process, and the most favoured style of the 'forties is a crabbed and rather gloomy synthesis of Yeats, Eliot, Hopkins, Ransom, Wilfred Owen and Laura Riding (at second-hand through her imitators). There have been no lively new literary

---

[1] Servidor.

fashions since 1936, when the outbreak of the Spanish Civil War warned the rest of Western Europe what was on the way and most young poets turned left-wing politicians; nor are any such fashions likely to crop up until café-life in Paris, and life at the elder English universities, regains something of its old happy-go-lucky ease; and until free-lance American writers, who are the shrewdest connoisseurs of fashion but depend on Europe for their inspiration, are able to travel about as freely as in the early 'twenties.

But will this ever happen? Writers of Western Europe are being warned that they must make their choice, before it is too late, between the Communist system and the big-business system. The Communist state demands verse which glorifies national achievement under Marxist theory and shows a complete divorce from European literary models; the big-business state demands verse which soothes the vanity and condones the near-illiteracy of the Hollywood-educated populace. The directors of neither system can afford to show a more merciful regard for individual sensibilities or divagations from orthodox taste than the Fascists whom they combined to overthrow; and both deride the aristocratic ideal to which poetry is traditionally committed. The writing of poems is therefore likely to become a more private affair than ever: the poet who refuses to make the choice between democracy and democracy will find that he has no public left but a few fellow-sufferers from the same anti-social obsession for 'Making.' The point is negatively and nostalgically made in the current issue of *Oxford Poetry*, for the last thirty years a fairly reliable preview of poetical fashions: it consists largely of what would be drawing-room verse but for the drawing-room's elimination from the modern living-quarters.

Checking the passages quoted in this chapter, I find that Mr. E. E. Cummings and Miss Marianne Moore have since rewritten some of the poems in which they occur; and hope that they will not mind my re-printing the original texts.

ANTHOLOGIES
with Laura Riding
(1927)

I

*TRUE ANTHOLOGIES
AND POPULAR ANTHOLOGIES*

In every language and at all periods, poems or fragments of poems are found which cannot be formally classified among the collected works of any known author; nor yet, because of their character and number, be each given the dignity of separate publication. Popular ballads unless forming part of a cycle, epigrams, epitaphs, squibs, stray lyrics and even longer poems which have irretrie·ably lost author and date, may well be united in a volume of non-classifiable verse; and this is always a legitimate use of the anthology.

In the days before cheap printing and dependable libraries the anthology was also justified as a secure portfolio for fugitive pieces by known authors, which might otherwise have perished. When at the beginning of the first century B.C. Meleager compiled his *Crown* of epigrammatic verse as a gift for one Diocles, 'weaving in the lilies of Anyte, the scarlet gopher of Antipater, the narcissus of Melanippides, the aromatic rush of Perseus, the young vine-branch of Simonides,' and so on, he was doing a service both to Diocles and to the poems, few of which would otherwise have survived. Mealeager added epigrams of his own to the *Crown*, but none written by any contemporary except those of his famous neighbour Antipater, and these probably for friendship's sake only: the poems of other contemporaries were left to their own fate. This compilation included none of the longer poems by the authors represented in the anthology, which Diocles might obtain from the copying-schools in manuscripts of formal length.

The *Crown* was an 'anthology,' a collection of flowers, but from remote or not readily accessible gardens and Meleager was a poet exercising an independent taste. Although he informed Diocles at the end of the 'proem' that the garland was not merely a personal gift to him but a common gift to all lovers of poetry, this was a rhetorical flourish rather than an acknowledgment of responsibility to a poetry-consuming public. Diocles circulated the manuscript among his friends:

169

it was copied and much admired. A hundred years later one Philippus added to it and brought it up to date, establishing it as a classic, an authoritative collection of short poems of a certain character; and where Meleager had sensibly used a mere alphabetical arrangement of first lines, Philippus set the bad example of arranging the poems in subject-categories.

By the time of the Antonines the use of anthologies seems to have been widespread; for instance, in the grave of a legionary of that period, in Egypt, a collection of regimental marching songs has been found. In the reign of the Emperor Justinian appeared Agathias, with the sinister surname 'Scholasticus,' the first thoroughgoing example of the popular anthologist. He made a collection of new epigrams modelled on the revised *Crown*, now a required educational text-book; which signalled the end of the anthology as a casual portfolio of poems. Agathias' anthology began with a servile panegyric of the Emperor, followed Philippus' vicious system of classification and included many contemporary exercises in the style of the early poems, even pseudo-dedicatory epigrams to the long-superseded Greek gods. It became a popular reciter for use in the intervals between courses of banquets, and at the same time a *Models for Verse Composition*; for Classical Greek was now a merely literary language and anyone who wrote for an amatory, funerary or convivial occasion looked to the two anthologies for authority.

Yet Philippus and Agathias did not find it necessary to give an appearance of 'solidity' to their collections in the style of the modern English school-anthology by slipping in, say, three or four nicely rounded incidents from the *Iliad* or *Odyssey*, a selected Homeric hymn, a seasonal excerpt from Hesiod, a messenger's speech of Aeschylus', a neat piece of stichomythia from Sophocles, a couple of Euripidean choruses, two or three odes of Pindar's, major poems by Sappho and Alcaeus; perhaps also the 'funeral speech of Pericles' or a purple patch from one of Demosthenes' *Philippics*, with an editorial comment: 'Though written in prose this may also be accounted great poetry.'

There have been portfolio anthologies of English verse from the earliest times: anthologies, for example, of ninth- and tenth-century charms and riddles, and of fourteenth-century carols and lyrics, and the famous 'Percy Folio' of minstrel ballads. All of these, however, were private manuscript collections not multiplied at the copying-schools: for the popular anthology developed only with the bookselling trade. Tottel's *Miscellany* of 1557 has at first sight much to recommend it. Tottel, a bookseller, collected the fugitive verses of court-poets of the elder generation, most of them dead, which might otherwise have been lost: they were poems written in the then new Italianate style, and originally intended only for manuscript circulation in the limited world of the travelled nobility. The *Miscellany* ran into eight editions in thirty years, its subscribers being evidently the country relations and wealthy would-be neighbours of this fashionable poetry-reading society; then it became a classic and a model for such later Elizabethan popular anthologies as *England's Helicon*, first published in 1600, which claimed to be a standard collection of the best contemporary lyrics. The 'Galleries,' 'Gardens,' 'Paradises' and 'Pageants' which followed in rapid succession, containing only poems in the courtly convention, are comparable with Agathias' collection: they provided 'occasional verse' of an amatory and declamatory kind for people with social ambitions whose taste in verse stood in need of education and refinement. A variation from these was the *Paradise of Dainty Devices*, published in 1576 by a printer named Disle, which was ecclesiastical rather than courtly. Love and Honour were replaced by graver and more didactic themes—'Think to Die,' 'Our Pleasures are Vanities,' 'Promise is Debt'; the collection also included a set of pieces appropriate to Holy Days, and a translation from St. Bernard of Morlaix. *Belvedere, or the Garden of the Muses*, printed at the same time and by the same publishers as *England's Helicon*, is, to quote A. H. Bullen, 'a collection of scrappy poetical quotations seldom exceeding a couplet in length,' anticipating the 'Beauties' of the late eighteenth century. But for the most part the Elizabethan anthologist restricted himself to short complete poems of the same general character: no lopped-off branches of the *Faerie Queene* were smuggled in, no speeches from *Tamerlaine*, *Gorboduc*, or the *Faithful Shepherdesse*. Chaucer, Gower, Lydgate and Skelton were not called upon for subsidies, nor was a section of popular balladry added, with an apologetic:

> Rude Rhymers though they be,
>   They boast a native wit:
> And through these gorgeous gardens may
>   Like nimble footmen flit.

The anthologists prided themselves above all on their modernity; a generation after the first publication of Tottel's *Miscellany*, the anthology was fast becoming a fashion parade. The following lines introduce Proctor's *Gorgeous Gallery of Gallant Inventions* (1578):

> See, Gallants, see the Gallery of Delights
> With buildings brave, imbost with various hue,
> With dainties decked devised of various wights,
> Which as time served unto proportion grew.
> By studies toiled with phrases fine they fraught
> This peerless piece filled full of pretty pith.

The monotony of these collections led in the seventeenth century to the publication of various anthologies of *Wit and Drollery* intended for the same reading public, which had, however, acquired through the theatres a literary interest in low life and clowning.

Tottel's *Miscellany* and Meleager's *Crown*, each the first of its line, contained no poems written for an anthology public, since such a public could be created only by a misuse of their anthologies. Meleager's excellence is more than an accident of date; he had no trade connexions and loved poetry for its own sake. Tottel, on the other hand, won his title as the Father of the English Anthology (Dr. Johnson also called him the Maecenas of the times) from an accident of date, not from the purity of his interest in poetry. Indeed, his scandalous rewriting of many of the poems included proves that but for this accident he would have been another worse Agathias. It was his eight editions which stimulated anthology competition and created the eventual confusion between true anthologies, that confine themselves to literary rescue-work, or have the excuse of being private scrap-books, and the all too numerous popular anthologies that turn poetry into a cultural packet-commodity.

In 1777 the Martins of Edinburgh began to print a series of *The Poets*. The London booksellers, alarmed at 'the invasion of what we call our Literary Property,' and probably also influenced by the prevailing encyclopaedic movement, determined, with Dr. Johnson as editor, 'to print an elegant and accurate edition of all the English Poets of reputation from Chaucer to the present time.' Forty of the most select booksellers met together, pooled their copyrights, and the printing soon began: but on a less ambitious plan than first intended, for they decided that English Poetry began with Abraham Cowley. However, in 1810, Chalmers' edition added the earlier poets; and English Literature was at last provided with a poetic *Corpus*. True, it included such tedious pieces as Warner's *Albion's England*,

Drayton's *Polyolbion* and Daniel's *History of the Civil War*, at full length, yet left out Shakespeare's and Marlowe's dramas; it included Ambrose and J. Philips, Watts, Dodsley, Tickell, Mickle, Smith, Jones and Sprat, yet left out Blake, Crashaw, Campion, Traherne, Vaughan, Marvell; it included almost all of Smart—except his *Song to David*. But it was a *Corpus*, the best which the publishers could furnish. The general public looked with pride not unmixed with dismay on this new acquisition. It was an impressive shelf-full, but was one really expected to read it all through? If so, did one have to start at the beginning and go on till one came to the end? Or might one skip? Charitable editors, friends of the booksellers, came to their help with further *Beauties of the Poets* modelled on the guides to previous less complete collections.

Shortly after the publication of Chalmers' edition the great poetry boom began. Not only were the elder poets securely indexed in Chalmers crying out to have their 'Beauties' exhumed for contemporary curiosity, but there were exciting moderns, too—the handsome, wicked, heroic Lord Byron, the romantic 'Waverley' Scott, clever Mr. Coleridge and retired Mr. Wordsworth, and Mr. Rogers the learned banker, and revolutionary Mr. Leigh Hunt and young Mr. ... er ... Shelley ('that custody case, you know') and tuneful Mr. Moore the Irishman. 'Let us have "Modern Beauties" too.' So they had them. Then the fashion came in of putting ancient and modern side by side in manuscript albums, the modern for pleasure, the ancient to counteract the pleasure—for this was a period with a growing conscience about hedonism.

The keeping of these private albums of poems which had made a particular appeal to the reader, each poem copied out in the reader's own hand, began as a disinterested hobby; and a few people still continue the custom to-day with pure enough motives. But the tendency to let the album lose its private character, by handing it about and allowing it to come into competition with other albums, soon destroyed the integrity of album-making. In the early nineteenth century the personal appeal became confused with the fashionable appeal. Because there was a sentimental cult for Chatterton, or because the elder critics agreed in accepting Shenstone as one of the Masters, or because Mr. Lamb and Mr. Hazlitt maintained that the Elizabethan Age, even without Shakespeare, had been quite as important an age of poetry as the Augustan, the private anthologist was kept so busy copying out page after page of verse that he had little energy left for enjoying it.

Of *Beauties of the Poets* there were many collections between 1780 and 1880. Three useful examples are Jane's *Beauties of the Poets*, a late eighteenth-century collection; Campbell's *Beauties of the British Poets*, published in 1825; and William Elwell's *The British Lyre*, published in 1854. Of Jane's anthology, which specialized in metronomic verse, the following oblique indictment occurs in a letter to Southey by John Jones, the Old Servant; who knew it only too well:

I soon engaged myself again, Sir (in 1795), with an old gentleman and his three nieces, whose names were Alexander, uncle and sisters of the present Lord Chief Baron, and I had not been in the family many months before, young as I was, I was made an upper Servant, and as I received a little card-money at times I soon was able to procure me some books, which I did by subscribing two or three quarters to the library, and the ladies were very kind to me, and often lent me others, and about this time, Sir, I bought the first and almost the only book I was ever master of, which was called Jane's *Beauties* and this I read over several times; but my chief reading now was history, and I made some poetical attempts but I kept copies of none of them excepting the epitaph on Molly Mutton, an old woman very well known about the streets of Bath at that time; but on some of my verses falling into the hands of the ladies, they were much amused with them, and, I believe, expressed regret that I had not been better educated. The housekeeper, Sir, was very kind to me, and on my expressing sorrow on her departure once when she was going to see her friends, she desired me to write something extempore in which my regret might be more strongly expressed, when in a few minutes I remember putting the following lines into her hand:

'There something is, my Martha dear,
    So amiable about thee,
The house is Heaven when thou art here,
    But Hell to me without thee.'

Jones' other poetical attempts were graver and more didactic.

Campbell's preface to his *Beauties of the British Poets* we must quote in full:

At no period of our history have we possessed such a galaxy of varied talent evinced in the poetry of the age as at present: and never with some few unfortunate exceptions has the vigorous nerve and intellectual grasp of our bards while throwing 'the drapery of moral imagination over our poor shivering nature' been more subservient to the interests of religion, or tended more effectually to promote the intellectual as well as the moral happiness of the rising generation. We have therefore in the present selection of the *Beauties of the British Poets* given to the productions of our living authors a longer space than is usually allotted to them in works of this nature: yet not to the exclusion of the writers of the olden time. For it has been our aim to bring together all the principal pieces of acknowledged merit and of intrinsic beauty which have undergone the test of the severest criticism and examination and have received the stamp of public approbation, together with many a charming anonymous production snatched with cautious hand as it floated on the stream of time towards the abyss of oblivion. While seeking for Beauties we have been careful to ascertain that no poison lurks beneath the flowers. Nothing has been admitted which has a tendency to offend delicacy or injure morality, and we have been as studious to select those passages which convey some solid instruction as those that are merely addressed to the fancy. Occasionally we have introduced a Critical Remark which we flatter ourselves will be an acceptable addition.

The promise of exciting modern work is not borne out by the index. Nothing of Keats is included, almost nothing of Shelley, less of Coleridge, a little inferior Wordsworth, no Blake. The modern writers given most space are Byron, Burns, Rogers, Moore, James Montgomery, Cowper. Not quite so much of Scott and Southey (copyright difficulties?), but their portraits form the engraved frontispiece to the two volumes. The longest poems are Pope's *Rape of the Lock*, Shenstone's *Schoolmistress*, Thomson's *Castle of Indolence* and Stillingfleet's *Essay on Conversation*, which between them take up at least a hundred pages. Shakespeare is represented by five short extracts from the dramas, not a hundred lines in all; each extract being given a moral heading such as 'Appearances are Deceptive,' 'The Power of Music,' 'The Course of True Love.' The eighteenth century is strongly represented, and there is a great deal of conventional 'Beauties of' verse-writing in the direct eighteenth-century tradition, of which this extract from Erasmus Darwin's *Upas Tree* is a neat example. He is speaking of 'Java's Isle':

> No spicy nutmeg scents the vernal gales,
> No towering plaintain shades the midday vales.
> No refluent fin the unpeopled stream divides,
> No revolant pinion cleaves the airy tides.
> Nor handed moles, nor beakèd worms return
> That mining pass th' irremeable bourn.
> Fierce in dread silence on the blasted heath
> Fell UPAS sits, the Hydra-tree of Death.

Elwell's *The British Lyre* has a lyrical preface. Note the missionary moralistic tone, now at its most resonant, but growing gradually fainter (except in definitely religious or educational anthologies) as the century wears on and as the advance of democracy makes the readers' enjoyment the determining commercial factor in the production of books. Note also the increased self-congratulation of the popular anthologist, tending more and more to drive the poets themselves into obscurity:

Three years have now elapsed since this little work first excited the attention of the Public, and if I may judge by the extensive diffusion it has enjoyed during that period, I have every reason to be satisfied with the appreciation of its readers. Filled with feelings of gratitude for the most hearty welcome allotted to my book, I consider it a delightful duty to express my thanks to its numerous friends and at the same time inform them that in this new edition I have endeavoured to improve the selection by inserting several modern poems which on account of the richness of their language, purity and beauty of their ideas, truly deserve the warm admiration of all lovers of English poetry. I now again launch *The British Lyre* into the vortex of public opinion, hoping its reception will prove as flattering to myself as in former times. With regard to the arrangement of the poems I need only quote a few remarks of a friend who kindly wrote the preface to the first edition: 'The book is divided into three parts. The first contains pieces relating to the works of God or the phenomena of "Nature" directing thought to all the lovely and awful demonstrations of the power and wisdom of the Creator, as described by the pen of poetic fancy. The second division relates to Man himself, to "Home and Country," to "Social and Domestic Affections"—and here all the elevated feelings of patriotism [N.B. this was the date of the "Indian Mutiny"], all the happy scenes of the heart are represented, while those deeper and sadder feelings, inherent to the frailty of man, are not forgotten. But after the praise of the beauties of Nature and the enjoyment of the high hopes of life, the third part, "Devotion," leads us to God Himself, shows us His Grace and Promises, our prospects of immortality, the consolation of public worship and of domestic prayers. Thus the author of this compilation will be found to have carried out the good idea of giving a clear description of "Mankind" by placing his selections under three heads, the first "The Place of our Existence," the second "Our Feelings and Actions during Life," and the third "Our Exit from this World and our Hopes for the Future."'

In the generation which has elapsed since Campbell's anthology, a great change has come over the Beauties. The eighteenth century has been almost entirely cut out. Pope is given a twenty-line part. Shenstone is dropped altogether. The Upas Tree is forgotten. Byron, Burns, Rogers, Southey, Moore, hold their own; but Montgomery,

Cowper and Scott are yielding pride of place to Wordsworth, Mrs. Hemans, Howitt, Barry Cornwall and Henry Kirke White. Coleridge, Shelley and Keats are gradually creeping up. Tennyson, as Poet Laureate, has established himself in about five pages. Shakespeare still moralizes on 'The Grandfather's Death-bed,' 'Mercy,' 'Flattery and Friendship.' The existence of the pre-Raphaelites is not yet recognized. A few seventeenth-century poets are revived: Waller, Marvell, Quarles, Vaughan, but each only in a short contribution. No poems of any size are included: though long poems are still represented by proxy of their Beauties.

The British Lyre is thus transitional to The Golden Treasury of 1891, the first popular anthology which settled the troublesome question of 'Beauties' and their extraction by claiming to be only a 'lyrical' anthology: this with satisfaction both to the compiler and his readers. The compiler was saved the labour of going through the longer works of Chaucer, Shakespeare, Pope, Cowper and company, and the readers were saved the duty of 'looking up' the context of each extract, and could content themselves with a good resolution to read these longer works at some indefinite future date. The Golden Treasury, which sold heavily because it ranged with greater freedom than its predecessors, and was at least ten years in advance of the literary taste of any rival, put the longer poems out of fashion. The editor of this 'modern classic' was Francis Palgrave, who worked with two unnamed assistants and was guided in his selection either directly or indirectly by the judgment of Tennyson. Indeed, it was as much Tennyson's influence through The Golden Treasury as the direct influence of his poems which gave the next two generations a Tennysonian view of the progress of English poetry. The Golden Treasury, with the 'additional poems,' has become the Dean of Anthologies, its original liberalism ossified. The editor of its one serious rival in circulation, Prof. Sir A. Quiller-Couch's Oxford Book of English Verse (1900), admits his obligations to it; the 'compiler cannot and does not wish to erase the dye his mind took from The Golden Treasury.'

Now, the private anthology which grows directly out of serious reading can be valuable to its compiler: it resembles, at its best, creation. A poem carefully chosen and copied down in the reader's handwriting becomes in a sense his own; it is the nearest that one who is not a poet can come to writing poetry. But a private anthology is tolerable only if it remains private. Mr. Robert Lynd, in introducing Sir Algernon Methuen's Shakespeare to Hardy anthology, quotes 'a young poet of our own time'[1] as testifying warmly to the therapeutic value of a good anthology for sick and disordered minds, and asks Sir Algernon and every other good anthologist to 'glow with pleasure at so startling a tribute to their usefulness.' But the possible medicinal value of an anthology for sick and disordered minds lies solely in the work which the sick and disordered mind does for itself by compiling this anthology. Even an honest private collection loses most of its virtue when published: the poems included have become part of the anthologist and become detached from their original context. This does not harm the anthologist, but he intervenes between reader and poem and thus prevents a direct introduction to it *by the poet himself*, who alone has the right to give this. The poems, for instance, included in Mr. Walter De la Mare's anthology *Come Hither* are so honestly his favourite poems that they seem a mere extension of the De la Mare atmosphere backwards through English poetry. This is a tyranny which no editor has a right to exercise over the reader. The Americans Bryant and Whittier, though their personalities were less fantastic, made typical poets' anthologies which were open to the same objections.

No matter in what good faith a private anthology is compiled, it becomes, when published, an organized theft of the signatures of the original poets; for the whole intention of a private anthology is to make the included poems the anthologist's own. Dr. Robert Bridges, in his *Spirit of Man*, goes so far as to suppress all signatures to the contributory poems, which occur, however, in an appendix, excusing their omission, and the omission of titles to the poems, on the ground that the book has to be read in sequence (as Dr. Bridges' new composite epic, we understand) and that titles or signatures 'might distract attention and even overrule consideration.'

The more honest the private anthology, particularly when the author is a well-known poet, the more dangerous is it when put on the market: its publication makes it appear an act of criticism instead of a mere expression of taste. Taste is the judgment which a person makes of a thing according to its congruity in his private scheme of life; criticism is the judgment which a person makes of a thing according to its excellence as compared with things like itself, regardless of its application to his private scheme of life. With taste, a poem is good because it is liked; with criticism, it is good because it is good. Now, it is all very well for a person to accept another's criticism if he is not original enough to make his own; for criticism, unlike taste, which is

[1] Servidor.

arbitrary opinion, can be tested. But when one person accepts another's taste he forfeits self-respect.

The poet as the private anthologist of his own work provides the only instance in which a private anthology makes a legitimate public anthology. Every one-man volume of verse is a selection from the poems which he wrote during a particular period of his life: even a full *Collected Edition* does not contain all the poems he ever committed to paper.

The Golden Treasury is a usurping private anthology, conscientiously compiled, and all the more formidable for that. Palgrave was not only an unsuccessful poet but a successful civil servant and educationalist; therefore well equipped to impose a personal taste (his own, guided by Tennyson's) as a critical canon on his public. In the poetical style which marks the preface of practically every popular anthology —for the anthologist, after months of laborious reading in other people's works, likes to give his own pen a good outing—he boasts:

> Chalmers' vast collection, with the whole works of all accessible poets not contained in it, and the best Anthologies of different periods, have been twice systematically read through: and it is hence improbable that any omissions which may be regretted are due to oversight.

Yet he mistook Darley for an Elizabethan! Recent 'lyrical' anthologists have so much respect for Palgrave's industry that they generally use the same list of authors, merely varying it with alternative poems of the same character as those which he (or Tennyson) selected.

The copying of anthologist from anthologist suggests sheep at a gap. Dr. Bridges, after compiling one private anthology, *The Spirit of Man*, an act of genuine if misapplied creation, and making the mistake of publishing it, was persuaded to publish another, *The Chilswell Book of English Verse* which, though it altered the proportionate weight given to the elder poets and included a few rather backward moderns, was only a *Golden Treasury-cum-Oxford Book of English Verse* in disguise. John Clare's 'I am: yet what I am none cares or knows' is the only Clare poem in the *Oxford Book of English Verse* and the only one which Dr. Bridges printed. This might pass as a case of great critics thinking alike, if it were not that Clare is far from being a one-poem man, and that Dr. Bridges evidently did not consult Mr. Edmund Blunden's recent and authoritative collection of Clare's poetry in which the proper text of the poem is restored: the *Oxford Book of English Verse* version was one rewritten by the asylum doctor who had charge of Clare's affairs at the time he wrote it. Dr. Bridges, to be blunt, borrowed and borrowed stupidly. Barnes' *Woak Hill*, similarly, has been so often anthologized in seven stanzas that few readers of poetry are aware that it has three other stanzas at the end which the poet thought necessary to the poem but which are always omitted. The painful first verse of Lamb's *The Old Familiar Faces* is also seldom given. The *Oxford Book of English Verse* protects us from the too poetic latter half of Donne's *Ecstasy*.

When *Annie Laurie* is included in an anthology it is long odds against the original version (written by William Douglas of Fingland in 1680, *not* by the late eighteenth-century Lady Scott) being printed even in an appendix, as Colonel John Buchan has done in his *Northern Muse*. Instead of:

> She's backit like the peacock,
> She's breastit like the swan,
> She's jimp aboot the middle,
> Her waist ye weel micht span :
> Her waist ye weel micht span
> And she hath a rolling ee . . .

we have Lady Scott's censored version in which Annie Laurie appears demure rather than wild:

> Her brow is like the snaw-drift,
> Her neck is like the swan,
> Her face it is the fairest
> That e'er the sun shone on:
> That e'er the sun shone on.
> And dark-blue is her ee . . .

O'Shaughnessy's *Ode* is always abbreviated. For 'Palgrave recognizing,' to quote a modern anthologist, 'the great difference between the first three inspired stanzas of Arthur O'Shaughnessy's *Ode* and the others, calmly and courageously dropped the final four.'

Re-titling is a common habit of Palgravians: we find Prof. Quiller-Couch re-titling as '*Vixi Puellis Nuper Idoneus . . .*' Wyatt's poem which Tottel had headed with *The Lover Showeth how he is Forsaken of Such as he sometime Enjoyed.* This reference to Horace successfully keeps down the passion of the poem, too strong for the popular anthology, to the commonplaces of which Horace is the Poet Laureate. The popular anthologist always prefers the most commonplace to the most poetic version of a poem. Prof. Quiller-Couch rejects the following as the last stanza of Wyatt's poem:

> It was no dream; for I lay broad awaking:
> But all is turned, thorough my gentleness,
> Into a strangë fashion of forsaking;
> And I leave to go of her goodnéss,
> And she also to use new fangleness:
> But since that I so kindly am servéd:
> I would fain know what she hath déservéd—

in favour of:

> It was no dream; for I lay broad awaking:
> But all is *turn'd now, through* my gentleness,
> Into a *bitter* fashion of forsaking;
> And I have leave to go of her goodness;
> And she also to use new-fangleness.
> But since that I *unkindly so* am servèd,
> '*How like you this?*'—*what hath she now deservèd?*

We conclude that Prof. Quiller-Couch went to Chalmers' *English Poets* first, following the example of Palgrave, his master, and there found the version which he has republished. It had been rewritten for a popular audience which could not be troubled with the archaic 'thorough' for 'through,' nor the 'strangë' for 'strange,' nor the inverted accentuation of 'servéd' and of 'déservéd,' nor the satiric use of 'kindly.' 'How like you this?' is patched in from a previous stanza to fill out the last line which, to a popular audience unable to appreciate its satiric meditative slowness, would read feebly enough. 'I would fain know' might be popularly regarded as padding, whereas it is the continued indignation of 'so kindly.' Prof. Quiller-Couch was careful to give the public what it could understand; since it was unlikely that anyone would go back behind Chalmers, no indication was given in the anthology that the text was not Wyatt's original. As a matter of fact, Chalmers, Palgrave and Prof. Quiller-Couch have a common source: Tottel. Apparently between the writing of the poem about the year 1536 and its printing in 1557 some hand, possibly Tottel's own, made these changes and supplied the poem with an explanatory title. Prof. Quiller-Couch is the popular anthologist copying from the popular anthologist; instead of getting the vexatious manuscript reading from Dr. Nott's edition long ago published from the Harrington MSS.

CA: N

Anthology footnotes are often disingenuous. For instance, though almost every popular anthology begins with *Sumer is Icumen In*, and almost every other popular anthology supplies a short footnote glossary, none has ever come clean with the line:

> Bulluc sterteth, bucke verteth.

Every possible polite explanation is given for *verteth* to distract attention from the poetic meaning that the buck, full of Spring grass, *farteth*, i.e. breaks wind.

The Golden Treasury being now a required educational text-book, Mr. T. Earle Welby publishes his *Silver Treasury of English Lyrics*. He admits Palgrave's as the classic anthology and tries not to compete but to supplement. His two tests are 'Is this poem, in its own sort, of rare excellence?' and 'Is it in Palgrave?' But in avoiding the Scylla of Palgrave, he sails dangerously near the Charybdis of Prof. Quiller-Couch. It would have been impracticable to admit both as classics, for the average reader cannot do with more than two standard anthologies, to give a hand to each.

In outward appearance a change has begun to come over the popular anthology in recent years, but this is a change only in journalistic technique. Instead of weightiness we tend to get lively sophistication; instead of gentlemanliness, a bland vulgarity; instead of confirmation of established taste, new discoveries not much believed in by the discoverer; instead of pompous flowery prefaces—no, they remain:

> Like the fabled fountain of the Azores, but with a more various power, the magic of this Art can confer on each period of life its appropriate blessing: on early years Experience; on maturity Calm; on age Youthfulness ...
>
> *The Golden Treasury*

> Poetry is the light that never was on sea or land, and the homely glow in the cottage window; the star in the sky and the fire on the hearth; the careless laughter of children and the dreams of the man of business; the glare of the footlights and the sacred flame of the altar; the jewels of the privileged few and the common coinage that everybody handles ...
>
> *The Bookman Treasury of Living Poets*

> All the Gems in this volume are not of equal brilliancy: the diamonds, rubies, emeralds and pearls of literature are few;—but there are other gems than these, of inferior value but still gem-like;—agate, cornelian, amethyst, turquoise, onyx and scores of others known to the lapidary and jeweller and prized by the public to whose appreciation they are offered.
>
> *One Thousand and One Gems*

Nor have I sought in these Islands only, but wheresoever the Muse has followed the tongue which among living tongues she most delights to honour.

The Oxford Book of English Verse

The poet touches life at every point; he paints all phases of human existence and in moments of exaltation he mounts to ideal regions and sees . . . the heavens opened and the angels of God ascending and descending. To such a vision the common man is not wholly blind. He knows without seeming to know what is beautiful and true.

From Shakespeare to Hardy

But there is no arbitrary isolation of one theme from another; they mingle and interpenetrate throughout, to the music of Pan's flute, and of Love's viol, and the bugle-call of Endeavour and the passing-bell of Death . . .

Poems of To-day

The books are handier to the pocket, more dashing though more perishable in format. But as with the brisking up of journalism, so with the anthologies: they have improved themselves with regard to everything but the one thing necessary, poetry—as the newspapers with regard to everything but truth. Their editors fall into five common occupational categories:

1. Irresponsible enthusiasts frequently acting in the name of a cause.
2. Minor poets, who wish to bully the public into accepting them as major poets through the leverage of their anthologies.
3. Professional critics who have easy access to the contributory volumes and are on good enough terms with publishers and poets to get copyright matter cheap.
4. The publishers themselves.
5. Poets with a reputation which the publishers are anxious to help them capitalize and so offset the comparatively poor returns their individual volumes usually bring in.

Their aim is to make a single book out of clippings from many books: to create a composite author who shall be a mean struck between all the poets included. But to strike a mean even, for instance, between Burns, Rogers, Tennyson and Clough, with only a century separating the first and the last, is plainly impossible. The result is the choice of a negative type of poem not proper to any of the poets: that is, not the sort of poem which either Burns and Clough must have written, but one that neither of them need have written. The intelligent but unread reader who wishes to find out which poets he would like to know better gets no help from the popular anthology: in an anthology everything reads, democratically, much the same. We would not go so far as to say that every poem in *The Golden Treasury* is uncharacteristic of the author, but even positive poems lose character by being anthologized. Poems by Shakespeare, Donne, Shelley, Keats, become affected by the same negative poison, to a point where they are almost unrecognizable; so faces in the Underground are made negative, as faces, by the spell of the cheap ticket which is the only link between them.

'Beachcomber,' of the London *Daily Express*, knows all about popular anthologies:

ANOTHER ANTHOLOGY

Mr. Dribble's 'Hundred Best Telephone Numbers' is all that an anthology should be. It is comprehensive and free from prejudice. Moreover, it includes many new numbers, the compiler having gone to the little-known outlying exchanges for fresh talent. 28443 Pobham, for instance, is a genuine discovery. Nearly all the favourite West-End exchanges are well represented, but one misses the superb 00010001 Mayfair. Also, one could have done with more Park numbers. It must be admitted, however, that the compiler has done his work so well that he has included numbers to suit all tastes. And if I were condemned to a life in prison or on a desert island, and were allowed to take six numbers with me, I should find them all in this anthology. One may conclude with the hope that each one of these hundred numbers may find an absorbing echo in at least one exchange.

I understand that the success of this anthology has emboldened Mr. Dribble to prepare a similar work, which will be called the 'Hundred Best Trains.'

Nevertheless, the true anthology survives, though growing scarcer every year. A. H. Bullen's *Lyrics from the Elizabethan Song-books* is a ready example, fully justified because access to the song-books themselves is difficult and the specimens he has rescued are decently representative. His *Lyrics from the Elizabethan Dramatists* may also be cited, though the dramas are more accessible than the song-books and the lyric is often too closely related to the play to justify its transplanting to an anthology. Another unexceptionable example is Prof. Child's *English and Scottish Ballads*, which is accurate, definite and well organized: it keeps to set limits, and within these, arranges poems which not only are otherwise inaccessible but gain by a collation of their widely scattered variants. In these, as in all true anthologies, the original texts are not modified for the convenience of half-educated readers.

But once a field has been covered well, as Prof. Child covered the popular non-literary English and Scottish ballad, as W. Carew Hazlitt in his four-volume *Early Popular Poetry* and his two-volume *Early Popular Scottish Poetry* covered the black-letter verse *fabliau*, as Chappell covered the field of early popular songs in his *Popular Music of the Olden Time*, there is nothing left to do but to cross the *t*'s and dot the *i*'s of these conscientious antiquarians and look for remoter fields of research. But there are not enough remote fields of research to go round, and the temptation to make a popular and uncritical *compote* of these scholarly collections is very strong. And once the research spirit is in abeyance, the conscientious observance of the original texts of fugitive pieces—a morality which first hardened only so late as 1822 with David Laing's *Select Remains of the Early Popular Poetry of Scotland*—is relaxed: and in nine cases out of ten the reconstituted poems, instead of recovering a clarity lost by the carelessness of the original scribe or printer, are further mishandled.

The true anthology, then, if it is not a strictly non-professional, non-purposive collection, such as the poet's or amateur's scrapbook, is a rescue anthology, at once textual and historical in emphasis. Since its object is to include as much material, irrespective of poetic quality, as will fully represent the field it purports to cover, it is committed in this sense to be uncritical; as the scrapbook is also uncritical in the sense that it has only a personal standard. The true anthology, in fact, is one which is in no way likely to become a popular anthology, since the general reading public asks from anthologies neither unauthoritative examples of private taste, nor historical material in the raw.

II

THE PERFECT MODERN LYRIC

A new type of poem has been evolved and popularized by the demands of the anthology-reading public. It is called 'the perfect modern lyric.' Like the best-seller novel, it is usually achieved in the dark; but certain critical regulations can be made for it. It must be fairly regular in form and easily memorized, it must be a new combination of absolutely worn-out material, it must have a certain unhealthy vigour or languor, and it must start off engagingly with a simple sentimental statement. Somewhere a daring pseudo-poetical image must be included, such as:

> If ye break faith with us who die,
> We shall not sleep, though poppies grow
> In Flanders fields.

or:

> The Master said:
>   'I have planted the Seed of a Tree,
> It shall be strangely fed
> With white dew and with red,
>   And the gardeners shall be Three,
>   Regret, Hope, Memory!'

If possible it must echo a familiar Biblical text.

Mr. W. B. Yeats' *The Lake Isle of Innisfree* is the most anthologized of all lyrics of this sort. True to type, it begins with the necessary sentimental statement: the Biblical 'I will arise and go,' padded with the poetical repetition of 'and go':

> I will arise and go now, and go to Innisfree.

The syllable 'free' suggests liberty, but to the realistic Irish peasant the island in question is known as Rat Island.

> And a small cabin build there, of clay and wattles made.

The smallness of the cabin suggests the enervation of the poet who will not even trouble to build himself a roomy retreat, and his complete improvidence against the damp of an Irish winter; this fatalism is likely to meet with a ready response from readers already enervated by much anthology-browsing. The most miserable touch is the proposal to *build* a cabin which he magically finds already *made* before he reaches the end of the line: suggesting the wish-fulfilment mechanism of the ordinary fatigue-dream.

> Nine bean rows will I have there, a hive for the honey bee.

Nine, because that is a poetical number, and beans perhaps in honour of Jack and the Beanstalk. How long the bean rows were, or who tilled them, does not appear. The reader is expected to react to the mystic 'nine' and suspect the presence of a deep allegory. But Mr.

Yeats is only dreaming, not exercising thought; 'nine' is a plain confession of muzziness. The 'honey bee,' too, is no more than a sugary synonym for the ordinary bee; and when the phrase 'a hive for the honey bee' is put in apposition to 'bean rows,' it can mean only that the poet, being too lazy to build his own skips, lets the bees swarm among his beans. But even so, the bees will never make their hive *in* the beans but will choose a hollow tree at some distance from the cabin. Note the ugly assonance of *bean* and *bees*.

> And live alone in the bee-loud glade.

Bee-loud is another would-be poetical phrase, but suggesting rather the abbreviations of a police-court report: 'Your worship, defendant used improper language while I was at my piano-practice. "Dee you," she said, "and dee your bee piano and the bee loud noises you make on it!"' As for sentiment, it is a weak repetition of two formerly much anthologized poems, Pope's *Ode to Solitude* and Roger's *A Wish*, cutting down the simple necessities of those earlier sentimentalists to a point far below subsistence level.

> And I shall have some peace there, for peace comes dropping slow,
> Dropping from the veils of the morning to where the cricket sings.

Again the poetical repetition to conceal the impoverishment of thought. In this second line we have the showy conceit which suggests profundity. Presumably the veils of the morning are the dawn clouds, and the place where the cricket sings is the cabin hearth: 'peace comes down the chimney every morning' is what Mr. Yeats really means.

The second half of the first line, because of 'for,' must grammatically explain the first half: owing to the slowness of the peace as it drops, the poet will be able to catch some of it at least as it comes down the chimney every morning.

> There midnight's all a-glimmer, and noon a purple glow,
> And evening full of the linnet's wings.

This is a further extravagance to set off the 'veils of the morning.' A-glimmering midnights are rare in Ireland; and linnets in Ireland, as elsewhere, are roosting by the evening. But 'midnight,' 'glimmer,' 'evening' and 'linnet' are poetical words and must go in, despite the sense: so is 'purple,' the easiest colour-disguise for feeble workmanship both in painting and poetry, and for that matter in music—purple begins as the colour of royalty and ends as the colour of anaemia and half-mourning. 'Linnet' is chosen from all the other birds partly because it was popularized by Keats, partly because it begins with *l* and the lullaby charm of the poem depends largely on an over-proportion of *l*'s to natural requirements. No modern poet, it is safe to say, with the exception of Mr. Edmund Blunden and Mr. Robert Frost, can distinguish a linnet from any other small bird with a squeaky voice even in strong daylight: but the linnet has become as fashionable in contemporary nature-verse as the lark and the nightingale used to be.

> I will arise and go now, for always night and day
> I hear lake water lapping with low sounds by the shore.

This is an attempt to pull the poem together, before it dissolves into mush, by reintroducing the idea of movement; but it is no real movement, only a repetition of the resolve taken in the opening line, which has not yet been, and indeed never could be, translated into action. The over-alliterative description of noises in the head reads like a pathological report, especially in view of the poet's previous auditory absorption in the buzzing of bees and the whirring of the linnet's wings.

> While I stand on the roadway, or on the pavements gray,

Is there an antithesis here between the roadway and the pavement? If so, it is not clearly made. And how does 'while I stand' square with 'I will arise'? Perhaps he stood on the roadway, careless of the traffic, but sat on the pavement. Why the 'pavement gray'? Is the inversion for the sake of the rhyme, or does 'gray' refer predicatively to the poet? Why all the *ay* sounds? Are they intended to create a melancholy urban sound in contrast with the Tennysonian vowel-variation of the preceding line; or is it just carelessness, and is the internal rhyme of 'way' and 'gray' unintentional?

> I hear it in the deep heart's core.

What he means is either 'in the core of my heart,' or 'deep in my heart.' But, unable to make the verse scan with only one of these phrases, he combines the two metaphors of *depth* and *centrality* of emotion in a way which defeats his meaning; for he has had to leave out the important word 'my' (it would have put too many heavy syllables at the end of the line), so that the possessor of the heart may be anyone or anything. Certainly, with whatever qualities the hero of such a simple-life romance might properly adorn himself, depth or centrality of emotion is not one of them.

Mr. De la Mare's *Arabia* is even muzzier:

> Far are the shades of Arabia,
>   Where the Princes ride at noon,
> 'Mid the verdurous vales and thickets,
>   Under the ghost of the moon;
> And so dark is that vaulted purple
>   Flowers in the forest rise
> And toss into blossom 'gainst the phantom stars
>   Pale in the noonday skies.

If we are to trust travellers, there are no shades in Arabia at noon except during sand-storms. There are no forests. The moon and stars are not visible at noon either there or anywhere else south of the Arctic Circle. The Arabians, princes and all, do most of their riding at night. Flowers do appear in certain Arabian districts each Spring, but grow low on the ground and are soon burned up.

> Sweet is the music of Arabia
>   In my heart, when out of dreams
> I still in the thin clear mirk of dawn
>   Descry her gliding streams;
> Hear her strange lutes on the green banks
>   Ring loud with the grief and delight
> Of the dim-silked, dark-haired Musicians
>   In the brooding silence of night.

Streams are not characteristic of Arabia except in the short rainy season, when they rush rather than glide. The lute is not an Eastern instrument in spite of the Authorised Version of the *Book of Daniel* (where they occur with harps, sackbuts and psalteries); and Arabian music is not sweet, but harsh, bare and monotonous like the desert.

> They haunt me—her lutes and her forests;
>   No beauty on earth I see
> But shadowed with that dream recalls
>   Her loveliness to me:
> Still eyes look coldly upon me,
>   Cold voices whisper and say—
> 'He is crazed with the spell of far Arabia,
>   They have stolen his wits away.'

The perfect modern lyric has a close affinity with the fatigue-dream. If this had been a poem of integrity, the word Arabia would never have been allowed to occur in it; either an actual place would have been chosen, such as Cambodia, where something, though not much, of what he says in the poem applies, or a new name would have been coined. But Mr. De la Mare has had a confused, luxurious dream in which the hackneyed lines 'I'll sing thee songs of Araby and tales of far Cashmere' have developed without any wakeful restraint into this foolish fantasy combining the silken Princes of Araby with the forests, flowers and silks of Cashmere and identifying the 'songs of Araby' with the Victorian song which celebrates them. The last stanza, which admits the craziness of the dream and its distortion of geographical fact, is its best ticket of admission into the popular anthology, where it will continue for many years to *cheat* people of a sigh and *charm* them to a tear.

Mr. Ralph Hodgson's much anthologized *Bells of Heaven*, with its humanitarian appeal for 'wretched, blind pit-ponies and little hunted hares,' is of the same category as *The Lake Isle of Innisfree* and *Arabia*. It offends us, certainly, to think of pit-ponies being kept down in the dark until they have lost the use of their eyes, and so it should; but only in proportion to other crimes of civilization. Pit-ponies are humanely treated underground, and being the property of the mine-owners and protected by the R.S.P.C.A. usually show fewer signs of wretchedness than the average miner or miner's wife and family. Thus the adjective 'wretched' can be fairly applied only to particular pit-ponies who happen to be wretched: but the cause of their wretchedness is not here specified. We should not insist on the weakness of 'wretched' if it were not matched by the 'little' hunted hares. Hares are not singled out for sport because they are usually small in size. Nor should mere size induce pity: mice are much smaller than hares and just as charming: but we destroy them without protest from Mr. Hodgson. Bugs and fleas are smaller still. The ugliness of hare-hunting lies in the hare's defencelessness, not in the relative size of man and hare. -

The first part of the poem runs:

> 'Twould ring the bells of Heaven
> The wildest peal for years,
> If Parson lost his senses
> And people came to theirs,
> And he and they together
> Knelt down with angry prayers
> For tamed and shabby tigers
> And dancing dogs and bears . . .

Dogs, generally fox-terriers, can be taught to dance only by the exercise of great kindness and patience, and enjoy doing their tricks; the same is true of bears. But Mr. Hodgson, who specializes in the breeding of bulldogs, may not realize this. The conceit of losing one's senses and coming to one's senses supports the whole burden of poeticality for this little piece and must be supposed to be wittily intended: but when one examines the antithesis it falls to pieces like the witticism of a dream examined in daylight. If 'Parson' is at present in his senses, and 'people' are out of theirs, one would suppose that all that was wanted was for Parson to kneel down and say the necessary prayers, and for the people thereupon to come to their senses. No, Parson has first to lose his senses. Yet if Parson loses his senses there will be no sensible prayers. Mr. Hodgson probably means that there is a callousness about Parson in his sensible moods which allows such things to continue without protest. But if in Parson, why not in the congregation? Why shouldn't they too lose their senses? If the first part of the antithesis is meant ironically, why not the second? Why should Parson come in for all the irony? And why should the Bells of Heaven be so enthusiastically rung at the receipt of prayers which are not contrite but indignant, and addressed to God? Must we suppose that the angelic bell-ringers dare to sympathize with 'people' in their new-found indignation, God corresponding in callousness with his representative on earth, Parson? Must God be persuaded to lose his senses in order to preserve the logic of Mr. Hodgson's humanitarianism?

The piece cannot be judged as poetry; it has to be judged as propaganda verse. But the first test of propaganda verse is whether it gives the message clearly, and *The Bells of Heaven* are, in Mr. Hodgson's hands, cracked. The next test is whether its remedial suggestions are plausible. Now, there is figurative sense in Shelley's:

> Men of England, wherefore plough
> For the lords who lay you low?

There is superficial sense in the temperance hymn beginning:

> Cold water is the best of drinks . . .

There is even a homely if fanciful wisdom in the eighteenth-century catch:

> Slaves to the World should be tossed in a blanket
> If I might have my will . . .

But all that Mr. Hodgson can suggest to improve the lot of (*a*) caged tigers, (*b*) performing bears and dogs, (*c*) pit-ponies, (*d*) hunted hares, is prayers to God by callous congregations miraculously converted to Sunday humanitarianism. The very inefficacy of the solution makes the poem delightful to anthology readers: they realize at once that they are not expected to do anything for the poor animals but read it.

Dr. Bridges' most anthologized poem begins:

> I love all beauteous things,
>   I seek and adore them;
> God hath no better praise
> And man in his hasty days
>   Is honoured for them.

Of course he loves all beauteous things. He loves them because he considers them beauteous, or he considers them beauteous because he loves them—it doesn't matter which. Naturally he seeks them and adores them. He seeks them because he adores them or he adores them because he seeks them—it doesn't matter which. Naturally also, this being the next thing on the list, he gives God praise, and he then gives man honour. The question, however, arises: Do the beauteous things belong originally to man or to God? Or must God and man litigate? 'Hasty' stands for 'quickly passing,' a commonplace distinction between immortal God and mortal man disguised by the far-fetched adjective and used merely to fatten a thin line.

> I too will something make
>   And joy in the making;
> Altho' to-morrow it seem
> Like the empty words of a dream
>   Remembered on waking.

'I too' can mean only that Dr. Bridges wishes to be classified as neither God nor man. 'And joy in the making'—by adding a new quality to his proposed creation, not known either to God or hasty man, Dr. Bridges suggests an antithesis, i.e.' God and man make beauteous things and are praised and honoured for them, but get no joy; I, on the other hand, am determined to get joy, although the impermanence of my creations gets me neither praise nor honour.' The 'dream remembered on waking,' a reminiscence of the Seventy-third Psalm, is a confession, like the closing lines of *Arabia*, that the poetic faculty is in abeyance here.

And what of Mr. John Masefield's *Cargoes,* which is to be found in almost every anthology in which *The Lake Isle of Innisfree, Arabia* and *I Love all Beauteous Things* are included? It begins:

> Quinquereme of Niniveh from distant Ophir,
> Rowing home to haven in sunny Palestine—

Niniveh has possibly been linked with the sea on Jonah's account, Mr. Masefield remembering that the prophet, afraid to pronounce doom on Niniveh, took ship from Tarshish. But Niniveh is on the river Euphrates, hundreds of miles inland from Palestine, so why a quinquereme of Niniveh should row *home* to Palestine is mysterious. Anyhow, the route from the land of Ophir (East Africa) to Palestine before the days of the Suez Canal was one no quinquereme could take unless it first casually circumnavigated Africa—Hiram of Tyre's Phoenician fleet which traded with Ophir was sensibly built on the Red Sea, with Solomon's right-of-way permission through Southern Judaea. And Niniveh had fallen long before quinqueremes were invented:

> With a cargo of ivory,
> And apes and peacocks,
> Sandalwood, cedarwood, and sweet white wine.

The circumnavigation of Africa is here lengthened by a voyage to the East Indies, or perhaps Polynesia, in search of sandalwood; but why these Mesopotamio-Phoenicians were such fools as to go to Ophir (where the gold came from) and to bring back not gold but cedarwood and wine, which were among the chief riches of Palestine, is not clear. The ivory, apes and peacocks are borrowed from the *Book of Kings,* but from a different chapter than the one dealing with Hiram: and they then came from India via Hadramout and the Red Sea with the Queen of Sheba. There is no finite verb in this stanza; which keeps the reader in suspense.

> Stately Spanish galleon coming from the Isthmus,
> Dipping through the Tropics by the palm-green shores,
> With a cargo of diamonds,
> Emeralds, amethysts,
> Topazes . . .

Cargo is rather a heavy term in this context: 'consignment' would be more plausible. The cargo would have been something bulkier; for instance, cotton, cacao, nuts, silver ingots, hard woods, sugar, and so on.

. . . and cinnamon, and gold moidores.

Well, then, believe it or not, the bulk of the cargo was cinnamon: the Spanish galleon was coming home from the Isthmus of Panama after trying unsuccessfully to plant a cargo principally consisting of cinnamon (from Ceylon) on the Mexicans. But why in the world were moidores among the cargo? Again some unsuccessful commercial transaction is indicated. The Spaniards took their chests of coined gold to the New World and were told: 'No, thank you, we have plenty of that yellow metal here.' This so chilled their stately hearts that they did not think of asking for some ordinary unworked bars of gold in exchange for steel knives, guns and other European manufactures. But they got the jewels all right, previously imported by the American natives from India, probably in barter for a small amount of Cinghalese cinnamon. There is no finite verb in this stanza either.

> Dirty British coaster with a salt-caked smoke-stack,
> Butting through the Channel in the mad March days,
> With a cargo of Tyne coal,
> Road-rails, pig-lead,
> Firewood, iron-ware, and cheap tin trays.

And still no finite verb; so we are evidently intended to hang these three nautical sketches on the wall and compare them. The main differences in the three exhibits are as follows: Verse 1, Oars; Verse 2, Sails; Verse 3, Steam. Verses 1 and 2, Romantic, scented cargo, long calm voyages; Verse 3, Prosaic cargo, short difficult voyages. The natural deduction to be drawn from these tabulated contrasts can only be that improvements in the methods of marine transport do not necessarily make for long, pleasurable voyages. Since this is hardly a sublime thought we look for a meaning of greater subtlety. The Tyne coal and road-rails give the clue. Where was the coaster taking them in the *mad* March days? Think a moment! Verse 1, Cedar and wine to Palestine; Verse 2, Moidores to Spain. Verse 3? Why, of course, iron and coal home again to Newcastle after a rattling voyage round the British Isles; in the course of which the cheap tin trays were re-imported into South Wales at an enhanced price.

There is a popular superstition that a poem, like the legendary female mind, is charming because it is illogical; that its elements need not tally closely with one another. Whereas really it is prose which does not demand so close a tallying: it can use dead metaphors, toy with false analogies, and record a succession of events bound together only by spatial or temporal propinquity. Prose describes something, it does not create something, so that almost any artifice that will strengthen the description passes muster: it is the idea, not the thing itself, which matters. But each element in a poem must tally with all the rest in every possible way. Each metaphor must be alive and reconciled to its neighbours; analogies must work out precisely; its events must have so complete an interdependence that a single idle or false word would spoil the poem's cohesion.

LOVING MAD TOM
(1927)

LOVING MAD TOM[1]

THE first occurrence of the ballad *Loving Mad Tom* or *Tom o' Bedlam's Song* is in a collection of manuscript songs and verses (British Museum, Additional MSS. 24, 665), called *Giles Earle his booke*, 1615; Earle was a friend of Thomas Campion's. It was first printed in *Wit and Drollery* (1656), next in an appendix to *Le Prince d'Amour* (1660), next in *Westminster Drollery* (1672). Disraeli popularized it in his *Curiosities of Literature* (1859).

1

From ye hagg & hungry Goblin,
y^t into raggs would rend yee,
& ye spirit y^t stand's by ye naked man,
in ye booke of moones defend yee
That of your fiue sounde sences,
you neuer be forsaken,
Nor wander from your selues with Tom,
abroad to begg your bacon
    while I doe sing any foode any feeding,
    feedinge—drinke or clothing,
    Come dame or maid, be not afraid,
    poore Tom will iniure nothing.

2

Of thirty bare yeares haue I
twice twenty bin enraged,
& of forty bin three tymes fifteene
in durance soundlie caged,
On ye lordlie loftes of Bedlam
with stubble softe & dainty,
braue braceletts strong, sweet whips ding dong
with wholesome hunger plenty,
    & nowe I sing &c:

---

[1] My acknowledgments are due to Mr. Jack Lindsay for textual research.

3

With a thought I tooke for Maudline
& a cruse of cockle pottage.
with a thing thus tall, skie blesse you all:
I befell into this dotage.
I slept not since the Conquest
till then I neuer waked,
Till ye rogysh boy of loue where I lay
mee found & strip't mee naked.
　　& nowe I sing &c:

4

When I short haue shorne my sowce face
& swigg'd my horny barrell,
In an oaken Inne I pound my skin
as a suite of guilt apparrell,
The moon's my constant Mistresse
& the lowlie owle my morrowe.
The flaming Drake and ye Nightcrowe make
mee musicke to my sorrowe.
　　while I doe sing &c:

5

The palsie plagues my pulses
when I prigg yor: piggs or pullen
your culuers take, or matchles make
your Chanticleare or sullen,
When I want prouant wth: Humfrie
I sup, & when benighted,
I repose in Powles wth: waking soules,
Yet neuer am affrighted.
　　But I doe sing &c:

6

I knowe more then Apollo,
for oft when hee ly's sleeping
I see ye starrs att bloudie warres
in ye wounded welkin weeping,
The moone embrace her shepheard
& ye queene of loue her warryer,
while ye first doth horne, ye star of morne:
& ye next ye heauenly Farrier.
　　While I doe singe &c:

7

The Gipsie snap & Pedro
are none of Toms Comradoes,
ye punck I skorne, & ye cutpurse sworn
& ye roring boyes brauadoes,
The meeke ye white the gentle,
mee handle touch, & spare not
but those y^t crosse Tom Rynosseross
doe what ye Panther dare not.
   Although I sing &c:

8

with an hoast of furious fancies
whereof I am comaunder,
with a burning speare, & a horse of aire,
to the wildernesse I wander.
By a knight of ghostes & shadowes,
I sumon'd am to Tourney.
ten leagues beyond the wide worlds end
mee thinke it is noe iourney.
   yet will I sing &c:

VARIANT READINGS

(W. here stands for *Wit and Drollery*; P. for *Prince d'Amour*;
West D. for *Westminster Drollery*; Dis. for Disraeli.)

I.—2. rend you, P. rend ye, W.   3. Spirits that stand, W. spirits
that stand, P. Spirits that stan, West D.   9. Nor neuer sing any Food
and Feeding, W.   10. Money (*for* feedinge), W.   12. For Tom, W.
   II.—2. O thirty, P.   5. the lovely, W. (*This version also runs lines*
5–6 *together: followed by Dis.*)   6. in stubble, W.   7. and whips, P.
8. And, P. and a, W.   9. Still do I sing, W. Yet did I sing, P.
   III.—3. thus —— tall, W.   a thing they call Skies bliss you all, P.
4. fell, W.   5. till the Conquest, W.   7. rogueing, P.   9. stript stark
naked, P.   10. And made me sing, W.
   IV.—1. When short I have shorn my Sows face, W.   2. Horned,
W.   3. Do I pawn my Skin, W.   I pawned my skin in an Oaken
Inn, P.   5. Morn (*for* moon), Dis.   6. lovely owl, W., *followed by*
Dis., and *omit* P.   Marrow, W. marrow, P.   7. *second* the *omit*, P.
9. While there I sing, W
   V.—1. The Palsie plague these Pounces, W.   The Palsie plagues,

these Palsies, P.   2. When I plague your pigs, P.   3. Calvers, P.
4. Chanty clear, P.   5. *Humphy*, P., I sup *carried back from next line*,
W., *also* Dis.   7. To repose, W., walking souls, W.   I walk in *Pauls*
with wandring souls, P.   8. And never, P.

VI.—1. At Mortal VVars, W.   I behold the stars at mortal
wars, P.   4. And (*for* in), W.   5. Embraces, W.   6. her Farrier, P.   7.
While the first doth horn The Stars of the Morn, W., the star in
the morn, P.   The starre of the morne, West D.   9. For still I do
sing, W.

VII.—1 The Gipsie, *Snapp*, and Pedro, W.   The *Jeepsie* snap and
Tedro, P.   3. The Baud I scorn and Cutpurse sworn, P.   5. The
Soler white and gentle, W.   The Sober white, West D.   The sober
Knight and gentle, P.   6. Me trace, or touch, W.   Me trace, and touch,
P.   7. Tom's Rhinoceros, W.   *Toms* rynoross, P.   8. the Panders, P.

VIII.—1. With a Heart of Furious Fancies, W., *same without
caps.*, West D.   3. of the ayr, P.   5. With a Knight, P., West D., W.

Francis Thompson rewrote the poem. His version, first printed in
The Dial, v., does not appear in his collected works, and I think that
the editors did right to exclude it. The original no more needed re-
writing by Thompson than Shakespeare's *Anthony and Cleopatra* needed
rewriting by Dryden. But why and how he rewrote it are points of
interest. Here are four of his eight verses:

1

From the hag and hungry goblin
That into rags would rend ye,
All the spirits that stand
By the naked man,
In the book of the moons, defend ye.
Beware of the black rider
Through blasted dreams borne nightly;
From Venus Queen
Saved may you bin,
And the dead that die unrightly.

2

With a wench of wanton beauties
I came unto this ailing:
Her breast was strewn

Like a half o' the moon
With a cloud of gliding veiling.
In her snow-beds to couch me
I had so white a yearning,
Like a moon-struck man
Her pale breast 'gan
To set my wits a-turning.

6

Hate, Terror, Lust, and Frenzy,
Look in on me with faces:
And monstrous haunch
And toad-blown paunch
Do show me loathed disgraces.
I hear on imminent cities
The league-long watches armèd,
Dead cities lost
Ere the moon grew a ghost
Phantasmal, viewless, charmèd.

8

As a burst and blood-blown insect
Cleaves to the wall it dies on,
The smeared sun
Doth clot upon
A heaven without horizon.
I dare not but be dreadless,
Because all things so dread are:
With a trumpet blown
Through the mists alone
From a land where the lists of the dead are.

Poor Tom is, in Thompson's handling, a Romantic Revival charac-
ter, but from the decayed end of the Romantic Revival—a Poe-esque
character wandering witless in a James Thomson *City of Dreadful
Night*. He has entirely lost his character as an Elizabethan stage-beggar,
exchanging a moon-struck innocence for shabby-genteel unwhole-
someness. He has even cultivated a squeamish horror of vermin,
though once, as he told King Lear, he would eat the swimming frog,
the toad, the newt and the water-rat; he would even drink the green
mantle from the standing pool and think nothing of it. Now the sight

of a squashed bug on the wall fills him with dread. Once he was on the easiest terms with his somewhat spiteful but quite familiar spirits; now they haunt him mysteriously and 'show' him 'loathed disgraces.' And his lady is no longer Maudline but an unnamed and mystical 'wench of wanton beauties,' a punk of the highest possible class, but a punk for all that: and punks the original Tom used to scorn. Thompson, in fact, was trying to intensify the poetic horror of the poem by releasing Tom from the squalor in which he found him—a squalor which caused Tom himself no disgust but only a gentle sorrow—and setting him to wander, adjectivally, in a cloudy no-man's land of literary fancy and literary remorse.

It was a great error in poetic judgment; as unfortunate as Robert Browning's when he provided a realistically grotesque itinerary for Childe Roland's brief, strange and sufficient journey to the Dark Tower—again improving on a furious fancy of Poor Tom's:

> One stiff blind horse . . .
>   With that red gaunt and colloped neck a-strain,
>   And shut eyes underneath the rusty mane.
> Seldom went such grotesqueness with such woe:
> I never saw a brute I hated so—
>   He must be wicked to deserve such pain.

'He must be wicked to deserve such pain' is poor Thompson's verdict on his Poor Tom—because he did not understand the original poem. His friend and protectress Alice Meynell had already purged the gold of its dross, as she doubtless put it to herself, meaning the literary part of the unliterary, by printing a severely cut and emended version in her anthology *The Flower of the Mind*. It consists merely of five four-line stanzas:

1. The morn's my lovely mistress . . .
2. I know more than Apollo . . .
3. The moon embraces her shepherd . . .
4. With a heart of furious fancies . . .
5. With a knight of ghosts and shadows . . .

Thompson embellished this refined version with enamel and filigree work.

Other poets have also picked and chosen. Edgar Allan Poe, Rudyard Kipling, Walter De la Mare have all used the last verse 'With a heart of furious fancies' as an introductory motto to a piece of romantic narrative (*The Unparalleled Adventure of Hans Pfaal*; chapter xv of

The Light that Failed; and *Henry Brocken*) and Mr. De la Mare has used 'the gold' again, after much the same refinement as Thompson's and Miss Meynell's, in his *Memoirs of a Midget.* The only case I know of a poet using a bit of the 'dross' for preference is Sir Walter Scott, who quotes a snatch of the ballad in *The Heart of Midlothian*:

> In the bonny cells of Bedlam,
> Ere I was ane and twenty,
> I had hempen bracelets strong,
> And merry whips, ding-dong,
> And prayer and fasting plenty.

But it is at least possible that Scott was repeating a verse of the ballad which had survived independently on the Scottish Border, a ballad that was originally, as I hope to show, all 'dross' and no 'gold.'

There are many obvious errors in the Giles Earle text (which we may call, for short, E) suggesting the unintelligent copying of a manuscript now lost (which may be guessed at as Q). We may be sure that Q was written in a double stanza like E, and not in a single stanza like all the other songs which go to the *Tom o' Bedlam* tune; and this is important, for when we come to examine the double stanzas in E we find that the 'gold,' as opposed to the 'dross,' is either present throughout each whole stanza, which holds together as a unit of thought, or else is confined to the second half of a stanza which does not so hold together. In no case does 'gold' begin the stanza and 'dross' close it. The poem is obviously the work of two authors: the 'dross' has a simplicity and brutality which suggest a popular origin, while the 'gold' is certainly the work of an educated writer. The first halves of the third and fourth stanzas:

> With a thought I took for Maudline . . .

and

> When I short have shorn my sow's face

could not have been conceived by the mind which added to the former:

> I slept not since the Conquest . . .

and to the latter:

> The moon's my constant Mistress.

The only tenable theory is that a cultivated writer took a poem which was 'dross'—a professional Bedlamite song, which we may call P,

written in single stanza form with a refrain, like all the other songs that
went to the same tune—and gilded it for use as a stage song that
would appeal to gallants as well as groundlings. Then if we are to
reconstruct P from E by an omission of all the work by the educated
author of Q, we must omit not only the conventionally chosen 'gold,'
but also any whole stanzas or second half-stanzas which have been used
to bridge the literary and unliterary styles. This gives a poem (with
the refrain as in E), consisting of the first half of stanza 1 (which Miss
Meynell did not regard as 'gold' and which Thompson included only
by a misunderstanding of its meaning); the whole of stanza 2, but
split up into two independent verses (following the hint in *The Heart
of Midlothian*); the first halves of stanzas 3 and 4; the first half of stanza
5—not the second, because the reference to Duke Humphry is a local
one which would be appreciated by the Bankside audience, but which
would hardly be understood in the country villages where the Bedlam-
ites did most of their trade; the first half of stanza 7—not the second
half, which is too magnificent. But something is missing. The appeal
to pity is incomplete: there is no summing up, such as one expects at
the end of a canting song. The missing element, which is the explanation
of Poor Tom's madness in terms of his love for Maudline, may be
supplied from a hint in the first half of stanza 3, 'With a thought I
took for Maudline,' and from the second half of the same stanza with
its reference to the roguish boy of Love and to the Conquest; it is
also suggested by the later-printed song *Loving Mad Tom* from *Wit
and Drollery* (1683), and by *To Find my Tom of Bedlam*, from *Wit and
Mirth* (1699), which is ascribed to Mad Maudline herself. The first four
verses of *To Find my Tom of Bedlam* run:

> To find my *Tom* of *Bedlam*, Ten Thousand Years I'll Travel;
> Mad *Maudlin* goes with dirty Toes to save her Shooes From Gravel.
> *Yet will I sing Bonny Boys, bonny Mad Boys, Bedlam Boys are Bonny;*
> *They still go bare and live by the Air, and want no Drink, nor Money.*

> I now repent that ever poor Tom was so Disdain'd,
> My wits are lost since him I crost, which makes me go thus Chained.
> *Yet will I, &c.*

> My Staff hath Murder'd Gyants, My Bag a long Knife carries,
> To Cut Mince-Pyes from Childrens Thighs, with which I feast the
>   *Faries,*
> *Yet, &c.*

My Horn is made of Thunder, I stole it out of Heav'n,
The Rain-bow there is this I wear, for which I thence was driv'n.
    Yet, &c.

It is unlikely that this song was sung in the villages by pretended female Bedlamites (Maudline may be a reference to another hospital for lunatics, St. Mary Magdalene's, corresponding with the Bethlehem Hospital from which Tom o'Bedlam took his name) though clearly P was so sung. It is merely a specimen of *Wit and Mirth* made for singing on festive occasions, and probably hawked as a ballad, like *The Aukreman* from *Westminster Drollery* (1661), and *The Vagabond* from *Wit and Drollery* (1662)—all sung to the *Tom o'Bedlam* tune. And it is unlikely that *Loving Mad Tom* (which we may call L) was sung professionally either, though it seems to contain lines borrowed from P. This poem runs as follows:

1

I'le bark against the Dog-Star,
    And crow away the Morning;
    I'le chase the Moon
    Till it be Noon,
And I'll make her leave her Horning.
But I will find Bonny Maud, *Merry Mad* Maud,
    And seek what e're betides her,
        Yet I will love
        Beneath or above,
    That dirty Earth that hides her.

2

I'le crack the Poles asunder,
    Strange things I will devise on.
I'le beat my Brain against *Charles*'s Wain,
    And I'le grasp the round Horizon.
But I will find, &c.

3

I'le search the Caves of Slumber,
    And please her in a Night Dream;
I'le tumble her into *Lawrences* Fenn,
    And hang my self in a Sun Beam;
But I will, &c.

4

I'le Sayl upon a Milstone,
And make the Sea-Gods wonder,
I'le plunge in the Deep, till I wake asleep,
And I'le tear the Rocks in sunder.
But I will find Bonny Maud, *Merry Mad* Maud,
And seek what e're betides her,
Yet I will love
Beneath or above,
The dirty Earth that hides her.

To Find my Tom of Bedlam reads like a companion piece to a *Loving Mad Tom* song in which the love element plainly occurs, though not necessarily to L. Another pair of companion pictures, *Forth from my Sad and Darksome Cel*, from *Wit and Mirth* (1699), and *Mad Maudline is Come*, from *Wit and Drollery* (1661), though printed earlier than L and *To Find my Tom of Bedlam*, are not of much interest except as confirming the love association of Tom and Maudline in a setting resembling that of E. *Forth from my Sad and Darksome Cel* recalls E in many points, particularly in a reference to the horning of the Heavenly Farrier.

Here, then, is my reconstruction of P, the professional song of the Abraham-men. The first verse is the sad soliloquy in explanation of insanity (supplied by analogy from *To Find my Tom of Bedlam*); the second verse is the salutation, recalling the customary 'lunatic bans' of which Edgar speaks in *King Lear*; the remaining verses, except for the last, are proof of harmless insanity; the last is the appeal for lovers' sympathy. The poem contains no mythological references: the Book of Moons is merely, I think, an astrological almanack carried by the 'Moon-men' (the gipsies):

P

1

In search of merry Maudline
Ten thousand years I'll travel.
Here's poor Tom goes with dirty toes
To save his shoes from gravel.
While he does sing 'any food, any feeding,
Feeding, drink or clothing?
Come dame or maid, be not afraid;
Poor Tom will injure nothing.'

2
From the hag[1] and hungry goblin
    That into rags would rend ye
The spirit that stands by the naked man
    In the Book of Moons defend ye!
While I do sing, etc.

3
Of thirty bare years have I
    Twice twenty been enragèd
And of forty been three times fifteen
    In durance soundly cagèd.
Now I do sing, etc.

4
In the bonny cells of Bedlam
    Ere I was one-and-twenty
I had bracelets strong, sweet whips ding-dong
    And prayer and fasting plenty.
Now I do sing, etc.

5
A thought I took for Maudline
    In a cruse of cockle-pottage:
With a thing thus tall—God[2] bless you all!—
    I befell into this dotage.[3]
So now I sing, etc.

6
When I short have shorn my sow's face
    And snigged my hairy barrel,
At an oaken inn I'll 'pound my skin
    In a suit of gilt apparel.[4]
But now I sing, etc.

[1] 'The Hag' was the mediaeval reminiscence of the Bronze Age Goddess 'Black Annis' or 'Anna.' She had a blue-black face and devoured young children.

[2] The substitution in E of 'Sky' for 'God' in this obscene passage—a common evasion of the Puritanical stage-censorship—proves that E was written for theatrical use.

[3] i.e. he thought about Maudline when he drank cockle-soup (shell-fish have a world-wide aphrodisiac reputation) which had a priapic effect upon him. 'Cockle-bread' was also an aphrodisiac.

[4] *swigged* for *snigged* and *horny* for *hairy* in E suggest that Giles Earle copied from a badly written manuscript. The passage means that when he shaved off his bristles and roughly clipped the shaggy hair off his body ('barrel' is the belly of a horse or ass) he lies down under an oak in the moonlight. 'Thou'rt brutish, shave thyself' was a contemporary Spanish catch-word.

7

The palsie plague my pulses
  If I prig your pigs or pullen.[1]
Your culvers take, or matchless make[2]
  Your Chanty-clear or Solan![3]
Yet do I sing, etc.

8

The gipsies Snap and Pedro
  Are none of Tom's camradoes:
The punk[4] I scorn and the cutpurse sworn
  And the roaring-boy's[5] bravadoes.
I do but sing, etc.

9

But I'll find merry mad Maudline
  And seek whate'er betides her,
And I will love beneath or above
  The dirty earth that hides her.
Till then I sing, etc.

I get the same feeling from L as from *To Find my Tom of Bedlam*:
one of conscious 'Wit and Drollery.' With the exception of the first
verse, there is a strained, ranting tone which occurs nowhere in E,
and I believe that this first verse is the final verse of Q, the first
theatrical version of the poem, omitted by Giles Earle from his
manuscript version with the same carelessness as allowed him to omit
the music for the song after ruling the lines for it; but that the author
of L happened to remember it and expanded it into a separate song by
using the second half of the stanza as a refrain and devising fresh
conceits in the style of *To Find my Tom of Bedlam*.

If this is so, Q can be restored as a poem by amending the obvious
corruptions of E and completing it with the first stanza of L. A young
Australian poet who is obsessed with the idea of making the theory of
la poésie pure apply to English poetry both in prospect and retrospect
recently praised the 'magic' of *Tom o' Bedlam*, as he knew it in E, for
its very meaninglessness. When I suggested to him that 'and the

[1] if I steal your pigs or chickens.
[2] take your pigeons or make a widower of.
[3] your cock or gander.
[4] Whore.
[5] Old soldier who blackmailed citizens into charity with oaths and threats.

lowlie owle my morrowe' should read 'and the lovely owl my marrow'
he was very angry indeed. If he had been consistent he would have
adopted as more poetic the still more corrupt variant readings of later
texts, given above—e.g. 'Toms rynoross' for *Tom* Rynosseross, and
'the Panders' for Panther. His view seems to be widespread; for
nobody has hitherto taken the trouble to make sense of 'swigged my
horny barrel' or 'cruse of cockle pottage.'

My conclusion that the first verse of L is the missing last verse of Q
is supported by the way it picks up the various loose threads of former
verses. It carries on the figure of the tourney, disposes of the moon
for her 'horning' the star of the morn (as mentioned in stanza 6), and
puts the necessary emotional emphasis on Maudline, the heroine of the
poem, who is scantily treated in E. So the poem ends with fierce force
as it began, not with the gentle and inconclusive 'Methinks it is no
journey.' So here is my tentative reconstruction of Q. It may have
lost other verses, but not many, because a theatrical song of this sort
was only a convenience for the scene-shifters; and scene-shifting on
the Elizabethan stage would not have taken longer than the time needed
to sing these nine stanzas.

Q

1

From the hag and hungry goblin
     That into rags would rend ye,
The spirit that stands by the naked man
     In the Book of Moons defend ye,
That of your five sound senses
     You never be forsaken
Nor wander from yourselves, with Tom,
     Abroad to beg your bacon.
While I do sing 'any food, any feeding,
     Feeding, drink or clothing?'
Come dame or maid, be not afraid:
     Poor Tom will injure nothing.

2

Of thirty bare years have I
     Twice twenty been enragèd,
And of forty been three times fifteen
     In durance soundly cagèd,

On the lordly lofts of Bedlam
  With stubble soft and dainty,
Brave bracelets strong, sweet whips ding-dong,
  And wholesome hunger plenty.
And now I sing, etc.

3

A thought I took for Maudline
  In a cruse of cockle pottage:
With a thing thus tall—God bless you all!—
  I befell into this dotage.
I've slept not since the Conquest,
  Ere then I never waked
Till the roguish fay of love where I lay
  Me found and stripped me naked.
And now I sing, etc.

4

When I short have shorn my sow's-face
  And snigged my hairy barrel
At an oaken inn I 'pound my skin
  In a suit of gilt apparel.
The Moon's my constant mistress
  And the lovely owl my marrow.[1]
The flaming drake[2] and the night-crow make
  Me music to my sorrow.
While I do sing, etc.

5

The palsy plague my pulses
  If I prig your pigs or pullen,
Your culvers take, or matchless make
  Your Chanty-clear or Solan!
When I want provant,[3] with Humphry
  I sup,[4] and when benighted
I repose in Paul's with walking souls
  Yet never am affrighted.
But I do sing, etc.

[1] dear companion.
[2] Dragon.
[3] need food.
[4] i.e. go to sleep supperless in Duke Humphry's Walk at St. Paul's.

6

I know more than Apollo,
　　For oft when he lies sleeping
I see the stars at bloody wars
　　And the wounded welkin weeping,
The moon embrace her shepherd[1]
　　And the Queen of Love her warrior,
When the first doth horn the Star of the Morn
　　And the next, the Heavenly Farrier.[2]
While I do sing, etc.

7

The gipsies, Snap and Pedro,
　　Are none of Tom's camradoes;
The punk I scorn and the cut-purse sworn
　　And the roaring-boy's bravadoes:
The meek, the white, the gentle
　　Me handle, touch and spare not,
But those that cross Tom Rhinoceros
　　Do what the Panther dare not.
Though I do sing, etc.

8

With an host of furious fancies
　　Whereof I am commander,
With a burning spear and a horse of air
　　To the wilderness I wander.
By a knight of ghosts and shadows
　　I summoned am to tourney,
Ten leagues beyond the wide world's end—
　　Methinks it is no journey.
Yet will I sing, etc.

9

I'll bark against the Dog-Star,
　　I'll crow away the morning,
I'll chase the moon till it be noon
　　And make her leave her horning,
But I'll find merry mad Maudline,
　　And seek whate'er betides her,
And I will love beneath or above
　　The dirty earth that hides her.
Till then I sing, etc.

[1] Endymion.
[2] i.e. The Moon cuckolds Lucifer, and Venus cuckolds Vulcan.

I suppose, in fact, that the author of Q discarded the introductory stanza of P in favour of the more dramatic start 'From the hag and hungry goblin,' fitted an explanatory second half to this stanza, and retained the final stanza as the final half-stanza of a song made by doubling the existing stanzas and inserting two entirely new ones. It was important to leave Tom with both feet on the earth at the end of the poem, after his visionary trip among the clouds.

As for the author of Q, he was a poet of the first rank and either the author of, or a collaborator in, a play in which rogues and vagabonds occur. Were it not such an invidious undertaking to ascribe even a very good poem to a writer of Shakespeare's majesty, I should immediately suggest that it was sung by Edgar at the close of the third scene of the second act of *King Lear*, as an interlude to give the scene-shifters time to prepare the arrangement 'Before Gloucester's Castle; Kent in the stocks.' Edgar has just announced his intention of becoming one

> Of Bedlam beggers, who with roaring voices,
> Strike in their num'd and mortified Armes,
> Pins, Wodden-prickes, Nayles, Sprigs of Rosemarie:
> And with this horrible obiect, from low Farmes,
> Poore pelting Villages, Sheeps-Coates, and Milles,
> Sometimes with Lunaticke bans, sometime with Praiers
> Inforce their charitie: poore *Turlygod*, poore *Tom*,
> That's something yet: *Edgar* I nothing am.

Must I play for safety instead and suggest Jonson's *Bartholomew Fair*, the song to be sung by Nightingale; or Middleton's *Roaring Girl*, the song to be sung by Trapdoor? These are the only two other possible dramatic contexts, but neither is anything like so suitable to the ballad as *King Lear*, where the outlawed Edgar plays Tom o'Bedlam and overlays the original dross of the beggars' ballad with the gold of courtly poetry. Indeed, if scholars are loth to accept Q as of Shakespeare's authorship they must assume a lost play by another hand in which the same unusual situation occurs; which would be silly. It will be recalled that Edgar attributes the loss of his wits to love. He warns Lear: 'Let not the creaking of shooes, nor the rustling of silkes, betray thy poore heart to woman.'

RUDYARD KIPLING
(1928)

RUDYARD KIPLING

THE superior critics of to-day have at last decided to admit Rudyard Kipling to their Hall of Fame and make the superior critics of yesterday who mocked him look foolish. They can justify their decision by pointing out that Kipling is an international figure; that he is the only Englishman not wholly an Irishman who has won the Nobel Prize; that he is a scholar, or at any rate speaks a good word for scholarship; that though a popular writer he dislikes the lower classes ('Serviles' as he calls them in his story *As Easy as A.B.C.*) unless they touch their caps to him; believes in the defence of the West; is widely travelled; and has deep respect for the French. Any popular romantic lapses of the past can be forgiven him in the light of such qualifications; and a further qualification, that he is unlikely to write much more, consolidates his position.

They are welcome to their new hero and there need be no embarrassing sequel, because Kipling addresses the larger public, the English People, On land and sea, Wherever Ye may be, and has no commerce with Bloomsbury. Their gesture of approbation is, in fact, superfluous: the elephant stops for a moment by the roadside and the beetle encouragingly lifts up a leg. Kipling is a great man in the most overt sense, the Lloyd George–Northcliffe sense; he is ordinary-minded though emotionally eccentric, the subject for mass-admiration, and no more to be argued away than the design on the postage stamp. The superior critics of yesterday knew that only too well. There is no point in parodying Kipling; he is not to be outdone. Or in suggesting that he is really no poet—that has been a popular commonplace since 1886—and the time is not yet ripe for suggesting that he really is a poet, after all. It would be false to pretend that he cannot write prose: he can, like any Frenchman. Or that he is unreadable: a set of Kipling has a sinister fascination for the reader, particularly one recovering from influenza—like old bound volumes of *Punch*. Finally, he is the literary aspect of the British Empire, the only possible literary aspect of a complex organization to which even the superior critics of to-day, as of yesterday, are unaccountably but inevitably affiliated.

Let us consider this British Empire. At first there was England, and England acquired overseas possessions of a casual sort: an accumulation of trading stations placed in various conveniently rich localities, widely separated, served by a powerful navy, and managed for the advantage of merchant companies in England. England was all that really mattered: although wherever possible the trade officials assumed control of the government of the country or district concerned and made themselves as comfortable as they could, there was no imperial sentiment floating about, or sentiment of any sort. Trading was a dirty, dangerous, and dishonourable game. Being honest with the natives meant being false to the shareholders of the merchant company; being honest to the company meant being extortionate to the natives. Since being honest to both meant a lean and perpetual exile, the traders usually compromised by being false to both. The only people who could afford to indulge in noble sentiments were the naval and military officers detailed to protect these posts: they had the traditions of their services to maintain, loathed their exile (which was seldom even profitable) and looked down on the traders. In other parts of the Empire white settlements, formed by religious refugees, fugitives from justice, freaks, misfits, black sheep, transported convicts, Scots, reformed prostitutes, and ex-naval ratings, had dispossessed the natives and become self-supporting.

Eventually the English found it convenient to take serious notice of their overseas possessions and knit them together into an Empire by every possible means; to make England more and more the trading exchange, administrative hub and exporter of locomotives, cretonnes and alarm clocks. They urged one another to think imperially. The difficulty was how to improvise the necessary imperial sentiment and pass it current in literary form. The Navy and Army were adequately provided with literary exemplars in the heroic pages of Smollett, Marryat, Campbell, Tennyson, Napier, and others. The Navy further knew that it had hearts of oak and that Britannia ruled the waves, and the Army knew that of all those royal heroes there was none that could compare, with a tow row row and a tow row row, with the British grenadier. But the Empire which the Army and Navy served had no idea at all how it looked in cold print, and continued to exist without official sentiment until well on into the reign of Queen Victoria. An occasional writer like Froude did his best to remedy matters, but in spite of his generous sacrifice of history to style made little headway. The Empire badly needed a Kipling, and at last got one—in India, towards the close of the eighteen-eighties. The trading posts in India had by this time been splendidly enlarged and regularized. The private trading company had been superseded by a public one, and most traders now drew their salaries as representatives of the Crown, like the soldiers and sailors. It was at last possible to be honest, though a trade official; it was safer too, except at the Native Courts. But it was difficult to hit a moral mean between the militant puritanism of the Mutiny heroes and the gentlemanly relaxation of European morals—excused by the climate—which had been a tradition of the traders since the time of Charles II; and without a fixed morality it is impossible to have sentiment; and without sentiment the English are lost.

Kipling was the moralist. At first, of course, he was looked on with suspicion and even detestation by the Anglo-Indians of the Mutiny tradition. *Departmental Ditties*, with its references to corsets and pink dominoes and the squeezed waists of other people's wives, was disgusting. *Plain Tales from the Hills* was intolerable: adultery was taken as a matter of course—their Simla might be Paris. Yet *Plain Tales from the Hills* scored a great success in London, where Simla seemed exotic and more than Parisian. The elder generation might expostulate against ' that cad Kipling' and even hint that he had ' a touch of the tar-brush'; but the younger, less actively religious, Anglo-Indians realized that to be part of Home literature made Simla morality respectable, and that they could now go to the limits of promiscuity which Kipling, in his over-colouring of the picture, allowed them. In return for this licence they had to accept, and live up to, certain qualities which he had attributed to them: emotional restraint, extraordinary conscientiousness in administration, love of truth and a sense of imperial brotherliness. The *Book of Joshua* which had been the *Field-Service Manual* of the Mutiny, had to be discarded—until next time. Killing the enemies of the Queen-Empress must in future be treated as a sport like pig-sticking, not as an act of expansion on the part of a chosen people; and bloody acts of vengeance like the many performed in the closing stages of the Mutiny were no longer to behoove the white man. Kipling has always recognized the origin of these acts. He is himself naturally inclined to hysteria and longs to indulge it; he admires Fuzzy-Wuzzy, the Dervish, above all the former enemies of the Queen, because he could froth at the mouth and break a British Square, spear and shield against rifle and Gatling gun. It is an admiration tinged with envy. He knows that many other Englishmen have the same shameful longing; but he knows that, though valuable in hand-to-hand fighting, hysteria must be kept out of tactics and administration. On this knowledge he continually harps. Throughout his works the spectacle of men on the point of hysteria but restraining themselves for reasons of pride, or else giving way and weeping and shooting themselves or their neighbours, constantly recurs. Two large-scale pictures of military and civil hysteria are to be found in *The Drums of the Fore and Aft* and *The Village that Voted the Earth was Flat.* Hysteria must be kept under control, then; the sahib must not let his angry passions rise with the temperature. Of course, the loyal cut-throats of a native regiment may ritually sacrifice a hundred Burmese warriors to open Heaven's gate for the soul of their slain white lieutenant, as in *The Grave of the Hundred Heads*—that is Eastern picturesqueness. But it is no longer a sahib's privilege even to kick or flog the peasant; though if a loyal native subordinate or an English private soldier (not quite a sahib) does so for the good of the peasant's soul it is not a bad joke. Nor may the native Princes be bled or blackmailed any more; though, again, if a non-sahib does so success-fully the sahib is permitted to smile, as in *The Man who would be King.*

At the same time that Kipling gave the Anglo-Indian administrator his *Deuteronomy*, he also gave the English private soldier in India his: in *Soldiers Three* and *Barrack Room Ballads.* This was another benefit, because British Grenadier sentiment was not consonant with the popular Victorian view of the common soldier as a lost soul badged for Hell by the very red of his coat, a view which was also held by the Anglo-Indians of superior rank. I own a copy of *The Church Catechism Explained*, a little book published at Cawnpore two years before the massacre, which takes its anecdotal illustrations from local barrack life. It is eloquent on the vices of the soldiery, their drunkenness, fighting, blasphemy, adultery; the only consolation given is that the soldier at least is not a wicked idolator like the Cawnpore Indian, and that several occasions have been noted of the spiritual conversion of soldiers and their subsequent retirement into decent civil life.

Kipling's proposed moral code was this: he condoned drinking bouts at hygienic intervals, he took something like the French view of adultery, he encouraged fighting with fists and belts as being an old English habit and better than running amok with rifle and bayonet, he delighted in oaths and ribaldry, and discountenanced piety while at the same time insisting on certain soldierly virtues such as loyalty, initiative, comradeship, steadiness under fire and, above all, personal cleanliness and care of arms.

The soldier accepted this practical code; or rather his Kipling-reading officers accepted it for him, as his godfathers; and so from 1887 until 1914 all time-serving soldiers grew more and more to be Kipling's Own—to a fantastic degree in the more imaginative cases. In 1914 a re-enlisted soldier was pointed out to me on the barrack-square at Wrexham; he had, it was said, deserted his regiment at Quetta with a comrade, passed on foot across the North-West frontier, and eventually surrendered to the British Consul at Jerusalem: ' 'E buried 'is chum by the way' the tale ended. Later, Kipling made the Merchant Service literary in much the same way, and gave it absolution in much the same terms. Later still, the Royal Navy, though conservative in religious matters, was not averse from submitting to the Kipling spell. The only two conditions which the sailors made were that he should be technically accurate in his writing and remember their religious sensibilities: these conditions he observed.

Kipling has always had the gift of knowing what his lowest-common-multiple audience will accept as a standard of convincing writing. About matters of administrative routine, climatic variations, drinks, polo, bee-keeping, frivolities and every sort of machinery he writes knowledgeably. About native Indian life, I gather from native Indians, superficially: here he plays on the Anglo-Indian prejudice in favour of the tough, savage, meat-eating, blood-feud-loving, fanatic hill-tribes-man, with his capacity for loyalty and heroism under the British Raj, and against the mild, philosophical, cunning, unwarlike, rice-eating plainsman, with a capacity for departmental detail and disloyal laughter. About barrack-room life, accurately in outline, fantastically in detail.

As an Anglo-Indian, one of his first tasks was to define the relationship between the religion of the white community and those of the various native communities. About conventional Christianity he has little to say, though heaven and hell are amusing abstractions to him, and droll irreverence about the crystal sea and St. Peter's register and the price of good pit coal is frequent both in his verse and prose. He is a capable amateur exponent of comparative religion and has a sentimental feeling for most Oriental cults; suttee appeals to his virile creed, so do hara-kiri and gongs and blood-sacrifice. He likes religions in which castes and degrees play a prominent part—the idea of Christian democracy he hates—but particularly those in which the fighting-man takes precedence over the priest and the politican. It appears that he is a Freemason; and this accommodating faith, to which every sahib in India, particularly every Army officer, must belong if he wants to get on, does ally itself with democracy. But it is only a mystical alliance: the craft merely affirms caste by allowing a temporary relaxation from caste while the Lodge is in progress.

Outside. 'Serjeant! Sir! Salute! Salaam!'
Inside. 'Brother,' an' it doesn't do no 'arm.

This, Kipling sees, is a neat way of squaring the notion of aristocratic militarism with that of imperial brotherhood. In his most recent volume *Debits and Credits*, he has recommended Masonry as a more effective organization for imperial usage than the Established Church.

Naturally, he realizes the practical necessity for religious toleration and is ready to believe in magic performances of a picturesque sort as potent in all cults. He insists, however, that the white man's magic is stronger than any, if it can be symbolized by the swastika amulet (Kipling's Own, again), having for its four arms The Sovereign, The Empire, The Job, The Girl who is Waiting; and if the white man does not, as in *The Mark of the Beast*, purposely offend some dusky god. Kipling's suppressed superstition is of the same sort as his suppressed hysteria: he knows that he shares it with most Englishmen and plays on their longing to indulge it. He allows them plenty of scope, so long as they do not lose their swastika amulet. Dreams, ghosts, visions, destinies, curses, warnings—he has exploited all these and many other varieties of lesser religious experience a hundred times over. Every now and then, of course, as in *My True Ghost Story*, he allows a merely rationalistic explanation; for the West must not allow itself to be hoodooed by the East. That was the point of Kim's reciting his multiplication table in order to neutralize the mesmeric spell of the native juggler. One gathers that one of Kipling's favourite authors is superstitious Aubrey, of the *Miscellany*, and that Kipling regrets his own date.

Kipling did have a spiritual experience of a major sort in the South African War: he came 'back to 'Ackneystadt, but not the same.' He had already realized that the far-flung Empire was capable of close spiritual integration and had written poems in that sense, his atlas wide open; the South African War, which he attended as war-correspondent, clinched the matter. (It is the greatest pity that Kipling was never a real soldier, admissible to the highest caste, for Dr. Johnson came near enough to the truth when he wrote that no man has a good opinion of himself who has not been one.) Not only did he then become aware of South Africa, but he met Australian, Canadian, New Zealand troops serving together. Lying on his back one night in the silent veldt he was aware of an Unknown God beaming down from beyond 'the 'igh inexpressible stars'; and thereupon mystically equated this Unknown God and the Genius of the British Empire—or that is how I reconstruct the event. It has always been touch and go with Kipling and his mysticism: he has kept his head fairly well, all considered. Just below the surface of his work lies the cranky conception of the English as one of the Lost Tribes, and the identification of this or that Continental power with the Beast of the Apocalypse; but he recognizes them as unsuitable beliefs, and repeats the multiplication table rapidly under his breath.

Having made the Empire mystico-literary in breadth from Mandalay to St. John's, Newfoundland, Kipling, now established in England, began to make it mystico-literary in depth. In default of the Lost Tribes myth he preached a mystic succession from the Roman to the British Empire. But mysticism needs supernatural agents; and since angels are Semitic inventions, and therefore only possible in a satiric setting or in hymns, the truly British fairy or *puca* had to do instead. But the pukka sahib could not be expected to admit belief even in a pukka *puca*; though he would dearly love to indulge the superstition. So Kipling's next scheme was to make English history exciting for a school-room audience, already captured by the *Jungle Books*, by turning it into fairy-stories, and to write just a little above his readers' heads so that the pukka sahib and the pukka memsahib could understand that the mystic message was really addressed to them. The message was that the morality of the public-school had prevailed in England among the lords ever since the Romans landed, and that the morality of the lesser breeds within the law, of the Hobdens and Orth'rises and of the loyal native auxiliary within the Empire, whether Pict, Tewara, Sikh, or Sioux, had likewise been constant.

It is curious that the Boy Scout movement, which began in the year that *Puck of Pook's Hill* appeared, did not find direct inspiration in this volume, or in its successor, *Rewards and Fairies*. The ritual of Oak, Ash and Thorn, and the spiritual tutelage of Puck, the first boy scout of the High and Far Off Times, would have suited it perfectly. Baden-Powell and Kipling were granted their inspiration for saving the youth of the Empire and making it clean and manly by the same South African stars. Kipling's sympathy with the movement is attested by his volume of *Sea and Land Tales for Scouts and Guides*; while Baden-Powell's antiphonic war-cry:

Cant. Ingonyama, Ingonyama!
(He is a lion, a lion!)

Dec. Invooboo, Invooboo!
(Nay, more, he is a hippopotamus, a hippopotamus!)

is pure Kipling, by *The Jungle Book* out of *Stalky and Co.*

Kipling is a pretty good historian of the present: he has never lost his journalistic gift for catching hold of a specialized vocabulary and working it up into a sentimental poem or short story. After mastering the jargon of the ship's engine-room, he worked up the locomotive jargon and the jargon of the garage, and finally was ready to Kiplingize the young Air Force and the Tank Corps too, if necessary. His greatest gift is making the casual remark pregnant with historical significance. Once during the South African campaign at a bar in Cape Town (or so I was informed by a man who swore he was there) Kipling was sitting with two New South Wales troopers. Kipling asked: 'What'll you drink?' The surly trooper did not answer him but, turning to his chum, remarked: 'Talking of wattles, Sam, do you remember the smell of the wattles at Lichtenburg when we rode in, in the rain?' Kipling noted the phrase and made a ballad of it. Afterwards, said my informant, a friend of his who 'knew his Kipling,' a resident at this same Lichtenburg, looked round for the wattles and found none. They are an Australian variety of mimosa, apparently. But that the scripture might be fulfilled, he sent to the Cape Town botanical gardens for a wattle or wattles, and reported his action to Kipling, who wrote to say that he was gratified. However, I recently met another Kiplingite at Port Said, where they abound, who told me that two miles from Lichtenburg is a grove of—well, some South African tree—which is a cousin of the wattles and does emit a wattleish smell in wet weather; he had always intended to write to Kipling and reassure him about it. Unfortunately it is not always possible to fulfil scripture retrospectively for Kipling. In the tale of *The Centurion of the Thirtieth*, for instance, the two main picturesque properties are the dwarfish Picts and the winged hats of the Northmen. Neither of these are now admitted by the historians. More recently he has gone badly wrong in dating the deaths of Scott and Jane Austen.

Kipling was one of the prophets of the war with Germany; but for a number of years he had also been a prophet of the invasion of British India by the Russians, and it never came off; so his score is one bull and one miss. He has always been a sensitive observer of racial prejudice

in the sahib class. Until Edward VII came to the throne he had nothing
against the Germans (after all, the idealized Widow of Windsor was
more or less a German herself), and there is even a sentimental German
with a thick accent who appears in one of the later Mowgli stories, an
official in the Indian Forestry Service, applauded for his sensible
administrative methods and knowledge of woodcraft.

When at last Kipling got his war, he behaved characteristically. The
hysteria rose very near the surface indeed. He even permitted the
sahibs, in a poem, to hate—a great relaxation of the code. In a peculi-
arly bloody story, *Mary Postgate*, he describes how a respectable
English governess let a wounded German airman die, in revenge for
the death of her old pupil, an English airman, and of a child killed by
a bomb. It is a neat evasion: a pukka sahib would have coldly and
distastefully fetched the German a drink and phoned for the ambulance,
in spite of the murdered child. (Possibly her old pupil had also acci-
dentally killed a child or two behind the German lines, but we must
not dwell on that.) At all events, the respectable governess was one of
the lesser breeds within the law; so, borrowing her old pupil's phrase,
she called him a 'bloody pagan' and waited for his death-rattle, which
cheered her up a good deal—*and* the war-bereaved sahibs who read
the account.

One of Kipling's literary problems is how to maintain the illusion
of the man of caste who never talks about what lies closest to his heart
—his mystic swastika—and yet explain the swastika in blackboard
terms for his readers. He has solved the problem more than once by
putting the sentiments into rough verse form, and leaving out the
aitches, or in flowery Havildar Major (see *In the Presence*). Or better
still, he has put them with prosaic vulgarity into the mouth of a member
of Parliament, so that they sound all wrong and the man of caste pulls
a wry face: this method is used successfully in the cadet-corps story in
Stalky and Co., and years later in *The Vortex* (1914). But for the most
part the sentiment is indicated, rather than expressed, by a casual,
shamefaced recital of great deeds, broken off with the dying close of
a *chota peg* on the veranda. Of course, he has written hymns full of
Ye's and Thou's and Lord God of Hosts, and the nemesis-averting
Recessional: 'Lord God of Hosts be with us yet, Lest we forget, lest
we forget,' and (though by another hand) the unblushing 'Land of
Hope and Glory,' which may eventually oust 'God Save the King,'
because its lines are longer, drearier, and therefore more suitable for
community singing. You would have thought that 'Land of Hope and

Glory' as authentic, though unsigned, Kipling would nauseate the sahibs, but hymns are privileged vehicles of even indecently religious sentiment (if the Thee's and Ye's are strictly observed): the regimental brass band plays hymns every Sunday in the Square. And so the hymns are condoned so long as Kipling will keep his prose clean.

In forty years Kipling has advanced his Empire, the literary one, through all the five continents and across all the seven seas. If you mount on the wings of the morning you meet him chattering of joysticks and Rusholme silencers, if you descend to the depths of the ocean he is there also, impersonating a submarine that found itself. Roll back two thousand years in history, he is hob-nobbing with Roman road-menders and Celtic gods. Advance a thousand years and he threatens you with appalling rays and aerial boards of control. Wider still and wider shall thy bounds be set, God that made thee mighty make thee mightier yet, With thy 'elio winkin' like fun, Three sides of a million-mile square, O'er a vast interstellar abyss, Are ye there, Are ye there, Are ye there? And if all the men who claim to have been at school with Kipling and are awarded free drinks as a tribute to the legend of *Stalky and Co.*, could be brought together, they would make a good-sized university.

Contemporary literature is strewn with his dilutions and extensions. The later Masefield in his *Sea and Land Romances for Scouts and Guides*, the later Wells in his novels of contemporary history, are ghosting for him. Mowgli gets popularized for Serviles and Americans as Tarzan of the Apes; Newbolt takes straight Kipling themes and writes them out in verse of greater spirit than Kipling himself can command: 'Drake's Drum,' 'Admirals All,' 'Play up, Play up, and Play the Game,' and the heroically conceived 'He Fell Among Thieves,' have a deeper popularity with the audience which Kipling created than any verses of Kipling's. Even Galsworthy has dipped into the sack and written of ships and Englishmen sweating in the jungle in a style easily recognizable as borrowed; and has constructed his best short story, *The Stoic*, in the carefully restrained Kipling manner, out of materials provided by a purposely vulgar Kipling poem, 'The Mary Gloster.'

Kipling's attitude to Americans is characteristic: he tolerates them only if they come to England and humble themselves as heirs who have lost their inheritance, and if they respect the hoary institutions and restrain their talk of wealth, remembering that the only caste which they have is a courtesy caste allowed them when visiting the estates of the real lords of creation. (No American has ever succeeded in localizing the American dialect which the Kipling American speaks. It is not New England, Southern, Middle West, or Californian, or a mixture of these; it is a literary convention.) But since Kipling, though denying them caste, gives them credit for humour, kindliness, mechanical knowledge, business ability, and so on, they forgive him and exchange grins when his back is turned, rather like the poor and foolish Babu. To humour him they come in cars, disguised in shell-rimmed spectacles and Kipling-American accents, honking through Burwash, Sussex, and stopping to chip souvenir pieces off his garden benches with their inevitable bowie-knives. They also collect his first editions. They are grateful for being caricatured.

The Irish have never, so far as I know, thanked Kipling for his view of them; they have even shown ingratitude. They have made a fool of him by overturning one of his strongest convictions, expressed in a shocking story, *The Mutiny of the Mavericks*, that an Irish regiment would never mutiny in India for political reasons: a battalion of the Connaught Rangers did so shortly after the Armistice, and the regiment was later, along with the *Mavericks*, the *Black Boneens*, and all the genuine regiments of that 'quaint, crooked, sweet, profoundly irresponsible, and profoundly lovable race that fight like fiends, argue like children, reason like women, and obey like men,' finally disbanded.

The French, to whom he has offered a verse garland, *France at War*, whose 'keen-faced *poilus*' he has actually admitted into an English heaven (see *On the Gate*), will probably treat him better—at any rate until their next war with us.

It must not be forgotten that Kipling wrote *Just-so Stories*, which is a favourite with all upper-class children who are not frightened by the end-of-the-worldish nightmare atmosphere of most of its pieces, or depressed by the confidential, rather cruel cheerfulness of the rest, and are old enough to be flattered by Kipling's appeal to them as grown-ups whimsically pretending to be children. I wonder whether it is really on account of the *Just-so Stories* and the *Jungle Books* that the superior critics of to-day (repaying a childhood's debt) are now making much of him?

[COMMENT 1949]

T. S. Eliot, o.m., this year's American-born Nobel Prize winner, has recently edited a selection of Kipling's poems; nothing could have been apter.

ESSAYS FROM *EPILOGUE*
(1935–1937)

I

NIETZSCHE

THE homogeneity of the Germans has been a matter of remark since the first histories of them were written—as Tacitus writes: 'A race with a distinct character: a family likeness pervades the whole, though their numbers are so great.' It is noteworthy that the four chief names of the race—*Deutsch*, *Allemand*, *Teuton*, *German*—convey this sense of congenital relatedness. *Deutsch* and *Teuton* are derived from the same word—meaning 'the people' in a corporate human sense. The Roman name for the race, as distinct from particular tribes, was *Germani*, which means 'the related ones'; it was a mishearing of *Wehrmann* (warrior), but the Germans accepted it as apposite. *Allemands* or *Alemanni* is *alle Männer* or 'all man.' Tacitus relates that their principal gods were Tuisto (the same as Teut) and his son Mannus (man), and that they sprang from the earth. That is, from the beginning Germans made a generic identity between the divine and the human.

Nietzsche was not only a German, he was increasingly conscious of what it was to be a German. *Ecce Homo*, his last book, is the most violent statement of Germanism on record; it was to him the most wonderful book, apart from his *Zarathustra*, ever written. Germans have a way of protecting themselves from an awareness of their own incoherence by telling themselves lies. Nietzsche piled lie on lie, but in the writing of *Ecce Homo* he must have come to understand himself, for the sequel was the madness which he had so long deferred: he allowed himself to disintegrate mentally and spent the rest of his life in an insane asylum. Tacitus observed how anxious Germans were, even when sober, to submit themselves to risks: they would stake their lives and liberties on a dice-bout. And reading Nietzsche—a man who, by pursuing Germanism to a desperate extreme, broke down in insanity—is for Germans an excitingly dangerous thing. Did not Nietzsche himself give warning that he who breathes the rare air of his lofty mountain-heights must beware? 'The ice is near, the loneliness is terrible.' Such cold and loneliness are metaphorical of loss of the comfortable sense of family warmth. Nietzsche is tempting the Germans to the abnormal; and they enjoy the temptation.

Ecce Homo was written in a condition medically interpretable as *euphoria*, which means to feel the highest well-being and capacity just before a complete breakdown. To begin with the physical background of this book is critically apt: Nietzsche himself was careful to explain his bodily condition by a running clinical commentary on the state of his health during the various periods of composition. The first chapter, 'Why I am so wise,' is largely an assertion of his own physical soundness and of the identity of physical soundness with spiritual well-being.

My circulation is slow. No one has ever been able to detect fever in me. A doctor who treated me for some time as a nerve patient finally declared: 'No! there is nothing wrong with your nerves, it is simply I who am nervous.' It has been absolutely impossible to ascertain any local degeneration in me, nor any organic stomach trouble, however much I may have suffered from profound weakness of the gastric system as the result of general exhaustion. Even my eye trouble, which sometimes approached so parlously near to blindness, was only an effect and not a cause; for, whenever my general vital condition improved, my power of vision also increased.

He blames the original physical exhaustion on the German climate and the German habits of over-eating, over-drinking, gathering round stuffy stoves, and on his own sedentary habits as a philological book-worm—from all of which he has long freed himself by escaping South. He makes no reference to his real ailment, a deep-seated venereal taint, though he must have been aware of it. 'I placed myself in my own hands, I restored myself to health . . . out of my will to Health and Life I made my philosophy.'

Ecce Homo is one long diatribe against spiritual and physical uncleanness.

I am gifted with a sense of cleanliness the keenness of which is phenomenal . . . I would die in unclean surroundings—I swim, bathe and splash about, as it were, incessantly in water, in any kind of perfectly transparent and shining element.

This bathing and swimming metaphor for spirituality is common to Nietzsche's writings; as all Germans give a spiritual significance to bathing and swimming. (Tacitus remarked on how much bathing the Germans did.) The Germans are also mountain-mad. By climbing they metaphorically express hatred of themselves for living in what

Nietzsche, speaking in spiritual terms, calls the Flatland of Europe. Nietzsche's supreme praise for his *Zarathustra* is 'the loftiest book on earth, literally the book of mountain air.' Swimming and mountain-climbing take a high yearly death-toll of Germans: the number of bathers drowned in the Rhine, and of climbers killed in the Alps, is excessive. It is characteristic of the Germans, too, that once one of them gets drowned in a foreign river or killed on a foreign mountain his example is always followed by others: they do not intend to get killed, only to tempt a danger which the death of one of them has Germanized. Nietzsche knew the falsity of the climbing urge. He addressed the Germans in his *Dionysus-Dithyrambs*:

> Ye mount?
> Is it true that ye mount,
> Ye loftier men?
> Are ye not, pray,
> Like to a ball
> Sped to the heights
> By the lowest that's in you?
> Do ye not flee from yourselves, O ye climbers?

In the same poem he also writes:

> Only the poet who can lie
> Wilfully, skilfully
> Can tell the truth.

The wish to arouse universal pity for suffering bravely borne is a characteristic of Germans for which Nietzsche had nothing but scorn and of which he wrote at length; yet he could not avoid the national idiosyncrasy himself. The year, he recorded, contained for him two hundred days of pure pain. Fear of physical indisposition makes the Germans of all people the most conscious of dietetic problems; and Nietzsche has not written twenty pages of this spiritual biography of himself as superman (the chapter heading is 'Why I am so clever'), before he feels himself obliged to note: 'In an enervating climate tea is not a good beverage with which to start the day: an hour before taking it an excellent thing is to drink a cup of thick cocoa, freed from oil.' In this strain he presses the double sense of the German word *Heiland*, which means both 'healer' and 'spiritual saviour,' one who makes whole.

Nietzsche felt strongly in himself the German dietetic dilemma: the choice between the two extremes of 'bestial' meat-gorging and drink-guzzling and the 'nonsense' of vegetarianism, to which he lent himself for a time. The guzzling and sousing is the natural German habit—Tacitus commented on it—and Nietzsche rightly linked it with German intellectual barbarity. Vegetarianism is the unnatural reaction, and Nietzsche rightly linked it with the 'beautiful soul' movement which he equally hated. Yet on the one hand he boasts of his own youthful prowess as a student-drinker at Pforta University, and on the other hand praises his *Dawn of Day*, written shortly after his severance from German cookery and drinking, for

... that sweetness and spirituality which is almost inseparable from ex-treme poverty of blood and muscle ... The perfect lucidity and cheerful-ness, the intellectual exuberance even, that this work reflects, coincides, in my case, not only with the most profound physiological weakness, but also with an excess of suffering. In the midst of the agony of a headache which lasted three days, accompanied by violent nausea, I was possessed of most singular dialectical clearness, and in absolutely cold blood I then thought out things for which, in my more healthy moments, I am not enough of a climber, not sufficiently subtle, not sufficiently cold.

Nietzsche blamed vegetarianism, or malnutrition, for the spread of the enervating Buddhist creed; and in modern Germany there has been a sympathetic affiliation between Tagore, Gandhi and Krishnamurti cults and the *Rohkost* cult. The 'beautiful soul' movement is apparently no modernism: the Germans have always been susceptible to Oriental religions. Tacitus was surprised by the presence of Isis rites in bar-barous Germany—Isis, he said, was symbolized by a galley to denote that her worship was imported.[1] He also remarked on the German desire to be thought well of by the outside world: 'They are peculiarly pleased with presents from neighbouring nations.'

Nietzsche loathed himself for being a German, and yet the im-moderacy and self-contradiction of his loathing was characteristically German. He took refuge in the lies that he was really a Pole: 'My ancestors were Polish noblemen.' But his mother was pure German, and his father, a Lutheran pastor connected with a petty Court, had a

---

[1] I have since come to the conclusion that Isis's galley was a moon-boat, such as was used in the cult of her counterpart Brizo of Delos, apparently the same goddess who was introduced into the British Isles in the second millennium B.C. as Brigit or Bride. This 'Isis' cult must have been brought into Germany by Bronze Age immigrants from the Northern Aegean. I now explain the schizophrenia in the German soul in terms of an unresolved conflict between their patriarchal Aryan strain and their matriarchal Mediter-ranean strain, which though recessive is attested by physical traits and numerous folk-customs.

pure German mother; the Polish strain was remote. He found comfort in the thought that when he travelled abroad he was never taken for a German, but usually for a Pole. Culturally he declared himself French. 'The Poles are the French among the Slavs.' 'I believe only in French culture and regard as a misunderstanding everything else in Europe that calls itself culture.' Referring to the *National Zeitung*, he says, 'a Prussian newspaper (this explanation is for the benefit of my foreign readers: for my own part, I beg to state, I only read *Le Journal des Débats*).' Again, in one of his poems he describes himself as Genoese (by residence of a year or two), linking himself with Columbus. His Polish blood made it easy for him, he said, to be 'a good European.' Yet he was hungry and lonely for Germany and constantly slipped back in his writings into 'We Germans.' One of his poems, *In Lonesomeness*, is the most ingenuous admission of this hunger:

> The cawing crows
>   Townwards on whirring pinions roam;
> Soon come the snows—
>   Thrice happy now who hath a home!

> Fast-rooted there,
>   Thou gazest backwards—oh, how long!
> Thou fool, why dare
>   Ere winter come, this world of wrong?

> Now stand'st thou pale,
>   A frozen pilgrimage thy doom,
> Like smoke whose trail
>   Cold and still colder skies consume.

Nietzsche supplemented the poem with *My Answer*, as if the stanzas had been addressed not to himself by himself, but to himself by some critic in Germany:

> The man presumes—
>   Good Lord!—to think that I'd return
> To those warm rooms
>   Where snug the German ovens burn.

> My friend, you see
>   'Tis but thy folly drives me far,—
> Pity for *thee*
>   And all that German blockheads are!

CA: Q

In *Ecce Homo* he makes another accidental confession, at the end of a passage about his Polish blood and '*this* side of the Alps' and the German inability to understand music: 'I do not know how to think either of joy or of the South without a shudder of fear.' And in spite of his passionate invective against everything German he continued to award the highest praise to German individuals. By the time he came to write *Ecce Homo* he had dropped most of his previous admirations—Wagner, Schopenhauer, Goethe; but he could still applaud Heine, Handel, Bach, von Ranke, Ritschl, Schultz, explaining them as either of foreign extraction or as belonging to a race of strong Germans now vanished. He accounts for his former adoration of Wagner by saying that Wagner's music was 'the counter-poison to everything German': it was all wrong, a German drug, but if one lived in Germany, as he himself had done, one needed it to keep alive at all. 'If a man wishes to get rid of a feeling of insufferable oppression he takes to hashish.' Yet he had once prospectively linked himself with Wagner in posthumous fame. 'When, in the summer of 1876, I took leave of Wagner in my soul . . . I took up arms, not without anger, *against myself* and on behalf of all that hurt me and fell hard on me.' One of his chief charges against Wagner's music is that it incites Germans not to marching or dancing, like strong old German music, but to a falsely spiritual *swimming*.

Nietzsche could not disguise the fact that German was the language in which he thought and felt and wrote. So he spoke of it as an obstacle the overcoming of which made his feats still more glorious. 'Before my time people did not know what could be done with the German language.' He boasted that he had even contrived to endow it with wit: the famous M. Taine had spoken of his *finesses* and *audaces*. Yet 'in order to cross the threshold of this noble and subtle world one must certainly not be a German.' German dyspepsia 'utterly excludes all intercourse with my books.' He has been 'discovered in St. Petersburg, Stockholm, Copenhagen, Paris, New York—everywhere but in Germany.' This curious appreciation of his work, in spite of the language bar, is easily explained: 'my readers are all exceptionally intelligent men.' At this point Nietzsche cannot help making an appeal to Germany as a poor misunderstood child cast off by his cruel parent. He writes winningly:

Wherever I go, here in Turin, for instance, every face brightens and softens at the sight of me. A thing that has flattered me more than anything else hitherto, is the fact that old market-women cannot rest until they have picked out the sweetest of their grapes for me.

Nietzsche was a clever tactician and knew it:

> Deceit
> Is war's whole art.
> The foxskin
> Is my secret shirt of mail.

This agrees with a statement in *Ecce Homo* about the natural depravity of 'us Thuringians,' but is in flat contradiction with a neighbouring statement that he fights only honourable duels—all fair and above-board.

His praise of everything French was well calculated. That a distinguished German classical scholar of good family and reputation had turned King's evidence against German culture was welcome news to the French—still smarting from their defeat in the Franco-Prussian War. Nietzsche's master stroke was the declaration that France had recovered her soul in this war. He even went so far in his flattery as to put Paris at the head of the places of 'pure dry air,' followed by Athens, Provence, Florence and Jerusalem, where genius was climatically at home. French critics praised him extravagantly and the French Government eventually subsidized a translation of his collected works. Nietzsche knew that it was useless to flatter the English into accepting him as a superman; London is not among the capitals where he claims to have been discovered. He seems to have decided that the best way of attracting the interest of Englishmen was to make disparaging remarks about their *niaiserie*, in the French style: he writes of them as 'mediocre,' 'unsophisticated' and 'benighted.' He even uses the French sneer at the size of English women's feet; and defends French classical writers—Molière, Racine, Corneille—against the claims made for Shakespeare's wild genius. But he cannot avoid the jealous, complaining intonation which the Germans inevitably fall into when talking about England. 'England's small-mindedness' was the 'great danger now on earth': herself and her colonies were needed for the European mastery of the world, under the spiritual leadership of a self-confident Germany.

He knew that he would get fame in Germany by repercussion: that he would be honoured as a great misunderstood German who had been honoured by the outside world, and that his apparent anti-Germanism would be understood and forgiven. A further shrewd move was his flattery of the Jews. He called the German Jews the honourable exceptions in national Philistinism; and as a result much of the impetus of the Nietzsche movement has come from Jews. The editor of the standard English translation, Dr. Oscar Levy, writes in his critical notes both as a militant Jew and a militant Nietzschean. He discounts the seriousness of the Nietzsche movement in France and expresses ' the firm conviction that if we could not obtain a hearing for Nietzsche in England, his wonderful and at the same time very practical thought must be lost for ever to the world—a world that would then quickly be darkened over again by the ever-threatening clouds of obscurantism and barbarism.' The Nietzschean cult in England has been confined to a very small group, mostly consisting of Scots; the one prominent person to champion him has been Bernard Shaw. Because of Shaw he has been accepted as a household reference, but at the price of being treated as a Shavian paradox.

Nietzsche wrote violently against Hegel, approving him only as a useful counter-poison to German sentimentality. Tragic sentimentality is another German characteristic. (The only other people in Europe to have it mixed, in the same way, with blood-thirstiness and philosophy, are the Lowland Scots.) He characterizes it:

. . . Good-natured; incontinent in small pleasures; always ready for tears; wanting to be able to get rid of innate sobriety and strict attention to duty and exercise; a smiling, indeed a laughing indulgence; confusing goodness and sympathy and welding them into one—this is the essential characteristic of German sentimentality; rejoicing at a noble magnanimous action; thoroughly self-satisfied.

This is the natural Germanism, the Germanism of the playwright Kotzebue, he says, on which foreign elements are inappropriately engrafted. Nietzsche's prose writings are the best possible evidence of this contamination for which he blames the Goethe cult. And in evidence of uncontaminated German sentimentality there are his poems, even those composed after his flight from Germany. For example, his two hymns to Friendship; and his two poems on the subject of an Italian tombstone on which was carved a relief of a girl stroking a lamb, with the inscription: 'Pia, caritatevole, amorosissima.' In the second of these poems occur the following lines:

> To-day, to-day alone,
> My soul to tears is stirred,
> At thee, the pictured stone,
> At thee, the graven word.

This picture (none need wis)
I kissed the other day.
When there's so much to kiss
Why did I kiss the—clay?

Who knows the reason why?
'A tombstone fool!' you laugh:
I kissed—I'll not deny—
E'en the long epitaph.

The anti-sentimental, bloodthirsty side of Nietzsche's Germanism is manifest in his glorification of war and his description of himself in *Ecce Homo* as 'the most terrible man who has ever existed,' on whose appearance follow cataclysmic world-happenings. Looking about Germany for companions in terribleness, he found them in Prussia, where there was an admixture of Slavonic blood.

The Brandenburg nobility and the Prussian nobility in general (and the peasantry of certain North German districts) comprise the most manly natures in Europe. That the manliest shall rule, this is the only natural order of things. The future of German culture rests with the sons of Prussian officers. We require an inter-growth of the German and Slav races and we require too the cleverest financiers, the Jews, for us to become masters of the world.

Nietzsche is nowhere so inconsistent as in his alternate recommendations, as a non-German German, for the blending and for the non-blending of national races and cultures. 'Our present-day Europe, the scene of a senseless, precipitate attempt at a blending of races . . .' 'What I am concerned with—for I see it preparing itself slowly and hesitating—is the United Europe. It was the only real work, the only impulse in the souls, of all the broad-minded and deep-thinking men of this century. Only in their weaker moments did they fall back again into the national narrowness of the "Fatherlanders".' In preaching the necessity for a consolidated European culture he either assigns the leading part to Germany or excludes Germany altogether. 'Wherever Germany extends her sway she *ruins* culture.' Now he applauds Goethe for introducing foreign culture into Germany, now he deplores the result: 'German culture is a sort of cosmopolitan aggregate.'

Nietzsche, in his attitude to women, is divided between a desperate need for their society and a fanatic desire to stand alone. One of the strongest German traits is the recourse to women in time of anxiety.

Tacitus writes about the Germans' readiness to take the advice of their women—'these, too, are the most revered witnesses of each man's conduct, and his most liberal applauders'; and about the tribal marriage-ritual—the husband presenting cattle and war-like gifts to the wife, the wife presenting the husband with arms, which he must not disgrace while married to her, and thus becoming the priestess of his honour. The wilful insensitivity of Germans towards their women in everyday life has in it an element of shame—shame of their dependence on them in moments of crisis. As in the time of Tacitus, Germans still have an uncomfortable feeling that 'something of sanctity and prescience resides in the female sex.'

Nietzsche advocated the total suppression of these feelings: Germans should learn to treat their women in the Oriental fashion in the manner of strong men. Woman's first and last function was child-bearing: in between, her function was to distract man and alleviate his troubles. In her distractive capacity Nietzsche insisted that she should take her cue from the man's desires, throwing prudishness to the winds: for 'love forgives all.' This is no easy task for her, he admits; man is so restless. She cannot keep his love unless she is essentially feminine, constantly whetting his sexual appetite by her fickleness. Such fickleness bars women from any part in public life or from any serious work. 'Women are so constituted that all truth disgusts them and that they try to be revenged on everyone who opens their eyes.' Yet 'the perfect woman is a higher type of humanity than the perfect man.' As for the divinatory and intuitive powers attributed to them, Nietzsche alternately pooh-poohed these powers and expressed the deep confidence in them which Tacitus mentions as a peculiar mark of Germanism. The most bitter of Nietzsche's many bitter charges against German women was that they were directly responsible for the barbarity of German culture; because they were such bad cooks, and because intellectual dyspepsia was identical with physical dyspepsia.

He gave them a complete exculpation, however, by saying that they really are not to be blamed; they are whatever man makes them. 'Man created woman—out of what? Out of a rib of his god,—of his ideal.' His own physical preference was for a majestic, contralto-voiced Germanic type—*petite* women were no women at all, he agreed with Aristotle. But this did not agree with his scorn for the size of English women's feet or with his intellectual demand for French daintiness and roguishness: he hated 'placid cows' as he hated the monogamic earnestness of German marriage which had so much impressed Tacitus.

'Bovine,' 'cows,' 'cattle,' were his strongest words of anti-German abuse. He wanted to be a bird; he had a bird-nature, he protested. And 'in order to become light and be as a bird, one must lose oneself—thus spake Zarathustra.' Nietzsche never succeeded in losing himself, only in contradicting himself; and the more self-contradictory he became, the more German—no soaring Pindaric or Napoleonic eagle, only a mad German ox entering into the spirit of the market-place by breaking loose from its herd and blundering into the booths.

II

COLERIDGE AND WORDSWORTH

While 'Life went a-maying with Nature, Hope and Poesy,' Coleridge had believed that human reality and poetic reality could be reconciled. At Cambridge he had decided not to pursue metaphysical speculation, but to seek a life of practical virtue and labour in ideal surroundings and in congenial company. He was always looking for friends. The closest friends he made were also poets, though not poets in the sense that he was. They were ambitious and stupid men, but not so stupid that they failed to recognize that the very qualities which they needed to improve their own work could be borrowed from his. Southey was the first. Coleridge drew him into a scheme for forming a pantisocratic community with ten other gentlemen and twelve ladies in the back-woods of America. Coleridge wrote at the time:

> . . . O'er the ocean swell
> Sublime of Hope, I seek the cottag'd dell
> Where virtue calm with careless step may stray,
> And dancing to the moonlight roundelay
> The wizard Passions weave a holy spell.

Southey abandoned this colonizing scheme as impracticable, and Coleridge never recovered from the setback. It returned pantisocracy to the barren region of speculation from which he had tried to escape: moonlight and the wizard passions, failing to reconcile themselves with virtue calm and the cottag'd dell, became disconnected and unreal.

He next won the friendship of Wordsworth. Wordsworth had himself recently met with a failure, but a more complete one than

Coleridge's. It is difficult at first to decide whether he was consciously aware when he was writing his poem *Nutting* of the meaning which underlay it, or whether he was deliberately allegorizing an incident in his life that did little credit to his social reputation. Composed in 1799, while he was on a walking tour in Germany, the poem is only a fragment 'struck out from the *Prelude* as not being wanted there.' It begins in the middle of a line and records a joyful holiday excursion which he had made as a boy, dressed up in ragged clothes beside Esthwaite Lake. He gets away all by himself to a part of the nut wood where none of his companions has been before; there he finds a virgin scene, a nut tree quite unravaged, 'tall and erect with milk-white clusters hung.'

> . . . —A little while I stood,
> Breathing with such suppression of the heart
> As joy delights in; and with wise restraint
> Voluptuous, fearless of a rival, eyed
> The banquet;—or beneath the trees I sate
> Among the flowers and with the flowers I played; . . .
> . . . a bower beneath whose leaves
> The violets of five seasons reappear
> And fade, unseen of any human eye.

So he pauses awhile to contemplate, secure in possession, and then beating down his sense of decency, rises up and ravages the boughs. 'But,' writes Wordsworth, 'unless I now, Confound my present feelings with the past, I felt a sense of pain when I beheld, The silent trees, and saw the intruding sky.'

So far there is nothing remarkable in the passage, which might fit well enough into the section of the *Prelude* celebrating childhood and school-time and there serve as a companion picture to little William's night adventure in the stolen boat on the lake. But three lines follow 'the intruding sky':

> Then, dearest Maiden, move along these shades
> In gentleness of heart; with gentle hand
> Touch—for there is a spirit in the woods.

and we are left wondering who this dearest Maiden may be—a riddle which in the childhood context has no answer. When we turn to the ninth book of the *Prelude*, 'Residence in France,' we wonder afresh what significance to the context the tale of *Vaudracour and Julia* can have there, in which:

> . . . Thou also, there may'st read,
> At leisure, how the enamoured youth was driven,
> To fatal crime . . .
> How, between heart and heart, oppression thrust
> Her mandates, severing whom true love had joined,
> Harassing both; until he sank . . . supine,
> Save when the stings of viperous remorse,
> Trying their strength, enforced him to start up,
> Aghast and prayerless. Into a deep wood
> He fled, to shun the haunts of human kind;
> There dwelt, weakened in spirit more and more;
> Nor could the voice of Freedom, which through France
> Full speedily resounded, public hope,
> Or personal memory of his own worst wrongs,
> Rouse him; but, hidden in those gloomy shades,
> His days he wasted,—an imbecile mind.

Wordsworth's secret was revealed only a few years ago. When he visited France in a burst of revolutionary enthusiasm in 1792 he had met at Blois a girl named Annette Vallon, seduced her and left her with a daughter, Caroline. His uncles deterred him from marrying Annette, and soon war between France and England separated the lovers, their correspondence was intercepted, and they did not meet again until ten years later.

The 'dearest Maiden' in *Nutting* is surely Caroline, then a child of six; the poem amounts to an apology for the wrong done to her mother. He asks the child to forgive his transgression, to be gentle with these shades of the past, but for which she would not be alive to enjoy the beauties of the forest of Blois. Wordsworth's sansculotte enthusiasm on his arrival in France is well conveyed in the phrase 'motley accoutrement, in truth, more ragged than need was.' It is curious that in *Nutting* the wood of latent meaning is the Forest of Blois, where Wordsworth seduced Annette, and the wood of manifest statement is in the Lake District; whereas in the *Prelude* passage, the wood where Vaudracour hid from human kind is, in the latent meaning, a wood of the Lake District, but in the manifest statement, a forest in France.

It is probable that Wordsworth wrote *Nutting*, with all but the 'dearest Maiden' passage, as part of the Childhood book of the *Prelude*; and that it was only when he reached 'Residence in France' that he suddenly recognized its symbolic reference to the Annette episode. He wanted to include it at that point as an allegory with the 'dearest Maiden' ending, and probably an introduction sketching the story of his unhappy romance. But caution reasserted itself: he printed *Nutting* separately and inserted as much of his confession at the Blois stage of his autobiography as the story of Vaudracour and Julia could carry off. These experiences had been Wordsworth's plunge into unreality, and he set himself to destroy all incriminating evidence of them. In *Vaudracour and Julia*, though recording the closeness of the tie which bound the two lovers and the spiritual collapse of Vaudracour after he had been separated from Julia by obedience to family orders, he so distorts the actual happenings as to acquit Vaudracour of all infamy and assist the drawing of the moral of human reality: the love was too idealistic, and should have remained unconsummated.

In the third book of the *Excursion* a further confession of guilt is put in the mouth of 'The Solitary,' whose account of his blameless wedded life and subsequent poetical activities does him only credit. Yet a sense of guilt prevailed over all Wordsworth's elaborate self-excusing. The Solitary is unbalanced by his wife's death: despair drives him to revolutionary politics and to Rousseau-istic experiment. Both activities proving fallacious remedies, he retires to the country-side to commune with Nature. He tells his visitors:

> Stripped as I am of all the golden fruit
> Of self-esteem; and by the cutting blasts
> Of self-reproach familiarly assailed;
> Yet would I not be of such wintry bareness
> But that some leaf of your regard should hang
> Upon my naked branches:—lively thoughts
> Give birth, full often, to unguarded words;
> I grieve that, in your presence, from my tongue
> Too much of frailty hath already dropped.

Coleridge had not been base. He had not wilfully retreated; he had merely not been able to find strength to cling to poetic reality. Strength, for him, came to mean human companionship and assistance. Wordsworth assumed a righteousness proportionate to his sense of guilt; and Coleridge, aware of guilt only in himself, did not realize, when he wrote to Southey that Wordsworth was the greatest man he had met, what his righteousness hid. The failure of the revolutionary principle in France to achieve ideal results seemed an *ex post facto* justification of Wordsworth's desertion of the cause, and of Coleridge's abandonment of the American plan. Between them they made this amendment to Godwin's ethical idealism, to which they had both been committed (the words are Coleridge's):

Those feelings and that grand ideal of Freedom . . . do not belong to men, as a society, nor can possibly be either gratified or realized under any form of human government: but belong to the individual man, so far as he is pure and inflamed with the love and adoration of God in Nature.

Instead of practising pantisocracy on an ideal shore, Coleridge decided to content himself with Wordsworth's scheme of deducing morality from Nature, as observed in the English countryside, and using this morality to soothe his spiritual dissatisfaction. Wordsworthian Nature did not, however, satisfy Coleridge; poetic reality still beckoned. So he persuaded Wordsworth to collaborate in *Lyrical Ballads*, which was to consist of poems of two sorts—those dealing with natural, and those dealing with supernatural, incidents. He made this concession to Wordsworth: that the supernatural incidents were to be put under the discipline of the natural emotions which they would excite. In Coleridge's *Ancient Mariner* the wedding-guest represents ordinary humanity, for whose benefit the mariner, a sinner redeemed from torment by the love he has suddenly felt for some beautiful water-snakes, attempts to confute poetic reality with moral counsels. But the poetic reality of his story has infinitely the greater force.

Among Coleridge's other contributions to *Lyrical Ballads* was *The Foster-Mother's Tale*. Here he tells of a youth who became very learned and 'ere his twentieth year had unlawful thoughts of many things.' He was put into a dungeon for heresy (dreaming there of green savannahs), but escaped to America; where he sailed alone in a boat up a great moonlit river, to live, a naked man, with the wild Indians: and was never seen again. In spite of the formal censure of the youth's behaviour, this is a strong plea for poetic reality. Wordsworth countered it, in the second edition of *Lyrical Ballads*, where it was reprinted, with a strong restatement of human reality—the poem *Ruth*. This is a tale about a romantic young man who, having lived in mistaken idealism among the American Indians, sang of green savannahs to an English maiden. He begged her to go back with him as his helpmeet. But he had learned the vices of the Indians, who were far from noble savages, and so betrayed her. His ship sailed without her. She went mad. Then, recovering somewhat, she lived an innocent life as a rustic tramp, playing on a hemlock pipe and communing with Nature; and Wordsworth promised her a Christian burial when she came to die. Coleridge had written the first part of *Christabel* in the same year: it was a still stronger plea for poetic reality—the 'frightful' beauty of Geraldine, the witch who infected with her wickedness the modest dutiful Christabel of his pretended preference. Not being able, without violence, to subject the poem to the human discipline which he had introduced into the *Ancient Mariner*, he did not offer it for inclusion in *Lyrical Ballads*.

Lewti, though at first included, was cancelled at the last moment: poetic reality was idealized in it as a beautiful Circassian for whom a lover vainly sighed. For *Lewti*, *The Nightingale* was substituted. Here Coleridge made his most formal disavowal of the witch, whom the nightingale's song had evoked in her aspect of Melancholy, saying that Melancholy was an idle illusion—for 'as thou my friend and thou, my sister' (William and Dorothy Wordsworth) had learned, the nightingale (poetry) was really a merry bird. To hold the other view would, he said, be to profane Nature's sweet voices, always full of love and joyance. But the poem itself, after the first three lines, which show the witch's influence, proves how far his poetic energy was sapped by such disavowals.

In Coleridge's poems the commonest symbol of the haunting presence of the witch is the moon. It occurs at the emotional peak of *The Ancient Mariner*, *Christabel*, *The Foster-Mother's Tale*, and *Lewti*. It is the main theme of *Dejection* (written four years after these poems) where he again addresses Wordsworth and tries to overbear melancholy with joy; but the moon has taken the shape of an Indian canoe and the Virtuous Lady Joy is routed. He records in this poem that he has been unable, in spite of Wordsworth's inspiration, to think of what he needs must feel.

The only poem in which he dared to find the moon good was *Frost at Midnight*; but he wrote it for his newly-born son Hartley, who might be blessed with the spiritual independence which he had failed to attain himself. In this poem he forgot all his Wordsworthianism, as he did in *The Three Graves*, written at the time that *Lyrical Ballads* was being prepared, but not included among them. In *The Three Graves* Coleridge savagely identified the sun, Wordsworth's god of joy and duty, with the mad vulgar mother who curses her two sensitive daughters and her son-in-law to perpetual unhappiness despite every virtuous endeavour on their part. In *Kubla Khan* he made his most complete recantation of human reality, indulging in a wanton luxury that came near to devilishness. *Kubla Khan* was written in the *Lyrical Ballads* period, but held back for a number of years, with the other unsuitable poems, until after his breach with Wordsworth: and then published only at the request of Byron, whom Wordsworth had taught Coleridge to regard as a representative, with Shelley, of the Satanic school of poetry. Even then he excused its composition as due to an opiate following the distress of mind produced by the calumny and ingratitude of men who had been fostered in the bosom of his confidence (Wordsworth not yet among them).

When friends failed him, Coleridge was always lost. As early as 1797, in his poem *To the Rev. George Coleridge*, published as the dedication of his *Poems*, he tells how much he has already suffered from disillusions and betrayals in his friendships:

> . . . through life
> Chasing chance-started friendships. A brief while
> Some have preserv'd me from life's pelting ills;
> But, like a tree with leaves of feeble stem,
> If the clouds lasted, and a sudden breeze
> Ruffled the boughs, they on my head at once
> Dropped the collected shower; and some most false,
> False and fair-foliag'd as the Manchineel,
> Have tempted me to slumber in their shade
> E'en 'mid the storm; then breathing subtlest damps,
> Mix'd their own venom with the rain from Heaven,
> That I woke poison'd! . . .

He then eulogizes the dedicatee as his earliest friend, whom he has loved as a brother and revered as a son. But in one copy of this book Coleridge wrote above the dedication: 'N.B. If this volume should ever be delivered according to its direction, *i.e.* to Posterity, let it be known that the Reverend George Coleridge was displeased and thought his character endangered by the Dedication.—S. T. Coleridge.'

Shortly after writing *Kubla Khan* he went with the Wordsworths to Germany. Parting from them there he took up metaphysics again, though he admitted its devilishness. On his return to England he showed a sudden surprising energy, writing vigorously on politics for the daily press. He renewed his friendship with Southey; and it was at this time that Southey gave him the first three stanzas and two further stanzas of *The Devil's Thoughts*. Allowed this licence by a friend whom by the standard of his own human deficiencies he could regard as a model human being, Coleridge let himself go as a devil, throwing the responsibility for his elaborations of the theme on the blameless origin of the nucleus. This poem and the later *Two Round Spaces on the Tombstone*, and *The Rash Conjurer*, all have a vigour which directly belies his pious affectations of childish innocence in

Something Childish but Very Natural, My Baptismal Birthday, A Child's Evening Prayer, Answer to a Child's Question—with which they are contemporaneous. The child poems were written in momentary reaction against metaphysics and in sycophantic imitation of Wordsworth's childishness, which was more proper to Wordsworth's narrow-minded obedience to authority. This vigorous mood did not last long. He lost his concentrating force and wrote less and less. He even had to depend on Southey for the support of his family—Southey who had abandoned his idealistic principles and become an industrious hack-writer, and was about to accept a pension from the Government for political services; and who held, moreover, an unfavourable opinion of Coleridge's work and habits. Coleridge and Southey were married to sisters; it was Southey who had forced Coleridge into marriage, and with a woman who proved to be chiefly interested, as Southey was, in worldly success.

Coleridge's inevitable break with Wordsworth was long delayed. At first there had been a fair exchange. In return for Wordsworth's friendship and moral stimulation, Coleridge had given him not merely a scholarly background to work against, but constant critical help in the use of language. (At the time of the breach Coleridge complained: 'I have loved with enthusiastic self-oblivion those who have been well pleased that I should, year after year, flow with a hundred nameless rills into their main stream.') But, like Southey, who had practically given up poetry for the journalistic successes of prose, Wordsworth now looked down on Coleridge. The Napoleonic wars had made a patriot of him: he portrayed an ideal England where duty and liberty met, a symbol of an urbanely poetical human reality. Coleridge had followed suit, but timidly. Patriotism and nature-worship in Wordsworth turned to preaching; preaching ended in ecclesiasticism. In 1802, for final self-justification, he had paid a brief visit to Annette at Calais, in company with his sister Dorothy, explained himself, and then returned to marry a Lake Country neighbour who made him a devoted wife.

In the complacent *Prelude*, addressed to Coleridge who had by then fallen far behind Wordsworth in popular success, the affection and gratitude expressed are little more than what he might have granted a wise old family servant, now in decay, who would be interested in the record of his young master's rise to eminence. Only at the end does he give Coleridge credit for being a poet too, playfully reminding him of the days when, before turning their minds to more serious tasks, they had 'wantoned together in wild Poesy'—he links Coleridge's *Ancient Mariner* and *Christabel* with his own *The Idiot Boy* and *The Thorn*—and encouraging him to spend the few remaining years of his life in raising a monument of glory to himself. He claims to have shown him the way and trusts that together they will instruct posterity:

Prophets of Nature, we to them shall speak
A lasting inspiration.

Coleridge, aware that since those wanton days he had written practically nothing, and impressed by Wordsworth's huge output, replied with *To William Wordsworth*, in the decayed family-servant style, humbly grateful for mention in a work that seemed a classic as soon as written. He said that on first hearing it read he burst into tears, realizing how he had wasted his own life; but that the tribute had given him some hope again and he now apologized for scattering poison-flowers of self-depreciation among the triumphal wreaths which were the author's due. He made a reference to Wordsworth's revolutionary visit to France, encouraging the legend that Wordsworth, glorious in his performances there, had left only because the revolutionary cause seemed hopeless, and was

. . . thenceforth calm and sure
From the dread watch-tower of man's absolute self.

A few years after the publication of *The Prelude* came the breach, subsequently repaired for good manners' sake, but in reality a final breach. Coleridge had lost confidence in Wordsworth and in himself; Wordsworth only in Coleridge. Coleridge continued to lament his own idleness; particularly he wished that he could have finished *Christabel*. But the second part, completed on his return from Germany, had turned out tedious and discouraged a third part.

Work without Hope draws nectar in a sieve,
And Hope without an object cannot live.

He was a 'Delinquent Traveller' and, no longer fit for 'America' (for true poetic experience, he meant), thought himself fit only to be enrolled among the criminal 'founders of Australian races.' But in *The Delinquent Travellers*, one of his best poems, he claimed for his unregenerate aberrancy, or delinquency, a higher poetic merit than for Wordsworth's social self-improvement. And he reasserted, however cynically, what he had expressed many years before in *Frost at*

Midnight—a confidence in himself as the destined father of poets, successful where he failed:

> —The Rogues! I see it in their faces!
> Receive me, Lads. I'll go with you,
> Hunt the black swan and kangaroo,
> And that New Holland we'll presume
> Old England with some elbow-room.
> Across the mountains we will roam
> And each man make himself a home:
> Or, if old habits ne'er forsaking,
> Like clock-work of the Devil's making,
> Ourselves inveterate rogues should be,
> We'll have a virtuous progeny;
> And on the dunghill of our vices
> Raise human pine-apples and spices.

He still clung by habit to the idea of friendship and virtue.

> Old friends burn dim, like lamps in noisome air.
> Love them for what they are: nor love them less
> Because to thee they are not what they were.

But he knew that he was for his fellows only a devil now—a cast-off, boring devil. In a piece called *Luther—de daemonibus* he wrote:

> 'The Angel's like a flea,
> The devil is a bore——'
> 'No matter for that,' quoth S.T.C.
> 'I love him the better therefore.'

As for the progeny of the first travellers to Australia: they have indeed turned out so virtuous that a few years ago the City Council of one of the State Capitals burnt all its early archives. 'Human pine-apples and spices' could not be bettered as a characterization of the pantisocratic modern Australian. Coleridge's son Hartley did become a poet, but repeated his father's failures. Coleridge's sons of the spirit were the pre-Raphaelites, headed by Dante Gabriel Rossetti. Of these only William Morris had the healthy energy for carrying the group's idealistic principles into orderly practice. But his Coleridge-like poetic beginnings—*The Defence of Guinevere*—were soon lost in his growing success as an importer of practical beauty into Victorian everyday life

—his printing, furniture, fabrics, etc. He continued to write, but what was not social-propaganda prose was interior-decorator verse applauded by the same 'liberal' public which had applauded the hard-working Southey.

III

KEATS AND SHELLEY

Keat's chief interest was the poet's relations with poetry, and the imagery he chose was predominantly sexual. Poetry for him was not a philosophical theory, as it was with Shelley, but a moment of physical delirium. The figure which Laura Riding has used[1] in characterizing Keats ('He ... disposed himself ... toward spiritual rape by a vigorous poetic personhead imagined as in pursuit of conquests') is one which occurs constantly in his poems. The first occasion is in *Sleep and Poetry*:

> O Poesy! for thee I grasp my pen
> That am not yet a glorious denizen
> Of thy wide heaven; yet, to my ardent prayer,
> Yield from thy sanctuary some clean air,
> Smooth'd for intoxication by the breath
> Of flowery bays, that I may die a death
> Of luxury, and my young spirit follow
> The morning sunbeams to the great Apollo
> Like a fresh sacrifice; or, if I can bear
> The o'erwhelming sweets, 'twill bring to me the fair
> Visions of all places . . .

Keats' contemporaries found in this sort of writing a quality which they interpreted as moral perversity. The slamming reviews which depressed him so much, because postponing the moment of poetic ecstasy which he identified with the moment of poetic fame, resulted rather from the critics' recognition of his perversity than from their obtuseness about his craftsmanship, or their prejudice against him as Leigh Hunt's protégé. Perversity, to the English mind, means any confusion of the usual functions and prerogatives of the two sexes, and Keats never seemed to be playing a *manly* role in his poems.

[1] *Poems and Poets, Epilogue II* (1936).

CA: R

Although he was male-minded enough in ordinary sexual business, as his letters to Fanny Brawne, and his song 'Give me women, wine and snuff,' show, the critics were right: he did mix the sexes in his poems. This resulted from his personalization of Poetry as an active female figure, and from his disavowal of the rape which the intellectual poet, as male, makes of Poetry—poems, in classical imagery, being the poet's children begotten of the Muse. He rejected traditional poetic psychology because the ecstasies it provided were banal and repetitious: not because he knew the nature of poetic experience, but because he had a greed of it and felt that it could not occur within the known, exhausted poetic conventions. So he reversed the traditional metaphor by making Poetry, as a dominant female, pursue the shrinking, womanish poet with masculine lustfulness.

Endymion was the stock classical figure of human youth and beauty lying asleep, secretly beloved by the watchful deity—the Moon. Keats, who had said that if poetry did not come to a poet as naturally as leaves to a tree it had better not come at all, used Endymion as the figure of a poet who, by putting himself into a recipient attitude, won without further effort 'the o'erwhelming sweets' for which his soul longed. (Keats used to court poetical inspiration by dressing up in traditional poetic robes and laurel crown.) Endymion first learns the technique of attracting goddesses by a study of Adonis in his bower; a heavenly guide conveys him there and, as if to give him a foretaste of amorous delights, cossets him with sweets—always associated in Keats' poems with poetic seduction—wine alive with sparkles, juicy pears, cream sweeter than nurse Amalthea skimmed for the boy Jupiter, and a bunch of blooming plums, ready to melt within an infant's gums. From Adonis' bower it was no long journey, by eagle-ride part of the way (to point the connexion with the seduced Ganymede), to a mossy bed where Endymion could fling himself on his back and presently clasp a naked waist above him. It was Dian, and he whispered to her:

> O known Unknown! From where my being sips
> Such darling essence, wherefore may I not
> Be ever in these arms?

The reviewers called *Endymion* 'indecent.' They wrote as classicists, and they were right in calling the poem indecent from a classical point of view: Diana should never have been equated in her sexual technique with Venus.

Hyperion started in a more 'manly' fashion. Hyperion was the Sun-Titan, an inexperienced youth, not yet converted into Apollo, the god of Poetry; the poem gives an account of this metamorphosis. Keats is said to have interrupted the writing of *Hyperion* because of the unfavourable reception of *Endymion*. *Endymion* was disliked because it did not reveal the author as a normal male being: critics did not analyse the nature of the abnormality, but decided that he was conceited in some unusual way. In a letter to his publishers, the more conventionally conceited, over-manly Byron wrote, for God's sake to send him no more Keats: and added abuse so indecent that his editors have deleted all but *manicon*, 'catamite,' which they print as 'mannikin.' Keats was aware that *Hyperion* was more spiritually ambitious than *Endymion*, and may have argued that it would be still less favourably received, for in *Hyperion* he was identifying himself with the god of Poetry. (The reaction of shame is recorded in his poem of apology to Delphic Apollo for having assumed his laurel-garland.) He did not understand that it was the mawkish quality of his ambition which critics disliked rather than the fact of his ambition. Hyperion is, in the end, not much more of a man than Endymion. He does not become the god of Poetry except by quasi-sexual relations with a female principle of reality described as Mnemosyne or Memory. She is an awful goddess, a supreme shape, and comes on him while he is half-asleep. He gazes into her eyes and:

> Soon wild commotions shook him, and made flush
> All the immortal fairness of his limbs,
> Into a hue more roseate than sweet pain
> Gives to a ravish'd nymph when her warm tears
> Gush luscious with no sob . . .
>   . . . So young Apollo anguish'd.
> His very hair, his golden tresses famed,
> Kept undulation round his eager neck.
> During the pain Mnemosyne upheld
> Her arms as one who prophesied.—At length
> Apollo shriek'd—and lo he was the God.

Keats toned down this passage when he eventually published it, leaving out the orgiastic pleasure of the ravished nymph, and making the climax less final:

> Apollo shriek'd—and lo from all his limbs
> Celestial . . .

At 'Celestial' the printed version broke off politically, as if he had cast his pen down in despair on reading the notices in the *Quarterly* and *Blackwood's*.

In *Sleep and Poetry* Keats had already begun this technique of sexual counter-changing; it is shown most clearly in his confused identity of the spirit of Poetry, which should have been female, with the slumbering Endymion and Apollo the mighty:

> A drainless shower
> Of light is poesy; 'tis the supreme of power;
> 'Tis might half-slumbering on its own right arm.
> The very archings of her eye-lids charm
> A thousand willing agents to obey.

His second volume, *Lamia, Isabella, The Eve of St. Agnes and Other Poems*, was given more favourable notices because he had disguised the indecency by taking the sexual figure one stage further. The conventional imagery had been of the male poet ravishing the Muse; his perverse improvement on this had been woman, a mannish Muse, ravishing the womanish poet. He now showed a definitely female figure inviting rape by a definitely male figure; but he told the story from the female point of view. By doing this he avoided the charge of perversity: he showed himself yielding to temptation as an apparently normal sexual adventurer, though to change his Muse into a conventionally feminine one he had to invest her with all his own sexual coyness. In *The Eve of St. Agnes* Madeline lies asleep but amorously expectant, while Porphyro at her bedside heaps up the extravagant jellies and candied fruits and syrops and spiced cakes in gold and silver vessels. Then she listens to his serenade of *La Belle Dame Sans Merci* and finally allows him to throb like a star among her dreams. The sweetmeats in these rape-scenes stand for the 'beauties' of poetry on which Keats laid more stress than on poetry itself. The 'beauties' were 'verisimilitudes,' or the ore with which every rift should be loaded: the poetic object was an illusion of glory in which the Muse was expected to indulge the passive poet. *The Eve of St. Mark* (not included in this volume) was written in the same vein. Bertha sat alone in her room in the Minster Square at Canterbury. Everyone was at church, and the streets were deserted. The stage was set for the lover to come along with his sweetmeats, soft drinks and musical instrument; to which blandishments Bertha could not but yield. She kept her virginity only because of Keats' failure to finish the poem.

Isabella and *Lamia* are both poems of self-pity. Isabella is the spirit of poetry luxuriously grieving for the poet who has been murdered by the 'ledger-men'—i.e. the materialists, the rationalists, the critics. They even rob her of the sweet-basil which grows from his dead head. Lamia, who in classical legend was a frightful demon-succubus, Keats treated as 'poor Lamia,' the Spirit of Poetry whom old Apollonius, the philosopher, stares at, sees as a snake and banishes from sight.

> Philosophy will clip an Angel's wings,
> Conquer all mysteries by rule and line,
> Empty the haunted air, and gnomèd mine—
> Unweave a rainbow, as it erewhile made
> The tender-person'd Lamia melt into a shade.

Lamia is the morbid figure of poetry made dismal by neglect—by the want of such honeyed flattery as Keats imagined fitting tribute from the poet. For all his absorption in romances of chivalry he never made Poetry into a Fairy Queen who demanded from her knightly poet active proof of his valour and devotion.

Keats wrote in a letter to Woodhouse that a poet was functionally irresponsible and had no identity, only yearning and fondness— allowing himself to be pressed upon and annihilated by stronger identities with whom he came into contact. In a letter to his brothers he glorified Shakespeare, in the same strain, as possessing the supreme poetic quality—'*Negative Capability*, that is, when a man is capable of being in uncertainties, mysteries, doubts, without any irritable reaching after fact and reason.' Keats felt himself torn between two demands: the demand of the critics and the sweeping demand of poetry itself. Between them he equivocated with that fluttering complaisance which he calls 'Negative Capability.'

In the same letter Keats writes:

Coleridge, for instance, would let go by a fine isolated verisimilitude caught from the Penetralium of mystery from being incapable of remaining content with half knowledge. This pursued through volumes would perhaps take us no further than this, that with a great poet the sense of Beauty overcomes every consideration, or rather obliterates all consideration.

Keats rightly felt that Coleridge had a poetic conscience which would not let him be content with random ecstasies. He wrote, further:

As to the poetic character itself (I mean that sort of which, if I am anything, I am a member: that sort distinguished from the Wordsworthian or egotistic Sublime: which is a thing per se, and stands alone) it is not itself— it has no self, it is everything and nothing—it has no character.

He was here distinguishing between Wordsworth's self-protective insensitivity to the pleasures of poetry and his own cultivation of poetry as the science of hedonics.

Shelley, who championed Keats as a victim of critical cruelty and saw him as performing something like his own philosophical arbitration between the human audience and poetry itself, displeased contemporary critics for reasons opposite to those for which they damned Keats.

It was not his professed atheism and Jacobinism which outraged popular feeling, so much as his spiritual hermaphroditism. Laura Riding in the essay quoted above shows how he tried to reconcile the opposite sympathies to which the poet is exposed: by a compromise in which judgment was evaded by a philosophical equating of the human with the poetic. At one time, indeed, he debated whether he should make philosophy or poetry his profession; and though he chose poetry, he tried to combine the philosopher and the poet in a Satanic character of superior physical and mental powers. In his *Defence of Poetry* he sets Bacon among the great poets and Shakespeare, Milton and Dante among the philosophers of the very loftiest power. Queen Mab is his first Queen of Poetry: but she does not have love-relations either with Oberon or with a mortal youth. She merely imbues the soul of a girl called Ianthe (Harriet Shelley) with a righteous, philosophical view of human affairs; the verses are annotated with astronomical data, recommendations for a vegetarian diet, and thoughts on the nature of time. She appears later as The Witch of Atlas, an energetic spirit who flies about with a winged monster of her own creation, called Hermaphrodite. Hermaphrodite is the poet-compromiser:

> A sexless thing it was, and in its growth
>   It seemed to have developed no defect
> Of either sex, yet all the grace of both,—
>   In gentleness and strength its limbs were decked;
> The bosom swelled lightly with its full youth,
>   The countenance was such as might select
> Some artist that his skill should never die,
> Imaging forth such perfect purity.

Towards the close of the poem Shelley gently rebukes Keats for con-
ceiving the Spirit of Poetry as sexed and therefore unpropitious for
the harmonious levelling of things which should be the poet's end:

> 'Tis said in after times her spirit free
> Knew what love was, and felt itself alone—
> But holy Dian could not chaster be
> Before she stooped to kiss Endymion,
> Than now this lady—like a sexless bee
> Tasting all blossoms, and confined to none,
> Among these mortal forms, the wizard-maiden
> Passed with an eye serene and heart unladen.

But the Witch is only a fanciful presentation of the Spirit of Poetry.
The poem closes:

> These were the pranks she played among the cities
> Of mortal men, and what she did to Sprites
> And Gods, entangling them in her sweet ditties
> To do her will, and show their subtle sleights,
> I will declare another time; for it is
> A tale more fit for the weird winter nights
> Than for these garish summer days, when we
> Scarcely believe much more than we can see.

First must come the serious business of smoothing out troubles of a
more immediate sort. Mary Shelley criticized the poem as having no
human interest; and he replied with some joking verses, acknowledging
the ineffectiveness of his vision:

> How, my dear Mary,—are you critic-bitten
> (For vipers kill, though dead) by some review,
> That you condemn these verses I have written
> Because they tell no story, false or true?
> What, though no mice are caught by a young kitten,
> May it not leap and play as grown cats do,
> Till its claws come? Prithee, for this one time,
> Content thee with a visionary rhyme.

But he never managed to synthetize into a single figure the poet, and
the philosopher, and the Promethean man of action on whose strategy
the miracle of human salvation seemed to depend.

IV

THE PASTORAL

Theocritus was a professional poet, attached for a time to the court of Ptolemy Philadelphus at Alexandria, and later to that of Hiero, tyrant of Syracuse. His more formal poems were panegyrics and hymns; the Eclogues were merely 'occasional verse,' half-humorous accounts of the shepherds and goat-herds he had met when on holiday in the Sicilian countryside. He selected on the whole the more sentimental passages in their lives for poetic record, but invented no Arcadian Golden Age for them—this was developed by his imitators. If the effect of the Eclogues is cheerful, it is because the climate of Sicily and its political security in Theocritus' time gave the shepherds an easy enough life—they had plenty of time for piping, unhappy love-affairs and their traditional contests of verse-improvisation. Theocritus lets them talk broad Doric and use coarse expressions. They know nothing of philosophy. No worship of nature as such is ascribed to them, though they have superstitions about the Nymphs and Pan. Their life is not idealized as superior to the town; and indeed, by contrast with the people of Syracuse, they appear foolish clowns. In the Twentieth Idyll, Eunica, a city girl of Syracuse, when made love to by one of the most eligible of neat-herds, spits thrice in her own bosom (as if to avert the ill omen that meeting a lunatic brings), and tells him that constant pipe-playing has roughened and deformed his lips and that he stinks of goat. The famous First Idyll, which contains Thyrsis' elegy for the dead shepherd Daphnis, is in no less realistic a vein than the Fifteenth Idyll, which describes the comic adventures of two Syracusan countrywomen on a visit to the Adonis festival at Alexandria.

Virgil's Eclogues were a formalizing of the more narrowly bucolic idylls of Theocritus. By this time the riches of the Sicilian countryside had been exhausted by improvident farming, and the life which the peasants led was as squalid and anxious as anywhere in the Roman Empire. But Virgil cared nothing for that: he used the pastoral situation as a convenient rostrum for moral philosophy, and though he kept a careful eye on the correctness of his shepherds' costumes and professional habits, gave them smooth lips and let them smell of civet rather than of goat. Moreover, when they mourn for Daphnis in the

Sicilian style, they do not mean Daphnis but Julius Caesar. And in the last Eclogue, Virgil's patron Gallus is wafted to Arcadia, where he sits in pastoral fancy-dress, mourning for Lycoris—in real life an actress in low comedy who has left him to go off with a soldier. The country deities gather pityingly about Gallus, and in this context the 'Where were ye, Nymphs?'is borrowed from Theocritus:

> Quae nemora aut qui vos saltus habuere, puellae
> Naïdes?

The Virgilian pseudo-shepherd was imported into English poetry by a scholastical Scottish monk, Alexander Barclay. The manner of early English poems had been bare and direct; the poets wrote in the shadow of a world of brutal fact—a cold, foggy world with only an occasional May Day or Christmas-tide interlude to relieve it. Their notion of poetry, which survived late in popular and provincial verse, was one of physical defeat. The Church, in consolation of this gloomy view, presented the holy world of Scripture, and especially the Gospels, as the supreme poetic reality. The popular poetic response was to bring Biblical characters into the immediate English countryside. Thus the English shepherd was an important figure in early popular carols because of his connexion with the Nativity; but remained an English country oaf, smelling of his flocks and smeared with tar:

> The shepard upon a hill he satt;
> He had on him his tabard and his hat,
> His tarbox, his pipe, and his flagat;
> His name was called Joly Joly Wat,
>   For he was a gud herdes boy.
>   Ut hoy!
> For in his pipe he made so much joy.

> The shepard upon a hill was laid;
> His dog to his girdell was taid;
> He had not slept but a litill braid,
> But 'Gloria in excelsis' was to him said.
>   Ut hoy!
> For in his pipe he made so much joy.

> .   .   .   .

> 'Now must I go there Crist was born;
> Farewell! I cum again to morn.
> Dog, kepe well my shepe fro the corn,

And warn well "Warrocke" when I blow my horn!'
                  Ut hoy!
        For in his pipe he made so much joy.

                .   .   .

'Jesu, I offer to thee here my pipe,
My skirt, my tar-box, and my scripe;
Home to my felowes now will I skipe,
And also look unto my shepe.'
                  Ut hoy!
        For in his pipe he made so much joy.

'Now farewell, mine owne herdes man Wat!'
'Yea, for God, lady, even so I hat;
Lull well Jesu in thy lape,
And farewell, Joseph, with thy round cape!'
                  Ut hoy!
        For in his pipe he made so much joy.

                .   .   .

The use of allegory in sermons and devotional books had only a superficial influence on popular poems. In *Piers Plowman*, for example, which is cast in allegorical form, the characters are ordinary English countrymen and their problems are those of immediate social behaviour. But whereas the mediaeval popular poet tended to record only his own direct experiences, the court-poet leaned towards allegory and converted it to unecclesiastical ends. He borrowed from contemporary Continental practice a new poetical world known as 'The Kingdom of Love,' which was geographically localized on a legendary Mount Cithaeron to which access could be had only in dreams. It was ruled by Love, a capricious, all-powerful Deity, whose severity to the lover could be somewhat mitigated by the intercession of his mother Venus (a parody of the Catholic ritual in which Mary intercedes between Christ and the sinner), and was haunted by powers such as Envy, Despair and Poverty, borrowed from ecclesiastical allegory, whose business it was to make the lot of lovers more difficult. The month in this kingdom was always May and the Kingdom consisted of a Royal Palace (some rooms of which were devoted to famous poets and orators) surrounded with interminable pleasure-grounds where the love-making knights and ladies wandered. This poetical world still kept a certain correspondence with the actual one. The scene was not impossibly fanciful, but merely a prolongation of summer well-being enjoyed in the gardens of royal palaces. The flowers in the parterres were the familiar rose, lily and pink; the rich clothes were the court-wear of state occasions and fine weather. Court-poems were a sweet conserve of brief summer joys for use with the salt-meat staple of the bad months. After a time poets, tiring of the sameness of their adventures in this Kingdom of Love, and especially of the morality figures which occurred in them, looked for a more poetically appealing Mount Cithaeron. They found it in the pastoral imported by Barclay, which was wholly irrelevant to their world of experience: Corydon, Phyllis, the Nymphs, Apollo, banks of hyacinth, asphodel meadows, the parsley-crown, the olive yard, and the lizard on the rock, being entirely un-English.

Barclay's treatment of the pastoral was moralistic. He borrowed not from Theocritus, but from Virgil through the fifteenth-century Baptista Mantuanus, who had adapted the Virgilian eclogue to the satire of court and city life. In his Fourth Eclogue Barclay attacks his contemporary, Skelton, as a 'rascolde poet' who had an immoral muse and who pandered to the taste of princes by celebrating viciousness. This is probably a reference to Skelton's *Tunnyng of Elynour Rummynge*, written in recollection of his sallies into low life, in company with Henry VIII, from the ideal pleasure-grounds of the royal palace of Nonsuch near Leatherhead. Skelton was almost the last classically educated English poet who could forget his Classics when looking at the countryside and not see Margery Milke-Ducke as Phyllis and Jolly Jacke as Corydon, or find 'behind every bush a thrumming Apollo' (John Clare's criticism of Keats).

The Elizabethan university-wits rejected Barclay's Mantuanian pastoral in favour of that of the Neapolitan Sannazaro: as better suited to their sophisticated literary purposes. (Barclay and Googe were from their point of view stuffy, old-fashioned writers spoiling good material.) They used the Arcadian scene as the ideal seat of literary leisure:

> Then amongst flow'rs and springs,
> Making delightful sport,
> Sat lovers without conflict, without flame;
> And nymphs and shepherds sings
> Mixing in wanton sort
> Whisp'rings with songs, then kisses with the same
> Which from affection came.
> The naked virgin then

> Her roses fresh reveals,
> Which now her veil conceals.
> The tender apples in her bosom seen;
> And oft in rivers clear,
> The lovers with their loves consorting were.

But they linked the pastoral with another contemporary fashion—
Euphuism—and made it ancillary to prose oratory. For Greene, Peele,
Lodge (from whom the scenario of *As You Like It* was borrowed)
and the rest, the shepherds were scholars proficient in the various
schemes and tropes of rhetoric learned from Sherry, Priscian, Donet,
Alexander, Moscellanus and Sysenbrotus. They applied these, however,
not to philosophy or theology or legality, but to the logic of love; thus
giving the knights and ladies of Mount Cithaeron a Renaissance
education. In Greene's *Menaphon*, a representative example of this
technique, academic niceness in prose writing is the chief consideration:

> Well, abroad they went, *Menaphon* with his sheephooke fringed with
> cruell, to signifie he was chiefe of the swaynes, *Lamedon* and *Samela* after:
> plodding thus ouer the greene fields, at last they came to the mountaines where
> *Menaphons* flockes grazed, and there he discoursed unto *Samela* thus; I tell
> thee faire Nymph, these Plaines that thou seest stretching Southward, are
> pastures belonging to *Menaphon*: there growes the cintfoyle, and the hya-
> cinth, the cowsloppe, the primrose, and the violet, which my flockes shall
> spare for flowers to make thee garlands, the milke of my ewes shall be meate
> for thy pretie wanton, the wool of the fat weathers that seemes as fine as the
> fleece that *Iason* fet from *Colchos*, shall serue to make *Samela* webbes withall;
> the mountaine tops shall be thy mornings walke, and the shadie valleies thy
> euenings arbour: as much as *Menaphon* owes shall be at *Samelas* command,
> if she like to liue with *Menaphon*. This was spoken with such deepe effects,
> that *Samela* could scarce keepe her from smiling, yet she covered her conceipt
> with a sorrowful countenance, which *Menaphon* espying, to make her merrie,
> and rather for his own aduantage, seeing *Lamedon* was a sleepe, tooke her
> by the hand and sate downe, and pulling foorth his pipe, began after some
> melodie to carroll out this roundelay.

Poetic writing had merely to be witty and 'sugared.' Thus the first
verse of Menaphon's roundelay:

> When tender ewes brought home with euening Sunne
> Wend to their foldes,
> And to their holdes
> The shepheards trudge when light of day is done.

Upon a tree
The Eagle *Ioues* faire bird did pearch,
There resteth hee.
A little flie his harbour then did search,
And did presume (though others laught thereat)
To pearch where as the princelie Eagle sat.

Sidney belonged to this school, but he was more classically inclined than the others: he inserted in his *Arcadia* three or four gentlemanly imitations of Theocritus.

In the *Shepheards Callender* Spenser tried to escape from this rhetorical paralysis and to make the pastoral a more serious—or at least superficially a more serious—poetic mode. Improving on Sidney's classicism, he engrafted the classical pastoral, in all its impure variety, upon native English rusticism, thus inventing a looser and yet more immediate pastoral technique. His Colin Clout, borrowed from Skelton, and his Piers, borrowed from Langland, graze their flocks in fields where Kentish and Arcadian trees and flowers and deities are mixed up together. Spenser here lent conviction to his composite, year-long poetical world by locating it in an idealistic folk-lorish countryside and thickening the atmosphere with quaint dialect words and obsolete forms borrowed from 'Old Tityrus' (Chaucer); it was essentially the same world, enlarged to more than Mandevillean range, over which the Faerie Queene ruled. Sidney, as a traditionalist, criticized Spenser in his *Apologie for Poetry*:

> The Sheapheards Kalender hath much Poetrie in his Eglogues, indeede worthy the reading, if I be not deceived. That same framing of his stile to an old rustick language I dare not alowe, sith neyther *Theocritus* in Greek, *Virgill* in Latin, nor *Sanaʒar* in Italian, did affect it.

But Spenser by the creation of this self-sufficient lunatic world, won the name of 'the Poet's Poet,' and Sidney is chiefly remembered as the dead shepherd of a classically incorrect pastoral of Spenser's.

Shakespeare was not classically educated, but picked up his classics as he went along; his treatment of country-people changes considerably in his later plays. In his early *Love's Labour's Lost* he caricatures the euphuists, showing in Costard's letter, read by the King, what the literal result would be if a real countryman tried to be a pastoral swain. Here also occur his Winter and Spring songs, which are critical demonstrations of real pastoral lyric: with Dick the Shepherd blowing his nail and Marion's nose all red and raw. Later, however, in *As You*

Like It, the aesthetic pastoralists are favourably contrasted with the true countrymen: the Clown is gross and stupid, not even idiot-wise like the fools in the tragedies, and only serves as a butt for Touchstone's euphuistic ruffling. In *The Winter's Tale*, one of his last plays, Shakespeare has all but capitulated to pastoral fashion. The shepherd, as Perdita's foster-father, is promoted to blank verse—hitherto all Shakespeare's countrymen have had to use country prose full of broad *a*'s and *ʒeds*. Even a country-dance of Satyrs is introduced. There is still a clown, but he is merely the low comedian. Finally, the island in *The Tempest* is a pasteboard Arcadia: no clowns and, instead of shepherds, classical gods and goddesses who descend by stage-machinery.

V

OFFICIAL AND UNOFFICIAL LITERATURE

In Chaucer's *Canterbury Tales* the official and unofficial literatures of his period occur side by side. The Knight's tale of *Palamon and Arcite*, typical official literature, is immediately followed by the Miller's tale, a purely criminal piece, and the Reeve's tale, in the same style but somewhat more obscene. Chaucer apologizes for the unofficial pieces, as in the Prologue to the Miller's tale:

> But this Millere
> He nolde his wordës for no man forbere
> But told his cherlës tale in his manére;
> Me thinketh that I shal reherce it here.
> And therefore every gentil wight I preye
> For goddës love, demeth not that I seye
> Of evel entente, but that I moot reherce
> Hir talës allë, be they bettre or werse,
> Or ellës falsen som of my matére.

At the finish he lets the prize for the best story be awarded to the Knight; but, by reporting the Miller's and the Reeve's contributions with the same force and skill as the Knight's and Parson's, he reveals how strong his criminal sympathies are. He himself, when asked by the Host for a contribution to the story-telling, begins a popular burlesque on chivalry, *Sir Thopas*. The Host interrupts him angrily after a few stanzas:

'Na moore of this for goddës dignitee,'

He is asked to tell another in better taste, which he does—the *Tale of Melibeus*, given in prose and consisting chiefly of irreproachable quotations from classical moralists. But the cutting short of *Sir. Thopas* is Chaucer's critical verdict that courteous-gentle and churlish-lewd are two worlds, and must keep their distance. 'Churlish' and 'lewd' were words of simple social designation corresponding with the modern 'the working classes' or 'the uneducated classes' or 'the masses'; but it was generally assumed that every churl was not only churlish and lewd, in the modern sense, but also a rogue. Only humane education was held to remove the taint of roguery; and until the late seventeenth century a condemned felon could save his neck by demonstrating his ability to read Latin.

Probably the first example in English literature of the courteous-gentle playing at the churlish-lewd—the gentleman as criminal—is Falstaff; but he is a comic speculation rather than an everyday character. The theme of the young gentleman merrily engaged in criminal activities and carrying the reader's sympathy with him was not popularized until the educated classes had been greatly enlarged and the lewd had begun to play at gentility: then came a counter-tendency of the gentle-born to play at lewdness. The eighteenth-century Mohocks who disturbed the peace of the Town at night, preying on citizens and beating up the watch, were not roughs but young gentlemen, who could justify their behaviour by quoting Classical precedents from Periclean Athens and Augustan Rome. *Tom Jones* is the purest literary example of Mohockism. Fielding, who was an Eton contemporary of Fox and Pitt, wrote *Tom Jones* as an extension of his criticism of Richardson's *Pamela*. Richardson was a stationer's apprentice who had been writing above his class, as if to prove how impeccable a show of courteous sentiment a man born lewd could make, after a little education, even when dealing with official upper-class themes of love and chastity; but who in Fielding's view had succeeded merely in being vulgar. Fielding purposely wrote below his class, as if to prove what vigour the upper classes could show even when dealing with such low themes as road-houses, whores and bastards.

Fielding, Sterne, Smollett and other eighteenth-century Mohock novelists were under a cloud throughout the Victorian age, which was dominated by Dickens. Dickens had read Fielding and Smollett as a boy and learned from them the charm of low-life scenes written in the high style; but, being born low down in the social scale, he could not afford to show the same sympathy with crime as they did —he made caricature-monsters of his criminals whenever they occurred. Since he did not confine himself to writing on upper-class topics, he had to go further than Richardson in pleading that the lower classes, so far from being necessarily lewd, churlish and common, had often greater gentility of spirit and virtue, even when uneducated, than the so-called gentle classes themselves. Thus official literature won the lower classes over as its strongest supporters. A new unofficial literature then came into being (a gentlemanly reaction against the vulgarization of official literature) which combined the lewd with the exotic and freakish. The obscene Limerick was the commonest vehicle, and the most polished examples of it were said to be the work of such distinguished poets as Tennyson, Swinburne, Henley and Stevenson. An official rehabilitation of Fielding and the other eighteenth-century Mohocks has followed, and new ventures in Mohock novel-writing—for example, by Norman Douglas, Aldous Huxley and Evelyn Waugh who write exclusively for the upper classes. E. W. Hornung's *Raffles* is not Mohock writing, but addressed to the wide semi-Victorian public. Raffles, the hero, is a gentleman cracksman, but not in any sense vicious. He lives an abstemious life, is loyal to his friends, keeps a clean mouth and burgles only the houses of rich swindlers and obvious cads.

Social control of obscenity in England is exercised in what seems a very haphazard way, but really in a simple continuation of the 'benefit of clergy' tradition; an obscene publisher is let off with a caution if he can 'read his neck-verse' in Latin, as proof that he is not a felon but merely a Mohock. Far more latitude is allowed the printed word (especially if the print is good and the price of the volume high and if Latin terms are employed) than the spoken word. Legal indulgence is strained to the utmost limit in the case of Mohocks, and it is only occasionally that such a limit is overpassed—Cleland's *Fanny Hill* in the eighteenth century and Joyce's recent *Ulysses* were both considered to come too close to the real thing to pass as gentlemanly jokes. So was *Lady Chatterley's Lover*. But D. H. Lawrence was not a simple Mohock; he was a man of the lewd class (from a mining district) reacting against the unnatural laws of genteel moderation imposed by Victorian education and claiming the right to rise by self-education to a gentlemanly disregard of conventional ethics: yet using the language of vulgar literacy to press this claim and never recovering his natural lewdness even in *Lady Chatterley*, where he achieves only a pathetic nastiness. This, of course, is an explanation of D. H. Lawrence in a purely social context, in which the three Sitwells are his stylistic opposites: naturally genteel, they renounce the sophisticated lewdness which is their new birthright as upper-class modernists and reclaim their old birthright of sophisticated decorum.

Mark Twain's *Huckleberry Finn* and *Tom Sawyer* contrast Huck, the true criminal, with Tom the Mississippi Mohock. Tom is the child of respectable upbringing who envies Huck his life as an illiterate, ragged river-bank loafer, and comes forward as a criminal mastermind to employ him. Huck takes him at his face value, and the result of their adventures in the first volume is that they become rich by accidentally exposing some genuine robbers and Huck is removed from his sugar-hogshead to a Christian home. He breaks away (in the second volume) and goes on criminal adventures of his own which are real enough to make *Huckleberry Finn* a far more enjoyable crime book than *Tom Sawyer*, where Tom is the false criminal force. The true character of Tom is revealed only at the end of *Huckleberry Finn*. He has been helping Huck to harbour a runaway negro slave, the property of a neighbour, who is trying to reach freedom and safety in a non-slavery State. Tom's plots for the negro's concealment are more literary than criminal—he always insists on 'style' in his doings—and Huck discovers finally that the negro is really a free man after all (liberated by his owner's Will since his escape) and that Tom has known this all along: Tom has been enjoying the sense of criminal activity without having it on his conscience that he has been conniving in the theft of a neighbour's property.

Fielding was something of a Tom Sawyer. As a London magistrate he made it his life's work to stamp out crime, with particular attention to gin, the criminal of drinks. But the English Mohock writer's affectation of criminal sympathies is somewhat different from Tom Sawyerism; it is a sophisticated, frankly experimental emotion, not a gentleman's wistful infatuation with lewd vigour.

VI

LUCRETIUS AND JEANS

Lucretius records a philosophic excitement in the strangeness of the material universe: a state of consciousness above the immediately physical but below consciousness of reality itself. The comfortable range of human thought reaches as far as the familiar strangeness of one's own being, and Lucretius could make a voyage of exploration outside his body without breaking its spell over his mind. Much the same sort of psychological adventuring has since been undertaken by Rimbaud and his successors, to whom the apparent impossibility of pursuing sensations beyond the limits of physical consciousness has implied the cruel inadequacy of the human mind to define truth; but Lucretius' work has a more direct connexion with the fanciful scientific cosmogony of Sir James Jeans than with the mental struggles of poets who have turned aside, from the straight path towards doom or resurrection, into a cerebral cul-de-sac. Science is concerned with isolating a minimum incident of certain duration—duration so certain that it need not be thought of as future, but only as the inevitable extension, by repetition, of the shortest, most instantaneous immediacy that can be conceived. Both Lucretius and Jeans, who demonstrates better than any other modern scientist the inevitable sentimentality of the scientific view, somehow manage to coax happiness out of the notion that some time, though not now, the universe must end. The outer immensity of space—since the practical realm of sensation lies within relatively meagre boundaries—is employed by both as a field for respectable scientific Corybantics. And they find in the little-ness of earth, and in the littleness of the individual, the source of a more workaday optimism: they make terrestrialism the capacity to isolate the particular local incident, or reality, from the general way of things—to perpetuate it in despite of the finality which lies at the end of the road. A still more striking resemblance between Lucretius' Epicurean science and modern scientific thought is their common impatience with causality, so that they even omit the demonstration of cause, as something in itself evil, or fatally governing. Lucretius was interested in causality only as the stimulus of effects; he did not much care what causes he ascribed to things—how ostensibly fallacious they were—so long as in ascribing a cause he clarified the effect which it perhaps precipitated.

A textual comparison of Lucretius' *De Rerum Natura* and Jeans' shortest and most poetical work *Eos: or the Wider Aspects of Cosmogony* strengthens this resemblance. As a popular historian Jeans is as unreliable as Lucretius—their first similarity. He asserts, for instance, that only in the past ten generations has the Earth ceased to be regarded as the centre of the universe. But Lucretius in the first century B.C. had explicitly stated that there could be no centre of the universe, because it was infinite; and this was not his own peculiar view but an Epicurean commonplace. Jeans also speaks of the atomic theory as the property of 'our scientific ancestors of half-a-century ago': unaware that John Dalton only revived 'scientifically' another Epicurean commonplace familiar to every classically educated Englishman. Jeans is excited at meeting Newton's anticipations, in his *Opticks* (1704), of present-day scientific theory; yet equally striking ones occur in Lucretius. For instance, Jeans' concept of space as being filled with wandering radiations from dead matter which contribute practically nothing to the sum of things is paralleled by Lucretius:

> Principio hoc dico, rerum simulacra vagari
> Multa modis multis in cunctas undique partis
> Tenvia . . . multo magis haec sunt tenvia textu
> Quam quae percipiunt oculos visumque lacessunt
> . . . simulacraque eorum
> Quorum morte obita tellus amplectitur ossa.

(In the first place I tell you that many images (reflections) of things wander about in many ways and in all directions, very thin . . . they are much thinner in texture than the images which strike the eyes and assail the vision . . . reflections also of those whose death is passed and whose bones are buried.)

Since this is only one of several parallels we may conclude that Jeans has not read Lucretius; yet there are numerous passages in *Eos* which would translate directly into Lucretian hexameters. For instance:

Under the action of great heat the outermost of the atomic electrons begin to break loose from the atom and fly off at a tangent, just as, when water is heated up, the outer molecules break loose and set off on independent journeys of their own. Finally the water is wholly evaporated; the heat has transformed it into a mass of gas (steam) in which each separate molecule flies along its own individual path like the bullets on a battle-field. In precisely the same way, the application of heat to the atoms causes successive layers of electrons to break loose from their moorings, and the atoms become smaller and smaller until finally no coherent structure remains but merely a powdered *debris* of atomic constituents, each nucleus and electron going its own way regardless of the rest.

The resemblance lies in the humanistic way in which they both write about their atoms, or particles, or molecules, or 'first-beginnings,' or 'seeds of things,' or electrons, or whatever invisible tininesses they happen to be discussing. 'Set off on journeys of their own . . . flies along its own individual path . . . each nucleus and electron going its own way regardless of the rest.' So Lucretius, talking of certain of his tininesses:

> Multaque praeterea magnum per inane vagantur
> Conciliis rerum quae sunt rejecta nec usquam
> Consociare etiam motus potuere recepta.

(Many of them, too, go wandering through space: they are rejected from the councils of things and have nowhere been able to ally their motions together even when admitted.)

Both Lucretius and Jeans are philosophizing in terms of infinitesimal units of matter or energy, or what-not—so insignificant that it is painfully headachy, except for scientific adepts, to bring the mind to bear on them at all, but which exist more tangibly than difficult generalizations because they answer troublesome questions 'beautifully' (Jeans' word). These infinitesimal units represent man in his most disorganized, irresponsible state; as the beautiful answers in which they assist are the most irresponsible answers. Leucippus invented them first, but they have been constantly recharacterized since his day in a variety of senses. To Leucippus they were infinitely small and indivisible. Later they had theoretically to be given 'parts,' to distinguish one atom from another; but only qualitative parts, the atom being still admittedly indivisible—which is Lucretius' view. Dalton 'weighed' his atoms but still forbade anyone to divide them: 'thou knowest thou canst not cut an atom.' Rutherford and Bohr, however, gave these qualitative parts separability, making a miniature solar system of each atom—which is Jeans' view. His 'atomic electrons' are infinitesimal parts of the atomic nucleus, of which the diameter is 'only a small fraction of the millionth of a millionth of an inch.' Yet Jeans writes about these *semina rerum* as Lucretius did in the passage quoted (*Multaque praeterea* . . .)—as if they were queer little idiosyncratic creatures of his personal acquaintance. Both writers are making every effort to be at home in a common-sense way in strange reality—to create an economical means of talking about universal problems, eliminating all the difficult aspects. So Jeans:

The infinitely great is never very far from the infinitely small in science, but it would be hard to find a more sensational illustration of the unity of science than that just given [i.e. the resemblance between atomic structure and the structure of solar systems].

In discussing the stars Jeans speaks of 'groups of bright stars moving in orderly formation through a jumble of slighter stars, like a flight of swans through a confused crowd of rooks and starlings.' So also Lucretius:

> . . . cum lucida signa ferantur . . .
> Flammea per caelum pascentis corpora passim.

(. . . when bright constellations, with fiery bodies, go grazing here and there across the sky.)

Both are fundamentally more interested in analogy than in theory. So Jeans says, in writing of cosmogony: 'One could hardly be prosaic if one tried.' And Lucretius: 'It is pleasant to drink at virgin springs of song, and to seek an illustrious chaplet for my head from fields whence the Muses have crowned no poet before me.'

Yet Lucretius' common sense is nonsense from the present-day scientific point of view. His wandering radiations or reflections, for instance, were offered as explanations of the fancies which men get in dreams about Centaurs and Chimaeras. That the world was not the middle of things he used as a final argument against the existence of upside-down animal life at the antipodes. His erratic stars were represented as possibly going in search of food. However, the only real difference between him and Jeans is that, though both are fancifully, and nonsensically, simplifying major universal problems, Jeans seems more respectably intricate in that he has a much greater accumulation of scientific hypotheses to deal with; his work is simplifying previous simplifications. In its design of substituting simple for complicated formulas of explanation, science was bound to grow more complicated itself, the more ambitious it became of being a completely adequate substitute for truth. But Lucretius' task was intricate in another sense: he had no complicated scientific apparatus at his disposal. He must constantly make the change-over from abstruse into practical language, and fortify his own system with abstruse explanations where it was incomplete; and he frequently complained of the inadequacy of Latin, compared with Greek, for abstruse statement, though simple statement was his object. Thus, Jeans' swan-flock figure is a complicated mechanistic nicety justifying a whole tradition of scientific rhetoric; while Lucretius' 'stars grazing across the sky,' though part of the plan which he shares with Jeans of fanciful simplification ('honey smeared round the medicinal cup of wormwood'), leave behind them an irksome linguistic difficulty. He would have liked his figure to convey of itself the analytic notion of freewill on the part of the stars, as well as the merely descriptive notion of erratic movement; but Latin exacted more explicit precision. He felt obliged to complete the description with suggestions of purpose in movement that the strict, descriptive Latin use of the word 'grazing' could not possibly convey.

Yet Lucretius was more devoutly scientific than Jeans and other scientists who no longer think of themselves as fighting a lonely and difficult battle against superstition—the superstition of those who do not want too easy an explanation. For, as between science and religion, it is science which is the bigot, science which wants to achieve mental peace by localized tricks of thought. Religion now indulges science, in so far as it keeps people in comfort and good humour by its charlatanism while the higher business is going on and in so far as it uses such pious language as 'in the service of mankind' to conceal the spiritually destructive nature of the service. The scientific battle is won and over-won. Scientists can draw what conclusions they like in the name of science and, so long as the public is convinced that 'people well up in science' treat these conclusions with respect, they will be accepted as pontiffs of practical truth—even when they are only improvising accounts of phenomena of which, by the nature of the analytical economies they practise, they can have none but the most arbitrary knowledge. Jeans speaks of the interior mechanism of the latest atom as confidently as if it were that of the latest aircraft engine.

Lucretius, not so comfortably placed, always emphasizes the tentative nature of his cosmogonal doctrine. Having said that one of many causes may explain the motion of stars—either that the whole sky may be driven by currents of air, or that the stars may, independently of the sky, be mechanically driven by internal force, or that they may be moved by tides in the ether, or that they may move consciously, in search of food—he ends by admitting that which of all these causes holds good in *our* universe it is difficult to say. Since there are so many various universes, as he has already shown by proving the infinity of matter in the total universe, each of these theories must hold good *somewhere*; and which one fits this particular universe, he will not rashly decide, for he must go step by step in a scientific spirit.

In present-day science such reservations have gradually dropped out, because scientists are careful to express their suppositions in mathematical formulas which, applied artistically to such problems as the structure of the atom or the inner temperatures of stars, give 'beautiful' results. They are applied only to safe, prepared cases—though remaining unworkable in unstereotyped ones: there must be a sympathetic equivalence between formula and case.

The mathematician need not hesitate to thrust his calculations right into the heart of the stars, and he can usually show, with something approaching very near to certainty, that at the centres of most of the stars nearly all, or perhaps quite all, of the electrons must have broken loose from their parent atoms leaving the stellar matter almost or quite pulverized into its constituent nuclei and electrons.

A beautiful result is as good as a demonstrable proof and can be superseded only by a still more beautiful result. 'Beauty is truth; truth, beauty,' wrote Keats as a chemist-contemporary of Dalton's. Lucretius, too, likes beautiful results; but he has no mathematical bludgeon at his disposal—only a store of imposing phenomenal curiosities, such as the action of a magnet on iron rings, the hurly-burly of motes in a sunbeam, the origin of forest fires in the rubbing together of twigs. He uses these as far as they will go. Unbeautiful results irritate him and in the last event he is reduced to his general reservation about the tentativeness of his doctrine. Thus, at one point he has been led to state that men once used to employ wild beasts in battle, such as lions and boars, against their enemies. He adds that this was an unbelievably foolish thing to do, because obviously the beasts would turn on their own masters with indiscriminate slaughter—but perhaps the men were reckless and did not care what happened to them, or perhaps the whole historical account which he has just given (with exciting detail) really belongs to the story of another universe altogether.

Lucretius is here doing what he always does when he stumbles against a piece of theory which seems humanly uncomfortable—he discounts its immediate applicability: such as that men were once born from wombs sprouting out of the earth, whose limbs were all wrongly placed on the trunk, so that they could not fend for themselves or reproduce their kind; or that the earth originally brought forth enormous monsters. His object is to rid men of terror, not to substitute scientific terrors for religious ones. He points out that an infinite variety of happenings and creatures obviously occur *somewhere* in the total universe, but that the natural laws current in other universes do not apply to this. A Chimaera, he says, obviously cannot occur in this world because the fixed laws which, according to our practical experience, rule the natures of lion, goat and snake (the components of a Chimaera) would be set in contradiction by such a mixture—and the final impossibility of a Chimaera is that it is held to breathe out fire, which would burn the goat-stomach of the creature.

Lucretius is no more an 'original' scientist than Jeans, though both may claim to have added their quota of interpretation and suggestion to the scientific aggregate. To avoid the charge of idiosyncratic madness they both ask authority for their work by citing previous scientists. What men have once thought—Democritus, Empedocles and Epicurus, Dr. Hubble, Prof. McLennan and Prof. Millikan—it is not unnatural to think again. Jeans has a bigger body of authorities to cite and a more compact corpus of scientific facts: he is able to draw on these facts for the human comfort which it is his chief interest to give. Thus, Jeans would be unlikely to support a scientific argument, as Lucretius does, with the fact that a leaden bullet slung from a military catapult melts when sent a long distance; he would have a mathematical formula pigeon-holed somewhere proving that the friction of the air is not great enough to make the lead anything more than somewhat hot to the touch. But his lack of historical accuracy, already referred to, suggests that, 'irreproachably scientific' though his work may be, this is only because he is writing when he is. Had he lived in Lucretius' time he would have been equally ready to believe, on Epicurus' authority, that clouds were bladders full of wind or water or fire, and that thunder probably came from their scraping their sides together, then bursting, discharging fire in the form of lightning and water in the form of rain: for it was a theory which fitted the known facts 'beautifully.' His own electrons and protons behave very much like Lucretius' clouds:

They are pure bottled energy; the continuous breakage of these bottles in the sun sets free the radiation which warms and lights our earth, and enough unbroken bottles remain to provide light and heat for millions of years to come.

The optimism which is the chief link between these writers is founded on extreme fear of mortal extinction. But both treat this fear as troubling only other people; for themselves, they are secure in the serene retreats of science. Jeans can write unconcernedly:

With an ardour equalled only by that of man's longing for personal immortality, many seem to desire that the universe itself should prove in some way to be immortal.

and Lucretius:

> Et quoniam docui cunctarum exordia rerum
> Qualia sint et quam variis distantia formis . . .
> Hasce secundum res animi natura videtur
> Atque animae claranda meis iam versibus esse
> Et metus ille foras praeceps Acheruntis agendus,
> Funditus humanam qui vitam turbat ab imo . . .

(And since I have explained the beginnings of all things and how they differ in their shapes . . . I must next explain in this poem the nature of mind and spirit, so as to cast that fear of Hell headlong out which affects man's life so deeply.)

Both cast out the fear by concentrating on the relative littleness and isolation of man in the total scheme of things; also by saying that, granted that *some time* human beings must face finality, mortal extinction will fall equally on everything. Both admit that the universe is running down and will come to an end one day. Lucretius insists that the end of this universe does not matter: there are always other universes. Jeans' view is much the same, though he does not speculate on other universes because he makes this one much more inclusive. Both comfort their readers by saying that it will be so long a time before the universe ends that they need not worry about the end. But both blow hot and cold according as they wish to affect their readers emotionally one way or the other, alternately insisting on the newness and on the oldness of the world for man.

In all probability the life in front of the human race must enormously exceed the short life behind it. *Jeans.*

> Verum, ut opinor, habet novitatem summa recensque
> Naturast mundi neque pridem exordia cepit.

(But my belief is that the universe is new and our world is new, and that it is not long since the beginning.) *Lucretius.*

So far as we can judge, our part of the universe has lived the more eventful part of its life already; what we are witnessing is less the rising of the curtain before the play than the burning out of candle-ends on an empty stage on which the drama is already over. *Jeans.*

Sed quia finem aliquam pariendi debet habere,
Destitit, ut mulier spatio defessa vetusto.

(But because she [Mother Earth] must have some limit to her bearing, she ceased, like a woman worn-out by old age.) *Lucretius.*

Similarly they blow alternately hot and cold in the matter of fixed laws and arbitrary phenomena. Jeans disposes of the idea that an original fortuitous combination of atoms made the universe, by a mathematical pronouncement that the chances for its fortuitousness are precisely one in $10^{420,000,000}$ (this last figure being short for a sum starting with 10 and ending in four hundred and twenty thousand million zeros); yet he concedes that *how* the universe was originally set going is shrouded in impenetrable mystery. When he comes to speak of the Earth itself he says that it is quite an unusual phenomenon, an astronomical freak, and that there are 'millions of millions' of chances to one (he does not give the precise figure) against the surface of any planet being in the same bio-chemical condition as ours to-day. So too Lucretius. He insists on the fixed laws, the decrees of fate, which govern everything. Yet he holds that the original atomic beginnings of things broke these eternal fixities by an accident; and that this resulted in the present universe, a compromise between fate (the fixed unalterable properties of things) and accident (things that come and go without prejudice to these properties).

Lucretius held that space was infinite, but that this universe (meaning as much of physical totality as people of his time could comprehend) was comfortably finite. His 'this universe' was a much more modest one than Jeans' 'this universe' because it did not include all matter, the infinitely greater part of which he held to lie outside in other universes. Jeans, while agreeing with Lucretius that space has no limit, and even with his contention that space and matter are co-extensive, makes 'this universe' include all the universes outside the visible one—and still declares it to be finite. How does he evade this paradox of finite limitlessness? By a word he has learned from Einstein, which curiously enough is the very word that Lucretius learned from Epicurus; a word that Epicurus used in evading the paradox of

how his originally fate-bound atoms started the hurly-burly of crea-
tion—namely, *clinamen*, or swerve. Lucretius writes:

> Quare etiam atque etiam paulum inclinare necessest
> Corpora; nec plus quam minimum, ne fingere motus
> Obliquos videamur et id res vera refutet.

(So I insist that the atoms must make a slight swerve; and not more than the
least possible, or we shall seem to be assuming oblique movements—which
is an untenable hypothesis.)

And Jeans writes that 'a general guiding principle, that of generalized
relativity, fixes a limit to space.' Light does not travel straight, but
with a *swerve* so slight as to have been unsuspected until only the
other day when the mathematicians discovered it accidentally. This
swerve denotes a curvature of space. So, if we were to go far enough,
we should only 'come back on ourselves'; travelling as fast as light,
we should come back on ourselves in one hundred thousand million
years. Lucretius used *clinamen* to account for human free-will, too.
The swerve is, of course, the very nature of scientific thought, as well
as the carefully irresponsible, disobedient nature of matter itself; and
it allows of infinity, or continuous duration, so long as people think
at individual random, as it also provides the comfort of finity, or
individual peculiarity of being.

Both Jeans and Lucretius feel the same embarrassment in talking
about divine being: and yet neither can resist mention of divinity.
There is no room for divinity in their self-like intellectual universe,
yet they cannot help introducing it emotionally. They both let it be
understood that gods or God (Lucretius preaches with missionary
zeal what by Jeans' time has become a scientific assumption) have
nothing whatever to do with things as they are; yet indulge their own
sentimentality and that of their readers in poetical references to the
divine. So Lucretius:

> Hunc tu, diva, tuo recubantem corpore sancto
> Circumfusa super, suavis ex ore loquellas
> Funde petens placidam Romanis, incluta, pacem.

(Goddess Venus, as you and Mars lie twined together in a divine sexual
embrace, please beg him charmingly to give us Romans peace.)

And Jeans, less naughtily:

And we cannot say how long the stellar matter may have been in the nebular state before it formed stars. Nothing in astronomy fixes with any precision the time since

> 'the great morning of the world, when first God dawned on chaos.'

The strongest note which they both of them strike is optimism as the counter-weight to fear—optimism derived from the admission and exploration of fear:

> ... we are standing at the first flush of the dawn of civilization. Each instant the vision before us changes as the rosy-fingered goddess paints a new and ever more wonderful picture in the sky ... *Jeans.*

> Diffugiunt animi terrores, moenia mundi
> Discedunt, totum video per inane geri res.

(Terrors of the mind flee away now, the walls of the universe open out, I see action going on throughout the whole of space.) *Lucretius.*

This lyricism necessarily brings its gloomy reaction. Lucretius, in spite of his serene philosophy, comes in the course of his argument upon several uncomfortable fatalities from which he swerves away, recovering his balance with difficulty. Eventually he gets into what motor-cyclists call a 'roll'—a slight skid inducing a greater and greater skid from which there is no recovery. He is discussing the plague at Athens. Hitherto he has been able to limit his digressions on uncomfortable topics to a few lines, though the account of the wild beasts in battle lasted for fifty before he could extricate himself. But in discussing the plague he goes on and on, trying to find some way of discounting this fatal horror, or of alleviating it; but can think of none. He is fascinated against his free-will by the ulcers, the retchings, the salty yellow spittle, the black bowel-discharge, the nose-bleeding, the desperate self-castration; and after a hundred and sixty lines he collapses at a point where the terrified survivors are brawling over the stinking and loathsome corpses of their relatives. There the whole poem breaks off.

Jeans ends in nightmare too:

> In any case, our three-days-old infant cannot be very confident of any interpretation it puts on a universe which it only discovered a minute or two ago ... And ever the old question obtrudes itself as to whether the infant has any means of knowing that it is not dreaming all the time. The picture it sees may be merely a creation of its own mind, in which nothing really exists except itself; the universe which we study with such care may be a dream, and we brain-cells in the mind of a dreamer.

VII

POETRY AND POLITICS
(with Laura Riding)

Poets who turn to politics nearly always turn to the popular sort and go as far to the left as they dare. When they concern themselves with aristocratic politics, this is largely for the pleasure of moving in refined society, on an island of proud retirement from the populace. Poetic virtue is, of course, not rooted in pride, nor does it involve retirement; it implies a close awareness of the conglomerate physical universe. But, though a poet does not seek substantiation of his virtue in aristocratic society, he finds there an atmosphere safe from the caprices of popular taste; aristocratic patronage of poets has, at least, caused less interference with their work than the patronage of the populace.

The populace now exercises a more tyrannical influence over English writers than ever before. This is due to a mistranslation of the democratic principle, that everyone has not only the right, but the obligation, to be responsible for himself, into a statement of historical achievement: that everyone has equal capability with everyone else. Democratic education inculcates the theory of universal talent, so that every reader feels himself the potential equal of any writer in the writer's own field; and the authors of most books published to-day are not true writers but semi-literate readers ambitious to earn money and fame by writing, and their books are forced on the market by sheer weight of advertising. Old-fashioned English firms, who have made it a point of honour to publish books written by true writers only, see the day coming when they must either invest most of their money in what they know to be trash, or else go out of business; many of them are already anticipating the day by buying ready-made best-sellers from the United States. But the Communist view of literature is even more destructive of the writer's integrity than the democratic view: it does not merely diffuse the essence of the literary consciousness and make practically every book by a true writer an unsound commercial proposition (a 'difficult' book). It denies the existence of any consciousness but the political, offering the author a devil's bargain: psychological adjustment to the physical world, fame and audiences guaranteed, if he will forget that he is qualitatively more articulate than the populace and assist the politician in making human values quantitative again. The object of Communism is to reintroduce into political consciousness all the physical impediments of which cultured aristocratic society has for centuries been purifying itself.

The democratic view of the literary consciousness is a sentimental error against which it is still just possible for the poet to hold his own: the democrat firmly believes himself the poet's friend. Thus the Prime Minister [Mr. Stanley Baldwin], addressing the Congress of the Universities of the British Empire at Cambridge in July 1936, asks for —more poets! But democratic poets, assigned the task of 'inspiring the world with a sense of unity and a sense of freedom.' He commends the comparative harmlessness of poets, in accomplishments so vague that their benefits cannot be calculated:

Great poets are scarce—scarcer, perhaps, than scientific men. I always feel that one of the tragedies of the world is the way in which the devil is using the discoveries of the chemist, and of those men who invented the internal combustion engine, for the destruction of mankind. No poet has done that. I do not think many of them did much harm in their lives, but they left us incalculable benefits for this world, and if the universities can conspire to produce more poets, more power to their elbow!

At the same time he pleads for the endowment of scientific research workers, to free them from financial anxiety:

In my view the men who are doing research and who have a special talent for that work, should be free, as far as possible, from teaching.

But the Chancellor of the Exchequer has recently declined to accept a motion for increasing the Civil List pensions in art, science, literature and learning from £1,200 (the figure at which it has stood for 100 years) to £4,000. The Chancellor states that there has been 'increasing difficulty in recent years in discovering a sufficient number of persons who can meet the two conditions of need and merit,' and that 'if the amount were increased, the tests applied to pensioners would have to be relaxed.' (The maximum pension is £120 a year, the average pension is about £60.) The democratic theory is that the poet either lives on inherited income, like Byron or Shelley, or makes literature a side-line to scholarly, ecclesiastical, educational or other wage-earning activity, like Herrick, or A. E. Housman, or T. E. Brown; or earns money by writing of a journalistic, dramatic or fictional sort with poetry as its fine flower, like Southey, or Wilde, or Kipling; but that if he does none of these things and prefers to concentrate on poetry and go hungry, the result is likely to be more incalculably beneficial still. That a poet is as much a research worker as the endowed scientist would never occur to any representative of democratic opinion. Mr. Baldwin is not serious in his plea for more poets: what he really means to assert is the need for more politicians. But we do not mean to suggest that poets should be endowed; those who pay the piper call the tune and the State, or any State-sponsored institution, is a dangerous patron of literature.[1]

Communism makes no provision whatever for the poet, but shrewdly designs his suppression. The poet who has to endure democratic publishing methods may still find dignity in the thought that he is not conspiring against himself, that he merely stands for the moment as a member of a preposterously large literary fellowship— the vanity of others is no outrage to his own dignity. But the poet who surrenders to Communism conspires in his own suppression. He consoles himself with the thought that the physical resurrection which is the ideal of Communism may eventually bring about the rebirth of poetry; yet he knows that poetry is never what will be, but always what is. He is a tired man, in search of a long physical rest; and once he lies down on the bed of Communism he will never rise again.

Fascism neither issues invitations nor makes any promises to the poet, though like Communism it attempts to arouse feelings of guilt in him towards his immediate physical world. It gives him a stern warning not to distract the public mind from that sense of triumph in physical existence which it is the Fascist object to cultivate. Fascism attempts to consolidate as adequate reality the nation's given physical properties; Communism, to render reality in physical terms and create new physical values to fill out the despiritualized universe. In Germany the given physical properties comprise the ideal of human self-sufficiency; in Italy, the authority for caprice of action. The Fascist poet is

[1] On leaving the Army after the last war but one, I swore an oath of poetic independence which I have kept ever since. The only job I took (for reasons of health) was that of Professor of English Literature at Cairo University, but I was my own master, had only one lecture a week to give, and resigned after a few months when difficulties arose with my French and Belgian colleagues. That was twenty-three years ago, and I have lived ever since by writing biography and historical novels: a profession which I find more easily reconcilable than most with being a poet. Shakespeare himself admitted the difficulty of a secondary profession in his sonnet about the dyer's hand; but to say that I am satisfied with my solution of the problem, how a poet should support himself without injury to his poetry, would be indecent—it would imply a greater satisfaction with my work than Shakespeare seems to have felt with his. (R.G., 1949.)

not invited to elevate and purify, he is merely permitted to cheer, and this forbidding attitude to poetry accounts for the fewness of the English poets who profess Fascist sympathies. The reaction against Fascism in the West has been a thoughtless rush of poets into the Communist ranks, though the real opposite number to the Communist poet is not the Fascist, but the Catholic, or Anglo-Catholic: the poet who escapes from the modern noise of factions into a noncommittal mediaevalism.

Politics have always covered two distinct kinds of problems: problems of administrative routine, and those that may be called 'questions of the moment.' The first kind includes views on the powers and responsibilities of public office, the creation or suppression of offices and, in general, the relations between the governed and the governing—these relations, or any other problem of administrative routine, tending to become a question of the moment whenever the emotional unanimity of the State happens to be broken. A question of the moment is, indeed, a substitute for some notion, such as the idea of God, or hereditary monarchy, or national glory, that has hitherto acted as a symbol of human co-ordination. It provides no new positive certainty to replace the discredited certainty, but is what the name implies: the raising of a question which the old certainty no longer answers. Excited concern with questions of popular representation, or of foreign policy, is bred from a collapse of faith: the 'antis' translate what would otherwise be problems of concrete routine into 'causes,' alleviating the discomfort of lost faith with a counter-irritant of fierce negation. For example, heated advocacy of popular representation is based on loss of faith in the notion of government itself, which depends on a belief in human capacity to govern. As a problem of concrete routine, popular representation calls for no evangelical ardour; one need only realize that human capacity to govern is qualified by many limitations in circumstances and human nature. Such a realization, when applied to the notion of government, increases political intelligence. But a curious contradiction results when popular representation is made into a counter-faith to the notion of government: though this is repudiated as historically erroneous, it is stated as an emotional absolute even in its repudiation. Much the same thing happens when economic problems are translated into causes; cynical analysis of the ways in which human nature has expressed itself economically for thousands of years becomes the means of elevating economic expression into an emotional absolute.

The confusion which centres in the habit of political causes may be described as human self-criticism developed into an ideal of human perfection that is believed in only strategically. An old-fashioned Socialist hymn begins: 'The people is a beast of muddy brain . . .' Yet, for the sake of political attack on the present governing classes, this beast is advanced as a figure of perfectionism. The ideas of God, of hereditary monarchy, of national glory, and even of popular representation, have successively broken down as symbols of human co-ordination; and now popular economics form the counter-symbol. If all co-ordinating energy were vested in any of these governmental ideals, thought, as such, would have ceased long ago and we should all be absorbed in the technical administration of daily life. Properly, politics represent the minutiae of community co-ordination, problems of community well-being, of rules for external life by which each member of the State interferes as little as possible with his neighbour's physical happiness. Religion and monarchy, for instance, are both political means for establishing a temporal condition of mutual non-interference between neighbours. But assuming such a temporal condition to have been established—what then? The ends of life are in thought, not in mere living. These true ends remain to be fulfilled: the discovery of reality, the definition of truth.

Because the principle of co-ordination which poets observe is not a physical one, they have the power, if they care to exert it, to disarm all physical interference threatened by their neighbours. We do not recommend anarchism, which is based on the sentimental fallacy that all people are exclusively poets: few people are. But most people are poets in some degree, and political reality is final reality for none but the rhetorical politician.

The origin of European politics is to be found in the perpetual disagreements which went on within each Greek city-state as to the best means of achieving physical prosperity amid the rivalry between states. Since that time, though states have become larger and more complex units, no political ambition has ever had any object other than that of physical prosperity, however idealistically phrased. The politician was then what he fundamentally still is: a servant charged with doing the routine-work of civic administration and with suggesting alterations wherever the provisions for public well-being might appear inadequate. The task was burdensome, invidious

CA: T

and not undertaken, at first, as a career but from public-spiritedness, and only by men too old to serve as soldiers or to work in the fields.

In Greece there were only three kind of political opinion, and these solely concerned the form of government suitable to a state at any given time: democratic, oligarchic or dictatorial. The same was true of Rome until the freedman-bureaucracy of the Empire put an end to all other forms. Politics in the ancient world meant struggles between rival clans for local supremacy within the various states. If clan strengths were evenly matched, there was an oligarchy; if one clan became powerful enough to expel its rivals, there was a dictatorship; if the dictatorship was too arrogant or too neglectful of the state's well-being, there was a revolution, to be followed either by a democratic régime, another dictatorship or a return to oligarchy. There might be rich variety of political incident to account for these changes—an unpopular war, an unpopular alliance, excessive taxes, uneven justice, an outrage of popular religious sensibilities; but economic theory never played a major part in the politics of the Classical world. The nearest equivalent to Socialistic activity was the occasional attempt of some bankrupt aristocrat to incite the debt-ridden mob to revolt and proclaim *tabulae novae*, the writing-off of all existing debts. Yet even here there was no intention of supplanting one economic method with another. Indeed, so long as slave labour was essential to national economy, any weakening of the existing economic structure would have been suicidal.

Thus the ancient world offered no temptation to make politics a subject for humanitarian poetry. Personal invective in lampoons, particularly at Rome, good-humoured satire, as in the plays of Aristophanes, prose speculation upon the most suitable constitution for states in general, as in Plato's *Republic*, and oratorical disquisition for oratory's sake on a local political theme, were politics' sufficient representation in literature. The politician remained the public servant, concerned before all else with his rather dreary administrative task on behalf of his often jealous and always suspicious fellow-citizens—except when war, or sudden national expansion, made him a figurehead of the nation's more grandiose physical ambitions. So it has been in Europe ever since. Pericles is remembered for his management of Athenian affairs during the period in which Athens exerted her full naval strength against Sparta; Richelieu for making France the proudest European power of his time; Pitt for his successful conduct of

British affairs during the Napoleonic wars; Disraeli for securing control of the Suez Canal and for adding India to the British Crown.

Archons at Athens, consuls at Rome, prime ministers in modern Europe—none of these is remembered after his death, as poets and even generals are remembered, unless some national emergency has given him symbolic prominence. Otherwise they are all rightly regarded as mere managing clerks, fulfilling the artificial role of elders to the children of the state. Citizenship in a state confers the benefits of immaturity on the populace; state officials must needs play the old-man parts, but they cannot be regarded as possessing more than theatrical maturity. The only apparent exceptions to the rule of political oblivion are men like Cicero and Demosthenes, who are celebrated not for what they did or stood for as statesmen, but for the polish and vigour of their eloquence: their utterances are assumed to have an educative value, as examples of incisive prose, for those who make politics their career. But the orators have never amounted to much as politicians, in peace-time at least; literary vanity prevents them from sinking their personalities in civic service.

In mediaeval Europe politics were concerned chiefly with the uncomfortable dyarchy by which every state was governed: the temporal and the spiritual rule. The temporal overlord was sometimes a willing ally and sometimes a threatening master and sometimes an unwilling slave to his spiritual overlord at Rome, or Constantinople or Avignon. The political grievance (politics necessarily involve grievance) was that the country had been impoverished by the double levy of taxes imposed by this system, the middlemen of each half of the dyarchy enriching themselves unjustly in the names of their superiors, the poor being victimized on every side. Complaints against ecclesiastical rogueries were more vocal in England than elsewhere because of its great distance from Rome, and already in the thirteenth century a large body of satirical ballads against the immorality and greed of the clerics had been circulating both in Latin and English.

The first English political poem with literary pretensions is Langland's *Piers Plowman*; its hero is the idealized country labourer. But Langland was no leveller: he believed in a strong king, supported by devout bishops and noble knights and lords, all attentive to the welfare of the people—a national front against the depredations of the bourgeoisie. The bourgeoisie consisted chiefly of parasitic clerics, but included also merchants and tradesmen whose dishonesties, he thought, should be kept in check by the King and his Parliament. Langland calls for governmental control of:

> Brewsters and bakers. bochers and cokes;
> For these aren men on this mold. that most harme worcheth
> To the pore peple. that parcel-mele buggen.

'The pore peple that parcel-mele buggen' means 'the wage-earning retail-consumer.' *Piers Plowman* was a semi-mystical political tract intended to be committed to memory by the uneducated commons— written in verse-form for greater verbal emphasis. But for a strong sense of social injustice, probably sharpened by the humiliation of his bastardy, Langland would never have come to be included in the roll of English poets; what he wrote was not a poem, but something between a work of philosophical speculation on possible remedies for the ills of the day and a diatribe against those who seemed immediately responsible for them.

Langland had much the same political opinions as Chaucer; but Chaucer was a poet and made a clean separation between his political opinions, which he expressed humorously, and his poetic energies. Politically, he supported John of Gaunt's party of feudalists against the growing power of the new nobility, the middle classes and the monks. In the *Prologue to the Canterbury Tales* Chaucer's most sympathetic portraits are those of the Knight, the Squire, the Franklin (or country gentleman), the Oxford Clerk, the Poor Parson and the Ploughman; his most unpleasant are those of middle-class characters —the Doctor, the Man of Law, the Friar, the Miller, the Reeve, the Shipman, the Cook, the Manciple, the Pardoner and the Summoner. His *Sir Thopas*, a burlesque on the rhymed chivalric romances of the day, is also a satire on the Flemish burghers of the party of Philip von Artevelde who had risen against their feudal overlords. But the 'cause' note is never heard in *The Canterbury Tales*.

The next poet, after Chaucer, who had strong political opinions was John Skelton. His satiric *Colyn Cloute* was versified for the same reason as *Piers Plowman* had been: an illiterate audience has a memory for verse, not for prose. *Colyn Cloute* is written down to the popular understanding and directed against the luxury and haughtiness of the lords of the Church who are a law to themselves, respect neither the King nor the people and bring the Church into disrepute. They have now gained ascendancy over the feudal nobility as advisers to the King, and outdo them in temporal pomp:

For the lordes temporall
Theyr rule is very small,
Almost nothing at all . . .
. . . Noble men borne
To lerne they have scorne,
But hunt and blowe an horne,
Lepe over lakes and dykes,
Set nothing by polytykes;
Therefore ye kepe them base
And mocke them to theyr face.

The political balance is thus upset, and the prelates, being men of
lewd birth and no learning, have nothing to recommend them socially.
But *Colyn Cloute*, like *Why Come ye Nat to Courte?* and *The Bowge of
Courte*, is clearly inspired less by political, than by private, feud.
Skelton, a poet and scholar, and formerly tutor and adviser to the
King, was a parish priest placed under the discipline of a notoriously
ill-living bishop, Nix of Norwich, and supplanted at court by Wolsey,
the ignorant upstart of 'greasy genealogy.' These verses do not come
within the canon of his real poems any more than his humorous
flytings against the Scots and against his rival poet Garnesh.

Henry's breach with Rome put a temporary end to all political
verse complaining of the evils of dyarchy. In the Elizabethan age,
though all the poets had patrons and identified themselves with them
politically, the nation was sufficiently united to make such partisan-
ship an incidental matter; satire was turned not against classes but
against specific persons or specific personal types. Only when a Puritan
Parliament reinstituted dyarchy, by forcing the King to cede it some
of his powers, was satire renewed as a political weapon, by Cleveland
and the Cavalier ballad-writers. During the Commonwealth a great
deal of anti-Puritan satiric verse was written—Butler's *Hudibras* the
most bitter and memorable—but little anti-episcopal or anti-royalist;
Milton was by nature a politician rather than a poet, and during the
Commonwealth abandoned his over-cultivated early lyricism for
politico-religious controversy in prose. He returned to poetry only
after the extinction of his political hopes, and then to a poetry with
both lyricism and political hate disciplined away, in which he attempted
to establish psychological equivalence between the religious and the
poetic temperament. His political verse consists merely of the lines on
'The New Forces of Conscience under the Long Parliament,' and four
sonnets: eulogies of Cromwell and Fairfax, and the sonnets on the

Piedmont massacre and on the unfavourable reception of his tract *Tetrachordon*.

Professional political verse began after the Restoration, when the fear of another civil war kept the two parties at arm's length: the satiric discrediting of the opposing party with the object of keeping them out of power. Sir John Denham, author of *Instructions to a Painter*, was the first of the anti-Court satirists; Marvell succeeded him. Marvell's satires were journalistic exposures and had great contemporary influence in consolidating what was later to be called the Whig party; they have no connexion with his real poems. The century which followed was the most active politically, and the most barren poetically, in modern English history. The field of political verse was divided between Dryden, Pope and their successors, who combined literary graces with politics, and obscure professional lampoonists with their vituperative ballads-to-the-tune-of, *Last Wills*, *Advices*, rhymed chronicles and the like. Now that the two parties, Whig and Tory, had ceased to represent any disagreement between rival governmental principles, political verse became purely factious and personal. Yet it was next to impossible for a poet to get a hearing without declaring for one party or the other and engaging in political journalism. Such writers as Defoe, Swift and 'Peter Pindar,' who earlier in the century would have been poets, 'sealed of the tribe of Ben' and discussing literature in the Devil Tavern, chose to become pamphleteers; none of them was above dickering with the opposing party and all squandered their poetic energy in satire or prose narrative of sociological cast. The recognized poets stood for formalism in technique, 'moralized verse' (as Pope put it), and escapist pastoralism.

It was a political change that broke the spell: the French Revolution created a third party—the Jacobins. Jacobinism introduced a naturalistic idealism into politics, and it was not surprising that in England the young men who felt themselves to be poets, in contrast with the intelligent nonentities who had gained chaplaincies and sinecures by party influence under the patronage-system, should respond sympathetically to a doctrine of anti-privilege. To Blake, a lower middle-class mystic, to Wordsworth and Southey, ebullient University undergraduates, to Coleridge and Shelley, eccentric young intellectuals, the doctrine of liberty, equality, fraternity was an invitation to adventures in freedom and poetry. Blake wore a red cap in the streets of London, Coleridge and Wordsworth came under suspicion of the anti-revolutionary police; Shelley sealed his letters with a revolutionary wafer, distributed political tracts in Ireland and wrote poems inciting agricultural labourers to strike. The notion of 'good' literature as the ally of revolutionary politics came into vogue. To survive as a poet, Blake soon found himself forced to change from revolutionary politics to revolutionary theology; and whether he did survive as such depends solely on the poetic value of the mystical poems which form the bulk of his work. Wordsworth and Southey tried to redeem themselves as poets by swimming towards the lifebuoy of literary respectability; Shelley died a martyr to his faith in the identity of politics and literature; Coleridge somehow managed to escape from the political welter with his soul intact, if not with a coherent poetical work.

By the time of the Reform Bill and the Abolition of Slavery, all idealistic political activity on the part of the poets had ceased, as well as the vigorous satire of the *Anti-Jacobin* and its successors which had made such activity seem absurd and indecent. It is noteworthy that the great Chartist Movement of the 'thirties and 'forties, which failed in its day but practically every demand of which came to be fulfilled by the end of the century, had no ambitious young University poets to support it. None was busied either with poetry or with politics, but all with humanitarian idealism, omitting the preliminary political stage, or with aesthetic idealism—ornate leisure. Romantic literary geniality was the aim both of the generation of Tennyson and of the pre-Raphaelites. William Morris, the most gifted of either group, did not become an active Socialist until late middle age.

The peculiar attraction which the political cause has for poets is to be explained by their rooted conviction that they are *good*. The goodness of poets and of poetry is unquestionable, but it is not a goodness to be piously exemplified in a partisanship of humanitarian causes. It is practically demonstrable only in poems written as poems—not as political, philosophical, aesthetic or musical displays; yet poets are sensitive to the challenge 'What is the moral justification of poetry?' because they are conscious of the intrinsic goodness of poetry. Goody-goody humanitarian causes draw them easily into membership by making them wince at the notion of all the injustices prevalent in the world of physical consciousness. Let it be declared as clearly as possible that the goodness of poetry is not moral goodness, the goodness of temporal action, but the goodness of thought, the loving exercise of the will in the pursuit of truth. Moral definitions may be invented for historical emergencies, but when a historical emergency passes, the moral definition passes with it: moral, or local, truth is finally unreal.

The pursuit of current morality is not the pursuit of poetry. The poet is concerned with that truth which is not a historical product but which is always there of itself because it *is* reality: he is concerned with final truth only.

VIII

POETIC DRAMA
(with Laura Riding)

Drama began as religious ritual and at its best remains so still, despite all technical modifications of the last two or three thousand years: any attempt to force a more complicated function on it has always weakened the dramatic spell. The object of religious ritual is to emphasize the reality of the human worshipper. Ritual involves acts of self-manifestation, or self-definition in its most vital physical sense. In the ancient Greek Mysteries the worshipper acted in conjunction with his god; in the popular drama the gods were theoretically present, but it was the human spectacle that occupied the attention of the audience, the performers imitating as impressively as they could the physical presences of the characters they represented. Dionysus, doomed patron of human vitality, presided over popular drama.

Drama, then, consists of a series of highly stressed acts by which a chosen set of characters are given immediate and intimate human reality for the purpose of making the quality of being human so vivid as to be undeniable. Its sincerity lies in its very exaggerations and artifices, in the conviction that this or this is what it is like to be human. That the characters chosen may be unusual as human beings is not a hindrance to drama, but rather an opportunity for constant exploration. The audience is given the sensation that to be human is something peculiar, exciting, sharply describable, yet something natural and true in the mass, no matter how fantastic-seeming in the individual. The fantastic, indeed, never makes good drama of itself. Drama must tame the fantastic to credibility; and the act of belief in the ritual presented to the audience must be matched by an act of belief in himself by every member of the audience. In this, the theatre maintains an identity with the church; besides articulating humanity, both institutions breathe out a confidence in humanity, which awakens indefinite hopefulness in the churchgoer and a precise emotion of pride in the theatregoer.

Although in Greek popular drama it is human reality that is articulated, this is done in contradistinction to the divine realities which are assumed to be somewhere not far off. But as philosophical definitions of the divine became more and more speculative, drama was bound to become more and more irresponsibly human: the dramatists grew ambitious in their quantitative analysis of humanity, humanity's divine counterpart grew less specific, less identifiable. The prerogative of defining human reality, which had belonged to the priests and mystagogues, was taken over from them for a time by the philosophers. But presently Christ supplanted Dionysus and pagan philosophy was taken over by the Church; and after the Renaissance religion was found too arbitrary, and philosophy too dry, to complement the newly consolidated sense of human reality. The poets then conceived of a reality which exceeded human reality and which would either, as drama, impinge on the senses of a massed audience with masterful force or else, as poetry, have only an internal effect and that only on isolated individuals. These alternatives have both been since realized and we may express their contradictory conjunction in terms of language. Language has now developed two different sorts of precision —dramatic, or conversation, precision, and poetic precision; the poetic is a necessary complement of the dramatic, though drama has arrogated to itself all the excitement of consciousness, casting on poetry a slur of esoteric fancifulness.

We do not mean that what is wrong with the drama is that it is not poetic; for drama does not, properly, include poetry. But it cannot have impressiveness unless it implies the existence of the other side of reality, the poetic face that is not turned to the proscenium: and impressiveness is the essence of drama, even in farce. Ancient popular drama implied the closed religious Mysteries; modern popular drama, to have ritual force, should imply private poetry. Its failure to do so in recent years indicates a general spiritual setback rather than a lack of dramatic technique; for nobody can deny the vigour of modern dramatic professionalism, and the cinema has reduced dramatic technique to a commonplace. That dramatists nowadays tend to choose their subjects from everyday life means not so much that they have grown more liberal, more conscious of the world outside the theatre, but rather that everyone now has a good stage-sense and a good stage-presence which he exercises in nearly every circumstance of life. Conversation itself has become more dramatic, more energetically colloquial. But the perfected excitement of mere living turns purposelessly back on itself, failing to imply a reality beyond its own. It is clear to everyone that such a condition cannot be wholesome: those who are most caught up in the machinery of modern excitement are the first to admit its madness.

Worse than this widening of the unbridgeable gap between dramatic and poetic realities, is the attempted introduction into the theatre of poetic realities, a colloquializing of these realities in dramatic contexts by the poets themselves. Some poets, humanly ill-at-ease on poetic ground, have transferred their entire poetic paraphernalia to the stage and there attempted to reconcile the two realities in a way that can only be called profanity. In *The Rock* and *Murder in the Cathedral*, for instance, T. S. Eliot is attempting a profane drama—more profane even than that of W. H. Auden, because he keeps his poetic paraphernalia solemn and well-conditioned, while Auden lets his run into farcical shabbiness. It is by no accident of personal theology that Eliot sets 'God' in the midst of his theatrical world: here is the assertion of a deliberately profane intention. Had the drama not been protected until recent times by a professional conscience which strictly limited its functions to the defining of human action, it would have become extinct long ago; its genius lies in this function and in no other. And were it not for a jealously maintained theatrical convention, these poets would not have found handy formulas for staging their profanities respectably; however, theatrical conventions having been continuously bequeathed in tail, any astute literary intelligence can still construct a stageable play.

Murder in the Cathedral combines telescopically all the literary devices of the ancient and modern stage. There is a little of everything. For example, late Elizabethan beauties:

> The purple bullfinch in the lilac tree,
> The tiltyard skill, the strategy of chess,
> Love in the garden, singing to the instrument,
> Were all things equally desirable.
> Ambition comes when early force is spent.

Classical French comedy wit:

> Farewell, my Lord, I do not wait upon ceremony.
> I leave as I came, forgetting all acrimony,
> Hoping that your present gravity
> Will find excuse for my humble levity.

Swinburnean Greek choruses:

c. : Death has a hundred hands and walks by a thousand ways.
p. : He may come in the sight of all, he may pass unseen, unheard.
t. : Come whispering through the ear, or a sudden shock on the skull.
c. : A man may walk with a lamp at night, and yet be drowned in a ditch.

Vachel Lindsay jazz:

> Are you washed in the blood of the lamb?
> Are you marked with the mark of the beast?
> Come down Daniel to the lion's den,
> Come down Daniel and join in the feast!

Bernard Shaw crossed with Euripides-in-school-translation:

What I have to say may be put in the form of a question: *Who killed the Archbishop?* . . . From the moment he became Archbishop he showed himself utterly indifferent to the fate of the country, to be, in fact, a monster of egotism, a menace to society . . . Now I have unimpeachable evidence to the effect that before he left France he clearly prophesied, in the presence of numerous witnesses, that he had not long to live, and that he would be killed in England . . . There can be no inference except that he had determined upon a death by martyrdom . . . I think, with these facts before you, you will unhesitatingly render a verdict of. Suicide while of Unsound Mind . . .

In an essay on Seneca published in 1927 Eliot had written:

Several scholars, Butler in particular, have called attention to a trick of Seneca of repeating one word of a phrase in the next phrase, especially in stichomythia where the sentence of one speaker is caught up in the next. This was an effective stage trick, but it is something more; it is the crossing of one rhythm pattern with another.

He gives examples. He gives examples, too, of Marlowe's Englishing of the trick:

> —Wrong not her birth, she is of royal blood.
> —To save her life, I'll say she is not so.
> —Her life is safest only in her birth.
> —And only in that safety died her brothers.

and adds: 'It is only a step (and a few lines farther) to the pun: *Cousins, indeed; and by their uncle cozen'd.*' So, because Seneca used the trick and 'several scholars' have noted it and Marlowe has made it respectable in English drama, in it goes into *Murder in the Cathedral*:

THOMAS: And if the Archbishop cannot trust the King,
                 How can he trust those who work for King's undoing?
THE TEMPTER: Kings will allow no power but their own;
                 Church and people have good cause against the throne.
THOMAS: If the Archbishop cannot trust the Throne,
                 He has good cause to trust none but God alone.

And it is only a step (a single line, in fact) to the pun:

> It is not better to be *thrown*
> To a thousand hungry appetites than to one.

The effectiveness of *Murder in the Cathedral* therefore lies in its appeal of dramatic astuteness, its well-documented ingenuities: in the cynical candour with which Eliot uses drama as a means of journalizing a poetic theme. He throws his theme to the audience, which is delighted to gnaw away at it—delighted because it has been confidentially told that not merely is it a very special bone, but it has been carefully cut away from the poetic corpse so as to reach the audience generously loaded with dramatic meat. In *The Rock* the profanity is less gracefully blended with dramatics. The chorus 'speaks as the voice of the Church of God' and expresses, irritably and awkwardly, in the traditional language of the Old Testament and the pulpit, the author's personal disappointment with the vulgarity of modern life.

> The Word of the Lord came unto me, saying:
> O miserable cities of designing men . . .
> Much is your reading, but not the Word of GOD
> Much is your building, but not the House of GOD . . .
> Will you build me a house of plaster with corrugated roofing,
> To be filled with a litter of Sunday newspapers?

Enter a parade of *Punch* unemployed, agitators and comic cockney workmen, expressing astonishment with 'Blimey!', 'Coo!', 'Lor'-love-a-duck!'; and of mediaeval ghosts mouthing Latin religious ritual, to set them off. A poetic effect is smuggled in by this stagey conjunction, expressive of the annulment of the time-sense by an ubiquitous sense of God; but, though the general pretence is poetic and the drama itself is offered as a convenience of truth, nowhere can any meaning be dissociated from dramatic artifice. The conclusion is merely a scholarly grafting of Blake's *Jerusalem* on the music-hall ballad 'I like London, I like Town, I really cannot see why people run it down; They always do the naughty things and leave the good things *undone*, *But* I'm very fond of Lo-ond-on!' As follows:

Ill done and undone,
London so fair
We will build London
Bright in dark air,
With new bricks and mortar
Beside the Thames bord
Queen of Island and Water
A house of our Lord.

Not only Seneca, but Kipling contributes to Eliot's theatrical tricks. In *A Truthful Song* the origin of the historical visions which appear to his bricklayers is explained:

> THE BRICKLAYER:
> I tell this tale, which is strictly true,
> Just by way of convincing you,
> How very little, since things were made,
> Things have altered in the building trade . . .

Euripides was profane in the same sense, and in his plays the popular drama of Athens went into corruption. It was temporarily redeemed by Aristophanes, and Comedy in general, and returned to healthy humanity. Comedy may be regarded as the dramatist's honourable escape from the temptation to identify dramatic veracity with poetic truth. He knows that he must not use his plays as the field of spiritual definition: he may decently concern himself with the moral values, the local values which human actions elucidate, but he cannot without profanity generalize these values as truth. Truth is not vested in action, but is subsequent to it; and action, the preliminary gesture of consciousness, is the substance of drama. In profane drama, it may be said, the poet—and it is only the poet who is capable of this profanity, as it is only the pious who are capable of sin—attempts to throw truth back into temporal action and confuse poetic with moral values and knowledge with action. Why? Because he feels lonely in poetic ground and hungers for human disorder. To introduce disorder into poetic values gives an illusion of realism to a timid poetic mind, the sort of mind that feels misgivings because of the discrepancy between itself and the mass consciousness of its time. Dramatic realities are supported by numbers, by the mass suggestibility of audiences, as poetic realities are not; it is therefore the timid, lonely poets who are most subject to the temptations of dramatic technique—those who are unhappy in poetry, as Eliot confesses himself to be.

Aeschylus and Sophocles, Euripides' predecessors, were dramatists who used poetic form as a means of restraint, as a discipline separating humanity from the gods with austere accuracy. Aeschylus confines himself in each play to the presentation of a simple story-pageant. In his earliest play, *The Suppliants*, the daughters of Danaus seek sanctuary with Pelasgus, King of Argos, from the impious marriage proposed for them with the sons of Aegyptus of Egypt. Pelasgus must choose between a conflict with men and a conflict with the gods to whom the Suppliants have appealed. In accepting the Suppliants he chooses a conflict with men. *The Persians* is a pageant of man and Nemesis, a dramatization of the arrival in Persia of the dreadful news of Salamis. *Prometheus Bound* shows the demi-god Prometheus bound in a cleft of rock in the Scythian desert, defying the might of Zeus by impiously cursing him in the name of Zeus' deposed father, Cronos. The remaining four of Aeschylus' seven surviving plays show more movement and verbal interchange and dramatic surprise, but each is a concentrated human demonstration. In *Agamemnon*, *The Libation-Bearers* and *The Furies* the moral implications of murder are dramatized. In *The Seven Against Thebes* the problem that Danaus faced reappears in another form, and Antigone similarly chooses to quarrel with men rather than with the gods.

By the time of Sophocles, competition for the annual dramatic prize at Athens had become acute; the dramatic spirit took on a professional energy. Plutarch records that Sophocles saw his own career in the following three stages: first, imitation of Aeschylus; next, making each word 'bite'; finally, suiting diction to individual character. His plots have the same concentrated character as those of Aeschylus (Antigone covers the same ground as *The Seven Against Thebes* and *Electra* is another version of *The Libation-Bearers*); but the stage is fuller, the plot subtler, the dramatic climax more consciously made. Man is ennobled by keeping at proud distance from the gods.

Euripides, let us repeat, was a profane poet; as we may think of Marlowe (though almost the earliest of the Elizabethan dramatists and having at first sight a resemblance in 'majesty' to Aeschylus, the earliest of the Athenians) as the Elizabethan Euripides. Euripides seems to have felt that the dignified perfection of Sophocles could be challenged only by novelty and irresponsibility. The religious conditions of the Dionysian festival kept him within certain bounds, as Marlowe later could not say openly what was in his mind when he made Tamerlaine taunt Mahomet and destroy his books (Mahomet being a surrogate for

Christ), or revile Jove (Jove being a surrogate for the Christian God), or let Dr. Faustus, under cover of invisibility, slap the Pope's face (the Pope being a surrogate for all Protestant bishops and priests). But within the imposed limits Euripides was as profane as he dared to be, making melodrama of the divine realities which his predecessors accepted religiously, using the stage merely as a convenience for popularizing his own eccentric values. He particularly enjoyed demonstrating the power of logic and rhetoric to justify indecent, foolish or crooked ends. He was no craftsman in the sense that Sophocles was; his plays are constructed with an almost deliberate clumsiness, the emphasis being episodic rather than cumulative, and the choruses no longer forming an integral part of the play, but serving merely as lyric interludes.

In *Medea*, which is accounted his best play, Medea is a bloodthirsty villainess, discarded by Jason for political not moral reasons, who takes bloody vengeance on his new wife Glauce and on her own children by him. In the end she flies masterfully away in a chariot drawn by winged dragons, unrepentant of her crimes. The cries of Medea's innocent children as they are being murdered and the horrific account of Glauce's death by poison are the strongest impressions left on the audience. The moral situation is a freak one, as it is in *Alcestis*, and excites only psychological interest. Euripides presents so many vicious or morbid characters not because he has a poor opinion of humanity, but because to do so gives him greater rhetorical scope; and the language which he applies to human paltriness acquires a pointed vehemence when applied to the gods. In *Alcestis*, Apollo and Death haggle over the soul of Admetus in what is almost a comic vein. In *The Bacchae*, the god Dionysus (Bacchus) in disguise tricks Pentheus into spying on the Bacchanals and then has him torn to pieces. Pentheus' only fault had been his protest against the immorality which went on when the girls of his household got drunk and rushed madly out into the woods. In this play, his last, and written for performance in Macedonia, a barbarian-Greek country, Euripides introduced an openly clownish scene—Pentheus being shown by Dionysus how to disguise himself as a woman; and the messenger's speech, telling how Pentheus was torn to pieces, is indecently horrific again.

In Shakespeare's plays we find drama and poetry side by side, unmixed. The plot is for the public; the poems which run parallel with the plot are Shakespeare communing with himself. It is this separation that makes it possible to stage his plays with dramatic success: the audience can disregard the poetic element because it has not been profanely mixed, as in Marlowe's plays, with the dramatic. Contrariwise, when they are silently read the dramatic element falls away: one is reading poetry. Profane poetic drama can interest only an audience that is cynical both about humanity and about poetry, and claims the author as a fellow-cynic. When silently read its one interest is in the satiric ideas which underlie both the action and the verse; but they have the rhetorical futility of propaganda—which, however eloquent, does not move those who disagree with it and flatters the intellectual vanity of those who do without stirring them emotionally, since the ideas vocalized are already familiar.

The drama of Shaw, by the way, is not profane; it is not drama at all, but prose argument, and should properly be compared with the *Dialogues* of Lucian. There is seldom any more drama in a play of Shaw's than there is, say, in Lucian's dialogue between Zeus and Cyniscus—when Cyniscus throws Zeus into argumentative disorder by his demonstration that the Goddess of Destiny ought to be punished for the sins of men because it is she who determines the course of human actions. The theatrical situation in Shaw is an artifice incidentally used to concentrate attention on his argument; as Lucian gives his argument greater point by putting it into the mouth of Cyniscus and standing Zeus by as a conversational butt. The only real character in Shaw's plays is Shaw himself, the philosopher turned demagogue. Lucian remained the philosopher, because his *Dialogues* were not intended for the stage. The dialogue-method, whether in prose or verse, is an innocent aid to banter; Theocritus used it so in his *Idylls*, and it is frequently to be found in shorter poems where the meaning is confined to the opposition of phrases between which there is a syllogistic play of sense.

Stephen Gosson, who was a poet as well as a divine, complained in *The Schoole of Abuse* (1579) against the temptations to profanity in drama:

Lacon when he sawe the *Athenians* studie so muche to set out Playes, sayde they were madde. If men for good exercise, and women for their credite, be shut from Theaters, whom shall we suffer to goe thither? Little children? *Plutarch* with a caueat keepeth them out, not as much as admitting the litle crackhalter that carrieth his maisters pantouffles, to set foote within those doores: And alledgeth this reason, that those wanton spectacles of lyght huswives, drawing gods from the heauens, and young men from them selues to shipwracke of honestie, will hurte them more, then if at the Epicures table, they had nigh burst their guts with ouer feeding. For if the body bee ouercharged, it may be holpe; but the surfite of the soule is hardly cured. Here I doubt not some Archplayer or other that hath read a litle, or stumbled by chance vpon *Plautus* comedies, will cast me a bone or ii. to pick, saying, that whatsoeuer these ancient writers haue spoken against plaies is to bee applied too the abuses in olde Comedies, where Gods are broughte in, as Prisoners too beautie, rauishers of Virgins, and seruantes by loue, too earthly creatures. But the Comedies that are exercised in oure daies are better sifted. They shewe no such branne: The first smelte of *Plautus*, these tast of *Menander*; the lewdeness of Gods, is altered and chaunged to the loue of young men; force, to friendshippe; rapes, too mariage; wooing allowed by assurance of wedding; priuie meetinges of bachelours and maidens on the stage, not as murderes that deuour the good name ech of other in their mindes, but as those that desire to bee made one in hearte. Nowe are the abuses of the worlde reuealed, euery man in a play may see his owne faultes, and learne by this glasse, to amende his manners. *Curculio* may chatte til his heart ake, ere any be offended with his gyrdes. Deformities are checked in ieast, and mated in earnest. The sweetenesse of musicke, and pleasure of sportes, temper the bitternesse of rebukes, and mitigate the tartenesse of euery taunt according to this

Flaccus among his friends, with fanning Muse
Doth nip him neere, that fostreth foule abuse.

Therefore they are either so blinde, that they cannot, or so blunt, that they will not see why this exercise should not be suffered as a profitable recreation. For my parte I am neither so fonde a Phisition, not so bad a Cooke, but I can allow my patient a cup of wine to meales, although it be hotte; and pleasant sauces to driue downe his meate, if his stomake bee queasie. Notwithstanding, if people will be instructed, (God be thanked) wee haue Diuines enough to discharge that, and moe by a great many, then are well hearkened to: Yet sith these abuses are growne too head, and sinne so rype, the number is lesse then I would it were.

The drama of Racine, Corneille, Molière, considered as poetic drama? Racine dealt with solemn classical themes, but limited their significance to strictly social contexts by making the characters more human, even, than we find them in ancient drama. It was essential that he should write in verse to safeguard the solemnity of his themes: the human situation, for the French eye, instantly transforms itself into farce. The verse dramas of Molière are not farces but unpleasantries; the unpleasant plays the same part in his dramatic consolidations of action as the solemn does in Racine's. Corneille breaks away from dramatic tradition by experimenting with psychological possibilities.

CA: U

His characters are grandiose speculations, his plots are unreal, internal —what his characters think rather than what they humanly do. We might, in fact, call him a profane dramatist if he had successfully dramatized poetic subtleties of character; but he failed to do so because the forces which moved his characters were not real even to him. He has written plays of caprice, of temperamental variation of character, which are pure drama in spite of his profane intentions: because audiences are always interested in what people do on the stage, regardless of the intellectual motive.

Corneille as a dramatist may be contrasted with Ben Jonson; Jonson's 'humours' are just as mechanical as Corneille's psychological distinctions of personality, but he is the better dramatist because he has disciplined poetic significance out of his psychological distinctions by making them part of a moral system, thus leaving his audience free to concern itself with action alone; whereas Corneille's audience must itself dissociate dramatic action from poetic significance. This kind of dissociation, whether made by the dramatist or left for his audience to make, provides the theatregoer with one of his chief amusements: his preoccupation with bare incident in defiance of what the author may have meant. The task of speculating on the author's meaning is then left to the dramatic critic, though the dramatist should, properly, have purified his material of meaning, and rested his plot on a causal succession of physically dramatic incidents. Dramatic incidents point to meaning, though they cannot contain meaning. The incidents in the better plays of Shakespeare's have this physical causality; but the 'meaning' piles up privately, poetically—it is what we come to after the show is over, when we are no longer part of the audience. Shakespeare's plays stand most firmly on our shelves as poems to the degree that they hold their own on the stage. *Timon of Athens*, for instance, is both dramatically and poetically poor because it lacks the vigorous interplay between plot and poetry that is found in *Hamlet* or *King Lear*. His Histories often flag because he has tried to exploit the interest attaching to a historical personality; when the result is only rhetoric. Though drama is concerned with the personal demarcation of action, and poetry with the personal demarcation of truth, neither poet nor dramatist ought to act as a personal publicity agent, even in retrospect.

HOW POETS SEE
(1939)

HOW POETS SEE

A POET should be aware of the way in which he looks at the world (in the most literal optical sense) and takes in what he sees; if he finds that he has contracted visual habits which prevent him from seeing things clearly or wholly, he should study to correct them. Here I record my own visual peculiarities with a mental resolve to correct them as soon as possible; and afterwards discuss the visual peculiarities of Keats, Wordsworth, Coleridge, Milton and Donne in relation to their poems.

I

In looking at any object, for example a house or a person, I concentrate my gaze on what I choose as the central point and focus it clearly, allowing the rest of the object to form a blur—of which however I apprehend the extent and general colouring. If after studying the central point I am still interested in the object, I look for other points of interest: thus, after long acquaintance with a person I know his single features by heart, but cannot recompose his face in memory. I must always have seen in the same partial way, because when thinking of the house where I spent my childhood, I remember the shapes of the different window frames, the look of particular bricks in the wall, the angle of the slate roof, but cannot recompose the general façade. In ordinary conversation I concentrate my gaze on both eyes of the person addressing me; in difficult conversation I tend to concentrate it on his right eye, and if the strain persists abnormally, I lose focus and he recedes into the distance, so that I see him whole, but small. I have, however, a perfect memory-sense by touch: I can remember the shape of any body or inanimate object I have once touched, and if I were asked to reconstruct the dimensions of a house in which I have lived for some years, I should imagine myself walking through it in the half-dark, and know just how the rooms stood in relation to one another, their size, the position of their furniture, and so on.

I never see people or objects against a clearly defined background, or separated from me by a clearly defined foreground. Background and foreground I make distinct objects: I see only with a fixed focus. (In walking, I always tend to swerve to the right of my indicated course: thus, I choose to walk on the left side of a person so that his proximity keeps me from straying.)

I never have clear visions of objects except in half-sleep or slight fever or great emotional stress.

In apprehending objects with no outstanding features which can be used as a central point—for instance, a haystack or an upturned packing-case—I tend to use as my arbitrary central point a position two-thirds of the way down the side to the left of me.

In visualizing a room, I walk across and around it in my imagination, unless there is someone in it, already moving, whom I can watch —in which case, I remain still.

I see well in the half-dark; by an effort to see all that there is, as well as by an abnormal expansion of the iris. The reaction of my eyes to light is very slow and I take more than the normal time to focus.

2

Keats was short-sighted. He did not see landscapes as such, so he treated them as painted cabinets filled with interesting objects. In *I stood tip-toe upon a little Hill*, one of his earliest poems, he explains his habit of seeing—or of not seeing. He did not look at the sky, but started from the farthest horizon, standing on tip-toe to survey as much earth as possible lying between him and it. Then, gloatingly, he let his eye travel up some small inviting path, in search of objects surmised to be there, though beyond the visual range of even the most long-sighted eye. His habit was to allow his eye to be seduced from entire vision by particular objects. He wrote, in *Calidore*, another early poem, that no healthy man could lightly pass by objects which looked out invitingly on either side of a boat as it progressed through beautiful scenery.

He saw little but what moved: the curving, the wreathing, the slanting, the waving—and even then, it seems, not the whole object in motion but only its edge, or high-light. To remedy this ghostliness of vision he invariably drew on his memory of how the objects felt, tasted, sounded or smelt. In *The Eve of St. Agnes*, for example:

> ... her vespers done,
> Of all its wreathèd pearls her hair she frees;
> Unclasps her warmèd jewels one by one;
> Loosens her fragrant boddice; by degrees
> Her rich attire creeps rustling to her knees ...

All that he has seen here is the twisted pattern of a seed-pearl hair ornament, and the moving neckline of a woman's shift as it exposed her body in falling.

He did not see faces as faces, but allowed himself to be held by the glitter of the eyes. He once wrote about a portrait of Spenser which had impressed him; here there was no glitter of eyes, so his attention was held by the arch of the eyebrows, and he records nothing else.

The first impression conveyed by his ballad *Meg Merrilies* is that he has given a detailed account of her looks; but in fact he has seen nothing except the glitter of her eyes in the moonlight, the movement of her brown hands as she plaits rushes, and her tallness. Similarly with the 'lady seen for a few moments at Vauxhall': he remembers the shine of her eyes against the evening illuminations and the rouged point of one cheekbone. Not having noted her lips, he tries to re-create them in sensuous memory by pressing his ear against them in his imagination; but what lives in his visual memory is the moving line of the wrist edge of her glove as she peeled it off her hand. In *La Belle Dame Sans Merci* he gives a general description of her face as 'full beautiful,' but the only particularity recorded is the wildness of her eyes; of the rest of her nothing is seen except the light movement of her foot through the grass, and the swaying length of her hair.

His eye could be readily caught by what moved suddenly or freakishly or with emotional effect:

> Scarce can his clear and nimble eye-sight follow
> The freaks and dartings of the black-winged swallow.

But for the most part his sight was turned inwards, to a mind-sight built up by the other senses, as in men who have gone blind early in life and can remember only in flashes what sight is.

> A lance ... reflected clearly in a lake
> With the young ashen boughs, 'gainst which it rests
> And the half-seen mossiness of linnets' nests.

He even deliberately externalizes colours that appear on the retina when the eye is shut:

> Lo, I must tell a tale of chivalry
> For large white plumes are dancing in mine eye—
> Not like the formal crest of latter days
> But bending in a thousand graceful ways . . .

3

Though Wordsworth tried to make accuracy and completeness of visual description, reinforced with religious or philosophical dogma, a substitute for poetic inspiration, he did at least look at the external shapes of things, and their relation one to another, and note them down conscientiously. He set out with the deliberation of a landscape painter. He records in *The Recluse* that as a boy he would choose, if possible, a look-out station which was aerial, though not giddy, with a depth of vale below and a height of hills above, and make it yield the most extensive possible field of vision. Thence he would gaze:

> From high to low, from low to high, yet still
> Within the bound of this huge concave.

In his early *Evening Walk* this habitual searching sweep of the eye is proved in action. It starts from the sky, rests on the hill-top, sweeps down the cliffs to the scree at the bottom, then up again by another line, and down again until the entire view is covered.

Every contributory object is seen against the background, the play of light and shadow is precisely recorded and nothing intruded (as with Keats) that is not visibly present. One downward sweep of the eye:

> While, near the midway cliff, the silvered kite
> In many a whistling circle wheels her flight;
> Slant watery lights, from parting clouds, apace
> Travel along the precipices base;
> Cheering its naked waste of scattered stone,
> By lichens grey, and scanty moss, o'ergrown;
> Where scarce the foxglove peeps, or thistle's beard . . .

Sixty years later he was still looking and recording in the same way In *Musings near Aquapendente* he wrote:

>   . . . remembrance holds
> As a selected treasure thy one cliff,
> That, while it wore for melancholy crest
> A shattered convent, yet rose proud to have
> Clinging to its steep sides a thousand herbs
> And shrubs . . . behold, how far and near
> Garden and field all decked with orange bloom,
> And peach and citron, in Spring's mildest breeze
> Expanding; and along the smooth shore curved
> Into a natural port, a tideless sea . . .

Then back again:

>   . . . while on the brink
> Of that high convent-crested cliff I stood . . .

Against Keats' *Meg Merrilies* might be set Wordsworth's *Old Cumberland Beggar*. Wordsworth saw him entire and studied him against various backgrounds, noting precisely how he walked, sat, ate, what was the colour of his face and hair; how he looked in the company of villagers and fellow-travellers, even what his field of vision was:

>   . . . on the ground
> His eyes are turned, and, as he moves along
> *They* move along the ground; and, evermore,
> Instead of common and habitual sight
> Of field with rural works, of hill and dale,
> And the blue sky, one little span of earth
> Is all his prospect . . . seeing still
> And seldom knowing that he sees, some straw,
> Some scattered leaf, or marks which, in one track,
> The nails of cart or chariot wheel have left
> Impressed on the white road—in the same line
> At distance still the same.

But he could describe the beggar so carefully only because he found him a picturesque subject for visual portraiture in the style of David Wilkie, not a friend or a live person. When emotion interrupted his visual habits, as in the *Lucy* poems, his descriptive power failed and he resorted to stock phrases: 'fresh as a rose in June,' 'fair as a star,' 'sportive as the fawn.' He gives us no hint of how Lucy looked, or walked, or sat or ate—only of how he himself felt about her before and after her death.

4

Coleridge's vision was of equal range and attention, but with a less studied choice of station than Wordsworth's, and his feelings were always derived from the sight; with Wordsworth it was a prepared feeling which determined the sight. Coleridge's anticipations of what he would see were often corrected by looking. In an early poem, *Reflections on Having Left a Place of Retirement,* he wrote

> . . . steep up the stony Mount
> I climbed with perilous toil and reached the top.
> Oh! what a goodly scene! *Here* the bleak mount,
> The bare bleak mountain speckled thin with sheep;
> Grey clouds, that shadowing spot the sunny fields;
> And river, now with bushy rocks o'er-browed,
> Now winding bright and full, with naked banks;
> And seats, and lawns, the Abbey and the wood,
> And cots, and hamlets, and faint city-spire;
> The Channel *there,* the Islands and white sails,
> Dim coasts, and cloud-like hills, and shoreless Ocean—
> It seemed like Omnipresence!

He saw with his heart as well as with his eyes, and before long learned to eliminate the merely descriptive from his poems. His letters are full of such passages as this:

We drank tea the night before I left Grasmere, on the Island in that lovely lake, our kettle swung over the fire hanging from the branch of a Fir-tree, and I lay and saw the woods, and mountains, and lake all trembling, and as it were *idealized* through the subtle smoke which rose up from the clear red embers of the fir-apples, which we had collected; afterwards we made a glorious Bonfire on the margin, by some elder bushes, whose twigs heaved and sobbed in the up-rushing column of smoke—and the Image of the Bonfire, and of us that danced round it—ruddy laughing faces in the twilight . . .

He wrote that it was a 'well-known fact' that what most impresses the eye and stays the longest in memory is 'bright colours in motion.' With Wordsworth, colour was seen not as an effect of changing light, but as a condition or category—as the 'red' in red-currants is an adjective of category, or the 'red' in red blackberries is one of condition. Blue sky or water to him meant calm weather; white road meant drought; grey lichens were a different variety from the yellow. The only critical use of colour I have discovered in Wordsworth's poems is the adjective 'grain-tinctured' applied to a cloudy sky. This anomaly has a grotesque possible explanation: an accidental punning transposition of Milton's 'skie-tinctured grain' (*Paradise Lost*, V, 280), applied to the Phoenix's lowest set of wings. Wordsworth was a draughtsman, who saw tone rather than colour and form rather than tone and composition.

Comparing Snowdon with the Peaks, Coleridge wrote (1800):

We have no mountains in the North equal to Snowdon, but then we have an encampment of huge mountains, in no harmony perhaps to the eye of the mere painter, but always interesting, various and as it were nutritive.

In a letter from Ratzeburg (1799) he had described at great length the effects of light on a frozen lake covered with mist.

When the sun peeped over the hills, the mist broke in the middle, and at last stood as the waters of the Red Sea are said to have done when the Israelites passed; and between the two walls of mist the sunlight burst upon the ice in a straight road of golden fire . . . intolerably bright, and the walls of mist partaking of the light in a *multitude* of colours. About a month ago the vehemence of the wind had shattered the ice; part of it, quite shattered, was driven to shore and had frozen anew; this was of a deep blue, and represented an agitated sea—the water that ran up between the great islands of ice shone of a yellow-green (it was at sunset), and all the scattered islands of *smooth* ice were *blood*, intensely bright *blood* . . . In skating there are three pleasing circumstances—firstly, the infinitely subtle particles of ice which the skate cuts up, and which creep and run before the skater like low mists, and in sunrise or sunset become coloured; second, the shadow of the skater in the water seen through the transparent ice; and thirdly, the melancholy undulating sound from the skate.

He was perhaps the first English poet who saw colour as colour: transient colour was a phenomenon which the ordinary eye was hitherto trained to disregard as idle, change of colour being seen only as it indicated what seemed material difference—colour of hair in youth and age, of the sky at dawn or dusk, of fruits as they ripened, of grass or leaves as they flourished or withered. For the rest, colour was emblematic, as purple for royalty, green for jealousy, white for purity; or distinctive, as 'my blue bowl, my russet nag, my red jerkin.'

Coleridge saw people not with the portraitist's eye but with the eye of feeling tempered with judgment. Here is his description of the poet Klopstock, whom he visited 'in a neat little parlour in a little commonplace summerhouse, one of a row.'

The poet entered. I was much disappointed in his countenance, and recognized in it no likeness to the bust. There was no comprehension in the forehead, no weight over the eyebrows, no expression of peculiarity, moral or intellectual, in the eyes, no massiveness in the general countenance. He is, if anything, rather below the middle size. He wore very large half-boots, which his legs filled, so fearfully were they swoln . . . His enunciation was not in the least affected by the entire want of his upper teeth . . . I looked at him with much emotion—I considered him as the venerable father of German poetry; as a good man; as a Christian; seventy-four years old; with legs enormously swoln, yet active, lively, cheerful and kind, and communicative. My eyes felt as if a tear were swelling into them. In the portrait of Lessing there was a toupee periwig, which enormously injured the effect of his physiognomy—Klopstock wore the same, powdered and frizzled. By the bye, old men ought never to wear powder—the contrast between a large snow-white wig and the colour of an old man's skin is disgusting, and wrinkles in such a neighbourhood appear only channels for dirt . . . It is an honour to poets and great men that you think of them as parts of nature; and anything of trick and fashion wounds you in them, as much as when you see venerable yews clipped into miserable peacocks. The author of the 'Messiah' should have worn his own hair.

5

Sight to Milton was painful; he loved light, but it hurt him. The only colour that he saw happily was green, which he dwelt on for its human comfort, especially the green of an arbour or grove shading the eyes from the sun, which spelt for him either natural innocence or an occasion for acts of mortal lust. The sentiment of *Il Penseroso* constantly recurs in his poems.

> And when the Sun begins to fling
> His flaring beams, me Goddess bring
> To arched walks of twilight groves . . .
> There in close covert by som Brook,
> Where no profaner eye may look,
> Hide me from Day's garish eie . . .

But, as a change from mere green and the 'shadows brown' of groves, he saw with pleasure the pale yellows, blues and pinks of Spring flowers.

In his *Comus* there is a famous debate in terms of sight on the subject of temperance, Comus arguing with the Lady against the waste of beauty in the Puritan-Stoic system of values. He holds that if all the world should in petulance feed on pulse, drink water, and wear only frieze, mankind would be strangled by the unused fertility of Nature:

> Th'earth cumber'd, and the wing'd air dark't with plumes . . .
> The Sea o'refraught would swell, and th'unsought diamonds
> Would so emblaze the forehead of the Deep,
> And so bestudd with Stars, that they below
> Would grow inur'd to light, and come at last
> To gaze upon the Sun with shameless brows.

But though he is here making a virtue of his photophobic weakness, interpreting it as humility and temperance, his secret ambition was to gaze on the Sun direct. While he had sight, twilight was the most 'genial' time of day for him; and it was only in his blindness that he gave way to his desire for the insufferable effulgence of sunlight on diamonds, beryl, polished gold or whatever else would shine. In *Samson Agonistes*, Samson does not long for colour and familiar sights —he longs only for light. Milton desired to be, in relation to the Sun or to solar truth, what the Son was to the Father. (*Paradise Lost*, VI, 719.)

> He said, and on his Son with Rayes direct
> Shon full, he all his Father full exprest
> Ineffably into his face received.

His eye was seduced by ringlets, mazes, curious knots, Gordian twines and quaint curves, which he intellectually rejected as wanton. From descriptions in his poems it is clear that the first thing that he saw in a woman was not her bright love-darting eye (as it was to practically all his contemporaries), but her hair. He was, in fact, a trichomaniac and if there was one passage in Classical literature which disturbed him emotionally more than any other, it must have been Apuleius' account of the same obsession in himself. (*Metamorphoses* II, 8.—*Cum semper mihi unica cura fuerit . . .*)

I have an obsession about hair. Whenever I meet a pretty woman, the first thing that catches my eye is her hair; I make a careful mental picture of it to carry home and brood over in private. This habit of mine I justify on a sound logical principle: that the hair is the most important and conspicuous feature of the body, and that its natural brilliance does for the head what gaily coloured clothes do for the trunk. In fact, it does a great deal more. You know how women, when they want to display their beauty to the full, shed their embroidered wraps and step out of their expensive dresses, and proudly reveal themselves with nothing on at all, aware that even the brightest gold tissue has less effect on a man than the delicate tints of a woman's naked body . . .

What joy it is to see hair of a beautiful colour caught in the full rays of the sun, or shining with a milder lustre and constantly varying its shade as the light shifts. Golden at one moment, at the next honey-coloured; or black as a raven's wing, but suddenly taking on the pale bluish tints of a dove's neck-feathers. Give it a gloss with spikenard lotion, part it neatly with a finely toothed comb, catch it up with a ribbon behind—and the lover will make it a sort of mirror to reflect his own delighted looks. And oh, when hair is bunched up thick in a luxurious mass on a woman's head, or, better still, allowed to flow rippling down her neck in profuse curls! I must content myself by saying briefly that such is the glory of a woman's hair that though she may be wearing the most exquisite clothes and the most expensive jewellery in existence, with everything else in keeping, she cannot look even moderately well dressed unless she has done her hair in proper style.

Fotis, I grant, needed no advanced knowledge of hairdressing: she could even indulge an apparent neglect of the art. Her way was to let her long, thick hair hang loosely down her neck, braiding the ends together and catching them up again with a broad ribbon to the top of her head; which was the exact spot where, unable to restrain myself a moment longer, I now printed a long passionate kiss . . .

If the woman's hair which Milton saw was bright and curled and dishevelled, like Fotis', he lusted; if it was smoothly braided he dared to love. It was only then that he noted the curve of her lips, and next the curves of her body. Vine-tendrils allured him so strongly that he seemed to see them in motion—'the gadding Vine,' 'the mantling vine that crawls'; and in *Comus*, the Genius of the wood claimed the power

> . . . to curl the grove
> With Ringlets quaint, and wanton windings wove.

With a man he first saw the brow, then the eyes beneath, then the hair. His descriptions of Adam and Eve are:

> His fair large Front and Eye sublime declar'd
> Absolute rule; and Hyacinthin Locks
> Round from his parted forelock manly hung
> Clustering, but not beneath his shoulders broad:
> She as a veil down to the slender waste
> Her unadorned golden tresses wore
> Dishevelled, but in wanton ringlets wav'd
> As the Vine curls her tendrils . . .

At Cambridge he wore very long hair and had the reputation of being narcissistic: 'Our Lady of Christ's' was his nickname. He cherished the recollection of his former good looks in his gouty old age and made blind Samson lament:

> . . . these redundant locks
> Robustious to no purpose clustering down.

In looking at scenery he seems to have started with his eye on the ground and raised it gradually upward to the tree-tops or wooded hills, and then lowered it as the light hurt his eyes, then looked 'from side to side in bredth.'

6

Donne, in his amatory poems, saw no more than the reflection of his own hopes and fears:

> I fixe mine eye on thine, and there
> Pitty my picture burning in thine eye.

He involved his mistress in this seeing:

> Our eye-beames twisted, and did thred
>   Our eyes, upon one double string . . .
> And pictures in our eyes to get
>   Was all our propagation.

And then blamed her for what had happened because of his own habit of self-looking:

> Send home my long strayd eyes to me,
> Which too long have dwelt on thee.

though in another poem he had begged the God of Love:

> Give me thy weaknesse, make me blinde
> . . . In eyes and minde.

He mistrusted the eye as seeing only the outward loveliness of a woman:

> For he who colour loves, and skinne
> Loves but their oldest clothes.

and:

I never stoop'd so low, as they
Which on an eye, cheeke, lip can prey,
    Seldome to them, which soare no higher
    Than vertue or the minde t'admire . . .

Every sight he saw was either negligible or unpoetic unless it could
be compressed into a striking image: as lead pouring in a stream from
the roof of a burning church, or the young preacher in his first sermon
singling out for violent harangue a lady whom he has wronged. For
the most part he borrowed his images either from popular literature—
the sick turquoise, the pregnant woman ready to travail at the sight
of some food she loathes—or from science: such images as celestial
and terrestrial globes, meridians, parallels, the Antipodes, appealed
to his inner sight for their regularity and comprehensiveness. His
outward eye he seems to have kept deliberately blinkered.

THE POETS OF WORLD WAR II
(1942)

THE POETS OF WORLD WAR II

I HAVE been asked to explain as a 'war poet of the last war' why so little poetry has so far been produced by this one. Yes: my publishers fastened the war-poet label on me in 1916 when *Over the Brazier*, my first book of verse, appeared; but when twenty years later I published my *Collected Poems*, I found that I could not conscientiously reprint any of my 'war poems'—they were too obviously written in the war-poetry boom.

Before explaining why no war poets have appeared after two years of World War II, I must point out that 'war poet' and 'war poetry' are terms first used in World War I and perhaps peculiar to it. In previous wars there had been patriotic verse and poems written in time of war, and even occasional poems written by soldiers on campaign—for instance, *Annie Laurie* by a Royal Scots subaltern during an early campaign in Flanders, and the ballads and theatrical prologues with which Major John André, the Deputy-Assistant-Adjutant-General, delighted British troops in America during the War of Independence. But none of these were war poems in the now accepted sense.

The war-poetry boom in World War I began with the death on active service of an R.N.V.R. sub-lieutenant, Rupert Brooke. The newspapers which had slated him as an impudent undergraduate versifier when his first poems were published a few months before, now paid him heroic honours. The sonnets in which he declared himself ready to die for an ideal England—rather than for the 'rolling ee' and 'jimp middle' of some Annie Laurie—were held to set a moral standard for young British manhood. They were not the only such poems written in 1914: *Into Battle* by Julian Grenfell, a young Lancer officer, expressed the sudden overwhelming sense of natural beauty which a soldier is entitled to recognize as a premonition of death; Grenfell was killed in France shortly afterwards. And Charles Sorley, a twenty-year-old captain in the Suffolks—promotion was quick in those days—wrote:

All the hills and dales along
Earth is bursting into song . . .

> Earth that bore with joyful ease
> Hemlock for Socrates,
> Earth that blossomed and was glad
> 'Neath the cross that Christ had,
> Shall rejoice and blossom too
> When the bullet reaches you . . .
> So sing, marching men,
> Till the valleys ring again.

Sorley was killed at Loos in October, 1915.

War poetry at first had a resolute, self-dedicatory tone but, as the war settled down to a trench deadlock, self-dedication became qualified by homesick regrets for the lovely English countryside, away from all the mud, blood and desolation—the theme of mud, blood and desolation being more and more realistically treated. The close connexion between war poetry and Georgian poetry must be emphasized: there was a contrastive interplay between the horrors of trench warfare and the joys of simple bucolic experience. Georgian poetry, in the derogatory sense now always applied to it, was bucolic joy which lost its poignancy when the war eventually ended.

When war poetry became a fashion in 1915, a good deal of it was written imitatively by civilians who regretted that age or unfitness prevented them from also 'making the supreme sacrifice.' (I notice that Stephen Spender in an article on the subject has accidentally included one of these civilians, Wilfred Gibson, among the dead soldier heroes.) Also, many soldiers wrote as though they had seen more of the war than they really had. Robert Nichols, for instance, whose brief and uneventful service in France with the Royal Field Artillery was ended by sickness, published an exciting and apparently autobiographical poem, *Attack*, about the feelings of an infantry platoon commander in a trench battle; and one of the realistic war poems for which I was best known in those days, *It's a Queer Time*, was written at my regimental depot in Wales some weeks before I had a chance of verifying my facts.

By 1917 war poems were being published by the thousand. A typical anthology was E. B. Osborn's bulky *Muse in Arms*, with authors drawn from almost every regiment or corps in the Army—all very gallant and idealistic but with hardly a poet among them. War poetry was a major export to the United States. Robert Nichols scored a great success there as a crippled warrior, reading Siegfried Sassoon's poems, mine, and his own to university and women's club audiences;

and when the United States finally came into the war, two American Rupert Brookes were found, Joyce Kilmer and Alan Seegar. *I have a Rendezvous with Death* and *Trees* were as widely popularized as Brooke's *If I should die, think only this of me* and *Grantchester*.

The character of British war poetry changed again in 1917, though what may be called the rank-and-file of war poets kept to the existing formulas. One of the two chief reasons for this was a realization by the more intelligent poets that the General Staff were sacrificing hundreds of thousands of lives in nightmare attacks which had no military justification; the other was the Conscription Act. Hitherto we had all been volunteers, and this had somehow been a consolation for the frightful conditions which trench warfare now implied. To be cannonfodder was dispiriting enough: to have perhaps unwilling conscripts foisted on our company was worse still. Siegfried Sassoon, a Royal Welch Fusilier, had begun as a typical war poet with:

> Return to meet me, colours that were my joy,
> Not in the woeful crimson of men slain . . .

written before he went to France. Now he was an angry veteran, raging sarcastically at the stupidity, callousness, incompetence and hypocrisy of the men who were running the war; and even taking the line that it ought to be stopped as soon as possible by a negotiated peace, and that the Germans were not the only people to blame. In July, 1917, badly wounded and shell-shocked, he refused to serve further in the Army, and later recanted only because he felt that he was being a traitor to the men left in France. I was his escort to the shell-shock hospital near Edinburgh to which he was committed, where we met for the first time the war poet whose name is always linked with his—Wilfred Owen. Owen had been invalided home from the Manchester Regiment in France as of no further use to them. The mental rhythm of the typical war-neurosis was one of jagged ups and downs: the up-curves represented a despairing nervous energy which, when converted to poetic use, resulted in poems terrifyingly beyond the patient's normal capacity; the troughs meant listless inept melancholia. Owen recovered, returned to France, won a Military Cross, and was killed just before the Armistice. Sassoon also returned to France and was again wounded in the head; but survived and wrote me a letter in verse beginning: 'I'd timed my death in action to the minute . . .' which I quote in the first edition of my *Goodbye to All That*.

CA: X

This historical account is almost sufficient in itself to answer the question, 'Why has this war produced no war poets?' In the first place it will be realized that the passing of the Conscription Act, a few months before World War II, made volunteer pride irrelevant and war poetry superfluous as a stimulus to recruiting. Next, the British Army has not yet been engaged on a grand scale with the enemy and, despite official reassurances, is not likely to be for some time. On the whole the soldier has lived a far safer life than the munition-maker whom in Word War I he despised as a 'shirker'; he cannot even feel that his rendezvous with death is more certain than that of his Aunt Fanny, the firewatcher. As for the beauty of the English countryside, he has seen far too much of it through a tent-flap during his dreary exile from home.

Finally, the army of World War II is not the amateur, desperate, happy-go-lucky, ragtime, lousy army of World War I. Its senior officers and N.C.O.s are practically all professionals; even its newest battalions are anything but ragtime; and it is being increasingly mechanized. Most of it is bored stiff with inactivity, and any sort of eccentric behaviour in officer or man is more sternly discountenanced than ever before in its history. (The right to eccentricity is only earned in battle.) The sort of soldier who in World War I would naturally have become a 'war poet' now feels a khaki-blanco mist rise between him and the world of his imagination. If the mist clears for a moment and he begins to write a poem it will probably be about his sense of difference from fellow-soldiers and his desire (in the words of *Aldershot*, a recent poem by John Waller) to:

> . . . shun the roar
> That is only echoing to the skies 'I forget, I forget.'
> Soldiers have made here a drear country
> Of barrack and ball-room, snack-bar and square, . . .
> Now all the world's darlings and Mother's heroes,
> The lonely, the lovely, the shy and the bold,
> Are made a machine or become hard-hearted . . .

Or he may feel like the speaker in Alun Lewis' *The Soldier*:

> I, within me holding
> Turbulence and Time . . .
> Feel the dark cancer in my vitals
> Of impotent impatience grope its way

Through daze and dream to throat and fingers
To find its climax of disaster . . .
But leisurely my fellow soldiers stroll among the trees.
The cheapest dance song utters all they feel.

But it is extremely unlikely that he will feel any qualms about the justice of the British cause or about the necessity of the war's continuance; so that, even if he has experienced the terrors of an air raid, he will not feel obliged to write horrifically about it, to draw attention to the evils of war. Poems about the horrors of the trenches were originally written to stir the ignorant and complacent people at home to a realization of what a 'fight to the finish' involved.

It should be added that no war poetry can be expected from the Royal Air Force. Though the airmen of World War I fought against worse odds and in crazier machines and led a far less disciplined life than their successors of to-day, there were no airman poets of note: the internal combustion engine does not seem to consort with poetry.

In World War I poems were written (by Doughty, Hardy, Davies, especially) which transcended and did not concern the war. Some were even the work of serving soldiers: such as *Moses*, a wild, poetic drama by Isaac Rosenberg, who was killed in the ranks of the Royal Fusiliers in April, 1918. Poems of equal quality and not directly concerned with the war are being written now, but few of them are published, because the paper shortage is so serious that the firms which specialize in publishing poems have decided to 'publish the work only of established poets,' and the established poets are finding little of importance to say.

ADDITIONAL COMMENT

(1949)

This article appeared in *The Listener* of October 23rd, 1941. Re-reading *Poems from the Forces* (1941), *More Poems from the Forces* (1943), and individual volumes of poetry published since by soldiers, sailors and airmen, I have come to the conclusion that Alun Lewis was the only poet of consequence who served and wrote in World War II; and he was accidentally killed in Burma, in March, 1944, before he had seen any fighting. No poets seem to have assisted in the Eighth Army's eccentric Libyan campaign; and young Sidney Keyes' death in action after a few days' service with the First Army has given his posthumous volume of poems more attention than it deserves as poetry: he was a synthetist of group-styles rather than a poet in his own right.

By the time that the rest of the British Army was at last engaged in grand-scale fighting the poets serving in it were too highly trained and conscientious as soldiers, and found the war too well-staged and exciting, to write defeatist war poems on the model of the 1917–18 sort; but what other sort was there to write? Even if they felt ambitious 'to be war poets,' the tortuous modernistic fashions in which they had been writing before their conscription were unsuited to the higher journalism which war poetry essentially is; and they disdained writing in the simpler styles which had served the poets of World War I. Deliberate heroism was so far outmoded as to seem vulgar or quaint. Besides, they saw no need to compete with the trained war-correspondent, who lived rough, brought his report back from the place of greatest danger and told the whole truth—even if part of the truth was afterwards censored. In World War I we had not been nearly so well served: W. Beach Thomas was no Alexander Clifford, and Philip Gibbs no Alan Moorehead. We felt bound to supplement the rosy official accounts of execrable battles, of which the writer had no first-hand experience, with unofficial sidelights on their realistic horrors. Only Mr. John Pudney has acquired a popular reputation as a poet of World War II—but he wrote as a professional verse-reporter, not as a poet, and throughout his service with the Royal Air Force he was doing liaison work, not merely fighting.

'MAD MR. SWINBURNE'

(1945)

'MAD MR. SWINBURNE'

AN OLD SAYING

Many waters cannot quench love,
　　Neither can the floods drown it.
Who shall snare or slay the white dove,
　　Faith, whose very dreams crown it,
Gird it round with grace and peace, deep,
Warm, and pure, and soft as sweet sleep?
Many waters cannot quench love,
　　Neither can the floods drown it.

Set me as seal upon thine heart,
　　As a seal upon thine arm,
How should we behold the days depart,
　　And the nights resign their charm?
Love is as the soul: though hate and fear
Waste and overthrow, they strike not here.
Set me as a seal upon thine heart,
　　As a seal upon thine arm.

This poem touches me in a peculiar way, for 'Mad Mr. Swinburne' is inextricably mixed in my childhood memories with such mythological figures of terror as the Ogre of Beanstalk Castle, the Bogy Man, the hosts of Midian prowling and prowling around, and Charlie Peace, the murderer who used to hide in his victims' houses, spread-eagled under a dining-room table-top. My parents lived on the fringe of Wimbledon Common over which in the late 'nineties my sisters and I used to be taken out most mornings by our nurse. Usually we went past Rushmere Pond and across to the Putney Road, which had a tall avenue of trees lining the Common side, with long wooden benches provided at intervals. This was Nurses' Walk and along crowded Nurses' Walk every morning at the same hour from his lair at 'The Pines,' Putney, came 'Mad Mr. Swinburne' rattling the two-pence in his pocket which was the daily allowance made him by his friend Theodore Watts-Dunton for a pint of beer at the near-by Rose and Crown Inn.

'Mad Mr. Swinburne' was said by some nurses to be 'Wicked Mr. Swinburne'—I suppose because he had once written some shocking poems, though this was not explained to me at the time—and many of them used to gather up their charges and hurry away at his approach. My picture of him is of a nimble and shrill-voiced gnome dressed in a biscuit-coloured suit with tails and talking insistently and shrilly at the top of his voice. He had wispy white locks and a tall hat perched at the back of his head; but this part is perhaps confused by a memory of Tenniel's Mad Hatter in *Alice in Wonderland*. His madness consisted chiefly in his addressing respectable nurses without an introduction and gazing ecstatically into their perambulators.

On one occasion 'Mad Mr. Swinburne' succeeded in catching me, having appeared suddenly from behind a tree near the Jubilee fountain, and bestowed some sort of blessing on me—I was too frightened to know what—but it had great literary virtue, as I afterwards learned, because Swinburne as a young man had received the blessing of Walter Savage Landor, and Landor as a child, the blessing of Dr. Samuel Johnson.

The rhythm in this poem is extraordinarily powerful and resurrects deep-sunken memories, but with a corrective vision of a little nimble old man no longer wicked, or ogreish, or mad, but drunk with universal love—the unhappy excesses of his youth and middle-age forgotten—and joyfully welcoming the Kingdom of Heaven in the persons of certain overdressed, overfed, priggish little late-Victorian children. I can still discern the insistent shrillness in the assonantal play of 'slay ... faith'; 'peace, deep'; 'sweet sleep'; 'nights resign'; 'hate ... waste'—at which technicians of the Miltonic and Tennysonian schools would virtuously shudder. For myself, I would not have the poem otherwise, though Swinburne of course had not the least idea of the meaning of the verses in the *Canticles*, out of which he has built it. It is the May-bride of Shunem, a well-watered village of Lower Galilee, who is addressing her lover of the year: 'Set me like an amulet on your right arm, the satchel (containing the Divine Name), turned towards your heart.' The Jewish editors of the Scriptures, unwilling to suppress this ancient collection of marriage songs, made them symbolic of the love of Israel for Jehovah; the Christian Church followed suit shamelessly by making them symbolic of the love of the Church for her Redeemer.

THE GHOST OF MILTON
(1947)

THE GHOST OF MILTON

IN 1942 while I was writing *Wife to Mr. Milton*, a historical novel about Milton's life with Marie Powell, his first wife, I felt his ghost haunting my writing-table with glowering eyes and minatory whispers; but refused to be daunted. The ghost has walked England in times of national crisis ever since Wordsworth conjured it up during the Napoleonic wars:

> Milton! thou shouldst be living at this hour:
> England hath need of thee: she is a fen
> Of stagnant waters: altar, sword, and pen,
> Fireside, the heroic wealth of hall and bower,
> Have forfeited their ancient English dower
> Of inward happiness. We are selfish men;
> Oh! raise us up, return to us again;
> And give us manners, virtue, freedom, power.
> Thy soul was like a Star, and dwelt apart;
> Thou hadst a voice whose sound was like the sea:
> Pure as the naked heavens, majestic, free,
> So didst thou travel on life's common way,
> In cheerful godliness; and yet thy heart
> The lowliest duties on herself did lay.

But the final effect of a year spent in reading Milton's works in bulk and detail, together with all the available historical evidence about his life, was a thankfulness that he was *not* living at that hour.

When my novel was published, the reviewers, both British and American, were inspired to righteous indignation. They accused me of 'guying Milton in preposterous fashion, in disregard of contemporary evidence, and reducing him to the stock figure of the ranting, long-nosed Puritan of farce'; of maliciously giving Marie, the supposed authoress of the story, a lively and charming character whereas, as all the world knew, she was a 'clod' and a 'manacle'; and of outraging history by my suggestion that Milton sent her home after a wedding-night fiasco and a month of unconsummated marriage, whereas, they said, the marriage was unquestionably consummated and it was Marie who deserted him. Worse, I had not allowed him to speak a single word of great poetry from the first chapter to the last. Two or three of them took their stand on *Lycidas*: nobody, they declared, could have written so perfect a poem and treated his wife as badly as I made out. One wrote:

Where is the 'sweet and affable deportment' recorded by the anonymous biographer who was probably his younger Phillips nephew; the 'delightful company, the life of the conversation, the unaffected cheerfulness and civility' remembered by his daughter Deborah; the courteous scholar, 'extreme pleasant in his conversation, and at dinner, supper, etc.,' described by Aubrey, Richardson, Edward Phillips and the rest? Where is the Milton who made such a tremendous social success with the polite Italians during his tour of 1638 and 1639? This vulgar bully and churl is not he. Nor is Mary credible. Far from being the dull girl, the 'mute and spiritless mate,' the 'image of earth and phlegm,' only good for physical intercourse, of the divorce pamphlets, here is a clever, lively, highly educated young woman, holding her own in conversation with Milton himself.

This reaction interested me as a proof of the extraordinary power still exercised by Milton's ghost, which on a plea of blindness has secured a charitable conspiracy of silence about his true character and actions. I had thought it only fair, since Milton's prejudiced account of Marie had so long held the field, to let her borrow my pen and say her say as the spirited daughter of a Royalist father—Richard Powell, J.P., lessee of the Manor House at Forest Hill, Oxford, a village within easy walk of Magdalen Bridge. But she wrote of Milton as a renegade Arminian and renegade Royalist, not as the prick-eared Puritan of farce: and if he ranted in her account, he ranted in pure Miltonic, not in Hudibrastic, style.

Since Marie was the writer, no 'contemporary evidence' as to events after her death was relevant, and it is certain that between Whitsun 1642 when, at the age of thirty-three, Milton went on a visit to Forest Hill to collect a large debt and astounded his household by bringing back not the money but the debtor's sixteen-year-old daughter, and May 6, 1652, when she died, having borne him four children, he wrote no poems at all. Apart from official correspondence, some occasional verse and a few rudimentary works of scholarship, his writing was wholly polemical and much of it vituperative and obscene. It would have been absurd for me to bring him on the stage spouting great poetry.

Jonathan Richardson, a sincere admirer of *Paradise Lost*, has given us the domestic background (*Explanatory Notes and Remarks on Milton's Paradise Lost* (1734)):

He had other domestic vexations, particularly that uncommon and severe one of the affront and scorn of a wife he loved and the continuance of it for some years, and this without allowing him time to know what conjugal happiness was. Many of his choicest years of life were employed in wrangling, and receiving and racquetting back reproach, accusation and sarcasm. Which though he had an arm and dexterity fitted for, 'twas an exercise of his abilities very disagreeable to him; as it must be to one accustomed to praise, as he was in his younger years . . .

No 'mute and spiritless mate' she! His ill-temper seems to have been partly due to constipation, for Edward Phillips goes out of his way to report the name of his favourite laxative. It is possible that later, after having known 'what conjugal happiness was' by marriages to Katherine Woodcock ('my late espoused saint') and to Elizabeth Minshull, and abandoned polemics in favour of religious epics, Milton may have become more cheerful, and behaved affably and civilly to guests, so long as they admired his genius and sympathized with his blindness and his crippling gout. But only to his guests, not to his three daughters by Marie.

Wordsworth's eulogy of Milton's inward happiness as he travelled on life's common way majestic and free as a Star is flatly contradicted by Richardson, who records that after the Restoration he was:

. . . in perpetual terror of being assassinated. Though he had escaped the talons of the law he knew he had made himself enemies in abundance. He was so dejected he would lie awake whole nights.

As for Wordsworth's view of his unselfishness and virtue, it does not bear even a casual scrutiny. He was egotistical, unscrupulous and grasping. Fundamentally he was interested in nothing but his own career; in hacking his way to the Temple of Fame over the dead bodies of his enemies, rivals and friends. Granted, he was a loyal servant of God, but he made God a shield and buckler for his own murderous campaign. Even in his Latin *Lament for Damon* (Charles Diodati), grief for his friend's death does not prevent the intrusion of a long passage about his own epical ambitions. He paid the price of blindness not so much for the defence of the Commonwealth as for the conquest of Salmasius: 'Conquering kings their titles take . . .' and he hoped that if he completely confounded Salmasius in his own field, he would succeed to the title of First Scholar of Europe. His austerities were not a gauge of his virtue: they were founded on a mystical belief in the magical power of chastity as a means to immort lity. But his ambitions proved his undoing. When the Civil War threatened and dramatic poetry went out of fashion he decided to win public fame by polemical writing, and this insensibly drew him into dishonesty. By the time he had been made Secretary for the Foreign Tongues to the Council of State (a proto-Fascist institution) and incidentally Assistant Press Censor—-why is this fact kept out of the text-books when so much stress is laid on the *Areopagitica?*—he had smudged his moral copy-book so badly that he had even become a 'crony' of Marchmont Needham, the disreputable turncoat journalist. The evidence that he arranged for the interpolation of an extra prayer into one of the many early editions of *Eikon Basilike* and then made it the subject of a scurrilous attack, in *Eikonoclastes*, on the memory of Charles I is fairly conclusive; and that he suspected that the book was itself a forgery does not make the action any less disgraceful. When the Commonwealth collapsed, he naturally returned to his early poetic ambitions.

The temporary hospitality he gave to Richard Powell when he brought his hungry and down-at-heels family to London after the capitulation of Oxford is often presented as an act of generosity; but the legal documents in the case tell a different story. That Powell had twice cheated him, first by borrowing money on worthless security and then by contracting to pay him a £1,000 dowry on the day he married Marie, but without any hope of doing so, does not exculpate Milton from the charge of moral baseness: he profited from Powell's helplessness—he was a dying man—to secure moneys from his estate to which a certain 'widow Ashcroft' had a prior claim; and he later defrauded Ann Powell of her 'widow's thirds.'

The Italian tour, quoted by the reviewer in evidence of Milton's social qualities, was undertaken before his marriage; and he evidently then felt that he was treading on classical holy ground and must put his best foot forward. He was anxious to show the Italians that a 'frozen Hyperborean' could be a man of charm, sensibility and erudition. The Italians have always been pleased to welcome distinguished Northerners who talk fluent Italian, know their Virgil, and write fairly correct little Italian love-poems. However, it is on record that Milton offended the religious susceptibilities of some of his hosts by tactless disputation, and that others found him uncomfortably strait-laced.

As for the early days of the marriage, Milton's nephew and pupil,

Edward Phillips, who was a child of eleven in 1643, recorded his impression forty-three years later that a few weeks after the marriage Marie went home to Oxford on a visit but did not return to London when summoned, her family being staunch Cavaliers and Oxford being the Royalist headquarters. The impression of his brother John Phillips, who was nine at the time, also recorded about forty-three years later, was that Marie did not like the 'reserved' life in Milton's Aldgate Street house and was encouraged by her mother to desert him. Earlier evidence, not easy to set aside, is Ann Powell's plea, July 16, 1651, to the Commissioners of Sequestration at Haberdashers' Hall, that she could not prosecute Milton for a debt he owed her because he was:

> ... a harsh and chollericke man, and married to Mrs. Powell's daughter, who would be undone if any such course were taken against him by Mrs. Powell, he having turned away his wife heretofore for a long space upon some other occasion.

Believing that each of these accounts had some truth in it, I did my best to reconcile them in the light of the military and political situation, the financial relations of Milton and his father-in-law, and the state of the divorce laws in 1643.

The marriage-night fiasco can be deduced negatively from the ideal account of Adam and Eve's honeymoon in *Paradise Lost* and positively from a variety of lesser sources. It is nowhere stated by Milton or any contemporary that the marriage was consummated but the reviewers considered this proved because, as one of them wrote, 'the whole gravamen of Milton's complaint was of the baseness and horror of a merely physical union between those whose minds are so far apart that the higher purposes of matrimony, cheerful society and intelligent and affectionate intercourse, are impossible.' He quoted from *Tetrachordon*:

> What courts of concupiscence are these, wherein fleshly appetite is heard before right reason, lust before love or devotion?

But this quotation was irrelevant since it refers only to the question whether a wife's misconduct is a better cause for *divorce* than incompatibility of temperament. The difference between dissolution and divorce under Canon Law, the authority of which Milton did not challenge, was that after a dissolution either spouse was at liberty to marry again; but after a divorce (for which a wife's adultery was a valid plea) the husband was entitled to separation only and would be committing bigamy if he married again. The violence of the four divorce pamphlets irresistibly suggests the effect on a chaste, sensuous, thirty-four-year-old he-virgin of frustrated consummation of marriage. Had there been consummation, Milton would never have found it in his conscience to attempt, in 1645, a technically bigamous marriage to 'Dr. Davis's daughter.' Clearly, he considered that since he had not been paid the marriage dowry; and since he had temporarily returned Marie to her father with her maidenhead intact; and since she had afterwards refused to come back to him; and since because of the Civil War there were no bishops available to dissolve the marriage, he had a right to consider himself free. It was fortunate for him that Marie came back in time: had bigamy been proved against him at the Restoration, as well as political crimes, neither *Paradise Lost* nor *Samson Agonistes* would have been written.

As for Richardson's story, related at second-hand, of the party of gentlemen, admirers of Milton's poems, who visited his youngest daughter Deborah (then married to a poor Irish artisan) early in the reign of George I, and asked for memories of her late father—surely it was only natural for her to tell them what they cared to hear? Addison, one of the visitors, made her a handsome present. But we have sworn evidence in the Canterbury Prerogative Court case, in which she and her sisters had overturned his nuncupative will, which shows their life with him to have been hateful. The will is shocking. Milton makes the non-payment of Marie's dowry the excuse for disinheriting his daughters by her:

The portion due to me from Mr. Powell, my former wife's father, I leave to the unkind children[1] I had by her, having received no part of it; but my meaning is, they shall have no other benefit of my estate than the said portion and what I have besides done for them, they having been very undutiful to me. All the rest of my estate I leave to disposal of Elizabeth, my wife.

My attitude to Milton must not be misunderstood. A man may rebel

[1] The reason of their unkindness is not far to seek. John Phillips records that:

'. . . excusing only the eldest daughter by reason of her bodily infirmity and difficult utterance of speech (which to say truth I doubt was the principal cause of excusing her) the other two were condemn'd to the performance of Reading, and exactly pronouncing of all the Languages of whatever Book he should at one time or other think fit to peruse. Viz. the Hebrew (and I think the Syriac), the Greek, the Latin, the Italian, Spanish and French. All which sorts of Books to be confined to Read, without understanding one word must needs be a Tryal of patience, almost beyond endurance; but it was endured by both for a long time, but broke out more and more into expressions of uneasiness.'

Deborah, 'his favourite,' escaped to Ireland three or four years before his death, as a lady's companion.

against the current morality of his age and still be a true poet, because a higher morality than the current is entailed on all poets whenever and wherever they live: the morality of love. Though the quality of love in a painter's work, or a musician's, will endear him to his public, he can be a true painter or musician even if his incapacity for love has turned him into a devil. But without love he cannot be a poet in the final sense. Shakespeare sinned greatly against current morality, but he loved greatly. Milton's sins were petty by comparison, but his lack of love, for all his rhetorical championship of love against lust, makes him detestable.

With all possible deference to his admirers, Milton was not a great poet, in the sense in which Shakespeare was great. He was a minor poet with a remarkable ear for music, before diabolic ambition impelled him to renounce the true Muse and bloat himself up, like Virgil (another minor poet with the same musical gift) into a towering, rugged major poet. There is strong evidence that he consciously composed only a part of *Paradise Lost*; the rest was communicated to him by what he regarded as a supernatural agency.

The effect of *Paradise Lost* on sensitive readers is, of course, overpowering. But is the function of poetry to overpower? To be overpowered is to accept spiritual defeat. Shakespeare never overpowers: he raises up. To put the matter in simple terms, so as not to get involved in the language of the morbid psychologist: it was not the Holy Ghost that dictated *Paradise Lost*—the poem which has caused more unhappiness, to the young especially, than any other in the language—but Satan the protagonist, demon of pride. The majesty of certain passages is superhuman, but their effect is finally depressing and therefore evil. Parts of the poem, as for example his accounts of the rebel angels' military tactics with concealed artillery, and of the architecture of Hell, are downright vulgar: vulgarity and classical vapidity are characteristic of the passages which intervene between the high flights, the communicated diabolisms.

The very familiarity of *Lycidas* discourages critical comment and it is usually assumed—though I disagree with this—that Dr. Johnson showed a lack of poetic feeling when he criticized the falsity of its sentiments and imagery:

It is not to be considered as the effusion of real passion: for passion runs not after remote allusions and obscure opinions. Passion plucks no berries from the myrtle and ivy, nor calls upon Arethuse and Mincius, nor tells of rough satyrs and fauns with cloven hoof. Where there is leisure for fiction there is little grief.

Milton's effusion was certainly not spontaneous; in 1637 he had been invited to collaborate in a projected memorial anthology in honour of Edward King, his late fellow-student at King's College, Cambridge, and was apparently the last to send in his piece. It is unlikely that his grief for King was any more sincere than the admiration he had expressed for Shakespeare seven years previously when similarly invited to compose a commendatory sonnet for a new edition of the Plays (the first of his poems to be printed[1]); and young King's appointment by Royal mandate to a vacant College Fellowship seems to have so embittered Milton, who considered that he had the first claim to it himself, as to turn him into an anti-monarchist. There is authentic emotion in *Lycidas*, but it springs, as in his *Lament for Damon*, from the realization that young intellectuals of his generation are as liable as anyone else to die suddenly;[2] Fate's latest victim might

---

[1] In the 1645 edition of his *Poems*, Milton is careful to date the sonnet '1630,' as if to show that the humble admiration for Shakespeare which he professes there should be discounted as youthful modesty. The only other reference he ever makes to Shakespeare is a patronizing mention in *L'Allegro* of (apparently) *As You Like It*:

Or sweetest *Shakespear* fancies childe,
Warble his native wood-note wilde.

The English poet for whom he felt the strongest antipathy was John Skelton, in whom poetic love was instinctive, whose conscience never made a coward of him and who openly repudiated all unnatural austerities while in the service of the Muse Calliope. Here I suspect retrospective jealousy in Milton, masked as virtuous scorn, for a man who had won degrees at three, not merely two, universities; whom Erasmus had described as 'the light and glory of English letters'; and whom Henry VIII, a poet himself, had crowned with laurel. It is not generally realized that Milton is referring to Skelton in his *Aeropagitica*:

'I name not him for posterity's sake, whom Henry the 8th named in merriment his vicar of hell.'

Milton has deliberately obscured the point of Henry's joke, which conveyed no moral censure: Skelton was Rector of Diss in Norfolk, and *Dis* was the Roman Underworld, or Hell.

[2] It was a silly death. The ship in which King was returning to Ireland fouled a sunken rock close to the Anglesey coast only a short distance from land and began to sink. The sea was calm but (like the Knave of Hearts and Blackbeard the Pirate) King had never learned to swim. There was no lifeboat handy, and the crew had apparently grabbed all the available empty casks. So he knelt praying quietly on the deck until he went down with the ship. The moral seems to have been lost on Milton: in his treatise *Of Education*, he recommends weapon-training, dancing, wrestling, riding and visits to the Navy as recreations that should supplement a young gentleman's study of theology and the liberal sciences, but makes no mention of swimming.

well have been John Milton, not Edward King; which would have been a far more serious literary disaster. It also springs, but more obscurely, from the Fellowship grudge—apparently the irrelevant attack, in the second part of the poem, on Bishops who are unfaithful to their flocks, was aimed at William Chappell, his hated former College tutor, recently promoted Bishop of Ross, as being the enemy who had secured King his Fellowship. Dr. Johnson was rightly scandalized by the sudden change at this point in the poem from 'the vulgar pastoral . . . in which appear the heathen deities Jove and Phoebus, Neptune and Aeolus . . .' to a satire on contemporary Church Government. He writes:

The shepherd is now a feeder of sheep and afterwards an ecclesiastical pastor, a superintendent of a Christian flock. Such equivocations are always unskilful; but here they are indecent.

When he adds that *Lycidas* 'has no art,' this is true only in the sense that it is a poem strangled by art. Johnson sturdily resisted the musical spell which the opening lines cast on more sensitive readers:

> Yet once more, O ye Laurels, and once more
> Ye Myrtles brown, with Ivy never-sear,
> I com to pluck your Berries harsh and crude,
> And with forc'd fingers rude,
> Shatter your leaves before the mellowing year.

and did not trouble to examine carefully the principles on which they were written.

So far as I know, nobody has ever pointed out that in the extravagantly artful interlacing of alliteration throughout this passage Milton is adapting to English metrical use the device of *cynghanedd*, or recurrent consonantal sequences, used by the Welsh bards whom he mentions appreciatively early in the poem. It may well be that he learned of the device when he visited the Court of the President of Wales, for whom he had written *Comus*, in 1634.

The initial consonants of the first lines are an alliterative interlace of Y.M.L. which is interrupted by the harshness of the alliterative pairs B.B., C.C., and F.F., and which, after *Shatter*, reappears to decorate the 'dying close.' The interlace of C.S.D. in the next two lines is linked to the foregoing with another B.B.:

> . . . leaves before the mellowing year.
> Bitter constraint, and sad occasion dear,
> Compels me to disturb your season due . . .

Then follows a more complicated interlace: a P.H.N.L. sequence connected to the C.S.D. sequence by a bridge of D's, and followed by a watery succession of W's to close the stanza.

> For *Lycidas* is dead, dead ere his prime
> Young *Lycidas*, and hath not left his peer:
> Who would not sing for *Lycidas*? he knew
> Himself to sing, and build the lofty rhyme.
> He must not flote upon his watry bear
> Unwept, and welter to the parching wind,
> Without the meed of som melodious tear.

It was naughty of Johnson to pretend that 'the diction is harsh, the rhymes uncertain, the numbers unpleasing': the sound of the poem is magnificent; only the sense is deficient. In the opening lines *Brown*, introduced for its resonance and as an alliterative partner to *Berries*, suggests a false contrast between myrtle leaves which go brown and ivy leaves that stay green; whereas both sorts of leaf go brown in old age and fall off after younger leaves have taken their place. Laurel is sacred to Apollo, the god of poetry; ivy to Dionysus-Osiris, the god of resurrection; myrtle to Venus, goddess of love. But ivy and myrtle drop out of the poem immediately and seem to have been introduced only for the melodious sound of their names; and though it is clear from the next lines that Lycidas' death, in August before the year has mellowed, has unseasonably forced Milton's hand, he does not explain why he has to shatter the leaves of these trees while plucking the unripe berries. If he needs the berries, though of these three sorts only myrtle berries are edible, when they ripen in mid-winter, he does not have to disturb the leaves; if he needs a wreath he can cut a young shoot and shatter neither berries nor leaves. Clearly *Shatter* is used merely for its violence of sound; the presumed sense is 'I have come to pluck your berries and leaves before the year has mellowed,' but this is not conveyed.

And if he needs a wreath, for whom is it intended? For himself, later to converse with Apollo and have his ears encouragingly touched, or for the laureate hearse of his fellow-poet? The exigencies of his complicated metrical scheme have blurred the logic of the stanza— *parching* and *melodious* are further examples of words chosen for their sound at the expense of meaning—but his musical craftsmanship has lulled successive generations of readers into delighted acquiescence, and in Johnson's words 'driven away the eye from nice examination.'

It is enough for them to catch the general drift: that a poet has died before his time, shattering the hopes of his friends, and that a fellow-poet, suddenly aware that he is human too, is fumbling broken-heartedly among the evergreens with a confused notion that he ought to weave someone—but whom?—a garland of some sort or other; and that he feels vaguely (but is too downhearted to work the theory out) that the Bishops are to blame for everything.

CA: Y

THE COMMON ASPHODEL
(1949)

THE COMMON ASPHODEL

THE poetic education given in the modern English literature class is meagre and wholly unpractical: it does not include a course in primitive religion, without a grounding in which such poems as *La Belle Dame Sans Merci*, *The Ancient Mariner* and *Tom o'Bedlam's Song* yield only a small part of their sense; or even in elementary nature study. One could, for example, get full marks by answering the classroom question 'What is Asphodel?' with 'A yellow flower mentioned by Homer as growing in Elysium, on soft beds of which the souls of the just were believed, in his time, to rest their weary limbs.'

But this answer would be inaccurate as well as insufficient. Pope who wrote in his *St. Cecilia's Day*:

> . . . Happy souls who dwell
> In yellow meads of asphodel

and Tennyson who wrote in his *Lotos-Eaters*:

> . . . Some, 'tis whispered, down in Hell
> Suffer endless anguish, others in Elysian valleys dwell,
> Resting weary limbs at last on beds of asphodel.

were seldom poets enough to check their botanical facts, and here they have blundered badly. Asphodel meads are not yellow and even ghosts would find asphodel beds extremely uncomfortable for lying about on.

The asphodel is a tall, tough-stemmed, handsome whiteish flower, known in England as 'king's spear', with bunchy leaves not unlike a daffodil's. ('Daffodil,' by the way, derives its name from 'asphodel'; and it may have been king's spear otherwise known as 'affodel', not the narcissus-like daffodil, which Milton ordered to fill its cup with tears at Lycidas' funeral. But the 'nectared lavers strewed with asphodel,' of *Comus*, are nonsensical whichever flower he meant.) It grows wild on the poorest soil in most parts of the Mediterranean countries, and the asphodel meadow through which, in the *Odyssey*, the dead walked should be pictured as rocky and waterless waste-ground with clumps of caper, spurge and lentiscus. Nor was Elysium even in Homer's time a place where the souls of the just were sent; it was where the souls of kings were privileged to go, irrespective of moral qualities. Their vassals and subjects, however virtuous, were not so blessed and had to descend to darker and less pleasant places underground. Elysium—the word is apparently pre-Greek—seems to have been originally a river-mouth islet to which the king's corpse was brought for burial, like King Arthur's to Avalon, and where he became an oracular hero. When this custom was discontinued in Mycenaean times 'the islands of the blessed' became a mere figure of speech and in the *Odyssey* they are vaguely located in the far West 'beyond the streams of Ocean, the White Rock, the Gates of the Sun and the Land of Dreams.' The White Rock was perhaps the Dover cliff-line.

Asphodelos as a flower name occurs nowhere in Homer; but four times as an adjective qualifying *leimon*, a meadow. It probably therefore stands for: *a*, not; *spod*, ashes (*spod* could become *sphod* in Attic Greek); *elos*, valley. If so, the *asphodelos leimon* is really 'the meadow in the valley of what escapes unburned,' namely of the king's soul which survives the funeral pyre; and *leimon* (formed from *leibo*, 'pour') may mean, rather, 'libation-place.' The connexion between these sepulchral islands and the asphodel, or king's spear, which is first mentioned by the early poet Hesiod, seems to be that it was a food plant. Although in Classical times asphodel and mallow were, proverbially, eaten only by the very poor, they must once, before corn was grown in Greece on a large scale, have been the staple diet even of kings. The asphodel has potato-like tubers, often as many as eighty to a single plant, which when baked in wood ash and eaten with salt and oil are said to be nourishing; Hesiod mentions an appetizing dish of baked asphodel beaten up with figs, but I do not know that anyone has sampled it in modern times. The seeds were also parched and eaten like corn, and even made into bread. Mallows are still popular in the south of France but asphodel has everywhere been ousted from the poor man's table by the potato; even the recent famine in the Greek islands failed to repopularize it. And the leaves are no fodder for sheep or goats, though pigs will eat the tubers if they are hungry enough.

Since the asphodel must have been the only food plant which the souls of heroes would find growing in profusion on their sepulchral islands, 'the dead,' as Sir Thomas Browne records in his *Urn-Burial*, 'are made to eat Asphodels about the Elysian meadows.' And since the tubers, like the souls, rose blessedly from the ashes of their wood-fire, the plant is likely to have taken its Greek name from the place, 'the valley of what escapes unburned,' rather than the place from the plant.

The later Greeks in defiance of the laws of etymology explained the word as formed from *aspis*, a viper, and *deilos*, terrible; which amounted to calling it 'snake's bane.' It was said that snakes could be kept at a distance by scattering its seeds on the ground; and the physician Nicander recommended the juice of the stems as a cure for snake-bite. These were guesses only and could easily have been disproved by experiment; but guesses based on primitive homoeopathic logic. Since the young stems closely resemble snakes; and since their royal flowers appear at the Spring Equinox when the Sun-god celebrates his victory over the Great Snake of winter; and since asphodels grow in Elysium where the blessed heroes walk; and since heroes are embodied in oracular snakes—therefore asphodel must be good against snakes. And since snakes were poetically connected with generation long before Freud exploited the symbolism, asphodel must also be a powerful aphrodisiac—as Pliny says it is. (This can also be easily disproved by experiment.) Pliny records that the stalks were hung up outside Italian farm-houses to keep off noxious spells: the theory probably being that common ghosts and demons, conjured up by witches to harm the inmates, would mistake the place for the asphodel meadows in the Islands of the Blessed, where they had no right to go.

Brockhaus' Konversations-Lexikon (1925) says that sugar and alcohol are now extracted from asphodel tubers, especially in the Languedoc. But the yield does not seem to be very high; an asphodel factory started five or six years ago in Majorca (where I live) during a sugar famine failed dismally, though the raw material is plentiful here and may be had for the carting.

I think that this is quite enough about asphodel.

INDEX